DATE DUE

CRISIS AND COMMAND

CRISIS AND COMMAND

The History of Executive Power from George Washington to George W. Bush

John Yoo

KAPLAN

PUBLISHING

New York

This publication is designed to provide accurate and authoritative information in regard to the subject matter covered. It is sold with the understanding that the publisher is not engaged in rendering legal, accounting, or other professional service. If legal advice or other expert assistance is required, the services of a competent professional should be sought.

Published by Kaplan Publishing, a division of Kaplan, Inc.
1 Liberty Plaza, 24th Floor
New York, NY 10006

Library of Congress Cataloging-in-Publication Data

Yoo, John.
  Crisis and command : the history of executive power from George Washington to George W. Bush / John Yoo.
       p. cm.
  Includes bibliographical references.
  ISBN 978-1-60714-555-4
  1. Executive power--United States--History. 2. Presidents--Legal status, laws, etc.--United States--History. 3. Constitutional history--United States.
  I. Title.
   KF5053.Y66 2009
   342.73'06--dc22
                                                    2009024862

Printed in the United States of America

10 9 8 7 6 5 4 3

ISBN: 978-1-60714-555-4

Kaplan Publishing books are available at special quantity discounts to use for sales promotions, employee premiums, or educational purposes. For more information or to purchase books, please call the Simon & Schuster special sales department at 866-506-1949.

CONTENTS

INTRODUCTION

CRISIS AND COMMAND completes a trilogy on the political, constitutional, and legal controversies provoked by al Qaeda's September 11, 2001, terrorist attacks on New York City and Washington, D.C. War acts on executive power as an accelerant, causing it to burn hotter, brighter, and swifter. It may burn out of control or it may flame out quickly. The American constitutional system has struggled from the birth of the Republic to figure out the right balance between energetic executive power and predictable, normal social activity; and the early years of the twenty-first century have been no different. The unconventional nature of the terrorist threat placed unprecedented stress on the Presidency and its relationship to the other branches of government. Al Qaeda's decentralized form demanded the reinterpretation of the rules of war, including the legitimate grounds for war, surveillance, targeting, detention, interrogation, and trial.

I was an official in the Justice Department involved in developing national security policy in the wake of the September 11 attacks. On the question of waging war, the President's constitutional authority had historically been paramount. Nonetheless, within weeks of the al Qaeda attacks, critics emerged claiming that Congress, rather than the President, should be making policy. In 2005,

I wrote *The Powers of War and Peace*, which explained my view of the original understanding of the Constitution's foreign affairs power, and applied it to post-9/11 questions about starting wars, entering treaties, and setting foreign policy. *War by Other Means* followed the next year. It explained the logic and legal authority behind the Bush administration's counterterrorism policies, though criticizing its political strategies. Both books argued that the Framers understood the Constitution to give the President the primary direction of national security decisions, with Congress retaining ample authority to check executive policy.

Some disagree with this reading of the original understanding. They object that the Framers' decisions at the end of the eighteenth century should not affect how we make national security policy at the beginning of the twenty-first. They argue that the Framers intended Congress to play the predominant role in setting national security and foreign policy and that legislative action invariably overrides presidential decision-making. Other critics believe that the original understanding of the Constitution has little or no application to contemporary separation-of-power questions. Ideally, they say, Congress should make the major peacetime policy decisions, the President execute them, and the courts adjudicate the cases. Both theories race toward the same finish line. Books with titles like *The New Imperial Presidency*, *The Terror Presidency*, or *Takeover: The Return of the Imperial Presidency* all proceed from the assumption that the President has no significant constitutional authority of his own but is bound to follow Congress's directions, even during war or emergency.

These works, and the contemporary zeitgeist they reflect, often overlook the importance of events like the Louisiana Purchase, the Emancipation Proclamation, or America's early assistance to Great Britain in World War II. This book explores a factor seldom consulted in debates over executive power today: history. A single volume cannot comprehensively examine the growth of executive power throughout our Constitution's 220 years, but it can deepen our understanding. I trace the genealogy of today's controversies back to the nation's first Chief Executive, George Washington, then describe how Thomas Jefferson, Andrew Jackson, Abraham Lincoln, and Franklin Roosevelt used the powers of their office in times of crisis. Stephen Skowronek has classified these men as the most transformative Presidents, the ones who disrupted the existing political order and replaced it with one of their own making.[1] Marc Landy and Sidney Milkis agree that these five Presidents are the "greatest" for their profound effect on the American political system of the day.[2]

This is not a coincidence. These Presidents are considered great precisely because of their boldness. Some made lasting changes to the political system; others altered the structure and powers of their office. But this alone cannot account for their success. Presidents such as Martin Van Buren, William McKinley, or Woodrow Wilson also wrought noteworthy political changes. Rather, our greatest Presidents became great by leading the nation through crises. "[I]f Lincoln had lived in times of peace," Theodore Roosevelt observed, "no one would have known his name now."[3] There is a significant, but misunderstood, link between the vigorous exertion of executive power and presidential greatness. By themselves, crises don't produce presidential excellence — just look at James Buchanan, Lincoln's predecessor, or Herbert Hoover, FDR's predecessor. Both responded to emergency — secession in one case, depression in the other — by withdrawing feebly into their shells. Chief executives can draw upon a deep well of constitutional authority when they act in the face of peril. Some may respond by bowing to Congress and respecting the status quo, but that course might perpetuate the very policies that failed in the first place. The qualities that define the executive — energy, speed, decisiveness, and secrecy, among others — are indispensable in emergency situations. The ordeals of the nation's founding, the Napoleonic Wars, the Civil War, or World War II were not overcome without Presidents of the day making use of the very broadest reach of their constitutional powers.

Some may read this book as a brief for the Bush administration's exercise of executive authority in the war on terrorism. It is not. It is a book about the constitutional and institutional history of the Presidency. It is not meant to be as comprehensive as histories that scour the life and times of a single Chief Executive.[4] I do not attempt to trace the evolution of the Presidency in a single frame, say, as a political actor, from Washington's patriot king to Teddy Roosevelt's rhetorical leader to today's campaign-in-being.[5] Instead, I seek here to provide a different perspective: to describe the relationship between the constitutional authorities of the office, and presidential success as measured by scholars of the Presidency. I examine how individual Presidents understood and used their constitutional authorities to deal with challenges, successfully or not.

This book is also written out of respect for Congress as well as the President. I have had the honor to serve as general counsel of the Senate Judiciary Committee under the chairmanship of Senator Orrin G. Hatch of Utah, a good and decent man as well as a steward of the Senate. I have the greatest respect for the awesome powers of Congress and the ways in which Congress and the broader political system can check any Chief Executive. It was Congress that forced the resignation of Richard Nixon through hearings, political pressure, spending constraints, and ultimately, the threat of impeachment. Today's critics of the Presidency underestimate the power of politics to corral any branch of government that goes too far. They give too much credit to appeals to abstract notions of constitutional balance to restrain a truly out-of-control President, or misread active responses to unprecedented challenges as challenges to the Constitution. The hyperbole in such rhetoric is manifest in overwrought yet commonplace invocations of "treason" or "tramplings" of the Constitution. Has the Constitution indeed been trampled on? History provides us with a guide.

Certainly, the fear that a President might abuse power for personal gain or to maintain his or her position has haunted America from her birth. Executive power, as the Founding Fathers well knew, always carries the possibility of dictatorship. In their own day, the great Presidents were all accused of wielding power tyrannically. Yet, they were not dictators. They used their executive powers to the benefit of the nation. Once the emergency subsided, presidential power receded and often went into remission under long periods of congressional leadership. When chief executives misused their powers, the political system blocked or eventually ejected the President. No dictator has ever ruled in the United States, yet critics of contemporary presidential power wish to work radical change in current practice out of fear of impending dictatorship.

Exercises of presidential power can go badly wrong, of course. Richard Nixon is the most salient example of presidential authority used for ill. He ordered the covert surveillance of political opponents, the infiltration of anti-war groups, and the harassment of critics — all on grounds of national security that were strained at best, and criminally deceitful at worst. He used executive privilege to conceal information from criminal investigators in the Watergate scandal, fired special Justice Department prosecutors, and ultimately resigned before his almost certain impeachment by the House of Representatives. After he left office, Nixon defended his actions in a television interview with David Frost, claiming in a damning over-generalization: "[W]hen the president does it, that means that it is not illegal."[6]

The broad exercise of presidential power is not confined to the twentieth or twenty-first centuries but represents the necessary expansion over 200 years of the constitutional powers of the office. It started with the Revolutionaries' effort to avoid executives who might become monarchs. By the time of the Constitution's ratification, however, the Framers' views had evolved in favor of an independent, forceful President. The Constitution devotes more of its attention to listing the powers of Congress, but it deliberately paints the President's powers in broad strokes. Our greatest Presidents, from George Washington on, have filled in these sketchy outlines with *deeds*, deeds that met national challenges, both foreign and domestic. Presidential power has grown with the nation's power, both in our constitutional law and in prestige and substance.

These conclusions are at odds with the prevailing scholarly accounts of the White House. Richard Neustadt, author of the most influential book on the Presidency of the last half-century, views the story of modern chief executives as a story of "presidential weakness."[7] Presidential power, Neustadt famously argued, is "the power to persuade." After examining Truman's firing of General Douglas MacArthur and his seizure of the steel mills during the Korean War, and Eisenhower's use of troops to desegregate the Little Rock schools, Neustadt concluded that resorting to formal presidential orders was "suggestive less of mastery than failure."[8] While Neustadt conceded that formal constitutional authority was part of a President's personal influence, he made clear that "the probabilities of power do not derive from the literary theory of the Constitution." Scholars following Neustadt find presidential power in characteristics such as communicative and political skills, organizational ability, vision, cognitive style, and emotional intelligence.[9] Neustadt would recommend that Presidents rely upon these skills and avoid any invocation of their constitutional powers.

A long-standing tradition in political science views executive power as a problem, not a solution. Woodrow Wilson, while still a young scholar, argued that the Framers had designed a defective Constitution. In 1885, he famously pressed for "congressional government" in which the President would be, in effect, a prime minister, at the head of the executive branch and the majority party in Congress. Wilson believed this the only way to coordinate both branches of government and overcome the debilitating effects of the separation of powers.[10] But by 1907, Wilson had changed his mind, putting his hopes in a President who would act as a powerful leader in national affairs.[11] Professor Clinton Rossiter, author of the classic *The American Presidency*, identified several duties incumbent on the Chief Executive, from "Protector of the Peace" to "Manager of Prosperity."[12] Rossiter worried that if the President did not use all of his formal and informal powers to lead the nation, the government would become "weak and disorganized." This view, echoed most recently by James MacGregor Burns, argues that the Constitution's original separation of powers divided the executive from the legislative far too well, creating paralyzed government as a result.[13] Presidential government, Burns observed, would "strengthen democratic procedures" and help achieve "modern liberal democratic goals."

For others, the problem is the reverse: the Constitution checks presidential power too little, not too much. After abuses of executive authority under Kennedy, Johnson, and Nixon, scholars argued that the political checks on presidential behavior had grown too weak and that a return to constitutional principles was necessary. Arthur Schlesinger, Jr., for example, who had praised the exercise of presidential power in his celebrated biography of Andrew Jackson, then as court historian to Kennedy, changed his tune after Vietnam. In *The Imperial Presidency*, he claimed that a "shift in the constitutional balance [of power]" between Congress and the President had occurred, one marked by "the appropriation by the Presidency, and particularly by the contemporary Presidency, of powers reserved by the Constitution and by long historical practice to Congress."[14] Claims that the Presidency has violated the Constitution's original design continues to characterize the work of some of the nation's leading law professors, such as Bruce Ackerman, John Hart Ely, Michael Glennon, and Harold Koh.

Both approaches assume that the Framers of 1787 designed the original Presidency to be a weak office, and that circumstances have expanded executive power far beyond its intended limits. One side welcomes this development; the other seeks to return to an eighteenth-century version of the Presidency. I believe that both sets of scholars underestimate the Framers' intentional desire to create a Presidency with broad, rather open-ended powers in specific areas, such as foreign affairs and national security. They meant to leave these boundaries flexible. And so, from the beginning, Presidents have acted forcefully to respond to emergencies and unanticipated events without consulting Congress. The Framers counted on politics to check and balance presidential initiative, not "parchment barriers." The Presidency could have evolved into a weak office whose occupants served as the Clerks-in-Chief to Congress. As it happened, the United States grew in size, population, and complexity, and the Presidency grew with it, in power and standing.

This insight can be traced at least as far back as Alexis de Tocqueville. In his classic *Democracy in America*, he observed that the Presidency was a relatively weak office because the armed forces were tiny, the nation was protected from Europe by the oceans, and no natural enemies sat along its borders. "The President of the United States possesses almost royal prerogatives, which he has no opportunity of exercising; and the privileges that he can at present use are very circumscribed. The laws allow him to be strong, but circumstances keep him weak." That would change, Tocqueville predicted, as America grew. It is in foreign relations "that the executive power of a nation finds occasion to exert its skill and its strength." If the national security of the country "were perpetually threatened, if its chief interests were in daily connection with those of other powerful nations," Tocqueville continued, "the executive government would assume an increased importance in proportion to the measures expected of it and to those which it would execute."[15]

This book will trace the history of presidential power from the founding of the Republic up to today's debates over the war on terror. Understanding the growth and nature of executive power requires an interdisciplinary approach, including political science, history, and law. To combine these fields is too rare. The origins of the "unitary executive" go back to Alexander Hamilton and before him to Montesquieu, Blackstone, Locke, and Machiavelli. The unitary executive theory, like the text of the Constitution, says that the President has the "executive power" of government — that is, the authority to manage the agencies and exercise powers inherently "executive" in nature, in particular the conduct of foreign policy. This vesting of power contrasts with the Constitution's grant of specified, or "enumerated," powers to Congress. Chapter 1 will discuss the creation of the Presidency, beginning with the colonists' experience with executive power, the problems with legislative supremacy during the Revolution, and the establishment of a strong, independent executive by the Constitution's Framers.

Following chapters will discuss individual Presidents and the use of their constitutional powers. No single volume could comprehensively discuss every President's relationship with his constitutional powers. Instead, Chapters 2 through 7 will focus on our great Presidents and contrast them with some of our worst leaders. In 2005, the *Wall Street Journal* and the Federalist Society asked 130

prominent historians, political scientists, economists, and law professors from across the ideological spectrum to rank each American
President on a scale of 1 to 5:

GREAT

1. George Washington 4.94
2. Abraham Lincoln......... 4.67
3. Franklin Roosevelt........ 4.41

NEAR GREAT

4. Thomas Jefferson 4.23
5. Theodore Roosevelt....... 4.08
6. Ronald Reagan 4.03
7. Harry Truman 3.95
8. Dwight Eisenhower....... 3.67
9. James Polk 3.59
10. Andrew Jackson ....3.58 [16]

Rather than put forward its own definition of greatness, this
book will examine the growth of the powers of these Presidents and
their effect on the nation's fortunes. All these Presidents believed
that their office was equal, and not subordinate, to Congress or the
courts and took for granted that the broad exercise of that authority was essential to their success. Several of these Presidents were, in
fact, responsible for some of the most explosive constitutional confrontations in American history. An enormous historical literature,
indeed, trumpets their "great" or "near great" status precisely because
they were so bold as to assert power with extraordinary vigor, and
precisely in the most contested or doubtful circumstances.

Chapters 2 through 7 will examine the history of some of
America's best and worst Chief Executives to understand the outer

limits and best uses of presidential power. Looking at the use of constitutional power through a few Presidents may seem questionable to historians, who usually try to understand an individual leader by presenting him in his every detail — hence the recent biographies examining the childhood, medical health, psychologies, and marital relations, among other things, of Presidents. I do not take issue with the broadening of presidential history, only here the focus remains on the intellectual, political, and legal development of the office. While important, the new social history does not provide as much useful context for an inquiry into constitutional powers as do political, diplomatic, and economic histories.

A related point is the importance of practice as a source of constitutional meaning. When confronted with any legal question, lawyers will turn first to judicial opinions as an authoritative source of interpretation. Supreme Court opinions parse the constitutional text in light of its original meaning, structure, history, and precedent. In separation-of-power questions, however, especially those involving foreign affairs and national security, judicial opinions are few and far between. There is no Supreme Court decision, for example, defining what the Senate may consider in giving its "advice and consent" to a treaty, or to a Supreme Court nomination, for that matter. The Supreme Court has never decided whether the President must receive a declaration of war or other form of congressional authorization before beginning military hostilities abroad. As then-Justice Rehnquist wrote for the Court in *Dames & Moore v. Regan*, "the decisions of the Court in this area have been rare, episodic, and afford little precedential value for subsequent cases."[17]

Historical practice has outsized importance because of this absence of judicial precedent or any other form of binding resolution of disputes among the branches of government. Practice reflects the understandings developed by the branches of government over time for reaching decisions in these areas. Presidents, for example, have never understood "advice and consent" to require personal consultation with the Senate before negotiating a treaty or choosing a Supreme Court nominee, and this because of a practice that began in George Washington's first year in office. Practice also represents the considered views of leaders of different branches over American history on separation-of-power questions. It is a record of the way in which government actors have adapted broad constitutional principles to discrete questions over time. The cumulative effect of their decisions may reveal sturdy truths about the way our government should best work within the system established by the Constitution. Justice Felix Frankfurter put the point well in the Steel Seizure case, *Youngstown Sheet & Tube v. Sawyer*, in which the Court blocked President Truman's takeover of steel mills during the Korean War: "The Constitution is a framework for government. Therefore the way the framework has consistently operated fairly establishes that it has operated according to its true nature. Deeply embedded traditional ways of conducting government cannot supplant the Constitution or legislation, but they give meaning to the words of a text or supply them."[18]

Studying practice closely may provide us with a quality of understanding similar to that enjoyed by courts. Judges usually avoid deciding questions until they arise in a real case, in part because the abstract principles are only tested in the context of actual parties, events, and facts. Similarly, it makes sense to examine executive power under these Presidents because the meaning of broad constitutional principles becomes sharper and clearer in the context of the challenges that they confronted. During periods of peace and domestic tranquility, Presidents, Congresses, and courts will cooperate much of the time, and so no occasion for the definition of their respective constitutional powers will arise. It is only during times of high stress on the political system when the principles of the constitutional framework clearly emerge. Two cautions are in order, however. First, just because practice exists does not make it right — the persistence of Jim Crow laws for almost 100 years does not, in my mind, make the separate-but-equal interpretation of the Reconstruction Amendments legitimate or correct. Second, practice may be wrong because earlier generations operated under poor information or did not confront the same types of circumstances that we do today.

These chapters on individual Presidents will show that the constitutional powers of the Presidency grew along with the President's political position as party leader and representative of a national majority. These powers involve control over the administrative state, law enforcement, the conduct of foreign policy, national security, and to the extent the Constitution is unclear, interpretation. The institutionally independent, unified executive and its powers were built through our history, by the hands of Presidents who guided America through the shoals attending its birth, rebirth, and rise to global preeminence. Presidential power has expanded with each crisis and emergency, to keep the nation out of the Napoleonic Wars, to purchase Louisiana, to free the slaves, to bring the nation into World War II, and to contain and defeat the Soviet Union. At these times, our greatest Chief Executives have vigorously used their powers to benefit, even to save, the nation.

This is not to say that Presidents can act unilaterally for very long, or that success inevitably follows executive initiative. Emergencies may call upon a President to lead, and robust exercises of presidential power can jolt the political system into recognizing new realities. But resistance and opposition almost always arise in response. Congress and especially the courts may try to defend the status quo. Presidents need the help of congressional majorities, well-organized political parties, or a passive judiciary for their policies to stay in place over the long term. Nonetheless, Presidents who hold narrow visions of their powers, or those who are overly deferential to Congress, such as James Buchanan, will experience failure in crisis. So, too, did Richard Nixon, who expanded presidential power in a time of war and foreign challenge but did so self-servingly against political opponents.

Nixon and Watergate prompted understandable concerns that the abuse of presidential power was a real threat to our democracy, yet permanently curbing executive power may prove even more damaging. The most radical critics of presidential power seek a return to an idealized system of government that has not existed for more than 100 years, ignoring the complexity of the world today. Congress is a large and unwieldy committee that rarely agrees on a single vision. Congress itself has chosen over the years to delegate enormous authority to the President — to regulate the environment, education, welfare, the Internet, and many other areas — precisely because it knows that the executive branch alone can bring management expertise to national problems. Our Constitution designed the executive branch to wield power effectively and flexibly, and our history has favored forceful, not constrained, Presidencies.

CHAPTER I

Beginnings

MOST JUDGES AND LAWYERS today do not hold the "originalist" view of Justices Clarence Thomas and Antonin Scalia that the Constitution should be interpreted in accordance with the Framers' understanding of the text. Yet, most Americans do believe that what the Framers thought they were doing is still the key starting point for any discussion of the powers of the government and the Presidency. Hence, studies of the Presidency usually begin with the Constitutional Convention of 1787.

The Framers thought long and hard about the question of executive power. In the words of historian Jack Rakove, creating the Presidency was "their most creative act." It was also their most ambiguous. Details of this new Presidency were left open, sparking controversy from the beginning.[1] In Europe, executive power had been the province of kings, not elected officials. Its exercise had caused social turmoil, revolution, and civil war. In the Framers' native Great Britain, restoration of the monarchy had followed. Taming executive power within a republican form of government became a central aim of the Framers of the new American Constitution.

Many scholars believe that the exercise of executive power today runs counter to the original constitutional design. This group argues that the Revolution against King George III was part of a larger rejection of executive authority and that the Presidency was intended to be a narrow, limited office. The Framers would never have intended to resurrect the same royal prerogatives that they had just fought a war to overthrow.[2] This view of the Presidency diminishes its constitutional authority and independence to that of a Clerk-in-Chief whose main duty is to execute Congress's laws. This interpretation profoundly misreads the political developments around the founding of America and the drafting of its Constitution.

It is true that the Revolutionaries rebelled against King George III and his perceived oppressions of the colonies, but it does not follow that they opposed the idea of executive power. To most who gathered in Philadelphia in the summer of 1787, post-Revolutionary efforts by the states to allow only weak executives with fragmented functions and powers had largely failed. Undermining the integrity of the executive branch had led to unstable, oppressive legislatures. The drafters of the Constitution came to Philadelphia in large part to restore the independence and unity of the executive branch — a republican, not a royal restoration.

EXECUTIVE POWER AND POLITICAL THOUGHT

EXECUTIVE POWER HAS always presented a conundrum: how to make the executive strong enough to promote the common good, but not so strong as to risk despotism. This problem remained vivid in the minds of the Framers. During the ratification of the

Constitution, Alexander Hamilton responded, in *Federalist 70*, to the fears of the Anti-Federalists that "a vigorous executive is inconsistent with the genius of republican government."[3] But in the very same paragraph, Hamilton went on to declare that "energy in the executive is a leading character in the definition of good government." How did the Framers go from the weak executives of their revolutionary state constitutions to the strong Presidency described by Hamilton?

What the drafters of the Constitution meant by executive power and how they viewed the Presidency require that we examine the constitutional thinking of the revolutionary and early national period in some detail. As intellectual historians Bernard Bailyn, Forrest McDonald, and Gordon Wood have shown, the writings of John Locke, Montesquieu, and Sir William Blackstone, set within the context of eighteenth-century British political history, had a profound effect on the Framing generation.[4] Political theory about the tensions between executive power and republican government go back at least as far as Niccolo Machiavelli, who is thought to have had little influence during his own lifetime but has become synonymous in the modern mind with coldhearted *realpolitik* at its starkest. Machiavelli deserves better than his popular reputation; J. G. A. Pocock titled his work on the roots of republican government "The Machiavellian Moment" in recognition of Machiavelli's key role in the rebirth of classic republicanism.[5]

Machiavelli invented the modern idea of the executive as the arm of government that both executes the laws and acts to protect the public welfare.[6] The rule of ancient consuls, emperors, and medieval kings did not rest on an idea of specialized function, but on a social class theory by which the royal class held power by divine right. Breaking with Aristotelian and Christian theories of political science, Machiavelli "liberated," in the words of Harvey C.

Mansfield, Jr., the executive from both natural law and religion.[7] The executive was, rather, the servant of necessity, bound to act in accordance with, in the absence of, or in extraordinary emergencies, in defense of the republic, even contrary to regularly constituted law. Machiavelli pointed to executive decisiveness and secrecy — princes were "quick" to execute and acted "at a stroke,"[8] unlike fractious senates. Acting *"uno solo,"* the successful executive's ambition will be turned to the common good, or else he will be held accountable for his failures — a concise early statement of today's idea of the unitary executive. Hamilton's description of the Presidency as able to act with "decision, activity, secrecy, and dispatch" echoes Machiavelli.[9]

Machiavelli challenged the thinkers who came after him to accommodate the executive's energy and decisiveness within the bounds of a formal constitutional order. Thomas Hobbes saw the executive as, ideally, an institution rather than a person. Hobbes believed sovereign authority should vest in one body, either a monarch or an assembly, and did not understand the executive and legislative functions to be distinct.[10] John Locke, in his *Second Treatise of Government*, gave birth to the modern separation of powers, dividing the executive from the legislative power and vesting these powers in different institutions. According to Locke, in the state of nature, every man holds the power to execute the laws of nature but gives up some of that power when joining the commonwealth. Locke saw the executive as primarily the servant of the laws. Because legislatures could not always remain in session, society requires "a Power always in being, which should see to the Execution of the Laws that are made, and remain in force."[11] The legislature held the "Supream [sic] Power" to set the rules of conduct, Locke said, while the executive remained subordinate in implementing the laws.

Locke envisioned a dominant legislature balanced by an independent executive with certain key lawmaking powers: the veto, the right to call or dissolve Parliament, and "federative" power over "war and peace, leagues and alliances, and all the transactions with all persons and communities without the commonwealth."[12] Though the federative and executive were "really distinct in themselves," Locke observed that "they are almost always united" because the former "is much less capable to be directed by antecedent, standing positive laws."[13] Locke's executive and federative functions were to be performed by the part of government that is always operational, swiftly adapting to new circumstances or dangers. Locke did not recommend separating the functions, which he predicted would lead to "disorder and ruin," by dividing "the force of the public" into "different commands."

Unanticipated threats were to be dealt with by prerogative, which, stripped of its royal origins, nevertheless allowed the executive, in an emergency, "to act according to discretion for the public good, without the prescription of the law, and sometimes even against it."[14] Like the federative power, the prerogative operated in a zone that general, antecedent laws could not address. "Many things there are which the law can by no means provide for, and those must necessarily be left to the discretion of him that has the executive power in his hands." The legislature was "too slow for the dispatch requisite to execution." Unlike the royal prerogative, the executive's authority had to be exercised in the public interest and for the common good. The existence of such power still raised the "old question" of how to resolve conflicts between emergency power and the standing laws. To Locke, there were no preexisting answers to this problem, and there was "no judge on earth" who could resolve it. Defining the executive prerogative's full scope beforehand would be simply impossible.

Montesquieu reinforced Locke's ideas with a unique twist. His 1748 *Spirit of Laws* inaccurately idealized the English constitution but became famous for the maxim that "when the legislative and executive powers are united in the same person, or in the same body of magistrates, there can be no liberty."[15] Montesquieu defined the legislative power as controlling domestic policy, taxing and spending, and establishing private rules of conduct. Following Locke, he viewed the executive power as enforcing the laws and conducting foreign relations. Montesquieu added a third branch of government, the judiciary, which Locke had classified as a law enforcement function. Apart from inventing the independent judiciary, Montesquieu did not fundamentally alter Locke's approach. Cited more than any other philosopher by Federalists and Anti-Federalists alike, Montesquieu was the prime exponent for the colonists of the idea of separating powers to safeguard liberty.[16]

Blackstone transformed these theories into something resembling constitutional law. In his *Commentaries on the Laws of England*, which was widely read in the colonies, Blackstone retained Locke and Montesquieu's distinctions among lawmaking, execution, and foreign affairs. The "making of the laws is entirely the work of a distinct part, the legislative branch, of the sovereign power."[17] It was a "sovereign and uncontrollable authority" on all domestic matters. Parliament could "do everything that is not naturally impossible." Blackstone's separation of powers, however, was based not on function but on social class — the King, Lords, and Commons represented different segments of society with their own attributes, such as power, wisdom, and virtue. Blackstone's mixed constitution protected liberty by ensuring that each social class participated in all government decisions.

Blackstone had much in common with Montesquieu and Locke. He defined the executive's primary job as prosecution of the laws and praised the British constitution's concentration of executive authority in a "sole magistrate of the nation" because it produced "unanimity,

strength, and dispatch."[18] In words that would be repeated during
the Philadelphia Convention (though often without attribution),
Blackstone criticized the idea of dispersing the executive power
among different officials. "Were it placed in many hands, it would be
subject to many wills: many wills, if disunited and drawing different
ways, create weakness in government." For that reason, Blackstone
concluded, the British constitution made the King of England "not
only the chief, but properly the sole, magistrate of the nation; all others acting by commission from, and in due subordination to him."[19]

Blackstone located the foreign affairs power in the Crown
because the King represented the nation, and large bodies could
not successfully conduct foreign affairs. "The king [had] also the
sole prerogative of making war and peace," exclusively exercised the
treaty power, could raise armies and navies on his own, and was "gen-
eralissimo, or the first in military command, within the kingdom."
Blackstone also recognized executive prerogative but limited it to
the "discretionary power of acting for the public good," which, if it
"be abused to the public detriment" would be "exerted in an unconstitutional manner."[20] Unlike Locke and Machiavelli, Blackstone
believed that Parliament could "lop off" or more "clearly define" the
prerogative; in other words, the prerogative could only operate when
the laws were silent, and not when they were in opposition. This
legislative check, however, was more apparent than real, because the
King possessed an absolute veto over legislation — restricting executive prerogative could happen only with the Crown's consent.[21]

The colonists' understanding of British political history also
influenced American constitutional thought during this period.
Struggle between the Stuart Kings and Parliament produced the
Civil War, Oliver Cromwell's Interregnum, the brief Restoration of
the Stuarts, and then the Glorious Revolution and ultimate settlement. While the political, economic, and social causes of this turmoil

were complex, the constitutional lessons were well known. Charles I refused to call Parliament into session for 11 years and sought to run foreign policy and the military without legislative funding. His efforts to evade Parliament led to his downfall. During the Restoration, the monarchy again tried to govern without Parliament, and again failed. After the 1688 Glorious Revolution, the monarchy and Parliament reached a settlement that clarified the latter's control over legislation, funding, and support of the military.

In the mid-eighteenth century, Britain was evolving from an executive branch personally centered on the King toward a cabinet system. The King ruled through a privy council usually composed of handpicked advisers and confidants. Parliament maintained its check on the executive through the power of the purse and its enactment of legislation. After the Glorious Revolution, the system developed into a nascent cabinet, whose members were chosen based on their ability to convince Parliament to adopt Crown policies, and ministers resorted to bribery and patronage to build legislative coalitions. In the mid-eighteenth century, for example, apparently one-third of all members of the House of Commons held offices appointed by the King, and another 5 percent benefited from government contracts. Patronage was the 1700s' version of today's congressional earmarks. Favors held legislators together when party discipline did not yet exist.

Change in the British political system had a profound impact on the colonists. The Revolutionary generation viewed these events through the lens of opposition ideology, which excoriated the Hanoverian Kings' efforts to manipulate Parliament, the permanent executive ministries, the new financial system backing the British Empire, and the spread of patronage and bribery throughout Parliament.[22] Corruption, standing armies, constant wars, and a large public debt sapped the British constitution's checks and balances and assaulted the rights and liberties of the British people. *Cato's Letters*, a tract of 144 much-quoted essays written by John Trenchard and Thomas Gordon, disseminated such ideas widely in the colonies — half of the private libraries of the day held a copy.[23]

The American Revolution was more than just a revolt against the idea of monarchy. Historians have puzzled over why the Framers rebelled when they were loyal British citizens, enjoying prosperity and growth, and victorious against France in the Seven Years' War. But victory brought a permanent military presence in the colonies and the need for heavier taxation, as well as trade regulation and monopolies imposed by Parliament. This contrasted sharply with London's previous policy of benign neglect, which had permitted the colonies to control their internal affairs and finances. Americans viewed the new taxation and regulation as nothing less than the overthrow of the checks and balances of the ancient constitution, and rebelled, not so much in an effort to curb executive power, but to maintain the historic balance between the Crown and Parliament on the one hand and the state assemblies on the other.

EXECUTIVE POWER IN THE CRITICAL PERIOD

INDEPENDENCE PUT AMERICAN theories of governance to the test, and they failed miserably. The Revolutionaries established one national charter, the Articles of Confederation, which soon proved crippled from lack of executive organization and leadership. The revolutionists wrote their state constitutions to undermine the structural integrity of the executive branch, and the results were legislative abuse, special-interest laws, and weak governments. Dissatisfaction with this state of affairs, even in a postwar time of relative peace and prosperity, led American nationalists to draft a new

Constitution that would create a stronger, more independent executive branch within a more powerful national form of government.
They would become known as the Federalists.

Scholars often misunderstand the Articles of Confederation.
Drafted in 1777 and ratified in 1781, the Articles established the first
American national government. Some have concluded that a power
was legislative, such as the power to make war, simply because the
Articles of Confederation granted it to the Continental Congress.[24]
Andrew Rudalevige is one such critic of presidential power who
believes that the Articles lacked an independent executive branch.[25]
This view mistakes the Articles of Confederation as creating a legislature, which it did not. As Chief Justice John Marshall recognized,
the "confederation was, essentially, a league; and Congress was a
corps of ambassadors."[26] It had no power of taxation nor power of
internal legislation, and it was not chosen on the basis of popular
representation. It had as much real legislative power in the United
States then as the United Nations has today.

Rather, the Articles of Confederation created America's national
executive, which inherited the Crown's imperial powers in the colonies, while the states retained their legislative powers.[27] It kept "the
sole and exclusive right and power of determining on peace and war,"
entering into treaties, and conducting foreign relations.[28] It had the
power to appoint committees and officers to administer federal law,
the central function of the executive. Congress's problem was not a
lack of executive power, but the way that power was organized and
supported. Initially, Congress created committees to carry out decisions, a design that proved disastrous with troops in the field fighting
the British. In 1781, Congress replaced committees with executive
departments headed by individual secretaries, an improvement, but
Congress continued to try to micromanage policy, and the executive
still lacked "method and energy," in the words of a young Alexander

Hamilton.[29] The states, which continued to control supply and internal legislation, failed to supply revenue to the national government or comply with its requests. This experience led General Washington to forever favor placing responsibility for executive action in a single, accountable leader.

Once peace arrived, Congress proved utterly incapable of handling its executive duties. It could not establish even a small military to protect northern forts near the Canadian border, which the British refused to hand over, in violation of the 1783 peace treaty.[30] Britain and France imposed harmful trading rules against American ships, while Spain closed the critical port of New Orleans to American commerce. American ambassadors could do nothing because Congress had no authority over commerce with which to threaten retaliation. It could not even approve an agreement with Spain, negotiated by John Jay, to reopen New Orleans and thereby the Mississippi, the chief route for American farm exports. Dissatisfaction with congressional weakness climaxed with Shays' Rebellion in August 1786. A mob of 1,500 men blocked the Massachusetts legislature from meeting, though the discontents soon scattered after a brief confrontation with state volunteers. Nationalists like Henry Knox and George Washington exaggerated the threat into 12,000 soldiers who had planned to rob banks and overthrow the state government. Congress's dismal record and the looming threat of chaos and disorder augured by Shays' Rebellion were at the forefront of the minds of the delegates as they met in Philadelphia.

Experimentation with the executive went to extremes in the states. Some eliminated the independence of the governor's office. In all but one state, the assembly elected the governor, making clear who served whom. Some states tried executive committees or required the governor's decisions to be approved by a council of state appointed by the legislature. As Professor Gordon Wood has observed, the councils often made the governors "little more than chairmen of their executive boards."[31] States limited the governor's term and eligibility. Most states either provided for the annual election of the governor, restricted the number of terms a governor could serve, or both. Pennsylvania tested the farthest reaches of radicalism by replacing the single governor with a 12-man executive council elected annually by the legislature.[32] The Revolution had occurred because the colonists wanted to maintain the independence of their legislatures from the control of the British King-in-Parliament. Their cure was to make the executive subordinate to the assemblies.

Some of the revolutionaries wanted to restrict the substance as well as the structure of executive power. Thomas Paine's *Common Sense* not only attacked the British monarchy, but it also called for an end to executives in the colonies. Paine proposed to his fellow Americans that they adopt governments run by legislatures, which would have only a presiding officer.[33] Thomas Jefferson's draft for the Virginia constitution merely gave the governor the title merely of the "Administrator."[34] Jefferson enumerated the powers the executive *could not* exercise: He could not dismiss the legislature, regulate the money supply, set weights and measures, establish courts or other public facilities, control exports, create offices, or issue pardons. The Administrator could not "declare war or peace, issue letters of marque or reprisal, raise or introduce armed forces, or build armed vessels...forts or strongholds." Although the draft ceded to the Administrator any remaining "powers formerly held by the king," there was little left.

But most states either gave the governor exclusive power to decide when to use the militia, or required that he consult the council before calling in the military. Although Virginia prohibited the governor from exercising any prerogative, it generally rejected Jefferson's advice and authorized the governor, with the advice of a council of state, to "exercise the Executive powers of Government."[35] States sided with John Adams, who for once had his day over his friend and future rival. Adams urged states to reproduce the forms and powers of the British constitution after adjusting for popular sovereignty. His plan called for a governor, a commons, and a mediating senate. According to Adams, "a people could not long be free, nor even happy whose government is in one assembly." Adams gave the governor a veto and control of the armed forces. He advised the adoption of an executive "who, after being stripped of most of those badges of domination called prerogatives, should have a free and independent exercise of his judgment, and be made also an integral part of the legislature."[36] Although the states experimented radically with the control of the executive branch, its substantive powers remained relatively unchanged.

The revolutionaries saw no need to reduce the substance of the executive power because they used constitutional structure to control their executives. Most state constitutions gave assemblies the power to choose the governors and allowed the executive to serve for only one-year terms, often with a limit on reelection. These states further bound their executives by requiring them to receive the consent of a council of state before exercising any independent authority.

Only one state, New York, freed its governor from these legislative shackles. British occupation of New York City for most of the war and the terrible state of its security (the state legislature had to meet in seven different locations during the first year of the war) gave its inhabitants a reason to break ranks on a vigorous executive.[37] New York vested "the supreme executive power and authority of this State" in a single governor. The people, not the assembly, elected him, and there was no limit on the number of three-year terms he could serve. No privy council was created to look over his shoulder, only a council of appointment and a council of revision to review the constitutionality of legislation.[38] The constitution vested him with the position of "general and Commander-in-Chief of all the militia, and admiral of the navy of this State," the power to dismiss or call the legislature into session and to issue pardons, and the duty to make recommendations for legislation and to "take care that the laws are executed to the best of his ability."[39] The first governor, George Clinton, won such success with these powers that the state returned him to office for 18 consecutive years, despite the British occupation. Clinton, wrote fellow New Yorker Gouverneur Morris, could not have been more suited to an office of such potential. He was a man "who had an aversion to councils, because, to use his own words, the duty of looking out for dangers makes men cowards."[40]

New York's definition of what fell within the executive power remained fairly unexceptional. Indeed, it was similar to those that Pennsylvania had given its pitiful executive. It was only when these powers were in the hands of an independent and unitary executive that vigorous government emerged. These lessons did not go unnoticed. New York's experience influenced not only the later constitution-writing efforts of Massachusetts and New Hampshire, but also the work of the Philadelphia Convention.[41] During the struggle for ratification, Publius — the pseudonym used by Alexander Hamilton, James Madison, and John Jay to author *The Federalist* — expressed the thoughts of many when he declared that the New York constitution "has been justly celebrated both in Europe and in America as one of the best of the forms of government established in this country."[42] As Charles Thach concluded, "[H]ere was a strictly indigenous and entirely distinctive constitutional system, and, of course, executive department, for the consideration of the Philadelphia delegates."[43]

The Framing generation had learned another corollary to this lesson. A legislature unbalanced by an independent executive brought

its own dangers. In states such as Pennsylvania, where the executive
had no veto, was straddled by a privy council, and was chosen by
the assembly, the legislature exercised virtually unlimited authority.
During the Constitutional Convention, James Madison argued that
"[e]xperience has proved a tendency in our governments to throw
all power into the legislative vortex. The Executives of the States are
in general little more than cyphers; the legislatures omnipotent."[44]
Legislative supremacy produced such "instability and encroachment" that if not checked, Madison predicted, "a revolution of some
kind or the other would be inevitable." Though the colonies had
won the Revolution, unrestrained state legislatures failed to follow
through on the 1783 Peace Treaty with Britain, imposed destructive
trade barriers, and passed laws that oppressed minorities and property owners. Despite the colonies' victory, the problems of government were so serious that historians came to describe these years as
the "Critical Period."[45]

Later constitutions followed New York's example. Massachusetts, which adopted its constitution in 1780, and New Hampshire,
which ratified a similar document in 1784, both provided for executives elected directly by the people with independent constitutional
powers. Those states, for example, gave their governors the authority
to make war, for offensive reasons as well as self-defense. Massachusetts's experience marks a sea change in attitudes toward the executive during the Critical Period. In 1778, the state legislature drafted
a constitution for ratification by the people that required the governor to carry out the laws of the legislature but gave him no independent constitutional powers. The people rejected the proposal, with
28-year-old Theophilus Parsons, a future chief justice of the state
supreme court, penning a historically significant critique known as
the "Essex Result." Parsons argued that the 1778 constitution violated the separation of powers by undermining the independence

of the executive and concentrating authority in the legislature. He
rejected the weak executive and called instead for a directly elected
governor who would share the power to veto legislation with a privy
council. Dividing authority over the military, in particular, was foolish: "Was one to propose a body of militia, over which two Generals, with equal authority, should have the command, he would be
laughed at." Control over the military, the Essex Result concluded,
should rest alone in the hands of the governor. Although Parsons recognized that the executive might try to expand his overall authority
through the exercise of his war power, he decided that the governor's
ability to respond quickly to emergencies justified centralization in
the governor. The executive must be one person, Parsons argued, to
clothe it with the speed and secrecy to enforce the laws internally
and to defend against external threats.[46]

Massachusetts's constitution of 1780 followed through on Parsons's arguments. It created a "supreme Executive magistrate," who
was elected directly by the people for renewable one-year terms. The
executive was to be Commander-in-Chief of the armed forces and
hold a conditional veto over legislation. With the consent of a council, the governor would make all appointments to the executive and
judicial branches. To the reformers who would attend the Philadelphia Convention, the Massachusetts constitution "came to stand for
the reconsidered ideal of a 'perfect constitution,'" writes Wood. It
"seemed to...have recaptured the best elements of the British constitution that had been forgotten in the excitement of 1776."[47] Its
enumeration of the powers vested in the Commander-in-Chief,
understood in light of the Essex Result, illustrates the contemporary understanding of the proper and most effective structure of the
executive branch.

New York and Massachusetts provided the models for the delegates who met in Philadelphia in the summer of 1787. The Framers

could have followed the path they knew best and treated the executive as Congress's Clerk-in-Chief, but instead they chose a less popular but more effective direction. By the end of the Critical Period's exuberant experimentation with dominant legislatures, states began to opt for executives very much like that of 1787. Why? As Gordon Wood has argued, the Framers believed that the 1776 constitutions had been the product of excessive revolutionary fervor. Unchecked by independent executives and judiciaries, the state legislatures had passed legislation infringing property rights, cancelling debts, and oppressing minorities. Factions, or special interest groups working at the expense of the broader public, had arisen. Unrestrained democracy had produced sharp and abrupt swings in policy that destabilized the newly independent states. The movement to restrain out-of-control legislatures, at both the state and national levels, proved so strong that Wood has likened it to a "Thermidorian" reaction.[48]

The object of this constitutional counterrevolution was a restored executive to check the excesses of the legislature, control law enforcement, appoint and manage government personnel, and conduct war and foreign relations. With Montesquieu's ringing injunction that liberty could only survive with a clear separation of the branches of government, the Framers arrived at the Constitutional Convention determined to create an executive that would be elected independently of the legislature and possess its own inherent authorities, so as to avoid the manipulation by the legislature that the revolutionary states had experienced, and to confound factions. As an authoritative work on the revolutionary constitutions has observed, "[T]he reaction against the colonial governor was so weak that it did not lead to parliamentary government with an executive committee of members of the legislature, but rather that within a decade the American system of presidential government evolved with full clarity and permanence."[49]

CHAPTER 2

Creation

WHEN THE DELEGATES to the Constitutional Convention met in the summer of 1787, the only thing that made them more uncomfortable than the Philadelphia heat was the topic of the executive. Madison's notes record that when James Wilson of Pennsylvania moved that the executive power be vested in a single officer, "a considerable pause" followed. It took Benjamin Franklin, who rarely threw his considerable prestige into the debates, to demand that "the gentlemen deliver their sentiments" because "it was a point of great importance."[1] But the Framers refused to consistently and directly address the chief problem — how to republicanize the executive. Rather, they reached a series of incremental decisions, many of them in committees or late in the convention.

Federalism dominated the convention: the representation of the small states in the Senate, the federal ability to tax and regulate individuals directly, and the issue of slavery. The Framers discussed the Presidency three times that summer but made little progress until the very end. Structure dominated: how many executives should there be, how chosen, and how removed? Sustained attention on the executive's substantive powers came only during the final rush near the Convention's end. With only two weeks to go, the draft located many executive powers either in Congress or the Senate. Then, a compromise was reached on the method for selecting the President; a logjam broken, powers soon migrated from the legislature to the executive. What emerged from the Constitutional Convention was a Presidency with its own independent powers, equal to those of the legislature, one that both in theory and in practice would prove to be up to the demands of future generations.

PRESIDENTIAL POWER AND WRITING A NEW CONSTITUTION

DISCUSSION BEGAN ON June 1 with the Virginia Plan, intro-duced by Virginia Governor Edmund Randolph and privately drafted by Madison. The Plan included two of the three core executive powers identified by Blackstone, Locke, and Montesquieu: to "execute the National laws" and to "enjoy the Executive rights vested in the Congress by the Confederation" such as foreign affairs,[2] but it lacked the veto over legislation or the power to pardon. Instead, it proposed a Council of Revision made up of the President and federal judges to review congressional acts. Madison broke the executive power down into the right to "carry into effect" the laws, to appoint inferior officers, and to perform other functions "not Legislative nor Judiciary in their nature" as Congress might delegate.[3]

What the Virginia Plan granted in substance, it took away in structure. Its executive would be chosen by the legislature, would serve only one term, and might consist of more than one person. Thus, it would have no claim to direct popular support nor ability to influence legislation. It would have resembled the parliamentary system of government that exists in much of the world today, in which the executive branch is simply the leader of the majority coalition in the legislature. While the Virginia Plan forbade members of the legislature from serving in the executive branch, legislative appointment of multiple executives would have made the office another arena for legislative deal-making. Cabinet officers would have felt beholden to their supporters in Congress rather than to the Chief Executive. Even in foreign affairs, a President directly selected by Congress would enjoy little independence. As Charles Thach observed, if the Virginia Plan had prevailed, "the American executive must have been of a type resembling in many fundamental ways the executive of modern Switzerland."[4]

Some wanted to create a weak President. Randolph believed an executive unified in one officer to be the "foetus of monarchy."[5] Roger Sherman supported legislative election of the President because he is "nothing more than an institution for carrying the will of the legislature into effect."[6] Sherman believed that Congress should appoint any number of individuals to head the executive branch, depending on the job at hand, and that Congress should be able to fire them "at pleasure." Early proposals that also won favor among the delegates limited the President to a single seven-year term. The main alternative to the Virginia Plan, the New Jersey Plan, proposed a multiple Presidency, chosen by the legislature and limited to one term.

Almost from the start, however, several of the leading lights of the Constitutional Convention sought to move the Presidency toward the New York model. Wilson argued early on for a single President to be directly elected by the people. Unification of the executive branch in one person would give the "most energy, dispatch, and responsibility."[7] He urged the delegates to toss aside Madison's council of revision, observing that a committee "oftener serves to cover than prevent malpractices." Wilson also wanted the President to have an absolute veto over legislation to protect his independence from legislative encroachment and to be eligible for an unlimited number of short terms, which would increase his popular accountability. Direct election by the people had proven both "convenient and successful" in New York and Massachusetts. Gouverneur Morris rose in support, commenting that otherwise, the President would become the "mere creature" of Congress and subject to "intrigue," "cabal," and "faction."

While a radical change in structure, Wilson's proposal broke no new substantive ground. Wilson agreed with Madison that the President's power was mainly to carry out the laws and appoint officers. Wilson "did not consider the Prerogatives of the British Monarch as a proper guide in defining the Executive powers. Some of these prerogatives were of a Legislative nature. Among others that of war & peace."[8] Charles Pickney agreed that the executive should retain his traditional powers, but that they should not include all of the Crown's foreign affairs authority. He "was for a vigorous Executive but was afraid the Executive powers of [the existing] Congress might extend to peace & war which would render the Executive a Monarchy, of the worst kind, to wit an elective one."[9] John Rutledge supported Wilson "for vesting the Executive power in a single person, tho' he was not for giving him the power of war and peace." Early supporters of an independent President worried that all of the "executive powers" would include making war and peace. But even the New Jersey Plan, noteworthy for its restrictions on the executive, declared that the President shall "direct all military operations; provided that none of the persons composing the federal Executive shall on any occasion take command of any troops, so as personally to conduct any enterprise as General."[10]

When the New Jersey Plan won supporters, Alexander Hamilton rose in support of a stronger executive. He proposed essentially a King, giving rise to lifelong suspicions that he was a closet monarchist. His "governor" would be selected by electors chosen by the people, and hold the office for life unless impeached for malfeasance.[11] It would not just execute the laws but would have an absolute veto, make treaties and appointments with the advice of the Senate, and direct the military. The governor would exercise "the supream [sic] Executive authority of the United States." Hamilton admitted that he took his inspiration from the British monarchy, practically guaranteeing that his proposals would go nowhere. Hamilton never made a formal proposal to the Convention but used a radical speech to push the delegates into a reasonable compromise.

By the end of the first week of discussion, the delegates agreed that a single individual should head the executive. By August, the executive would become "Commander in Chief of the Army and Navy of the United States, and of the Militia of the Several States," and receive the power to execute the laws, to appoint officials, to call Congress and recommend legislation, to receive ambassadors, and to grant pardons. Out of concern over executive aggrandizement, the Senate initially received sole power over treaties and appointment of ambassadors, as well as the power "to make War; to raise Armies; to build and equip Fleets" and powers over taxation, spending, and the regulation of commerce. The Senate served as an executive council, modeled on those of the states, which shared executive power with the governor. Senators were to be elected by the members of the House rather than appointed by the state legislatures.[12]

Further work on the executive awaited resolution of the most contentious issue of the Convention: the debate over whether Congress would represent the population or the states. In the Great Compromise of July 16, 1787, the small and large states finally agreed to a bicameral legislature with a Senate with equal voting power among the states, a decision that had a profound effect on the Presidency. As Jack Rakove has argued, as the Senate became the protector of state interests, it lost its special justification to manage foreign affairs. The Great Compromise rippled outward, affecting both federalism and the separation of powers.

The Senate's transformation gave a new urgency to those who wanted a President to serve as a counterweight to Congress. Even Madison, who had included legislative selection in the Virginia Plan, now joined Wilson and Morris. "It was essential," he argued, "that the appointment of the Executive should either be drawn from some source, or held by some tenure, that will give him a free agency with regard to the Legislature."[13] Morris laid out an innovative case for a strong independent executive. Reversing Montesquieu's contention that republics could only be small, Morris argued that only a President with vigorous powers could hold such a large nation as America together. Roger Sherman of Connecticut and Charles Pinckney of South Carolina objected that the people were too uninformed to choose the best candidate, that state favoritism would prevail, or that demagogues would dominate. Morris responded that an independent executive would balance Congress. Allow legislative selection of the executive, Morris warned, and the President "will not be independent of it; and if not independent, usurpation and tyranny on the part of the Legislature will be the consequence."

Over the next few days, the Convention wavered between selection by the legislature or by electors chosen by the states or the people. Discussion ranged from whether the electors from faraway states could travel to the national capital to vote (an important consideration in the day of horse and sail) to whether foreign nations would bribe legislators. The delegates also went back and forth over the veto. In the first week of discussions, the convention agreed to a limited veto with a council of revision in which the President and members of the judiciary could block unwise, unjust, or improper laws. Instead of serving as a check on the executive, the council responded to fears that the executive would lack the political "firmness" to stand up to the legislature *without* support from the judiciary.[14] Eventually, the Convention eliminated the council but kept the President's limited veto.

A small group of delegates, known as "the committee of detail," took on the job of winnowing down the principles approved in June and July. It produced a draft Constitution in early August. Wilson, the consistent supporter of an independent executive, headed the committee, and it showed. The Constitution now vested "the executive power of the United States" in one man. The President served as Commander-in-Chief and held the right to appoint inferior executive officers, veto legislation, carry out the laws, issue pardons, receive ambassadors (the primary means of carrying out foreign affairs in the eighteenth century), and recommend legislation.[15] The draft kept the powers to appoint judges and make treaties with the Senate, and gave Congress other elements of the British monarch's authority, such as raising armies, making war, and regulating commerce.

Based on the most powerful state executive of the time, New York's, this draft became Article II of the Constitution. Far from favoring a weak executive, the Framers had chosen the strongest republican model available. Presidential power continued to gain as the end of the Convention drew near. On August 15, the delegates decided that a qualified veto was necessary to protect against congressional abuse. Wilson remarked that "the prejudices [against] the Executive resulted from a misapplication of the adage that the parliament was the palladium of liberty,"[16] and where "the Executive was not formidable," people would likelier equate the "legislature and tyranny." Morris pressed for an absolute veto to guard against "encroachments of the popular branch of the Government." "If the

Executive be overturned by the popular branch," he warned, "the tyranny of one man will ensue."[17] Supporters of a strong executive even succeeded for a time in setting the votes needed to override a presidential veto at three-quarters of both houses of Congress, rather than the two-thirds we have today.

War was next on the agenda. On August 17, Charles Pinckney moved that the power to "make war," then vested in Congress, be transferred to the Senate alone, because the former's "proceedings were too slow."[18] The Senate, he thought, would be small and more familiar with foreign affairs. Pierce Butler of South Carolina responded that the Senate would suffer from the same problems as Congress, so the war power should be given to the President, "who will have all the requisite qualities, and will not make war but when the Nation will support it."

James Madison and Elbridge Gerry of Massachusetts (who in later life would become the author of salamander-shaped electoral districts) proposed that the Convention amend Congress's power from "make" war to "declare" war. According to Madison and Gerry, the amendment would make clear the President's authority to "repel sudden attacks."[19] Roger Sherman of Connecticut opposed that change because he wanted the executive to "be able to repel and not to commence war." Gerry responded that he "never expected to hear in a republic a motion to empower the Executive alone to declare war." George Mason of Virginia opposed "giving the power of war to the Executive," because he "was for clogging rather than facilitating war; but for facilitating peace." Yet, Mason supported the amendment. Rufus King of Massachusetts defended the proposal because giving Congress the power to "make" war "might be understood to 'conduct' it, which was an Executive function." With that comment last in mind, the delegates approved the Madison-Gerry amendment with eight states in favor and one against.

The final understanding of the delegates remains controversial to this day — perhaps because the amendment was made at the equivalent of 5:00 P.M. on a Friday.[20] Yet, their changes to the war power made two things clear. First, the power to "declare" war was a narrower subset of the broader power to "make" war. Second, the changes to the war power followed the general trend near the end of the Convention to transfer authority to the President.

Congress's power to declare war was not the only aspect of the war power. Declarations of war often followed the outbreak of combat and had the legal function of defining the status of hostiles and neutrals.[21] The Declaration of Independence would have been the legal model uppermost in the delegates' minds. Issued more than a year after fighting had broken out with the British, the Declaration articulated the grievances against Great Britain, the grounds for the resort to armed hostilities, and the remedies that would bring the war to an end. When lawyers referred to the power to begin or to commence war, they used language broader than "declare." The Articles of Confederation had provided that Congress enjoyed "the sole and exclusive right and power of determining on peace and war," and South Carolina's constitution conferred the power to "commence" war upon its legislature.[22] Article I, Section 10 of the Constitution declares that "No State shall, without the Consent of Congress…engage in War, unless actually invaded, or in such imminent Danger as will not admit of delay." This is just the language and the procedure favored by modern scholars who believe that Congress ought to have the final say on war. But the Framers turned from that language and divided the war powers between the President and Congress. Congress has a powerful influence over war through funding, but giving Congress the power to "make" war would encroach on authority best shared with the executive.

The Convention soon followed by ending the Senate's monopoly on treaties. Some delegates, such as Charles Pinckney, believed that the Senate should "manage foreign affairs" and perform a variety of executive functions, but on August 23 the Convention gave the President the right to make treaties, subject to the Senate's approval. Madison observed that "the Senate represented the States alone, and that for this as well as other obvious reasons it was proper that the President should be an agent in Treaties."[23] Rakove has laid out a strong case that these "other obvious reasons" included a concern about the Senate's unrepresentative nature and a new respect for the President's democratic accountability.[24] Although most commentators describe the treaty power as shared between the President and Senate, the Constitution weights matters heavily in favor of the former. The Constitution locates the treaty power in Article II, where presidential powers reside, not among Congress's powers in Article I. It gives the President the "Power to make Treaties," conditioned on "the advice and consent" of the Senate. The President decides whether to start negotiations, negotiates terms, and even after the Senate consents, determines whether to conclude the treaty. Combined with the authority to receive ambassadors and his general executive power, the President's role gives the executive branch the effective ability to control the setting of foreign policy and diplomatic relations with other nations.[25]

Not until the very end did the Convention forge the crucial democratic tie between the President and the American people. On the last day of August, the delegates referred undecided questions to a committee of unfinished business, composed of one delegate from each state. Four days later, this committee returned with a proposal for the Electoral College, which was approved two days later. It represented a compromise among supporters of state involvement, popular election, and congressional choice, but its shift toward selection by the people is unmistakable. Supporters of an independent executive, such as Wilson, Madison, and Morris, had fought against any system that gave the states or Congress control over the selection of the President.[26] At the same time, it is undeniable that many of the Philadelphia delegates were suspicious of undiluted direct democracy, which had caused the problems in the states that had brought them together. They wanted a virtuous President who would pursue the national interest, even if that meant sometimes resisting the temporary passions of the people. The rise of political parties to filter and then support a few candidates had not yet occurred. Parties would have been associated in these delegates' minds with "factions" subversive of the public good.

The Electoral College was the Framers' answer to the threat of legislative supremacy and demagogic popular leadership. State legislatures would set the process for choosing electors, which would amount to the number of the state's Representatives and Senators. These electors would then vote for two candidates, one of whom had to hail from another state, to reduce the influence of home-state favoritism and regionalism. Electors would meet in their states and send their votes to the President of the Senate, who would open them and count them in Congress. The winner would become President, and the runner-up would become Vice President. If no one received a majority, members of the House would choose the President from the top five vote-getters, with each state delegation casting a single vote.

Hamilton and Madison believed that the Electoral College would achieve both of their goals by enlarging the sphere to select the President. Demagogues would be less likely to reach the nation's highest office if voted upon by a national electorate. As Hamilton wrote in *Federalist 68*: "[I]t will require other talents, and a different kind of merit to establish him in the esteem and confidence of the whole union, or so considerable a portion of it as would be necessary

to make him a successful candidate" for the White House.[27] Gouverneur Morris declared in the Convention that an "election by
the people at large throughout so great an extent of country could
not be influenced by those little combinations and momentary lies
which often decide popular elections within a narrow sphere."[28] Or
as Hamilton explained: "Talents for low intrigue, and the little acts
of popularity may alone suffice to elevate a man to the first honors in
a single state."[29] But a nationwide election would prevent the worst
from rising high. Morris had predicted earlier in the Convention
that the people "will never fail to prefer some man of distinguished
character or services," or of "continental reputation."[30]

Looking back, the Electoral College resembles a Rube Goldberg
contraption, a complicated system of voting devised to avoid both
direct popular selection and any formal role for Congress and the
states. The states still have a role, because the number of electoral
votes per state includes Senate seats, and because elections with no
majority winner are thrown to the House to be decided on a one-
vote-per-state basis. This backup system provides for legislative influence if no continent-wide favorite emerged in the Electoral College.
Recognizing that this process posed the same problems as congressional election of the President, Madison and Hamilton by the end
of the Convention supported selection of the President by only a plurality of electoral votes. They lost that question to the small-state delegates. Still, except for this, the President's election did not depend
on Congress, and the President would be broadly representative of
the American people.

Further transfer of powers from the Senate to the President followed. The President's control over treaties and the appointment of
ambassadors, with Senate participation, was formalized. Aside from
its veto over treaties, the Senate no longer had any role in foreign
affairs; it was now the President who enjoyed the initiative in inter-

national relations. Morris argued that this was correct because the President was "the general Guardian of the National interests."[31] The Senate also lost the authority to appoint federal judges. Now, the President would appoint with the Senate's "advice and consent." Like treaties, the Appointments Clause placed the President in the lead position: The President nominates first, and after receiving Senate consent, makes the appointment. Combined with his duty to take care that the laws are faithfully executed and his authority to appoint all inferior executive branch officers, the appointment of judges ensured that the President would control the enforcement of the nation's laws. One last decision before the close of the Convention did not go the President's way — the vote to override a presidential veto of legislation was reduced from three-quarters of Congress to two-thirds, which diminished the President's role in the legislative process but still guaranteed that the President could defeat most bills attacking executive power.

Scholars disagree about the significance of these last-minute changes. The struggle over foreign affairs has produced the sharpest recent conflicts about the scope of presidential power. Several leading law professors argue that the Framers intended only limited exceptions from a general congressional control over foreign affairs and national policy. Other scholars, such as Clinton Rossiter have, over the years, made the case that the Framers intended to vest the foreign affairs power in the President.[32] Some historians argue that presidential power grew out of distrust of the Senate, while Edward Corwin famously observed that the Constitution "is an invitation to struggle for the privilege of directing American foreign policy."[33] Whatever the precise intent of the Framers, Anglo-American constitutional and political tradition as described by Locke, Montesquieu, and Blackstone, and put into practice by British Kings and Parliaments, lodged the foreign affairs power in the executive. Nothing in the new constitutional text and its surrounding discussions moved that baseline. Perhaps more important, the renovated Presidency ensured that future Presidents would hold the initiative in setting policy and executing it. George Washington lost no time in doing just this, and the First Congress acquiesced to it.

With its work done, the Convention decided to adjourn for the last time. Throughout the debates, Benjamin Franklin had stared at George Washington's chair, which bore the image of a rising sun. On that last day, Franklin told the Convention that during the last three months he had wondered "whether it was rising or setting. But now at length I have the happiness to know that it is a rising and not a setting sun."[34] In part, Franklin's optimism was triggered by the innovation of the American Presidency. Hoping to tame the executive with popular selection, a radical choice in a world of monarchies, the Convention empowered the new government with an independent executive who held the authority to enforce the laws and to manage foreign affairs. Left unaddressed was the third leg of the executive's historical powers, the prerogative to override written law when crisis or emergency dictated. Yet, the executive power had been established so as to allow future occupants of the Presidency to claim inherent authorities, among them the conduct of foreign policy and the protection of the national security.[35]

PRESIDENTIAL POWER AND
THE RATIFICATION PROCESS

AFTER PHILADELPHIA, the political momentum behind constitutional reform moved to the states. Leading accounts of the Presidency often overlook the state ratification process: Schlesinger's iconic *Imperial Presidency* and Michael Genovese's more recent *The Power of the American Presidency*, for example, limit discussion of

the state debates to a few quotes from *The Federalist*.[36] Other leading
books jump straight from the Philadelphia Convention to the Washington administration, or only begin in 1789.[37] The Constitutional
Convention, encapsulating discussion and votes at a single time and
place, is understandably more straightforward to study, whereas the
ratification process took place over the course of a year at unruly
conventions spread across the country, in open-air and closed-door
meetings, and in letters and newspaper articles.

Yet, the ratification debates arguably have greater political
legitimacy than the Philadelphia Convention. Madison and Wilson
themselves admitted that the Philadelphia Convention proposed,
but had no authority to establish, a new Constitution. The Constitution itself proposed to replace the Articles of Confederation only
after the approval of specially elected conventions of nine states. Ratification gave the Anti-Federalists the opportunity to challenge specific provisions and to force its supporters, the Federalists, to explain
how they would work in practice. Adoption of the Constitution was
no sure thing. Of the five states that ratified within four months,
only Pennsylvania experienced significant Anti-Federalist resistance,
and still the Federalists there prevailed by a margin of two to one.[38]
But in the critical states of Massachusetts, Virginia, and New York,
the voters had elected a majority of Anti-Federalist delegates. Without these states, the Constitution surely could not have succeeded;
Virginia, in particular, was the key to ratification. The Constitution survived in Massachusetts only narrowly, by a vote of 187–168,
apparently after Federalists promised Anti-Federalist John Hancock
the Vice Presidency; in Virginia by only 88–80; and in New York by
only three votes. The narrow margins and the economic and political
significance of these states make their understanding of the Constitution particularly important.

One factor influenced ratification above all others — George

Washington. It is impossible to overstate the influence of the "Father of the Country" on Americans of the founding generation. Washington had led a ragtag, outmanned, and outgunned army to victory over one of the most powerful nations in the world, then prevented his army from undermining civilian control, famously surprising a meeting of officers who had planned to launch a military coup (known to historians as the "Newburgh Conspiracy"). When he began to read a document to them with the words, "Gentlemen, you will permit me to put on my spectacles, for I have not only grown gray but almost blind in the service of my country,"[39] officers in attendance wept, and the conspiracy collapsed. He achieved worldwide renown as a modern-day Cincinnatus when, at the end of the war, he returned all power to Congress and retired to private life, and then placed his considerable prestige behind the Constitution by agreeing to chair the Philadelphia Convention. As Pierce Butler wrote afterward, he did not believe that the President's powers "would have been so great had not many of the members [at Philadelphia] cast their eyes towards General Washington as President; and shaped their Ideas of the Powers to be given to a President, by their opinions of his Virtue."[40] That prospect no doubt allayed fears about abuses of executive power.

When the Constitution went to the states for ratification, only the text of the Constitution was before the voters; Madison's notes of the Convention debates remained secret until his death in 1836. The enfeebled governorships of the Pennsylvania or Virginia constitutions had been abandoned in favor of an independent executive in the New York and Massachusetts mold. Leadership was centralized in one person, eligible for unlimited terms, fully responsible for the executive branch, to be chosen by an Electoral College, not Congress. No advisory council diluted the President's authority or responsibility. Instead, he had the power to appoint executive branch officials,

Justices of the Supreme Court, and lower court judges, subject only to the advice and consent of the Senate. The President would have a qualified veto, giving him a share of the legislative power as well as the means to defend himself from any congressional efforts to strip him of his powers. He could issue pardons, adding to his control over law enforcement through the Take Care Clause.

The President would also be the Commander-in-Chief of the nation's military, take the lead role in treaties and in appointments, and have exclusive power to execute the laws. A legal point probably only dimly perceived by the public, but certainly well understood by the lawyers of the Convention, Article II places the open-ended "executive power" of the United States in the President, in contrast to Article I, which says that Congress is to have only those "legislative powers herein granted." The idea of the prerogative was left unaddressed, and the exact division of power over foreign affairs unresolved. Students of executive power, from Machiavelli through Blackstone, or of British constitutional history, would have recognized the traditional powers of the executive in the new Constitution.

The new Congress attempted to repair the defects of the state assemblies. The representative national legislature had its own powers of taxation and funding, and the authority to directly regulate private conduct independent of the whims of the states. Congress held significant foreign affairs powers of its own, including raising and funding the military, declaring war, defining punishments for violations of international law, and regulating interstate and international commerce. Yet, it no longer had "the sole and exclusive right and power of determining on peace and war" nor the sole authority of "entering into treaties and alliances," as it had had under Article IX of the Articles of Confederation. The Framers thought that dividing these powers would stimulate executive initiative in war and peace, checked by legislative control over funding and domestic regulation as in Great Britain.

Anti-Federalists attacked the new Constitution as a repudiation of the Revolution, focusing mainly on the powerful national government and the absence of a bill of rights. They charged that the new executive was nothing but the return of monarchy in a different guise, but on specifics their arguments were disorganized and scattershot. Federalists had the advantage of controlling the agenda. Anti-Federalist opposition nevertheless forced the Federalists to describe the separation of powers as they expected it to work in practice, and the reasoning behind the grant of executive power.

Anti-Federalists quoted Montesquieu's warning that the executive and legislative powers had to be separate; they predicted that these parchment barriers would fail without the checks and balances of social classes as they existed in the mother country. They attacked the establishment of a Senate, which resembled the aristocratic House of Lords, and complained that the Senate would bully both the House and the President to do its bidding. George Mason made the Senate a centerpiece of his explanation for refusing to sign the Constitution. Its role in treaties, appointments, and impeachments, he wrote, "will destroy any Balance in the Government, and enable them to accomplish what Usurpations they please upon the Rights & Libertys of the People."[41]

Eager to find fault with the new Constitution, some Anti-Federalists even thought the delegates had not gone far enough to empower government leaders; some thought that there should be no division between executive and legislative power to serve as a brake on the government. One Anti-Federalist writer, "Cincinnatus," decried the "absurd division" of the executive power between the President and the Senate, which "must be productive of constant contentions for the lead, must clog the executive of government to a mischievous, and sometimes to a disgraceful degree."[42]

Some warned that the new office of President might turn into a monarchy. "Cato," one of the first widely circulated Anti-Federalist writers (almost all political writers during the Revolution and early American national period wrote under pseudonyms, many drawn from significant figures in ancient Roman history), asked in New York, "[W]herein does this president, invested with his powers and prerogatives, essentially differ from the King of Great-Britain?"[43] An "Old Whig" in Pennsylvania maintained that the Constitution's powers made the President "in reality to be a king as much a king as the King of Great-Britain, and a King too of the worst kind; an elective King."[44] The "Federal Farmer," considered by historians to be the most able and moderate of the Anti-Federalist writers, worried that the lack of term limits might give a single man or family control of the office for decades and that the right to appoint officers would lead to corruption like that of Georgian England.

Anti-Federalists linked the Commander-in-Chief role to the prevalent dread of standing armies. "Brutus," another leading Anti-Federalist pamphleteer, warned that "the evil to be feared from a standing army in time of peace" went beyond military support for their leader to the danger of military coups, saying that the "equal, and perhaps greater danger, is to be apprehended from their overturning the constitutional powers of the government, and assuming the power to dictate any form they please."[45] There would "not be wanting a variety of plausible reasons to justify the raising" of an army, he warned. "Tamony" became the target of Hamilton's wrath for writing, "[T]he commander of the fleets and armies of America,...though not dignified with the magic name of King, he will possess more supreme power, than Great Britain allows her hereditary monarchs" because armies could receive funds for two years at a time and "his command of a standing army is unrestrained by law or limitation."[46]

A President at the head of the armies, supported by a Senate combining all three powers of government (the Senate passed legislation, participated in making treaties and appointing officers, and tried impeachments), could become corrupt and crush the liberties of the people. The Federal Farmer predicted that the new central government would be unable to execute its powers "without calling to its aid a military force, which must very soon destroy all elective governments in the country, produce anarchy, or establish despotism."[47]

The Federalists responded that to limit government power in emergencies would be foolhardy. These powers, Hamilton argued early in December 1787, "ought to exist without limitation."[48] Echoing Locke, he observed that the nature and scope of emergencies were "impossible to foresee." Because the "circumstances that endanger the safety of nations are infinite," Hamilton warned, "no constitutional shackles can wisely be imposed on the power." Agreeing with his *Federalist* coauthor, Madison chimed in: "The means of security can only be regulated by the means and the danger of attack."[49] Madison concluded, "It is vain to oppose constitutional barriers to the impulse of self-preservation. It is worse than vain; because it plants in the Constitution itself necessary usurpations of power." A Constitution with a weak government and executive, some Federalists argued, posed an even greater danger of tyranny, for to survive in a dangerous world, the nation would be forced to resort to actions the Constitution forbade. Insecurity was ever-present in the Framers' minds, for the new republic was hemmed in to the North by the British and to the South and West by the Spanish.

This argument played into Anti-Federalist concerns about a centralized government that mingled specific powers. Federalists admitted that the Constitution did not fully separate legislative, executive, and judicial functions, but pointed to the British and state constitutions that granted the executive a veto over legislation.

A better safeguard than complete separation, they argued, was to give each branch incentives and the authority to check each other. In *Federalist 51*, Madison wrote that power needed to align with self-interest: "Ambition must be made to counteract ambition. The interest of the man must be connected with the constitutional rights of the place." Competition among the branches would present the best protection. "The great security against a gradual concentration of the several powers in the same department, consists in giving to those who administer each department, the necessary constitutional means, and personal motives, to resist encroachments of the others."[50]

Madison's reliance on structural checks and balances was a 180-degree turn from the enthusiasms of the Revolution. As Wood has emphasized, the revolutionaries put their faith in legislatures as exemplars of popular sovereignty. The people could do no wrong, so why restrict the power of their representatives? By 1788, Federalists had come to see unlimited legislative power as presenting its own problems. In a democracy, James Madison wrote in *Federalist 48*, the legislature held broader powers and access to the "pockets of the people." He warned that "it is against the enterprising ambition of [the legislature], that the people ought to indulge all their jealousy and exhaust all their precautions."[51] He had seen the "impetuous vortex" of the legislature in action in Virginia and Pennsylvania, and thought a strengthened executive was needed to guard against unwise popular passions acting through the legislature. "In republican government the legislative authority, necessarily, predominates." So, "the weakness of the executive may require, on the other hand, that it be fortified."

Hamilton followed Madison's contributions to *The Federalist* with a more detailed and sophisticated discussion of the executive branch. While the divisions within a legislature might encourage deliberation, they also tended to subject government decisions to "every sudden breeze of passion" or "every transient impulse," especially those created by the flattering "arts of men."[52] Hamilton saw that legislative sovereignty had its drawbacks, when the legislature sold out the long-term common good for short-term popularity or political gain — a conventional idea today, but a radical one then. This situation called for executive intervention. A vigorous executive could protect against those "irregular and high-handed combinations which sometimes interrupt the ordinary course of justice," and would provide a security against "enterprises and assaults of ambition, of faction, and of anarchy."[53] An executive did not owe an unjustified and "unbounded complaisance" to every sudden breeze of popular passion, nor did he have obligations toward the "humours of the legislature." A popularly elected executive serving a set term in office could block "imperious," impetuous, or unwise legislative acts that merely catered to a popular mood. In his famous discussion of judicial review in *Federalist 78*, Hamilton used the same logic: each branch owed its ultimate constitutional responsibility to the people, not to the legislature, and could use its unique powers to negate unconstitutional actions of the other branches.

The revolutionary state constitutions had created obstacles to good government, persuading the Convention delegates that a strong executive and republican government were not incompatible but mutually reinforcing. "A feeble execution is but another phrase for a bad execution," Hamilton argued in *Federalist 70*, "and a government ill executed, whatever may be in theory, must be, in practice, a bad government."[54] "Good government" required "energy in the executive," and a vigorous President was now seen as "essential to the protection of the community from foreign attacks" and "the steady administration of the laws."

Energy, in turn, depended on four pillars: unity, duration, financial support, and "competent powers." First was "unity" in office. Concentrating executive power in one person would bring "[d]ecision, activity, secrecy, and dispatch," Hamilton wrote, echoing Machiavelli. To diffuse executive power among multiple parties, or to require the approval of a council of state, would endanger virtues needed for good government. Authority would be weakened, and confusion among many opinions would reign, frustrating the government's ability to respond to "the most critical emergencies of the state." A plural executive would "conceal faults and destroy responsibility," allowing blame for failure to be shifted and avoiding accountability of punishment by public opinion. A "cabal" within a council would "enervate the whole system of administration" and produce "habitual feebleness and dilatoriness." Hamilton pointed out, insightfully, that the British constitution had established a council precisely in order to hold ministers responsible for mistakes, to maintain the fiction that the King could do no wrong. Under a republican government, the buck should stop with the Chief Executive, who should not be hampered with divided responsibility, nor free to deflect blame onto a committee. "A council to a magistrate, who is himself responsible for what he does, are generally nothing better than a clog upon his good intentions, are often the instruments and accomplices of his bad and are almost always a cloak to his faults."[55]

Federalists in the state ratification conventions amplified Hamilton's appeal. In the Pennsylvania ratifying convention, James Wilson observed that "we well know what numerous executives are. We know there is neither vigor, decision, nor responsibility in them."[56] The Constitution placed executive power in a "single magistrate," so as to bring "strength, vigor, energy, and responsibility" to the execution of federal law.[57] Governor Randolph, who had disagreed in Philadelphia, now concurred in Virginia: "All the enlightened part of mankind agree that the superior dispatch, secrecy, and energy with which one man can act, renders it more politic to vest the power of executing the laws in one man."[58] The second pillar of executive power was duration in office. In all but two of the revolutionary states, executives were chosen annually. "Where annual elections end, tyranny begins," went the revolutionary era slogan. Most states also placed term limits on their executives to prevent "the danger of establishing an inconvenient aristocracy," in the words of the Pennsylvania constitution. Federalists rejected the idea of term limits because short terms contributed to instability, leading to rule by the whim of the majority. In *Federalist 71,* Hamilton explained that a longer term would promote stability as well as "the personal firmness of the executive magistrate, in the employment of his constitutional powers." A longer term with the opportunity for reelection gave a President the time to "plan and undertake the most extensive and arduous enterprises for the public benefit." If his term were too short, popular opinion would sit foremost in the President's mind, and short-term political gain and hopes for reelection would come before the public interest. Longer terms created less rotation in offices and shifts in policy as new Presidents took office. A "change in men" would create "a mutability of measures."

Eligibility for reelection would allow the nation to gain from the experience and qualities of successful executives. The two-term tradition took hold with Washington and was only codified after Franklin Roosevelt's unprecedented four victories. For the Federalists, the prospect of reelection would encourage the chief executive to pursue policies in the broader public interest. Influenced by David Hume, the authors of *The Federalist* designed a system of government that would harness private interest to the national benefit.[59] This was nowhere more true than in the design of the Presidency. Hamilton described "the love of fame" as "the ruling passion of the noblest minds." Pursuit of fame would encourage Presidents to confront difficult challenges, but only if they could win reelection and their labors be rewarded.

The third pillar was "adequate provision for its support." The Constitution removed the President's salary as a tool of legislative gamesmanship by prohibiting its change during his term. An irreducible salary and lifetime appointment are regarded as the foundation for the independence of federal judges. The Framers wanted the President to be accountable to the people, but they also wanted the President to be as independent of Congress as the courts. "The Legislature," Hamilton warned, "with a discretionary power over the salary and emoluments of the Chief Magistrate, could render him as obsequious to their will, as they might think proper to make him."[60] Congress has more such authority over judges, as it could theoretically raise judges' pay in exchange for favorable decisions, or punish the courts by never raising salaries during a judge's lifetime. A President's guaranteed salary for a four-year term gives him somewhat greater freedom from congressional control.

The fourth pillar of the Presidency was "competent powers," both enumerated and explicit, and unenumerated and inherent. In beginning his discussion of the President's powers in *Federalist 72*, Hamilton observed that the "administration of government" falls "peculiarly within the province of the executive department." It included the conduct of foreign affairs, the preparation of the budget, the expenditure of appropriated funds, and the direction of the military and "the operations of war." Officers who exercised these powers were assistants to the President who should be appointed by the executive and "be subject to his superintendence." Both, however, were constructions that came from no specific grant of authority in the constitutional text, only Article II's vesting of the general executive power in the President.[61]

Chief among the President's enumerated powers was law enforcement. "The execution of the laws and the employment of the common strength, either for this purpose or for the common defense, seem to comprise all the functions of the executive magistrate,"[62] Hamilton observed. The general grant of the executive power and the duty to "take Care that the Laws be faithfully executed" both restrict and empower the President. They make clear that the President cannot suspend the law of the land at his whim, as British kings had, but they also give the President authority both to enforce the law and to interpret it. Enforcing the law gives the President the right to compel the obedience of private individuals, and even states, to the Constitution, treaties, and acts of Congress. At critical times in American history — the Washington and Jefferson administrations, the Civil War, the civil rights revolution — Presidents have even called on military force to fulfill this constitutional obligation.

Enforcement implies interpretation. In order to carry out the laws, an executive must determine their meaning. Sometimes those laws will be clear, as when the Constitution sets the minimum age for a President, but more often than not, the laws are ambiguous or delegate decision-making to the executive. Judicial review usually arises after a law's passage and enforcement, and it requires that a case be brought. The executive must often interpret the laws before a dispute reaches the courts. In situations where a law creates no private right to sue, or the constitutional issue involves a political question immune from judicial review, the courts may never even be able to take up a case that raises the right question, effectively giving the executive or Congress the final say. With the current move to judicial supremacy and the decline of the political question doctrine, the courts are, however, choosing to address more such issues of law.

Hamilton regarded the gravest threat to the separation of powers to be the "legislature's propensity to intrude upon the rights and to absorb the powers of the other departments."[63] Skeptical of "a mere parchment delineation of the boundaries," Federalists believed instead that each branch needed "constitutional arms for its own defence." For the executive, that weapon is the veto. Today, Presidents often veto bills on policy grounds, needing the support of only 34 Senators to prevail. More often than not, constitutional objections are left to the courts. This is almost the reverse of the Framers' expectations. In *Federalist 73*, Hamilton explained that the veto would allow the President to deflect "an immediate attack upon the constitutional rights of the executive." Blocking an act of Congress would have been regarded at the time as aggressive for courts, but not Presidents. Between 1789 and 1861, Presidents vetoed roughly two dozen bills for constitutional reasons; the Supreme Court struck down only two.[64] Jefferson even doubted whether he could veto a law for anything but constitutional reasons. Under this view, if a bill only made bad policy, a President had no choice but to sign it. This problem did not trouble Publius. The veto would not just serve as a "shield to the executive" but would "furnish[] an additional security against the enaction of improper laws." For him, the President could veto laws because they were too partisan, too hasty, or "unfriendly to the public good."[65]

Some have argued that if a President believes a law is unconstitutional, he has no choice but to veto it, and if his veto is overridden, he has no choice but to carry out the law faithfully.[66] They cite the Constitution's Take Care Clause as support. Textually, however, this argument ignores the fact that the Constitution is the highest law of the land. The obligation to faithfully execute the laws requires the President to obey the Constitution first above any statute to the contrary—as the Supreme Court recognized in *Marbury v. Madison*, judicial review flows from the principle that a court cannot enforce a law that conflicts with the Constitution itself.[67] To require the President to carry out unconstitutional laws would defeat the larger purpose behind the veto. James Wilson, for one, anticipated that Congress might seek to grab executive power: "[T]he legislature may be restrained and kept within its prescribed bounds by the interposition of the judicial department. In the same manner the President of the United States could shield himself and refuse to carry into effect an act that violates the Constitution."[68] As Akhil Amar has written, "In America, the bedrock principle was not legislative supremacy but popular sovereignty. The higher law of the Constitution might sometimes allow, and in very clear cases of congressional usurpation might even oblige a president to stand firm against a congressional statute in order to defend the Constitution itself."[69]

The veto power and the refusal to enforce unconstitutional laws are aspects of executive control over law enforcement. Another is the inherent discretion to prosecute some laws more vigorously than others, which is a less confrontational, but equally significant, aspect of the executive's discretion to allocate limited government resources in accordance with its policy preferences. Presidents may decide to devote few investigatory resources to enforce laws with which they disagree, while transferring more to priorities on their agenda. The pardon power enhances this discretion. A pardon is not subject to review by any other branch; President Jefferson used the pardon to free persons convicted of violating criminal laws that he regarded as unconstitutional. The pardon power was reinstated after several state constitutions had removed it from the executive during the revolutionary period. However, as Hamilton predicted and President Gerald Ford's pardon of President Nixon proved, the main check on abuse is public opinion.[70]

At the time of the Constitution's framing, executive power was understood to include the war, treaty, and other general foreign affairs powers. Under the British constitution, the Crown exercised the powers over war and peace, negotiation and communication with foreign nations, and control of the military. Parliament retained exclusive control over the purse, domestic regulation, and raising the army and navy. When the colonies declared their independence, these powers were assumed by the national government under the Articles of Confederation — while the Continental Congress served as the country's executive, it lacked any true legislative powers. Thus, when the Framers ratified the Constitution, they would have understood that Article II, Section 1 continued the Anglo-American constitutional tradition of locating the foreign affairs power generally in the executive branch.[71]

Hamilton and the other Federalists did not look to the executive to manage war and peace for tradition's sake. They understood the executive to be functionally best matched in speed, unity, and decisiveness to the unpredictable high-stakes nature of foreign affairs. As Thomas Schelling has written, a nation-state would want "to have a communications system in good order, to have complete information, or to be in full command of one's own actions or of one's own assets."[72] Rational action on behalf of the nation in a dangerous world would be best advanced by executive action. Edward Corwin observed that the executive's advantages in foreign affairs include "the unity of office, its capacity for secrecy and dispatch, and its superior sources of information, to which should be added the fact that it is always on hand and ready for action, whereas the houses of Congress are in adjournment much of the time."[73]

The Framers intuitively understood the concept. State refusal to support the Continental Army had frustrated Washington throughout the Revolution. Congress had suffered from grave collective action problems, which eventually forced it to form executive committees. After independence, American leaders worried that they would lose in the peace what they had won in the war. The young nation was hemmed in by the great powers: Spain, France, and Great

Britain. States were engaged in trade wars. Foreign nations exploited divisions between the states, which split along sectional lines over foreign policy. The Continental Congress had negligible armed forces at its command (barely 1,000 soldiers on the borders and no seafaring navy), while the state militias had proven to be undistinguished fighters. With America's position in the world precarious, concern about foreign relations was as important as domestic issues in the Framers' thinking.[74]

Threats to the national security led to greater centralization of foreign affairs power in the executive. Article II gave the President the roles of Commander-in-Chief and Chief Executive. "Of all the cares or concerns of government, the direction of war most peculiarly demands those qualities which distinguish the exercise of power by a single hand," Hamilton wrote in *Federalist 74*. "The direction of war implies the direction of the common strength," he continued, "and the power of directing and employing the common strength forms a usual and essential part in the definition of the executive authority." It was for this reason, Hamilton argued, that the Constitution vested executive authority in one person, rather than the multimember executives of the Continental Congress and the states.[75]

The executive's control, however, was incomplete. Making treaties would remain executive in nature — the power remained in Article II — but because of their status as supreme federal law would require Senate consent. While the President would control military operations and diplomatic relations, he would not have the power to raise the military, issue the rules for its governance, nor enact any legislation with domestic effect. Appropriations for the military could only run two years, giving Congress a regular opportunity to review the executive's foreign policies.

Not wishing to make themselves easy political targets, Federalists downplayed comparisons of the President's powers with those of the British Crown. They emphasized the Presidency's fixed term, its obedience to the Constitution and the laws, and its lack of independent funds. Hamilton observed that the British King was a permanent, hereditary monarch, with an absolute veto and the right to raise armies and navies and declare war. By contrast, he argued in *Federalist 69*, the President is Commander-in-Chief, in which his authority was nominally the same as the King's, "but in substance much inferior to it," because the President could not declare war or create the military. Hamilton's rhetoric got the better of him here, as even in Britain by this time, Parliament exercised the power to raise armies. The only real difference between the King's and the President's military powers was Congress's power to declare war. Tellingly, Hamilton did not define the meaning of "declare."

Federalists ultimately referred to British history to explain the checks on executive power. In the Virginia ratifying convention, the Anti-Federalists were led by the fiery oratory of former governor Patrick Henry, still famous for his "Give me liberty or give me death" speech. Henry claimed that the Constitution "squints toward monarchy" because the "President may easily become a King." "If your American chief be a man of ambition and abilities, how easy is it for him to render himself absolute!" Henry exclaimed. At the head of an army, the President "can prescribe the terms on which he shall reign master" and will violate the laws and "beat down every opposition."[76] The Senate and the President might conspire to vote the executive a permanent military with which to impose an "absolute despotism," or the President might simply declare himself king.

Federalists countered that a President could never succeed in establishing a military dictatorship, because the other branches could stop him using their own constitutional powers. This marked a significant turning point in the theory of executive power. Federalists did not respond with the traditional checks-and-balances approach of mixed government. Unlike the Anti-Federalists, the Federalists did not believe that an aristocracy existed or was likely to rise, or that the President would represent a particular social class. Instead, they defended the Constitution by arguing that the separation of powers would rely on functionally defined branches of government — executive, legislative, and judicial — checking each other.[77] In response to Henry, Federalists pointed to Parliament's funding powers as a check on war. Madison agreed with Henry that "the sword and the purse are not to be given to the same member," but he disagreed that the American government combined the two. "The sword is in the hands of the British King; the purse in the hands of the Parliament. It is so in America, as far as any analogy can exist."[78] Federalist George Nicholas argued that Congress's sole control over establishing and funding the military "will be a powerful check here."[79] Both Nicholas and Madison drew upon the examples of political conflict from British history to support the idea that government functions, rather than social class, would provide balance to the government.

Although it would have been to their advantage, the Federalists did not argue that Congress's power to declare war — or judicial review — would check the President. Instead, the ratification debates show that they expected each branch to exercise its unique powers to block unconstitutional or mistaken decisions. In another area of foreign affairs, for example, Federalists argued that Congress could contain the executive's treaty power (already conditioned by the Senate's advice-and-consent role) by refusing to enact laws or appropriate funds needed to bring the United States into compliance.[80] The Constitution created a division of labor in which the President, Congress, and the courts cooperate, but also compete, to promote the national interest. After the Revolution, the weakening of the executive branch and the dominance of the state assemblies had thrown that healthy competition out of joint. For the system to succeed, the Presidency had to have the independence and powers to allow it both to stand up to Congress and to properly pursue its own functions, which included the powers over foreign affairs, administration of the laws, and the protection of the national security.

CONCLUSIONS

IN RATIFYING THE CONSTITUTION, the people rejected the radical innovations of the Revolution. Defenders of that status quo, who had promoted a republican faith in the legislature's purity in transmitting popular wishes, had lost. Gone were the multiple executives, advisory councils, and legislative selection of the governor. Yet, Federalists did not advocate a return to the past. The Presidency was not founded on divine right. The Constitution created a republican executive to be elected by the nation as a whole, with a connection to the people independent of Congress. The possibility of reelection would keep the President mindful of the approval of the electorate, but with a different time horizon than the two-year members of the House and the six-year Senators. The executive would be a truly coordinate and independent branch of the government.

The new Constitution rehabilitated the executive both structurally and substantively. Through the ratifying conventions, the people rejected the revolutionary view of executives as largely controlled by the legislature. By the end of the ratification, the Federalists had succeeded in enacting a constitutional plan that restored the executive's core powers while making it directly responsible to the people as a whole. They had republicanized the executive, or in Harvey Mansfield's words, they had "tamed the Prince." It would be the job of future Presidents to realize the Framers' vision of an energetic and empowered executive, but one constrained by a Constitution and the political system that would grow from it.

CHAPTER 3

George Washington

A SINGULAR FACTOR influenced the ratification of the Constitution's article on the Presidency: all understood that George Washington would be elected the first President. It is impossible to understate the standing of the "Father of the Country" among his fellow Americans. He had established America's fundamental constitutional principle — civilian control of the military — before there was even a Constitution. Throughout his command of the Continental Army, General Washington scrupulously observed civilian orders and restrained himself when a Congress on the run granted him dictatorial powers. He had even put down, by his mere presence, a potential coup d'etat by his officers in 1783.[1] Washington cannot be quantified as an element of constitutional law, but he was probably more important than any other factor.

The Revolutionary War had revealed Congress to be feeble and the states to be unreliable. Washington had exercised broad executive and administrative authorities that went well beyond battlefield command to keep the army supplied. This experience made Washington a firm nationalist who supported a more effectively organized and vigorous national government. Though he barely spoke at the Constitutional Convention, Washington placed his considerable prestige behind the enterprise. During ratification, he launched a one-man letter-writing campaign to encourage Federalists throughout the country, and particularly in his critical home state of Virginia, to win the Constitution's approval. Washington remains the only President to be elected by a unanimous vote of the Electoral College.

Because the American republic grew so successfully, we tend to treat Washington's decisions with an air of inevitability, but the constitutional text left more questions about the executive unanswered than answered. Article II vested *the* executive power of the United States in a single President, but it did not list its components (unlike Article I's enumeration of legislative powers). It did not create any advisors, heads of departments, or a cabinet, not to mention a White House staff; specify how the President should interact with Congress, the courts, or the states; nor describe how the President and the Senate were to exercise their joint powers over treaties and appointments.

Washington filled these gaps with a number of foundational decisions — several on a par with those made during the writing and ratification of the Constitution itself. His desire to govern by consensus sometimes led him to seek cooperation with the other branches. He was a republican before he was a Federalist, but ultimately Washington favored an energetic, independent executive, even at the cost of political harmony. Washington centralized decision-making in his office so that there would be no confusion about his responsibility and accountability, and his direct orders sped quickly through the small federal bureaucracy. He took the initiative in enforcing the law and followed his own interpretation of the Constitution.

To Washington, the departments and their secretaries served only as "dependent agencies of the Chief Executive." As Leonard White has written, the President made "all major decisions of administration" and took full responsibility for them.[2] He managed diplomatic relations with other countries and set the nation's foreign policy. At the end of his two terms, the Presidency looked much like the one described in *The Federalist*. Hamilton's outsized performance as Secretary of the Treasury helped, but the real credit goes to Washington.[3]

None of this was foreordained. Washington could have chosen to mimic a parliamentary system with cabinet secretaries who represented different factions in the legislature or a balanced government with executive branch officials drawn from an aristocratic social class. He could have assumed the function of a head of state and given department secretaries freedom over their jurisdictions. Or he could have considered the Presidency as Congress's clerk, draining any initiative from the job and committing himself solely to carrying out legislative directions. He might even have thought of himself as the servant of the states (he certainly did not; on a trip to Boston, President Washington refused to call on Governor John Hancock, instead forcing an ill Hancock to come to him first).[4]

Washington ranks in the most recent scholarly poll as our nation's greatest President. Some might think that his high standing rewards him, like Jefferson, for his achievements before he assumed office, but this view understates the second source of his greatness — establishing a stable government under law that has endured to this day. Washington led the nation through its first growing pains, restored the country's finances, kept the nation out of a dangerous European war, opened the West to American expansion, and saw the Constitution through the appearance of the first political parties (something the Framers did not foresee and would have opposed). Washington did all of this without seeking popularity and without enjoying what we would think of today as political talents. He was a natural leader, one of the finest horsemen of his age, and a tall and strong man. He had single-handedly ended a riot among northern and southern soldiers on Boston Commons by grabbing the leaders in each hand and shaking them into submission. Washington was stern, distant, and concerned above all about his reputation. He carried himself with gravitas, projected a demeanor of republican simplicity and virtue (hence the fable about the cherry tree), and yet struggled his whole life to control a ferocious temper. Every President since Washington's day has had the impossible task of measuring up to his founding example.

ESTABLISHING THE PRESIDENCY

AFTER HIS ELECTION in early 1789, Washington took his time getting to the nation's capital in New York City. He wanted to give Congress time to count the electoral votes, avoid the appearance of unseemly eagerness, and allow the people to see the physical symbol of the new national government. Once installed, Washington made clear who was in charge.

Three approaches to organizing the executive branch existed.[5] Some Senators believed they would share administrative authority because of their say over appointments and the example set by the state advisory councils. A second view, identified with Alexander Hamilton, held that department heads would perform the same positions as ministers in Great Britain; they would exercise significant independent discretion and coordinate the making of policy in Congress and its implementation by the executive. Washington chose a third, which resembled the organization of his military command. The President alone would exercise the executive power.

He would receive advice from his department secretaries, who would supervise the inferior officers in their agencies. All matters of executive policy would come to him. He would either make all significant decisions or delegate them. Administration, in the words of historian Forrest McDonald, was "highly personal, after the fashion of the pre-bureaucratic eighteenth-century world."[6]

Washington's initiative became apparent within a month of his inauguration. Even though there were no federal laws to enforce nor positions to fill, Washington quickly took over the existing administrative machinery of the Articles of Confederation. He ordered the ministers of war and foreign affairs and the Board of Treasury to provide him with "an acquaintance with the real situation of the several great Departments, at the period of my acceding to the administration of the general Government" and a "full, precise, and distinct general idea of the affairs of the United States."[7] He made clear that subordinate executive branch officials were his assistants, rather than independent power centers. Washington wrote that the "impossibility that one man should be able to perform all the great business of the State, I take to have been the reason for instituting the great Departments, and appointing officers therein, to assist the supreme Magistrate in discharging the duties of his trust."[8]

Washington could not have accomplished this alone. He had a willing and able ally in the 38-year-old Congressman from Virginia, James Madison. Even though he had played the leading intellectual role in the drafting of the Constitution, had cowritten the newspaper editorials that would become *The Federalist*, and had led the forces for ratification in the Virginia convention, Madison had barely won election to the House due to Patrick Henry's opposition. Once there, Madison promoted Washington's policies — a position that would not last into the second term. Madison is what we would today think of as a coalition builder: organizing behind the scenes, ceding political credit to others, acting through committees and larger bodies, yet always moving others toward his preferred goal. What he lacked in political gifts — he was short, fearfully shy, and had a weak voice — he more than made up for in his genuine intellect, willingness to work the longest hours, and meticulous preparation. It is no wonder that he has always been a favorite of scholars.

Madison took the lead in enacting legislation to establish the government, from the constitutional amendments that became the Bill of Rights to the first direct national taxes in American history. Madison likewise managed the debate over the establishment of the first great executive departments, what Daniel Webster would later call the "Decision of 1789."[9] The key issue concerned the authority to remove the heads of the departments of Foreign Affairs, War, and the Treasury. Four possibilities existed. First, the Constitution may have intended that the President exercise the power alone, with the Senate's role in confirmation being the sole exception from his general control over appointments. Second, it could have reserved the right to the President and Senate together, under the idea that the same process should be used to reverse a decision as to make it. Third, removal might only occur through impeachment. Or fourth, the Constitution could leave the power to Congress, as part of its power under the Necessary and Proper Clause, to establish the departments in the first place.

Decision of this question had profound implications for presidential control of the executive branch. The constitutional text is silent as to whether cabinet officers must obey presidential orders, and Chief Executives to this day back up their commands with the implicit threat of removal. If cabinet members could only be removed by impeachment, or with the advice and consent of the Senate, they would feel little fear when ignoring presidential directives. Congress also recognizes this relationship between removal and control, and

since the New Deal has tried to impose conditions on the removal
of officials who work for the independent agencies. The 1978 Ethics
in Government Act, for example, created an independent prosecutor
by prohibiting his or her removal except for committing a felony or
other violation of the law. Impeachment or congressional discretion
over removal would have created even greater disruption by transferring effective control over subordinate executive officials to the
legislature. Only an inherent removal power in Article II's undefined
grant of the executive power allowed control of subordinate officers
by the President.

When Congress took up the issue of national finance on May 19,
1789, Madison proposed three departments: War, Foreign Affairs,
and Treasury. Each department would have a Secretary, appointed
by the President with the advice and consent of the Senate, but
removable by the President alone.[10] Amendments to require Senate
approval of removals failed, and Madison's proposal won a considerable majority.[11] Specific bills detailing each department's functions
came before Congress a month later, whereupon opponents of executive power again attempted to strike recognition of the President's
removal authority.

Madison argued that the President's standing as Chief Executive
gave him the inherent power to fire subordinates. "Is the power of
displacing an executive power?" Madison asked the House on June
16. "I conceive that if any power whatsoever is in its nature executive
it is the power of appointing, overseeing, and controlling those who
execute the laws."[12] The Constitution only allowed a single exception
to the President's power in the Senate's advice and consent function.
Congress could not add others. "If the constitution has invested all
executive power in the President," Madison said, "I venture to assert
that the Legislature has no right to diminish or modify his executive
authority."

While there were dissenters, the First Congress clearly believed that Article II's vesting of the executive power in the President was more than a stylistic device. Madison's supporters amended the bills to make clear that Congress was not granting the President the power to remove, but only recognizing his constitutional authority to do so.[13] In the Senate, which we would expect to be more jealous of its prerogatives, the removal provision encountered more difficulties. The Senate deadlocked 10–10 on the bills to create the Departments of Foreign Affairs and War because of the removal question. Vice President Adams broke both ties in favor of the House versions, handing the administration a victory. The Treasury bill raised a different variation of the executive power issue. Critics thought the power of the Department was too great, particularly its authority to "digest and prepare plans for the improvement and management of the revenue, and the support of the public credit," which they believed properly rested within Congress's power of the purse. They sought to divide leadership of the Treasury into a board, as under the Articles of Confederation, and to limit the President's removal power because the Department exercised legislative powers. Again, Madison succeeded in convincing the House to create a Treasury Department with maximum authority and energy, but within the President's control, and again the Vice President broke a Senate tie in the administration's favor.[14]

Members of the legislative and executive branch would recognize that the "Decision of 1789" represented Congress's own constitutional understanding of the President's executive authority to remove subordinate officials. In the course of the debate, supporters of presidential removal argued that the Chief Executive bore the constitutional obligation to faithfully execute the laws. This required that subordinates aid him "in the administration of his department."[15] The President's power to remove gave him the power

to make sure that these officials enforce the laws as he wished. Giving Congress or the Senate a role in removal would make the President a "mere vapor" and would place "the Legislature at the head of
the Executive branch."[16] As Madison wrote to Jefferson, the House
vote was "most consonant to the text of the Constitution, to the
policy of mixing the Legislative and Executive Departments as little
as possible, and to the requisite responsibility and harmony in the
Executive Department."[17]

Washington's cabinet nominations met far less opposition than
the creation of their offices. Hamilton was nominated, confirmed,
and took office as Secretary of the Treasury all on September 11,
1789. Henry Knox was confirmed as Secretary of War the next day,
and Thomas Jefferson was nominated for Secretary of State two
weeks later and was confirmed in a day. In choosing these officials,
Washington did not pursue the same objectives as Presidents today.

Washington did not become President as the head of a political party and did not campaign for a "mandate," nor did he seek
nominees who agreed with a particular program or agenda. Washington chose men he called the "first Characters," who had already
held positions of trust in state government, the Confederation, or
the Continental Army. They were to be both strong on merit and
geographically diverse. Washington believed that selecting nominees who were held in the highest regard in their communities
would encourage respect and "affection" for the new national government.[18] He balanced the major cabinet appointments among Virginia, New York, and Massachusetts; his Supreme Court nominees
hailed from six different states. His interest in "first Characters" at
times outweighed his interest in harmonious relations: Hamilton
and Jefferson quickly became deeply divided over economic and
foreign policy, such that Washington did not even have his cabinet
meet as a group until his second term under the pressures of the

French Revolution.[19] Nominees had to be "friends" of the national government; no Anti-Federalists would assume federal office. While making his first appointments, Washington wrote that he would not "bring a man into office...whose political tenets are adverse to the measures which the general government are pursuing." This, he believed, would be "a sort of political Suicide."[20]

Given his interest in local reputations, Washington might have welcomed the Senate's participation before selection of a nominee. Article II's advice-and-consent structure might have given rise to a joint Senate role in choosing the nominees — otherwise, what would distinguish "advice" from "consent"?[21] But Washington would have none of it. Even before he had chosen his cabinet officers, Washington had assumed the responsibility of nominating customs collectors, who would represent the national government in every major city and port. For Savannah, Washington chose a former revolutionary army officer named Benjamin Fishbourne, who was serving in the same capacity for the state of Georgia. Fishbourne became the first nominee to be rejected by the Senate.

The Senate adopted a resolution seeking face-to-face meetings with the President for every open office and appointed a committee to meet with Washington to work out the procedures. Washington promptly nominated another candidate and rebuffed the idea of formally meeting with the Senate to choose executive officers. He wanted to make clear that he was the Chief Executive and that members of the executive branch were his assistants. While Presidents, including Washington, have always informally consulted with members of Congress in selecting federal officers and judges, they have ever since relegated the Senate's constitutional function to the approval of *their* nominees.

Once installed, cabinet members understood that Washington was responsible for the actions of the entire executive branch.

Writing to his own administration 12 years later, Jefferson described Washington as sending a stream of questions, requests, and orders to his department secretaries and meeting with each of them on a regular basis, usually over breakfast, to discuss matters until he was fully satisfied. This unending circulation of reports, letters, and paperwork — backed up by the President's constitutional authority to require "opinions in writing" — kept him "always in accurate possession of all facts or proceedings in every part of the Union, and to whatsoever department they related."[22] Washington "formed a central point for the different branches," Jefferson wrote, allowing the President to promote "unity of object and action among them." Given his wartime experiences, as Forrest McDonald has observed, Washington felt little need to delegate foreign or military affairs, sometimes reducing Jefferson and Knox to the status of glorified clerks.[23]

Hamilton exercised unusual leadership over the establishment of the national bank not because of any constitutional or statutory independence, but because Washington remained uninterested in finance. Washington also trusted Hamilton because of his wartime service as his trusted aide-de-camp and upon the recommendation of Robert Morris, who had overseen revolutionary finances. Hamilton's grand design was unique in another respect. It was the only time that the administration managed legislation through Congress. In general, Washington took a hands-off approach to the legislature. In his first annual address to Congress (delivered in person), he put aside his original plan to propose legislation and instead spoke generally about commerce, farming, and manufacturing; promoting science and the arts; and implementing the Constitution.[24] He questioned whether he could do anything more. "It rests with [Congress] to decide what measures ought afterwards to be adopted for promoting the success of the great objects, which I have recommended to their attention."[25] Today's practice of lobbying Congress or threat-

ening a veto to affect policy outcomes would have been quite foreign
to our first President.

Creating the nation's financial system was the exception. Hamilton proposed that the national government assume the wartime
debts owed by the Confederation and the states. To repay at close to
face value, Hamilton wanted to issue bonds funded by new taxes on
imports. His plan essentially refinanced the national debt by con-
solidating multiple loans into one large, regular mortgage payment.
It created a permanent debt, which Hamilton believed would provide a stable currency (with the government notes), expand credit
within the economy, and give the financial and merchant classes
(who would hold the notes) a stake in the government's success. It
also needed a national bank to loan the government money and handle its interest payments, and to make open market transactions in
government bonds.[26] Assumption of the state debt made it through
the First Congress, but only after Hamilton, Jefferson, and Madison
had reached a deal over dinner. Jefferson supported the financial legislation when Hamilton agreed that the national capital would rest
on the Potomac.[27]

Hamilton worked tirelessly to build public and congressional
support for his grand design. While the core of Congress's constitutional powers lay in the purse strings, the complexity of public
finance and spending caused legislators to vote up or down passively
on Hamilton's initiatives. Still, Hamilton's plan caused Washington
to consider the first use of the veto. Madison and Jefferson worried
that the proposed system would duplicate Britain's corrupt political
and social system. Influenced by British oppositionist ideology, they
associated a national bank with the Crown's influence over Parliament, the movement of economic power away from farms to the cities, and the rise in the political power of the financial classes. Even as
Hamilton's proposal passed both houses overwhelmingly, Madison

attacked it for lacking any specific textual basis in the Constitution
and exceeding the Necessary and Proper Clause. Madison reversed
his anonymous position in *The Federalist*, where he had argued in
favor of a broad reading of the federal government's powers.[28]

Washington asked Jefferson and Attorney General Edmund
Randolph for their opinions, and even asked Madison to draft a veto
message. Randolph concluded that the Tenth Amendment limited
the powers of Congress to set up a bank. Jefferson argued that the
creation of a bank was not "necessary" to achieve a legitimate purpose, and that to give the Necessary and Proper Clause a broader construction would burst the Constitution's careful limits on national
power.[29] Hamilton responded that the Clause was a grant of power
that allowed the government to enact means that were not just "necessary," but useful. The Necessary and Proper Clause empowered
the government, rather than limiting it to steps that were absolutely
indispensable.[30] Hamilton's opinion would strongly influence the
Supreme Court's opinion in *McCulloch v. Maryland*, which upheld
the constitutionality of the bank 20 years later.[31] Washington signed
the bill two days after he received Hamilton's written opinion.

Washington understood the President to have the independent right to decide on a bill's constitutionality. If he had deferred
to Congress, he would not have asked his cabinet, and he did not
think of waiting on the courts to decide. Washington appears to
have believed that he should only veto legislation he thought clearly
violated the Constitution. Jefferson himself had advised Washington to use the veto only if his mind was "tolerably clear" on the bill's
unconstitutionality.[32]

Washington did not issue a veto until 1792 for a bill that allo-
cated Representatives to different states in a clear violation of the
Constitution's requirement that every state receive no more than one
member for every 30,000 citizens.[33] While Washington left behind

no written thoughts about the veto, it seems that his reasoning was similar to the logic of *Federalist 78* and *Marbury v. Madison*. As the delegation of authority from the people to their political agents, the Constitution represents the highest law. No branch of the government can engage in any act that breaches its terms. A President has a constitutional duty to use his powers, including the veto, to prevent violations of the Constitution. As Jefferson wrote in his bank opinion, the veto was "the shield provided by the Constitution" to prevent Congress from exceeding its enumerated powers.[34]

Washington did not seek to transform his veto into a broader right to advance his policy views. Glenn Phelps argues that Washington signed legislation on international trade and senatorial pay that ran strongly against his own policy preferences.[35] Still, Washington did not believe his legislative function was limited to guarding the Constitution. His only other veto blocked spending legislation with no constitutional infirmity. In the last days of his Presidency, Congress passed a bill eliminating two cavalry units on the Western frontier. This clearly rested within Congress's constitutional authority to raise and fund the military, but Washington nonetheless rejected the bill because it immediately stopped the pay of troops far away on the frontier, where they were most needed.[36] Washington thought Congress's plan made for poor military strategy, something he knew more about than anyone in the United States.

ENFORCING THE LAW

WASHINGTON DID NOT believe that his executive power was limited to the hiring and firing of officials. Procedural in nature, that view places the President in charge of all of the personnel within the departments and agencies, but does not recognize any powers of substance. An important constitutional dimension of the Presidency, however, flows through Article II's requirement that the President "shall take Care that the Laws be faithfully executed." While Presidents have believed that the Take Care Clause includes the interpretation and enforcement of federal law, critics have argued that it only acts to prohibit the President from suspending a law duly enacted by Congress.[37] Under this theory, Article II's vesting of the executive power mandates only a single President, and not much else. More sophisticated scholars, such as Lawrence Lessig and Cass Sunstein, maintain that Congress's power to establish the agencies includes the right to decide who is to enforce federal law, even so far as to vest the execution of law in entities independent of the President.[38]

This was not Washington's view. He believed that the executive power held both substantive and procedural dimensions. The President's primary authorities of substance centered in foreign and military affairs, but a significant part was domestic. Washington believed that a combination of his authority as Chief Executive and the Take Care Clause gave him the power and responsibility to carry out federal law. This included directing anyone, regardless of his position, who might participate in enforcing the law. Washington, in his vigorousness, even set precedents followed by no other President after him such as personally leading troops in a show of force against a rebellion.

Scholars have long observed that the Constitution leaves unclear where "administration" falls among the executive, legislative, and judicial branches. For Washington, that function lodged with the Presidency, just as Hamilton had argued in *The Federalist*. Our first President believed it crucial to set a visible precedent of vigorous and effective execution of the laws to contrast the strength of the new national government with the weaknesses of the old. Washington's choices were all the more important because of the First Congress's great mass of legislative activity. Unlike its predecessor, the First

Congress immediately exercised many of its enumerated powers. It established the executive departments, the federal courts, tax and customs rules, a system for the sale of the Western lands, intellectual property rights, bankruptcy regulations, and navigation rules. Some functions were performed by "mongrel" offices (Randolph's description of the Attorney General because it lacked a department) that fit uneasily in a clean tripartite separation of powers. The Post Office seems to have operated with significant independence; federal prosecutors were appointed by the courts and reported to the Secretary of State; and the Secretaries of War and State and the Attorney General reviewed patent applications.[39] But the great mass of federal law was to be carried out by the new departments, with Treasury having the greatest number of employees (500 versus 22 in the other departments) to collect taxes and customs duties. Washington took control of these officials from the very start.

As with Shays' Rebellion, Americans' suspicion of taxes put the young government to the test. One of the subroutines of Hamilton's financial program imposed an excise tax on the manufacture of liquor. Whiskey was an important article of commerce, going beyond the impressive drinking ability of Founding-era Americans. Distilling allowed Western farmers to transform their crops into a more transportable form, to the point where whiskey even served as a form of frontier currency. After Congress adopted the tax in 1791, protests occurred in the western parts of Pennsylvania (one of the leaders was Albert Gallatin, who would become Jefferson's Treasury Secretary), Virginia, Kentucky, and the Carolinas. Armed resistance broke out three years later, the first significant internal challenge to the new federal government. It would not be the last time that Americans would break the law to defend their beverage of choice.[40]

Washington employed a strategy of political patience backed up by the threat of force. When trouble first arose, he issued a proclamation declaring that resistance to the tax was "subversive of good order, contrary to the duty that every citizen owes to his country, and to the laws, and of a nature dangerous to the very being of a government."[41] Citing his authority under the Take Care Clause, Washington ordered all courts and officials to enforce the tax and to punish lawbreakers. He sent a note to state governors expressing his "entire confidence" that they would "cheerfully" promote "a due obedience to the Constitutional Laws of the Union." Governors were not even officers of the federal government, but Washington believed that he could command them to enforce the law.

Washington then adopted a wait-and-see attitude. Congress amended the law to moderate, but not eliminate, tax enforcement, and Hamilton experimented with measures to encourage compliance. Armed resistance still broke out in the summer of 1794, when tax officers began to issue arrest warrants in western Pennsylvania, with trials to be held across the state in distant Philadelphia. About 500 militiamen skirmished with a dozen regular soldiers and burned the home of the federal tax inspector on July 16. On August 1, about 7,000 armed men marched on Pittsburgh; federal officials fled to escape tarring and feathering.

Washington believed he had a personal responsibility to enforce the law. Hamilton, Knox, and Attorney General William Bradford recommended calling out the state militias under federal control, while Randolph, then Secretary of State, urged reconciliation through a federal commission. Washington took both courses. The Constitution gives Congress the authority to provide for the calling of the militia to "execute the Laws of the Union, suppress Insurrections and repel Invasions." Under the 1792 Militia Act, the President can call out the militia once a federal judge finds that forces too powerful for the courts are blocking enforcement of the law.

The administration provided the facts of the rebellion to Justice

James Wilson, who made the required findings. On August 7, Washington issued a proclamation that the western Pennsylvania area was in a state of insurrection, ordered the rebels to return to their homes, and declared his intention to call out the militia. He ordered 12,500 troops from Maryland, New Jersey, and Virginia, in addition to Pennsylvania. Washington also sent commissioners to offer amnesty to any who would swear an oath to obey the laws. His strategy was remarkably successful: a large majority took the oath, while an army of nearly 13,000 (the popular call for troops met with more volunteers than asked) rode through the area in September. They found only 20 rebels, the rest having scattered.

Washington had moved swiftly, issuing his proclamation and calling out the militia only six days after the attacks on federal officials began. He had not waited for federal judges to trigger the Militia Act, but instead went directly to Justice Wilson for a finding of insurrection. He had not consulted Congress, but instead limited discussion of the options to his cabinet, from whom he ordered opinions, and to the state governors, who had to supply the troops. His relationship with the governors is particularly instructive. Under the Articles of Confederation, the governors and legislatures of the states routinely ignored requests for legislation or supplies made by the Continental Congress. Washington turned this unhealthy relationship upside down. When Pennsylvania's governor claimed that a resort to force was unjustified, Washington responded that the nation's response would not depend on the state's views, and ordered him to supply militia to serve under federal command. Washington believed that when state governors enforced federal law, they were subordinate to him, even if he could not remove them.

Washington led the army *personally*. He rode at the head of the troops, followed by Hamilton and the governor of Pennsylvania, in a show of the new government's strength. Washington's actions were remarkably popular, far more than anyone in his cabinet anticipated, and he followed them with a message to Congress that described the resistance as an insurrection, treason, and a challenge to federal authority.[42] Congress so approved of Washington's careful use of his powers that it permanently reenacted the Militia Act in 1795 and removed the 1792 Act's requirement that the President seek judicial approval before calling out the militia—all that was required now was a presidential proclamation.[43]

A less dramatic, but equally revealing, episode in the aftermath of the Whiskey Rebellion further illustrates Washington's control of all aspects of federal law enforcement. Defending the modern independent counsel law, today's critics of executive power argue that prosecution does not fall within presidential control. They have pointed to the fact that in 1789, Congress created no Justice Department—the Attorney General was the sole officer whose job was to advise the President and to represent the United States before the Supreme Court. In the first Judiciary Act, Congress placed the appointment of federal district attorneys in the courts and did not make them explicitly responsible to the Attorney General or the President. Washington did not believe this made federal prosecutors independent. After the Whiskey Rebellion, he ordered Pennsylvania's federal prosecutor to drop the cases against two rebels, and after his Neutrality Proclamation (to be discussed shortly), Washington directed U.S. attorneys to collect information and prosecute violators.[44] This is not to say that Washington exercised the type of centralized control over prosecution that Presidents do today. Given the distances of communication and travel, local federal officials enjoyed a broad discretion that their modern counterparts can only dream of.[45] Still, Washington believed he could issue direct orders to anyone who carried out federal law, and none of those on the receiving end appears to have disagreed.

The handling of the Whiskey Rebellion rebels set another important law enforcement precedent that counterbalanced the legislature's plenary control over domestic legislation. Just as the President can direct the prosecution of cases to the letter of the law, he can also moderate the law's harshness. Washington's decision to drop the two Whiskey Rebellion cases made clear that he possessed the discretion to choose which cases to prosecute and which to let go. The executive branch would not seek to punish every infraction of federal law. Prosecutorial decisions would be based on a host of considerations, such as the resources available, deterrent effect, retribution, and the seriousness of harm. Under President Jefferson, these considerations would include disagreements with Congress over the policies and constitutionality of the criminal law. A President could refuse to prosecute offenders of a law that he believed violated the right to freedom of speech or religion, even if Congress disagreed.

Washington's offer of amnesty also revealed an important presidential power — to stay a mechanical application of the law to yield more important national benefits. The Constitution's grant of the pardon power could have been read to allow the President only to release individuals already convicted of a crime, though the historical evidence suggests that the Framers believed it would be used to offer rewards to criminal conspirators who cooperated with the government.[46] Washington used the pardon power for a broader purpose, that of restoring order and allowing the government to show magnanimity. Nothing in the Constitution explicitly thrust these goals on Washington, but as Chief Executive he took the establishment of a strong government and the protection of the national interest to be his unique responsibilities. It is a sign of how strongly Washington shaped the office that even today we automatically assume that Presidents enforce the laws guided by their own understanding of the public good.

PROTECTING THE NATION:
FOREIGN AFFAIRS AND THE WARS OF EUROPE

PRESIDENTS OWE THEIR privileged position in foreign affairs not to politics alone, but to the Constitution and to our first President. Washington established from the beginning that the executive branch would assume the leading role in developing and carrying out foreign policy. He did not go unchallenged. In defending Washington's foreign policy initiatives, Hamilton first publicly argued that the President is vested with all of the government's executive power, except that specifically transferred to another branch by the Constitution. Presidents ever since have taken the initiative in foreign affairs by relying on their constitutional powers.

The Constitution's text does not explicitly grant much to the President beyond the undefined executive power, the Commander-in-Chief role, and the right to receive ambassadors. He must share the treaty and appointment powers with the Senate, while Congress receives the powers to declare war and issues letters of marque and reprisal (government permission to privateers to conduct hostilities against an enemy), to raise and fund the military, and to regulate foreign commerce, among other powers. There have been periods where early Presidents deferred to Congress's foreign policy leadership, though with poor results — witness President Adams and the 1798 Quasi War with France or President Madison and the War of 1812. Indeed, the conventional wisdom among many legal scholars is that the Constitution gives Congress control over foreign affairs, and that Presidents have inappropriately seized power over war and peace.[47] As a practical matter, however, the President today can launch the nation into war without explicit congressional consent, enter or end international agreements, interpret international rules on behalf of the United States, and control diplomatic relations with other nations. These decisions, from President Truman's decision to wage the Korean War to Jimmy Carter's termination of the mutual defense treaty with Taiwan, have sparked political controversy and claims of presidential overreaching. It might not have been Washington's original intention to develop the executive so completely, because he devoted much of his first term to establishing the national government, appointing its officers, and fixing the nation's finances. When he turned to foreign affairs in the early months of his Presidency, he seemed to think that the Senate would perform the role of an advisory council on diplomatic matters. In contrast to his approach to appointments, where he considered the Senate's role to be limited to review of his nominations, Washington apparently believed that the Constitution required him to consult with the Senate before sending ambassadors to negotiate. As we will see, however, our first President quickly came to the conclusion that the executive would have to play the primary role in determining the nation's foreign policy.

War Powers

WAR REMAINS ONE of the most hotly disputed questions in constitutional law today. Some claim that the original understanding of the Constitution requires Congress to authorize all wars because of its power to declare war. Defenders of the executive branch rely on the modern practice of Presidents launching significant wars without congressional authorization. Opponents of this view have relied on a 1793 statement by George Washington rejecting a plea that the United States attack the Creek Indians. "The Constitution vests the power of declaring war with Congress," Washington wrote to Governor William Moultrie of South Carolina, "therefore no offensive expedition of importance can be undertaken until after they shall have deliberated on the subject, and authorized such a measure."[48] Some scholars claim this shows Washington's agreement that Congress must enact legislation authorizing all military hostilities abroad. David Currie, for example, concludes that the "first three presidents," Washington included, "took an appropriately narrow view of their authority as Commander in Chief," a view he believes was faithful to the decisions of the Constitutional Convention.[49]

War in the early years of the Republic was not so simple. The administration sought Congress's cooperation when it needed increases in the size of the army, military spending, or the approval of agreements — in other words, those areas where the Constitution specifically provided for a legislative role. When it came to political and military strategy, however, Washington and his advisors mostly acted alone. Under our first President, the United States waged war against only one enemy, the Indian tribes located in the neighborhood of present-day Ohio. By the time of the ratification, friction between Indians and American settlers in the West had grown, and some tribes had refused to respect the terms of the peace with Great Britain.[50] British leaders, for their part, hoped that the Indians would create a buffer state that would limit American expansion in the Northwest. Washington and Knox pursued a peaceful settlement with the tribes, but they prepared for war.

In 1789, it would have been impossible for Washington to conduct military operations without Congress's active cooperation. This was not because of the power to declare war; there simply were no troops for the President to command. After assuming office, Washington reported to Congress that the existing army numbered only 672 officers and soldiers, scattered across the frontier. By comparison, Indian tribes menacing Georgia could field 5,000 warriors for battle.[51] Under the Articles of Confederation, Congress had established a force to protect the frontiers "from the depredations of the hostile Indians" and police the public lands.[52] In order to wage any kind of campaign, Washington would have to convince Congress to create a standing army. Living in a world with a large peacetime army and navy, we easily forget that Chief Executives of the eighteenth and nineteenth centuries had to seek ad hoc creation of a military force to fight any significant conflict. Congress's power of the purse and its authority to establish the military gave it a functional veto over any war, and the ability to limit the nature of a conflict through the structure of the armed forces.

Congress quickly provided for the continued existence of a small permanent army. It also gave the President the authority to call out the state militia "as he may judge necessary" to protect settlers against "the hostile incursions of the Indians,"[53] but enacted no statute declaring war on the Indian tribes. Aside from the militia authorization, Congress placed no restrictions of any kind on the use of the regular armed forces. The natural conclusion is that Congress recognized the President's powers as Commander-in-Chief to decide how to use the forces once created. It is possible that Congress believed it was simply reauthorizing the army under the same conditions and purposes as that of the Confederation Congress, but we need not depend on inference. During the House debates, some in Congress objected to the bill's language because they believed it gave the President the unconstitutional power to start a war.[54] Others wanted to add language to the bill to force a more aggressive strategy on the administration. Madison argued that Congress should not specify where troops should be based nor for what purposes they should be used. "By the Constitution, the President has the power of employing these troops in the protection of those parts [of the country] which he thinks requires them most."[55]

Washington's actions in 1789 show that he believed that once Congress created the military, he had the authority to decide whether and how to use it. Even before Congress had approved the continuation of the regular army, the administration ordered General Josiah Harmar to begin disrupting Indian activities in the area of what would become Cincinnati. In October, Washington ordered Arthur St. Clair, governor of the Northwest Territory, to mobilize 1,500 militiamen and launch punitive operations against the Wabash and Illinois Indians, should they reject diplomatic overtures.[56] These troops were not enough. Federalists had long thought that state militias performed poorly and were unreliable and badly trained. Knox believed that at least 2,500 regular troops would be needed to quell the hostile Indian tribes in the Ohio region.[57] A few months later, Washington requested an increase in the permanent army to 1,200, and Congress obliged. Continuing its practice from 1789, Congress passed neither an authorization of hostilities nor a restriction on the use of regular troops.[58]

Washington settled on war with the Indians in the Ohio region that summer. On June 7, 1790, Washington ordered Harmar and St. Clair to organize a punitive expedition into Indian territory to destroy bandits who were harassing settlements and apply pressure for a peace agreement. Washington soon expanded his aims: to field an army of 2,000 troops, roughly 1,600 of them militia, to attack the major villages of the Ohio tribes and to construct a permanent garrison to block their ties to the British.[59] As military historian Richard Kohn has written, the "2,000 man, two-pronged expedition fully committed the military, political, and moral prestige of the United States government."[60] Washington informed Congress about the scope of the Indian problems to justify increases in the army and the right to call out the militia, even going so far as to forward copies of his correspondence with St. Clair.[61] But he sought no authority from Congress for his plan to drive more than 150 miles into enemy territory.

The offensive met with disaster. In October, Harmar's expedition lost about 200 men in a battle with the Indians and withdrew back to base, leaving its dead, wounded, and arms behind. When news arrived in Philadelphia, disgust reigned. Washington ordered another offensive by a new army of 3,000 troops with plans to construct a series of forts throughout the Indian territories. He informed Congress of his intentions in a December 8, 1790, speech and requested another increase in the size and funding of the army.[62] Some members of Congress disliked the strategy, and others opposed the extra spending, but news of Indian massacres on the frontier overrode any opposition. The second expedition fared even worse: on November 4, a surprise attack by a force of 1,000 Indians completely destroyed St. Clair's force. The regular American army ceased to exist, and the western United States was laid open to attack — it was the most devastating American military defeat since the early days of the Revolution.[63]

When the news arrived in December 1791, the capital was stunned. Washington came under withering attack, and critics accused the administration of mismanagement, poor strategy and policy, and a failure of leadership. Washington and Knox decided to escalate with a large, professional army that could permanently defeat the tribes. Washington did not seek statutory authorization for offensive operations or a declaration of war, nor did he seek congressional ratification of his strategy, but he needed legislative cooperation to expand the military. Washington sent Congress a flood of information about the failed St. Clair expedition, conditions in the Northwest, and a request to quintuple the size of the standing army and triple military expenditures to roughly $1 million a year. Jeffersonians in Congress viewed the new military as yet another piece of the Hamiltonian plan to duplicate the corrupt British political, economic, and military system. Although opposition was fierce, and public dissatisfaction with the administration's Indian policy was widespread, Congress gave Washington what he asked for. It placed no limits on the use of the troops but did include a new restriction — that the troops be demobilized "as soon as the United States shall be at peace with the Indian tribes."[64] Jeffersonians also included some bitter medicine by conducting an investigation into the St. Clair disaster and issuing a report attacking the administration for mismanagement.[65]

The 5,000-man army brought victory. Washington ordered General "Mad Anthony" Wayne to undertake offensive operations against the Indians (he was even authorized to attack the British forts in the area, if assured of "complete success"). Diplomatic overtures failed because their success and British encouragement had convinced the tribes to seek complete American withdrawal from the Ohio region. Wayne spent all of 1792 and early 1793 assembling and training his army, even as Jeffersonians in Congress attacked the administration's strategies and attempted to cut the size of the regular army in half. In August 1794, Wayne won a decisive victory at the Battle of Fallen Timbers, which permanently broke Indian military resistance in the area. Historians today credit the battle with opening up large-scale settlement of the Northwest Territory and ending British efforts to hem in American expansion. It was a resounding success for Washington's Indian policy and vindicated his reliance on a professional military establishment.

Washington's success in the Indian wars did not follow a simple process of Congress's declaring war first, followed by executive implementation of war policy. Congress never authorized offensive military operations; at most, it had allowed the President to call out the state militia to defend settlers from Indian attacks. A more complex process took hold, one characterized by presidential initiative and leadership, balanced by congressional control over the size and shape of the military. Washington and his advisors decided on the mix of negotiations and force, the timing of offensive attacks, and the overall strategy. Congress respected Washington's discretion to make these decisions, but it had a veto through its control over the organization and growth of the military. If it had wanted to favor diplomacy, Congress could have limited the army to 1,000 troops or fewer. Congress's power to control the President's initiatives came not through formal legislation or declarations, but via its monopoly over funding.

In most areas of domestic affairs, Washington played a relatively passive role and left matters to Congress, but not so with military affairs. From the very first bill continuing the 700-man army through the expansion to a regular army of 5,000, the Washington administration took the initiative without fail. Each increase was first developed and then proposed by the executive branch, and while some in Congress had a different view — particularly over the balance between regular army and militia troops — the legislature as a whole never refused the Commander-in-Chief's requests. In the Republic's earliest years, Washington set an example of executive leadership upon which future Presidents would draw. At the same time, Washington took all of the political responsibility for the success or failure of the Indian wars, and Congress displayed little eagerness to fight him for it. Blame for the crushing defeat of St. Clair's forces was laid wholly at the administration's doorstep, but at the same time Congress deferred to the President's request for more troops to undertake even more ambitious operations. Presidential power allowed Washington to take the initiative when the nation's security and interests demanded it, but it also bore with it the heavy responsibility for failure as well as success.

Some might argue that these military conflicts have little constitutional significance because they involved the Indians, rather than nations.[66] But by all indications, the Washington administration acted as if the normal rules of war and diplomacy applied. In cabinet meetings on military strategy, President Washington declared that "we are involved in actual war!"[67] Indians in the Ohio region could field a military force as large as the United States Army, while the tribes in Georgia had a force five times greater at their command. When the Washington administration wanted to reach a negotiated settlement, it considered the agreements to be treaties and submitted them to the Senate for consent.[68] Three decades would pass before the Supreme Court classified the Indian tribes as semi-sovereign, dependent nations.[69] Winning the conflict with the Indians was critical to America's national security, and the government treated it as the war that it was.

CONSENT BUT NOT ADVICE

ON SATURDAY, AUGUST 22, 1789, even before Congress had created a Secretary of State, Washington personally visited the Senate to take its temperature on a possible Indian treaty. With Knox in tow, the President came prepared with a short paper on the problem and a list of seven questions he wanted answered by the Senate. As Vice President Adams read the questions aloud, street noise from outside disrupted the proceedings. Adams repeated the questions again. Senators asked that all relevant treaties and related documents be read aloud, and then asked for the questions again. Senator William Maclay of Pennsylvania moved that the whole matter be referred to a special committee. Washington lost his temper, jumped up, and left the chamber with the words: "[T]his defeats every purpose of my coming here." Some report that Washington muttered as he stormed out that "[I] would be damned if [I] ever went there again."[70] Apparently, he returned the very next Monday, and the Senate agreed to all of his questions, but no President, Washington included, ever again consulted in person with the Senate.

By trying to include the Senate, Washington revealed that it was ill-designed to play a formal role in treaty negotiations. Because international politics required secrecy and subtlety, the Senate's formal function in the future was limited to consent, but not advice. This episode also demonstrated, as Stanley Elkins and Eric McKitrick have observed, that the President was more than simply a prime minister. To be effective, the office required a certain level of prestige and independence that precluded a personal appearance before the Senate for permission to conduct negotiations. Washington's instinct to take firm control over the nation's diplomatic relations cemented this institutional dynamic. Upon taking office, Washington began to issue directions to John Jay, then Foreign Minister under the Articles of Confederation, and immediately dictated diplomatic relations with other nations.[71] He assigned ambassadors to their missions, subject to Senate confirmation, and issued their instructions, removed them when necessary, and sometimes sent special envoys without senatorial advice and consent.[72] In creating and funding the State Department, the First Congress recognized the President's special rights in foreign affairs by not delegating any duties to the Secretary of State other than those assigned to him by the President. As Sai Prakash and Michael Ramsey have argued, there would have been no need for the Secretary if the President did not already have a preexisting foreign affairs power.[73] Congress funded the department simply by appropriating a lump sum and leaving pay and employee grades to executive discretion.

Washington wanted to protect his authority to set the rank of diplomatic officials and asked the Secretary of State for his opinion. Jefferson responded, "The transaction of business with foreign nations is executive altogether."[74] The only exceptions were those functions given to the Senate, which were "to be construed strictly" in favor of the President's authority. Which envoys to send, where to send them, their diplomatic grade, and their instructions, both public and secret, Jefferson concluded, "all this is left to the President; [the Senate] is only to see that no unfit persons be employed." The stuff of ambassadorial rank and negotiating records may seem trivial today, but in the eighteenth century they were the main instruments of foreign policy. Nations sent ambassadors on missions to negotiate agreements with instructions that left them a few goals and great flexibility on the terms; an ambassador's diplomatic rank signaled his nation's attitude toward a country. In 1794, Washington sent John Jay, the former foreign minister and Chief Justice at the time, to Britain with instructions to reach the best settlement possible of America's outstanding differences. His choice sent a strong signal that the United States wanted an amicable relationship. Echoing Madison's arguments during the removal debates, Jefferson believed these decisions fell within the President's authority because foreign affairs remained executive in nature.

Jefferson would regret his support of executive authority as he came to oppose Washington's foreign policies toward France and Great Britain. The beginning of the French Revolution in 1789 set off wars in Europe that would last a quarter-century. Eventually, the United States became entangled and barely escaped with its independence intact. But Washington kept the United States out of the conflict, giving the nation time to develop its strength and confidence. In guiding the young republic between the Scylla and Charybdis of Britain and France, he imposed a policy of neutrality based on the constitutional understanding that he held the authority to set foreign policy, interpret and even terminate treaties, and decide the nation's international obligations. Washington paid a steep price: his policies divided his government, sparked the creation of the first political party, and turned future presidential elections into partisan affairs. Neutrality in the European wars ruined Washington's hopes for a government ruled by consensus and left him disgusted with politics.

After the beheading of King Louis XVI, France declared war on Great Britain and Holland on February 1, 1793.[75] Edmund Genet, the new regime's ambassador to the United States, arrived two months later. News of war threw the American government into a quandary over the 1778 treaties with France, which had been crucial to the success of the Revolution. Article 11 of the Treaty of Alliance called on the United States to guarantee French possessions in the Americas, which implied that the United States might have to defend France's West Indies colony (today's Haiti).[76] Article 17 of the companion commercial treaty gave French warships and privateers the right to bring captured enemy ships as prizes into American ports.[77] Article 22 prohibited the United States from allowing France's enemies to equip or launch privateers or sell prizes in American ports.

Genet attempted to rouse the American people against Britain. Demanding that the United States honor the treaties, he authorized American ships to raid British shipping. The cabinet split over a response. Jefferson deeply hated Great Britain, admired the French Revolution, and suspected Hamilton of duplicating the British political system. For his part, Hamilton loathed the French Revolution, and his financial system depended on good relations with Britain. Upon learning of the French declaration of war, Hamilton, "with characteristic boldness," immediately urged Washington to suspend or terminate the treaties.[78] The young Treasury Secretary simply could not help meddling in the affairs of others, especially those of the Secretary of State. Hamilton believed that Britain's control of the seas and its trading system made good relations with London paramount. While a change in government did not automatically void treaties with another state, he argued that the uncertain status of the French government and the dangerous wartime situation allowed suspension of the treaties.[79] While Jefferson agreed that military participation in the European war was out of the question, he believed the United States was obliged to fulfill the treaties. (Under the Articles of Confederation, he had served as minister to France.)

On April 18, Washington sent a list of 13 questions to Hamilton, Jefferson, Knox, and Randolph and ordered a cabinet meeting for the next day — establishing a regular mechanism of presidential decision-making.[80] Almost all of Washington's questions involved the interpretation of the 1778 treaties. Question four, for example, asked: "Are the United States obliged by good faith to consider the Treaties heretofore made with France as applying to the present situation of the parties?" Washington ordered them to give an opinion on whether Article 11 applied to an offensive war launched by France, whether the United States could both observe the treaties and remain neutral, and under what conditions the United States could suspend or terminate the treaties.

Washington's questions produced a deceptive unanimity in the cabinet. Everyone agreed that a proclamation of neutrality should be issued, but in order to assuage Jefferson's concerns, the word "neutrality" was not used. Indeed, given the distance of the United States, its military weakness, and its strategic irrelevance to the European theatre, neutrality was the only realistic option. Two other questions received the same unanimity. The cabinet agreed that the President should receive Genet as France's ambassador, making the United States the first nation to recognize the government of revolutionary France. The members further agreed that consulting Congress was unnecessary. The executive branch would decide the nation's position on the European wars. Adjourning the meeting without reaching the other questions, Washington asked his advisers to submit written responses on whether to suspend or terminate the 1778 treaties.

No one in the cabinet disputed that the President held this power under the Constitution. On April 28, Jefferson, later joined by Randolph, argued that international law did not permit the suspension or annulling of a treaty because of a change in government.[81] Because he believed that France was unlikely to ask the United States to defend the West Indies, Jefferson recommended that the administration do nothing. On May 2, Hamilton and Knox argued that the civil war in France allowed the United States to suspend the treaty, or even terminate it because of the new circumstances threatening American national security.[82] They read the treaty to apply only to defensive wars, not to one in which France had attacked first. Telling Jefferson that he "never had a doubt about the validity of the treaty," Washington decided against suspension the next day.[83] On the question of the West Indies, Washington decided to remain silent, a wise choice, as Jefferson's prediction proved correct and France did not seek American aid.

Washington issued his decision in a proclamation drafted by Randolph.[84] Recognizing a state of war between France and the other European powers, he announced that the United States "should with sincerity and good faith adopt and pursue a conduct friendly and impartial toward the belligerent [sic] Powers." Washington further saw fit to "declare the disposition of the United States to observe the conduct aforesaid towards those Powers respectfully" and "to exhort and warn the citizens of the United States carefully to avoid all acts and proceedings whatsoever, which may in any manner tend to contravene such disposition." The proclamation also stated that the federal government would prosecute those who "violate the law of nations, with respect to the Powers at war." His proclamation was a determination that American obligations did not require entry into the war on the side of the French. After a year, Congress implemented his interpretation into domestic law by making it a crime for a citizen to violate American neutrality.[85]

Although the Continental Congress had negotiated and ratified the 1778 treaties, Washington never asked about its intentions.[86] None of his cabinet members wanted to interpret the treaties in the light most favorable to France. Both Hamilton and Jefferson grounded their appeals in the national interest, international law, and common sense. Neither expressed a belief that consultation with Congress or the Senate was necessary or advisable. Washington and his cabinet proceeded on the assumption that it was the province of the executive branch to interpret treaties, and so set foreign policy, on behalf of the United States. They even believed that the President had the authority to terminate the 1778 treaties. Hamilton argued that the President could terminate if necessary, but recommended only suspension. Fighting a rearguard action, Jefferson did not raise a constitutional objection. Even though Hamilton convinced Washington to declare neutrality, it is doubtful that Jefferson could have produced any other outcome — the United States simply was not going to enter the war on France's side, at least not for another two decades.[87]

The proclamation provoked one of the great constitutional debates in American history. In a series of newspaper articles that summer, Hamilton adopted the pseudonym of "Pacificus" to defend the President's constitutional authority.[88] Hamilton began with the position that foreign policy was executive by its very nature. Congress was not the "organ of intercourse" with foreign nations, while the judiciary could only "decide litigations in particular cases." Declaring neutrality, therefore, must "of necessity belong to the Executive." It drew from the executive's authority as "the *organ* of intercourse between the Nation and foreign Nations," as "interpreter of the National Treaties in those cases in which the Judiciary is not competent," and as enforcer of the law, "of which treaties form a part." Hamilton argued that treaties, as well as the rules of international law, were part of the laws to be carried out by the executive, and "[h]e who is to execute the laws must first judge for himself of their meaning." Last, but not least, Hamilton believed the executive could declare neutrality because of its "Power which is charged with the command and application of the Public Force."

Basing his claims on the constitutional text, Hamilton argued that the President's authority derived from Article II, Section 2's grant of the executive power. The Constitution already made the President Commander-in-Chief, maker of treaties with the advice and consent of the Senate, receiver of ambassadors, and executor of the laws. But "it would not consist with rules of sound construction to consider this enumeration of particular authorities as derogating from the more comprehensive grant contained in the general clause." Article II's enumeration of powers "ought...to be considered as intended...to specify and regulate the principal articles implied in the definition of Executive Power; leaving the rest to flow from the general grant of that power...." For Hamilton, the Senate's role in making treaties was only a narrow exception from the general grant of executive power to the President and "ought to be construed strictly." When the Constitution sought to transfer traditionally executive powers away from the President, it did so specifically, as with the power to declare war. "The general doctrine then of our constitution is, that the Executive Power of the Nation is vested in the President," Hamilton concluded, "subject only to the exceptions and qualifications which are expressed in that instrument."

Madison, however, expressed surprise and concern over the President's Proclamation of Neutrality. In a letter to Jefferson, Madison claimed Hamilton had talked Washington into an "assumption of prerogatives not clearly found in the Constitution and having the appearance of being copied from a Monarchical model."[89] His immediate criticism was that the proclamation intruded on Congress's power to declare war. Jefferson explained that although he had agreed in the cabinet that the President could declare neutrality without consulting Congress, that he nonetheless held constitutional concerns. When Hamilton's Pacificus essays — defending the President's power to declare neutrality — appeared in the press, Jefferson begged Madison: "For God's sake, my dear Sir, take up your pen, select the most striking heresies and cut him to pieces in the face of the public."[90]

Under the pseudonym "Helvidius," Madison took issue with every point of Hamilton's constitutional arguments.[91] He dismissed Locke and Montesquieu's classification of foreign affairs as executive in nature because they were "evidently warped by a regard to the particular government of England." Making treaties and declaring war were legislative powers because they had the force of law; therefore, the President could not exercise them. "The natural province of the executive magistrate is to execute laws, as that of the legislature is to make laws," Madison wrote. "All his acts therefore, properly executive, must presuppose the existence of the laws to be executed." The Constitution vested the power to declare war in Congress and gave the Senate an equal share in the treaty power, confirming that they set private rules of conduct made the law of the land by the Supremacy Clause. To allow the President a share of the legislative power "is an absurdity — in practice a tyranny."[92]

Madison's deeper argument was that placing the power to start and wage war in the same hands risked tyranny. "Those who are to conduct a war cannot in the nature of things be proper or safe judges whether a war ought to be commenced, continued, or concluded."[93] Why? Because, according to Madison, "war is in fact the true nurse of executive aggrandizement."[94] In war, "physical force is to be created," "the public treasures are to be unlocked," "the honors and emoluments of office are to be multiplied," and "laurels are to be gathered," and all are to be placed at the disposal of the executive. It is an "axiom," therefore, that "the executive is the department of power most distinguished by its propensity to war." Pacificus's broad reading of the vesting of the executive power in the President, Madison retorted, was nothing less than an effort to smuggle the British Crown into the Constitution.

History has looked more favorably on Hamilton's arguments than Madison's. Helvidius claimed rather unpersuasively that foreign affairs were legislative in nature or shared between the branches, and he never directly addressed Hamilton's argument about Article II's vesting of the executive power in the President.[95] It was difficult for Madison to deny that Article II granted the President some unenumerated powers, in light of his arguments during the removal debate. Madison ultimately rested on the narrower point that the President could not interpret treaties in a manner that prevented Congress from exercising its own plenary constitutional power to declare war.[96] The proclamation, however, did not prevent Congress from declaring war, if it wished. Washington's actions only had the effect of preserving the status quo.

Despite the partisan divisions, the Helvidius-Pacificus debates and the neutrality controversy demonstrate some common ground. No one doubted that the President held the initiative in foreign policy, nor did Madison take serious issue with the idea that the executive had the power to interpret or even terminate treaties. Madison and Jefferson were making a broader argument against unenumerated executive powers and the structural point that those powers could not be used to supplant Congress's own authorities. Hamilton agreed with this up to a point, noting that Congress's power to declare war gave it the final word on whether the United States was in a state of war with another country. The Constitution's explicit grant of a specific power to Congress prevents the President from usurping that power, just as Congress cannot use its own plenary powers to invade the proper scope of the executive. We can see this balance in Washington's unsuccessful efforts to prosecute individuals for violating the proclamation. Only Congress could regulate the conduct of citizens within the United States, and it was not until Congress enacted criminal legislation that prosecutions could succeed.[97]

The proclamation set one of the most important precedents for executive power: Presidents henceforth would exercise the initiative in foreign affairs. Jefferson and Madison wanted to limit the executive's powers where they were perhaps needed most — in foreign affairs. But the growth of the nation and its interests would place increasing pressure on their constitutional vision. As the effect of foreign affairs on the nation grew, the powers of the office would respond to keep pace. Still, Hamilton's view required no prerogative, no ability of the President to act outside of the Constitution when necessity demands. He believed that the Constitution gave the President, through the grant of "the executive power" of the government, all of the authority necessary to handle exigencies and unforeseen circumstances. Jefferson and Madison, on the other hand, fought against an elastic reading of presidential power, and as Jefferson's opinion on the bank showed, generally in favor of a strictly limited federal government. This would force them, surprisingly, into the position of relying on the theory of an extra-constitutional presidential prerogative when they assumed power in 1800.

EXECUTIVE PRIVILEGE

WASHINGTON'S LARGELY successful efforts to keep the United States out of the European wars called on him to define executive power one last time in his last year in office. The occasion was the Jay Treaty, which sought to resolve long-term issues plaguing Anglo-American relations. Great Britain continued to occupy forts within the Northwest Territory, which under the 1783 peace treaty it was required to evacuate, on the ground that British creditors could not recover pre-revolutionary loans made to Americans. British officials in the area caused constant trouble by encouraging local Indians to oust the Americans from the territory. A more immediate difficulty was Britain's naval war against France. American merchants and shippers were profiting handsomely by selling to both belligerents, with the trade between the Caribbean colonies of the two great powers being especially lucrative. In 1793, Britain declared an embargo against France, seized neutral ships carrying contraband including food, and seized sailors on American ships who were allegedly British deserters. Later that year, Britain imposed a blockade on the French West Indies trade, leading to the immediate seizure of 250 American merchant ships in the area.[98]

Britain's seizures of American shipping stoked a war scare. Congress rejected proposals for a 15,000-man army but agreed to a temporary embargo on Great Britain and the construction of six daring new frigates, America's first blue-water navy. After news came that Britain had rescinded its embargo of the French West Indies, Washington sent Chief Justice Jay to London as a special envoy to settle all outstanding disputes. Jay reached an agreement in November 1794, which arrived in the United States in March. In Jay's Treaty, Britain agreed to evacuate the Northwestern forts, allow limited American trade with the West Indies, grant most-favored-nation tariff treatment to American imports, and create an international commission (the first of its kind) to arbitrate the debt claims, the seizures of American ships, and the U.S.-Canada border. Jay failed to reach any settlement on slaves carried off by British forces at the end of the Revolution or to get British commitment to the principle that neutral ships could carry goods to any of the belligerents. Under the circumstances, it was probably the best deal possible: it ended the British threat to the Western territories and kept the peace for another 17 years. Many historians today consider the Jay Treaty a success and another example of Washington's leadership.[99]

Opposition by Jefferson's supporters was so fierce that it cemented the emergence of the two-party system in American politics. In June 1795, a 20–10 Federalist majority in the Senate barely approved the treaty (except for the provision on the West Indies trade, which it rejected). Washington ratified the treaty in August. When the text became public, large protests erupted throughout the country. Jeffersonians sought to capitalize by blocking measures in the House needed to implement the treaty, such as changes in tariff schedules and appropriations for the compensation of British claims. Hoping to reveal embarrassing details within the administration, the House voted 62–37 in March 1796 to request all of the papers related to Jay's mission. On earlier occasions, the administration had supplied papers in response to congressional investigations, one into St. Clair's defeat by the Indians, the second into allegations of financial irregularities by Hamilton. Although he cooperated with Congress on these occasions, Washington had taken the view that he could refuse if the disclosure of the information would harm the public interest.[100] Even if the Presidency could lay claim to a right of executive privilege, the benefits of harmony with the legislature and maintaining public confidence in government would usually prevail.

This time, Washington chose to place the confidentiality of

executive deliberation above good relations with Congress. Only five days after the House sent its request, Washington responded that it had no constitutional right at stake. To allow the House to see the papers would create "a dangerous precedent."[101] The Constitution had vested the power to make treaties in the President, with the advice and consent of the Senate, because of the need for secrecy in diplomatic relations. Expanding the House's role would undermine the nation's ability to keep secrets and make it difficult, if not impossible, to manage foreign affairs effectively.

Washington observed that the Framers had explicitly rejected any role for the House in treaty-making, and had included the Senate to protect state interests — a fact he knew well as President of the Constitutional Convention. The House had an obligation to implement the treaty, as it had already carried into effect without question all previous ones. If the House had a legitimate constitutional claim to the papers, Washington might comply, but here he need not consider it. "It does not occur that the inspection of the papers asked for can be relative to any purpose under the cognizance of the House of Representatives," Washington wrote, "except that of an impeachment which the resolution has not expressed."[102] Jeffersonians were shocked, Federalists overjoyed. Efforts to block the treaty soon lost steam, in part because of Washington, in greater part because the restoration of the international carrying trade sparked an economic boom.

Debate has continued to this day over whether Washington correctly refused the House's demand for information. He did not describe his claim as "executive privilege" or ground it in a broad theory of the President's right to protect internal communications and advice, as the Supreme Court would in the Watergate tapes case.[103] Washington kept his claim carefully circumscribed to the House's exclusion from treaty-making. He had turned over all of the papers to the Senate as part of the process of advice and consent. Washington, however, clearly believed that his right to withhold information from Congress extended beyond that narrow context. In 1794, the Senate requested all diplomatic communications between the American envoy to France (who was then Gouverneur Morris) and the Secretary of State. Attorney General William Bradford advised that the President could withhold correspondence whose revelation would harm the public interest, and the other members of the cabinet agreed. Washington provided the correspondence but informed the Senate that he had not given them material that, in his judgment, ought not to be publicly communicated.[104]

Washington's arguments have broad implications. He consciously ignored the House's legitimate constitutional right to gather information to appropriate money and regulate trade.[105] To say that the House had a right to the documents only if it were considering impeachment was an overstatement, to say the least. Washington based his refusal in part on the need for secrecy in foreign affairs, referring to the harm that would arise if the government could not act with discretion in negotiating agreements. While limited to treaties, Washington's decision would provide the foundations for future Presidents to expand their right to keep from Congress and the courts any information whose disclosure would harm the national interest.

CONCLUSIONS

OUR CONSTITUTION USUALLY grants those elected to the Presidency their legitimacy; with Washington, it was the reverse. His standing as the Father of the Country bestowed legitimacy on the Constitution. It is hard to imagine another member of the founding generation who could guarantee that the Constitution would overcome the centrifugal forces of its early years. Washington placed at the service of the young government his record as the general who had won the nation's independence, and his reputation for republican virtue etched in memory when he had stepped down from command.

Washington was not the greatest simply because he was the first. He did more than serve as the ceremonial head of government. Understanding instinctively that his actions set the example for his successors, Washington made decisions that fulfilled the Federalists' hope for independence and energy. He reserved to the executive control over the selection of government nominees; treated all subordinates as part of a unitary executive branch, with himself at the top; and fought to keep the internal deliberations of his advisers confidential.

Washington believed he had to interpret the Constitution independently in executing his powers, whether by signing proposed bills or implementing those on the books. When it came time to enforce national laws and policies, Washington led the troops personally to demonstrate the energy and authority of the new government. In foreign affairs, Washington read the Constitution to give him the executive's traditional leading role, including the interpretation of treaties and international law, the deployment of military force, and the conduct of diplomatic relations. He moved forcefully to keep the nation out of the European wars and to reach a settlement with Great Britain.

Washington demonstrated that a President could not succeed without his constitutional powers. The Framers did not account for, and were openly hostile to, political parties. They believed that a President should stand above parties, which were seen as temporary factions assembling against the national interest.[106] From the very beginning, Washington saw his office as advancing a set of policies, a program, which required the cooperation of the executive and legislative branches. Washington's administration devised the national banking system and the assumption of debts. It developed the policy of neutrality in the wars between Great Britain and France and set the nation on a hostile military course with the Indians. Washington understood the Presidency as giving him, not Congress, the initiative in defining foreign and domestic security policy.

Institutional independence included recognition of the other branches' prerogatives. Only the legislature could create the bank, approve the Jay Treaty, or fund the troops on the frontier. While Washington was dismayed at the open partisanship of the Jeffersonian opposition, his administration began the first experiments in the coordination of executive and legislative branches through a common political party. Washington would even recognize perhaps the ultimate limitation on the Presidency. By stepping down after two terms, Washington introduced a republican rotation in office, a precedent unbroken until Franklin D. Roosevelt, which proved to be a political bulwark against executive tyranny. By combining constitutional independence with constitutional self-control, Washington set the example of a republican executive that his successors would follow.

CHAPTER 4

Thomas Jefferson

WHILE NOT ONE OF the top three of our nation's "greatest" Presidents, Thomas Jefferson consistently ranks as one of the "great" after Washington, Lincoln, and FDR. No doubt, he owes some of his high standing to his achievements before and after his time in office. He drafted the Declaration of Independence, founded the University of Virginia, and served as governor of his state and envoy to France. He was an architect, scientist, farmer, and inventor. Yet, Jefferson was a bundle of contradictions, so much so that historian Richard Ellis titled a recent biography *American Sphinx.* Jefferson was perhaps our nation's most eloquent spokesman for human freedom, but at the same time kept slaves and fathered illegitimate children with one. As Leonard Levy has shown, he was a master of rhetoric in defense of civil liberties, but did not hesitate to use government power to pursue critics and opponents. He criticized the growth of federal power yet exercised it to limits rarely seen in American history to enforce an embargo. He demanded responsible, effective government but suffered from migraine headaches that prevented him from fulfilling his duties at times of high stress, both as governor and President.[1]

Nowhere do these contradictions seem to arise more sharply than with regard to Jefferson's views on executive power. Jefferson is widely thought to have opposed a strong Presidency. While drafting the Virginia constitution, he attempted to strip the governorship of many of the executive's powers and re-title the position as that of "Administrator."[2] While envoy to France, he faulted the proposed Constitution because it contained no presidential term limits. He worried that once elected, a President would be returned to office for life. "I am not a friend to a very energetic government. It is always oppressive," he explained to Madison.[3] He praised the Constitution because it created "one effectual check to the Dog of war by transferring the power of letting him loose from the Executive to the Legislative Body."[4] While Secretary of State, Jefferson adopted a theory of strict construction to oppose Hamilton's broad interpretation of the Constitution's implied powers — first with the creation of the national bank, then with the proclamation of neutrality — and he organized America's first political party against the "monocrats" who were allegedly reinstalling features of the British monarchy in the United States. While President, Jefferson sought to reduce the size of bureaucracy and the military, lower taxes, enhance majority rule, and center the nation in his vision of an agrarian republic. He characterized his election "as real a revolution in the principles of our government as that of 1776 was in form," by saving the country from a Federalist Party that favored the executive.[5]

In office, however, Jefferson claimed the right to interpret the laws at odds with the courts and Congress, bought Louisiana even while doubting the act's constitutionality, shepherded legislation through Congress, and tied the legitimacy of the Presidency to the will of the majority. His actions belie the straw man of a weak Jeffersonian

Presidency, a fact not lost on his contemporaries. Hamilton said that during their time in the Washington administration, Jefferson "was generally for a large construction of the Executive authority" and was "not backward to act upon it in cases which coincided with his views."[6] This was Hamilton's idea of a compliment. Henry Adams would conclude, in his magisterial history on Jefferson and Madison, that the former exercised presidential power "more completely than had ever before been known in American history."[7] Many political scientists ever since have considered Jefferson an example of principle giving way before political expediency.[8]

A growing minority of historians and political scientists, including Jeremy Bailey, Ralph Ketcham, David Mayer, and Gary Schmitt, argues that this contradiction proceeds from a false starting point. It is assumed that Jefferson favored a weak executive because he sought a limited national government. The two ideas, however, need not conflict. Jefferson indeed wanted a government of limited constitutional powers balanced by states possessing significant sovereignty. In his draft of the 1798 Kentucky Resolutions, Jefferson argued that the Union represented only a compact between the states, rather than a national government representing one people. But within that framework, he favored a clean separation of powers that made each branch of the federal government supreme in its own sphere. For those matters properly classified as executive in nature, the President would govern, subject to the explicit exceptions and power sharing set out in the Constitution. He favored an executive branch headed by one individual, free of a council of advisors, to enhance executive accountability and responsibility, and sought to reconceptualize the office as the representative of a popular majority, elected to carry out an agenda. Jefferson embarked on a major innovation in presidential power, that of the President as party leader, which allowed him to promote a national program by coordinating the activities of the executive and legislative branches. Jefferson made the Presidency more powerful by making it more popular.[9]

Jefferson profoundly affected the Presidency by introducing the concept of the prerogative. He advanced the theory, clearly following Locke, that the President could act outside the Constitution to protect the national interest in moments of great crisis or opportunity.[10] In this, he differed from Hamilton and the Federalists, who believed that the formal powers of the President were flexible enough to address any national emergency. "The circumstances that endanger the safety of nations are infinite," Hamilton had written as Publius, "and for this reason no constitutional shackles can wisely be imposed on the power to which the care of it is committed."[11] Jefferson, however, followed a strict constructionist approach to interpreting the Constitution, which resisted a broad reading of the President's formal powers. The prerogative allowed Jefferson to protect the country in unforeseen circumstances and keep his constitutional principles. As in the Louisiana Purchase, he could act beyond the Constitution when necessity demanded it. In exchange, the President had to throw himself upon the people for approval of his unconstitutional act. That check reinforced Jefferson's innovation of placing the legitimacy of the Presidency on national election and his representation of the will of the majority.[12]

Jefferson's conception of the executive power was the product of the lessons of experience. As governor of Virginia during the Revolution, when British forces had American troops on the run, Jefferson came to appreciate matching the executive's powers to its responsibilities. In discussing proposals for Virginia's new constitution, Jefferson argued that the executive power did not reach as far as the British Crown's prerogatives, but at least included the power to enforce the laws and other powers not judicial or legislative in nature. During the Constitutional Convention, Jefferson advised friends that the Constitution should create an independent executive branch. "I think it very material to separate in the hands of Congress the Executive and Legislative powers," he wrote. "The want of it has been the source of more evil than we have ever experienced from any other cause."[13] As Secretary of State, Jefferson believed that control over foreign relations was one of those executive powers, from which the Senate's role in treaty-making was only a narrow exception. While he urged Madison to write against Hamilton as Helvidius, Jefferson agreed with the rest of Washington's cabinet that the President should declare neutrality.

Jefferson entered office after a bitter campaign. Jefferson considered the Federalists to be monarchists who wanted to duplicate the British political and economic system. In the election of 1800, his Republican Party swept Federalist majorities out of Congress, and John Adams out of the White House. But Jefferson tied in the Electoral College with his party's vice presidential candidate, Aaron Burr, even though his party intended that Jefferson become President. Under the rules of the Electoral College, each elector voted for two candidates, with the Vice President simply the runner-up. The tie threw the election into the lame-duck Congress, where Federalists entertained various schemes to deny Jefferson the Presidency, including swinging it to Burr or refusing to choose anyone at all. Hamilton apparently feared Burr more than Jefferson, and the Federalists eventually gave the latter the victory. The Twelfth Amendment, ratified in 1804, finally required electors to vote separately for President and Vice President, but the election of 1800 would be resolved in the House, and Jefferson would owe his selection to his claim that the President should represent the will of a national democratic majority.

The election represented the transfer of power from one political party to another without fighting or bloodshed, a rare thing in those days. In his inaugural address, Jefferson famously said, "We are all Republicans: we are all Federalists," to underscore the belief in representative government shared by all. Once in office, though, Jefferson reversed much of the Federalists' system. He unraveled the Hamiltonian financial structure by reducing government expenditures, cutting taxes, and retiring the national debt. This would pull the heart out of the network of financiers, merchants, and bureaucracy and reorient the country toward agriculture, western expansion, and a limited national government. However, his opposition to Federalist policies did not imply a rejection of the powers of the Presidency. Jefferson's characterization of the Hamiltonian system as monarchic was not an attack on executive power, but a criticism of the British system of executive corruption of the legislature. Jefferson would not hesitate to expand presidential power to achieve his own policies.

PERSONNEL

JEFFERSON'S FIRST STEPS in unwinding the Federalists' system occurred in the area of personnel and law enforcement. Jefferson introduced the idea that the members of his cabinet, and most of the subordinate executive officials subject to presidential appointment, should hail from his party. Washington had sought the best characters for his cabinet, hence the selection of Jefferson himself as Secretary of State. Jefferson chose only Republican leaders for his cabinet, with Madison as Secretary of State and Gallatin as Treasury Secretary. Jefferson did not immediately turn out all federal employees and replace them with party supporters, but he gradually replaced half by the end of his first term.[14] He had little problem refusing to sign the commissions of officers who had received "midnight appointments" at the end of Adams's term (one of them leading to the foundational Supreme Court decision in *Marbury v.*

Madison) or having his majorities in Congress repeal the Judiciary Act of 1801, which had created several new judgeships with Federalist occupants.

Jefferson's effort to supplant Federalist officials with Republicans was more than the realization that personnel shape policy. It created an alternative path for presidential control of the executive branch. Washington had relied on the constitutional principle that he was personally responsible for taking care that the laws were faithfully executed. All officials within the executive branch were there to assist him in carrying out that constitutional duty, and hence must be within his direct control. Jefferson supplemented this line of authority with the discipline of party politics. His appointees enforced administration policies because Jefferson headed the executive branch, and he headed their political party.

Jefferson became the inventor, though not the most ruthless practitioner, of the spoils system. Some states, such as Connecticut, experienced "a general sweep" of Federalists out of national offices, while others saw a more gradual replacement. The desire to reward the party faithful after the election only partially explains Jefferson's actions. Jefferson believed the executive branch represented the people as much as the legislature, and so he wanted Republicans to have the same share of offices as they had of the popular vote. He understood that executive officers make policy choices beyond robotically executing the law. By the end of his administration, Jefferson had placed party members in two-thirds of all executive offices. Because of Jefferson, today we accept with little controversy that Presidents may choose their own party members for most important government positions. That Jefferson had to rely on partisan considerations in appointments suggests that relying on formal constitutional powers is simply not enough to control the executive branch.[15]

LAW ENFORCEMENT

J EFFERSON'S VIEWS ON law enforcement laid a strong claim to presidential equality with the other branches. Among the most hated pieces of Federalist legislation were the Alien and Sedition Acts of 1798, which made it a crime to defame or libel the government (with truth as a defense). Jefferson and Madison had secretly drafted the Kentucky and Virginia Resolutions, which suggested that the states could resist unconstitutional federal laws. Parts of the Acts expired at the end of the Adams administration, but Jefferson proceeded to pardon the ten individuals convicted under the law and ordered all prosecutions dropped. "A legislature had passed a sedition law. The federal courts had subjected certain individuals to its penalties of fine and imprisonment," Jefferson wrote in 1811. "On coming into office, I released these individuals by the power of pardon committed to executive discretion, which could never be more properly exercised than where citizens were suffering without the authority of law, or, which was equivalent, under a law unauthorized by the constitution, and therefore null."[16] Even though the courts and Congress had found the Alien and Sedition Acts to be constitutional, Jefferson used his power as President to prevent the laws from being executed.

Jefferson's decision was rooted in a strict view of the separation of powers and the right of each branch to interpret the Constitution for itself. He utterly rejected the notion that the courts have the last word on the meaning of the founding document. In a letter to Abigail Adams explaining his actions, Jefferson asserted that the executive and judiciary are "equally independent" in reviewing the constitutionality of the laws. "You seem to think it devolved on the judges to decide on the validity of the sedition law," he wrote. "But nothing in the Constitution has given them a right to decide for the

Executive, more than to the Executive to decide for them. Both magistracies are equally independent in the sphere of action assigned to them."[17] While the courts can view a law as constitutional and allow cases to move forward, the President can hold a different view and refuse to bring prosecutions against those who violate the law and pardon those already convicted. In an 1819 letter, Jefferson cited his reversal of the Sedition Act convictions to show that "each department is truly independent of the others, and has an equal right to decide for itself what is the meaning of the constitution in the cases submitted to its action; and especially, where it is to act ultimately and without appeal."[18] While Jefferson did not challenge the courts' right to interpret the Constitution, he denied that the judiciary's conclusions bound him in the exercise of his own responsibilities.

Jefferson's vision went further. He believed that Presidents ought to use the veto only when they were fairly certain that Congress had passed an unconstitutional law; he did not appear to think that he should veto laws because he disagreed with Congress's policy choices. On the other hand, Jefferson viewed his right to interpret the Constitution as extending beyond the President's role in the legislative process. As the Alien and Sedition Acts episode shows, he believed a President could decline to prosecute laws that in his opinion violated the Constitution. Similarly, Jefferson would not have expected the courts to feel bound by the views of the President and Congress on the constitutionality of the laws that they enact.

JUDGES

RELATIONS WITH THE judicial branch plagued the Jefferson administration. Federalists had a strong hold on the judiciary, and Jefferson thought of it as the last redoubt of his political opponents. "They have retired into the judiciary as a stronghold. There the remains of federalism are to be preserved and fed from the treasury, and from that battery all the works of republicanism are to be beaten down and erased."[19] He believed that it was wholly appropriate for the executive and legislative branches to alter the personnel of the judicial branch in order to change the outcome of its decisions. Jefferson felt no unease in having Congress repeal new judgeships, postpone Supreme Court terms to influence decisions, and in his most ambitious effort, remove judges in an effort to change the direction of the law.

Republicans in the House began by eliminating the new judgeships created by the Federalists in 1801. They followed by attempting to remove the judges who were left. In 1803, Jeffersonians began impeachment proceedings against John Pickering of New Hampshire, a Federalist district judge who happened to be crazy and a drunk. His mental sickness while chief justice of the state supreme court had led to efforts to oust him, and when a seat on the federal bench opened, state leaders promoted their way out of the problem by recommending Pickering.[20] In 1804, the Senate voted along strict party lines that Pickering's erratic behavior on the bench satisfied the "high crimes and misdemeanors" standard and removed him from office. Jefferson had written to the House to pass along complaints about Pickering and ask Congress to perform its constitutional functions.

Pickering was only target practice for bigger game. Justice Samuel Chase, a signer of the Declaration of Independence and former Anti-Federalist, had infuriated Republicans with his political outbursts on the bench, which included an attack on universal manhood suffrage and the Judiciary Act of 1803. Jefferson wrote a letter to a Maryland Congressman suggesting impeachment: "Ought this seditious and official attack on the principles of our Constitution, and on proceedings of a State, to go unpunished?"[21] His majority in the House obliged, beginning impeachment proceedings on the day of Pickering's conviction. But the Senate refused to convict, establishing the precedent that impeachment would not be used to overturn judicial decisions.

Jefferson's attack on the judiciary is conventionally understood as a defeat, and in terms of constitutional principle it was, but in terms of immediate politics, Jefferson came out ahead. After its decision in *Marbury*, the Supreme Court would not invalidate another federal law until *Dred Scott* a half-century later. The challenge to the judiciary effectively removed any threat that the federal courts would stand in the way of Jeffersonian legislation or presidential actions. Instead, the Marshall Court devoted itself to defending the prerogatives of Congress by vindicating the powers of the national government against those of the states. Jefferson's expanded view of the rights of the President and Congress against the judiciary, while constrained by the Senate in the end, helped him remove an obstacle to his policy agenda.

Jefferson's confrontation with the courts gave birth to another invocation of executive power. While Washington had refused to disclose treaty documents to the House, Jefferson withheld information from the judiciary. The occasion was the Burr conspiracy, whose historical details still remain unclear. In 1805, Aaron Burr (after killing Alexander Hamilton in a duel while no longer Vice President) hatched a scheme to launch a military expedition in the American Southwest. Depending on the account one believes, Burr either sought to attack Spanish possessions and bring them into the United States, or to detach territories from the United States and create for himself an independent empire, or some combination of the two. Burr had several private dinners with Jefferson at the White House while he secretly advanced his plans in Washington. In the end, one of the coconspirators, General James Wilkinson, turned against Burr as he was forming his troops, arrested him and other plotters, and sent them to Washington for trial.

Burr was prosecuted for treason before Chief Justice John Marshall, sitting as a federal trial judge in Virginia. Burr's defense sought information in Jefferson's possession, including reports on the conspiracy sent to the President. Marshall issued a subpoena for the documents, but Jefferson refused to acknowledge the Court's right to force the executive to produce information for its proceedings. He explained to the federal district attorney that a court's subpoena could not override the Constitution, which "enjoins his constant agency" in leading the American people.[22] Returning to his consistent view that the separation of powers required independence for each branch of government, Jefferson argued that the executive would become subordinate to the judiciary "if he were subject to the commands of the latter, and to imprisonment for disobedience." Proposing an argument that Bill Clinton would try, unpersuasively, before the Supreme Court, Jefferson argued that responding to the commands of the judiciary would "keep him constantly trudging from north to south and east to west." Jefferson would be "the sole judge" of what government documents to make public. As a compromise, he sent a limited set of documents to the U.S. attorney and ordered him only to release portions needed in the interests of justice. Marshall did not pursue the subpoena any further, and Burr and his coconspirators were acquitted. Jefferson's short-term political wishes were frustrated — he was convinced that Burr was guilty of treason and had virtually convicted him in a special message to Congress — but he established the first true precedent of executive privilege.

FOREIGN AFFAIRS: WAR

IT IS IN FOREIGN AFFAIRS that fans of Jefferson can make their best claim for his inclusion in the list of greatest American Presidents. While Jefferson used his powers as Commander-in-Chief to wage a successful offensive against the Barbary states — inspiring the lyric "to the shores of Tripoli" — his most important presidential act involved an exchange of property rather than cannon shot.

Despite his earlier attacks on executive power, Jefferson did not seek to withdraw the President's powers in war. Jefferson had planned to reduce the federal budget by cutting the military to the bone, but events caused him to depend on the navy maintained by the Adams administration. The immediate cause was relations with the Barbary pirates. Although history remembers them as bandits, they did in fact inhabit autonomous regions — Algiers, Tripoli, and Tunis — within the Ottoman Empire, and an independent nation, Morocco. Their leaders preyed upon the shipping of other nations, seized their cargos, and sold their sailors into slavery. Under the Continental Congress, the United States had paid tribute (amounting to $10 million under Washington and Adams) to allow American shipping to proceed unhindered.[23] Jefferson's accession to the Presidency coincided with demands for higher payments and the impressment of a U.S. Navy frigate by the Dey of Algiers.

Having long disliked paying the Barbary tribute, Jefferson decided to send the Navy to put an end to the insults to American shipping. In a meeting on May 15, 1801, the cabinet unanimously agreed that Jefferson should send a squadron to the Mediterranean as a show of force. No one in the cabinet, including Madison and Gallatin, believed that the President had to seek congressional permission to order the mission. The only legislative action was a statute enacted on the last day of the Adams administration, requiring that at least six existing frigates (American frigates at this time were the best in the world) be kept in "constant service" — an effort to prevent Jefferson from reducing the navy to zero. Jefferson and his cabinet thought that the statute could be read to allow the President to send a "training mission" to the Mediterranean. The cabinet also agreed that the President had constitutional authority to order offensive military operations, should a state of war already be in existence because of the hostile acts of the Barbary powers. "The Executive cannot put us in a state of war," Gallatin said, "but if we be put into that state either by the decree of Congress or of the other nation, the command and direction of the public force then belongs to the Executive."[24] Jefferson and his advisors believed that the Constitution only required Congress to declare war to undertake purely offensive operations against a nation with which the United States was at peace. As Abraham Sofaer has observed, Jefferson and his advisors assumed they had the authority for the expedition simply by virtue of Congress's creation of the navy forces that made it possible — a position no different from that taken by President Washington in the Indian wars.

Jefferson was clear on this in his orders to the naval commanders. The Secretary of the Navy ordered Commodore Richard Dale to proceed to the Mediterranean and, if he found that any of the Barbary states had declared war on the United States, to "chastise their insolence" by "sinking, burning, or destroying their ships & vessels wherever you shall find them."[25] Dale could impose a blockade and take prisoners, going well beyond simply protecting American shipping from attack. Upon arriving and discovering that the Bashaw of Tripoli had declared war, Dale issued orders to his squadron to attack any and all Tripolitan vessels. Lieutenant Andrew Sterett, commanding the 12-gun schooner *Enterprise*, encountered a 14-gun Tripolitan corsair on a resupply mission to Malta in August 1801.

The *Enterprise* fought for three hours and killed half the corsair's crew, cut down its masts, threw its guns overboard, and set it adrift. Sterett could not keep the prize, because he was on the outward leg of his resupply mission, but his actions produced broad approval in the United States and a joint resolution applauding the crew.[26]

The President portrayed his orders differently to Congress in December 1801. He claimed that he had not authorized offensive operations, that Sterett had acted in self-defense, and that the *Enterprise* had released the corsair because Congress had not authorized offensive operations. "Unauthorized by the Constitution, without the sanction of Congress, to go beyond the line of defence, the vessel, being disabled from committing further hostilities, was liberated with its crew."[27] While some scholars have viewed Jefferson's words as presidential acceptance of Congress's control over war, Jefferson did not accurately represent Sterett's attack, the decision to release the captured warship, or the nature of the orders to Commodore Dale, nor did he reveal his thinking or that of his cabinet when those orders were cut. Jefferson followed by requesting that Congress authorize offensive operations. During the subsequent congressional debates, no one questioned the constitutionality of Jefferson's orders to the Mediterranean squadron, and several Congressmen argued that the President had the power to order hostilities because of the existing state of war. Congress ultimately chose to delegate broad powers to Jefferson to take whatever military measures he thought necessary as long as war continued.[28]

Jefferson's message to Congress presents an example of a President's rhetoric not matching his actions. He claimed a constitutional limitation on presidential power that neither he nor his cabinet had previously raised, though one that ran in favor of Congress. He had sent American forces into a hostile area and ordered them to undertake offensive actions without any plausible congressional authorization. On the other hand, Jefferson did not act as aggressively as Presidents today. His orders to attack Tripoli responded to a declaration of war by the enemy. He could justify his orders on the ground that Congress had created the forces and that a state of war already existed, the position taken by the cabinet and supported by Hamilton in a newspaper essay. According to Hamilton, "[W]hen a foreign nation declares, or openly and avowedly makes war upon the United States, they are then by the very fact, already at war, and any declaration on the part of Congress is nugatory: it is at least unnecessary."[29] Hamilton had things right as a matter of international law at the time, and most agree that he was correct on the Constitution. Presidents should not have to wait to seek authorization from Congress when another nation has already attacked or declared war upon the United States.

Efforts to solve the Barbary problem turned to another form of warfare, covert action. Shortly after the dispatch of the squadron to the Mediterranean, the American consul at Tripoli suggested that the United States help the brother of the Pasha to overthrow the government. In August 1802, Madison authorized American naval and diplomatic personnel to cooperate with the brother, and in May 1804 the cabinet voted to provide him with $20,000. The American consul at Tunis provided another $10,000, helped the pretender to the throne assemble a mercenary army, and ordered the Navy to transport him covertly to Tripolitan territory. The brother captured one of Tripoli's major cities in 1805, forcing a peace treaty with the United States that freed American prisoners, granted privileges to U.S. shipping, and ended the war. While Jefferson's actions certainly fell within Congress's broad authorization to "cause to be done all such other acts of precaution or hostility as the state of war will justify, and may, in [the President's] opinion, require," the President chose not to inform Congress of these secret measures until six months after the peace treaty was signed. No one objected, and Congress even bestowed a tidy sum on the brother for his cooperation.[30] Jefferson would set the precedent for future covert action against threats to national security, with Congress's main check remaining the power of the purse.

Jefferson acted with swiftness during another military confrontation, this time with Great Britain. On June 22, 1807, the British warship HMS *Leopard* stopped the smaller American frigate USS *Chesapeake* as it was leaving Norfolk, Virginia. The *Leopard* was under orders to search for British deserters hiding on American vessels. When the *Chesapeake*'s captain refused to allow a search, the *Leopard* fired on the unprepared ship, killing three and wounding 18, and then removed four alleged deserters. The attack provoked outrage throughout the country and prompted demands for war. Without consulting Congress, which was not in session, Jefferson ordered all American waters closed to British warships. He redirected funds for the nation's fortifications devoted to New York, Charleston, and New Orleans and ordered the purchase of significant amounts of military stores and ammunition, including materials to construct 100 gunboats. Jefferson also sent orders to James Monroe in London to demand reparations and punishment of the *Leopard*'s commander. When Congress convened in October, Jefferson did not claim that the purchases were legally authorized, but instead sought after-the-fact approval because the "emergencies facing us" justified his actions. Jefferson relied on the power to act in moments of crisis to defend the nation, even in areas like spending, which the Constitution had specifically given to Congress. Congress agreed and voted overwhelmingly to appropriate the funds that Jefferson had already spent.[31]

THE LOUISIANA PURCHASE

WHILE FULL OF daring exploits, war with the Barbary pirates was not the central concern of American national security policy. America's future depended on relations with Great Britain, France, and Spain, which held the key to neutrality and westward expansion. Spain controlled New Orleans, through which exports using the Mississippi had to pass. Without access to the Mississippi, transporting goods over land from Ohio to the East took longer than sailing from New York to London. The British Empire was America's primary trading partner, receiving about 50 percent of its exports, and the Royal Navy effectively controlled the Atlantic. France was also an important trading partner — Americans had grown rich selling goods to the antagonists during the latest round of European wars — and it controlled the Louisiana territory to the West.

Jefferson's purchase of Louisiana defused this hazardous situation. He avoided war with France and Spain and doubled the size of the nation. He made possible the fulfillment of Republican political economy and foreign policy: to conquer the territory to the West without war, open Western settlement by controlling the Mississippi, and maintain America's neutral status. The Louisiana Purchase created the possibility that Jefferson's "empire of liberty" would be continent-wide, but it required Jefferson to put aside his vision of strict constitutional construction and adopt a broader vision of executive power, one that permitted the nation to take advantage of the great opportunities thrown its way.

While it was not the product of luck, the Louisiana Purchase must have seemed like the intervention of Fortune in the fate of the Americans. The retrocession of Louisiana back from Spain to France (France had lost the territory to Spain at the end of the Seven Years' War) gave Napoleon dreams of an American empire. An expedition to restore control in Santo Domingo, which had been taken over by a slave rebellion led by Toussaint L'Ouverture, failed. Another mission to send troops to Louisiana could not leave port due to winter ice, and in late 1802 Spanish officials closed the port of New Orleans to American shipping while they awaited the handover of the territory to France. Jefferson sent envoys to Paris to buy New Orleans and West Florida (which today comprises the portions of Mississippi and Alabama that lie along the Gulf of Mexico, along with parts of Florida and Louisiana), aided by a secret congressional appropriation of $2 million. Federalists proposed negotiating from a position of strength by invading New Orleans and West Florida first,[32] but Jefferson privately had been willing to go even further, entertaining a possible alliance with the hated British against France to seize Louisiana.

When American ministers arrived in Paris, they received a gift. Napoleon decided to sell not just New Orleans, but the entire Louisiana territory. The first ambassador on the scene, Robert Livingston, did not believe the offer was genuine, but when the second envoy, James Monroe, arrived, they quickly decided to exceed their instructions and buy all of Louisiana for about $15 million. The Louisiana Purchase doubled the size of the United States, gave it permanent control of the Mississippi and New Orleans, and dislodged France and Spain as serious threats to American national security in the West. "This removes from us the greatest source of danger to our peace," Jefferson wrote to his son-in-law.[33] Played differently, the United States could have been drawn into the Napoleonic wars, which would have proven disastrous, and found itself hemmed into the Eastern seaboard. Jefferson's reputation as one of America's greatest Presidents was sealed on the day that the Louisiana treaty was signed.

But in order to buy Louisiana, Jefferson had to change his vision of the Constitution. Jefferson had believed that the Constitution did not permit the acquisition of new territory or its incorporation into the Union as new states. The Constitution has no express provision providing for the addition of territory, though Article IV, Section 3 gives Congress the power to "dispose of and make all needful Rules and Regulations respecting the Territory or other Property belonging to the United States." Some later argued that this clause assumes that new property could be added in the future, but as Gary Lawson and Guy Seidman have pointed out, this interpretation runs counter to the text of the clause and its placement in the Constitution.[34] The clause describes the power to make rules and dispose of property, but it does not empower the government to add new territory in the first place — it could be read to apply only to the territory of the United States as it existed in 1789, such as the Northwest Territory. Even before he sent Monroe to negotiate for New Orleans, Jefferson had raised doubts before his cabinet.

Jefferson also doubted whether new territory could become states. The Constitution provides for the addition of new states, upon the approval of Congress, and it prohibits the formation of new states out of the borders of existing states without their consent. Jefferson apparently worried that this prohibition also applied to the creation of new states from the territory of existing states. His Attorney General, Levi Lincoln, agreed and advised that the boundaries of existing states be enlarged to include the Louisiana Purchase.

Jefferson and his cabinet sought refuge in a position that was "virtually indistinguishable" from Hamilton's arguments in the debates over the Neutrality Proclamation and the Jay Treaty. Gallatin argued:

1. The United States as a nation should have an inherent right to acquire territory.

2. Whenever that acquisition is by treaty, the same constituted

authorities in whom the treaty-making power is vested have a constitutional right to sanction the acquisition.

3.   Whenever the territory has been acquired, Congress should have the power either of admitting into the Union as a new state, or of annexing to a State with the consent of that State, or of making regulations for the government of such territory.[35]

In other words, the federal government has powers that extend beyond those explicitly set out in the Constitution, including the sovereign powers held by all other nations. Gallatin claimed that the treaty power vested the federal government with the ability to exercise these inherent national powers. This broad reading of the executive power allows the President and Senate together to exercise power that is nowhere set out in the Constitution but must be deduced by examining the rights of other nations in their international affairs. As the primary force in treaty-making, this power would redound to the President's benefit. Gallatin's opinion concluded that the people had implicitly delegated the authority to acquire territory to the national government by vesting it with the powers to make war and treaties, and govern the territories.

This was strong drink for a man who believed that the Constitution did not allow a national bank. Jefferson accepted Gallatin's reasoning, though he predicted that new territory would enter the Union as a matter of "expediency" rather than constitutional principle. Perhaps he felt he was making only a small compromise when all that could be hoped for was New Orleans. When Jefferson learned that Livingston and Monroe had succeeded beyond his wildest dreams, the constitutional doubts resurfaced. To John Dickinson, he admitted in August 1803 that "our confederation is certainly confined to the limits established by the revolution. The general government has no powers but such as the constitution has given it; and it has not given it a power of holding foreign territory, and still less of incorporating it into the Union." He confessed that "an amendment to the Constitution seems necessary for this."[36] Jefferson did not limit himself to private letters to friends, but expressed his views to his close ally in the Senate, John Breckinridge of Kentucky. "The Executive in seizing the fugitive occurrence which so much advances the good of the country, have done an act beyond the Constitution," Jefferson wrote in August[377] It was now up to Congress to support the unconstitutional act. "The Legislature in casting behind them metaphysical subtleties, and risking themselves like faithful servants, must ratify & pay for it, and throw themselves on their country for doing for them unauthorized what we know they would have done for themselves had they been in a situation to do it." Jefferson believed it was best to admit openly the violation of the Constitution and seek popular support, which he believed was healthier for the constitutional system. "We shall not be disavowed by the nation," he predicted, "and their act of indemnity will confirm and not weaken the Constitution, by more strongly marking out its lines."

Jefferson even personally drafted at least two constitutional amendments adding Louisiana, but events forced him from the luxury of his strict-constructionist beliefs. Shortly after he wrote to Dickinson and Breckinridge, Jefferson received a dispatch from Livingston in Paris that Napoleon was having seller's remorse. Livingston reported that Napoleon would seize any delay or request for changes as an opportunity to renounce the agreement. Jefferson worried that the delay of a constitutional amendment would give France the opening it needed, though both Madison and Gallatin thought France would not back out, and no one in the cabinet thought a constitutional amendment was necessary. Jefferson sent letters to Congress asking that constitutional objections to the treaty be dropped, and that "nothing must be said on that subject which may give a pretext for retracting; but that we should do sub silentio what shall be found necessary."[38]

Jefferson's most remarkable exchange came with Senator Wilson Cary Nicholas. Nicholas warned that any public statement by Jefferson against the constitutionality of the Purchase might sink the treaty in the Senate. Jefferson agreed that "whatever Congress shall think it necessary to do, should be done with as little debate as possible, & particularly so far as respects the constitutional difficulty." Still, he could not resist the opportunity to restate his belief that the Constitution did not envision the addition of new states from territory not already part of the nation in 1789. The opposite construction, advanced by his cabinet and by Nicholas, too, would allow the United States to add "England, Ireland, Holland, [etc.] into it." Broad rules of interpretation, Jefferson warned, would "make our powers boundless" and would render the Constitution "a blank paper by construction." Jefferson claimed that when faced with a choice between two readings of the Constitution, "the one safe, the other dangerous, the one precise, the other indefinite," he would choose the "safe & precise" and instead "ask an enlargement of power from the nation where it is found necessary."[39]

Jefferson had claimed authority for the President to act outside the Constitution itself when circumstances demanded it. If he had interpreted the powers of the executive narrowly, he would have put the Louisiana Purchase in danger. But it was Jefferson's strict constructionist views that created this dilemma in the first place. His reading of the Constitution seems mistaken and has never been the view of any of the three branches of government since. Article IV, Section 3 gives Congress the authority to admit new states and then adds the qualifier that when new states are formed from existing states, those states must consent. The broader power, without that qualification, must apply to something (otherwise, why not just make all admissions subject to state consent), and that something must be the creation of states out of new territory. As Lawson and Seidman argue, the Admissions Clause, as it is known, merely declares that "new states may be admitted by the Congress into this Union." Second, Article II's vesting of the executive power in the President contains a power to address national emergencies and crises. Jefferson could have read the executive power to include the authority to acquire the Louisiana Territory because of the threat to the national security if it had remained in the hands of other nations.

Instead, Jefferson chose to keep both Louisiana and his constitutional faith by turning to the prerogative. Jefferson's political dexterity made him flexible enough to take advantage of this great national opportunity, even to the point of adopting a vision of presidential powers potentially broader, in some ways, than that of Hamilton. Washington had established the legitimacy of the national government by keeping his energetic executive within its constitutional bounds. Hamilton had given theoretical punch to Washington's actions by arguing that the Constitution had to include the power to address every national emergency, and that this power would naturally reside in the executive. Jefferson, however, approached the Presidency more in keeping with Locke's theory of the prerogative. In his letter to Breckinridge, Jefferson had bypassed constitutional objections to the Louisiana Purchase by comparing his position to that of a guardian who acts beyond his authority but in the best interests of his ward. He had to seize the opportunity "which so much advances the good of the country." In response to the firing on the *Chesapeake*, Jefferson again acted beyond his constitutional powers. In both cases, Jefferson claimed that unforeseen circumstances, produced either by necessity or by opportunity, required him to exceed his legal powers to protect the greater good. Following Locke, Jefferson looked for ratification for his *ultra vires* decisions — "an indemnity," as he wrote to Breckinridge — from the people through their representatives in Congress.[40]

Jefferson explained his embrace of the prerogative more completely after he left office. In an 1810 letter, he addressed the question of whether "circumstances do not sometimes, occur, which make it a duty in officers of high trust, to assume authorities beyond the law."[41] Jefferson thought the question was "easy" in principle, though could be "embarrassing in practice."

> A strict observance of the written laws is doubtless *one* of the high duties of a good citizen, but it is not *the highest*. The laws of necessity, of self-preservation, of saving our country when in danger, are of higher obligation. To lose our country by a scrupulous adherence to written law, would be to lose the law itself, with life, liberty, property and all those who are enjoying them with us; thus absurdly sacrificing the end to the means.

Jefferson followed with examples of military necessity: Washington destroying private property during the Revolutionary War to gain a tactical advantage; Jefferson himself as governor of Virginia seizing men and material to defend the state from the British. Even more interesting was Jefferson's use of the prerogative to defend several of his decisions as President. One was the possibility of purchasing the Floridas, even though Congress had made no appropriation — the implicit reference to Louisiana was obvious. "Ought the Executive, in that case...to have secured the good to his country, and to have trusted to their justice for their transgression of the law?" Jefferson's answer was yes. Another example was the purchase of military supplies after the attack on the *Chesapeake*. A third was General Wilkinson's arrest of the Burr conspirators without trial or right of habeas corpus. In all of these situations, Jefferson believed, "a law of necessity and self-preservation" was at stake, and that law "rendered the *salus populi* supreme over the written law."

Acting beyond the written Constitution was not for the weak of heart or the low in status. Obeying the higher law of protecting the nation was a duty of the highest elected officers, Jefferson believed, not those "with petty duties." It could only be called upon during genuine moments of crisis, not when "consequences are trifling, and time allowed for a legal course." In normal times, "overleaping the law" was worse than "a strict adherence to its imperfect provisions." The elected leader is susceptible to a sharp backlash if he misjudges popular opinion. According to Jefferson, "It is incumbent on those only who accept of great charges, to risk themselves on great occasions, when the safety of the nation, or some of its very high interests are at stake." Jefferson trusted that his fellow Americans would be forgiving; they would "put themselves in his situation" and judge his decisions based on what he knew at the time.

Several difficulties emerge from Jefferson's adoption of Locke's theory of the prerogative. He did not explain when the nation's security is truly at stake — when it triggers the prerogative and when it does not. Jefferson admitted that it would sometimes prove difficult to identify the line between acting within the law and invoking the prerogative. He compared the judgment needed to that of a good officer who knew when to act as he thought best because his orders did not anticipate an unforeseen case or extreme results. One clear case is protecting the nation from attack, as in the example of the Revolutionary War, the Burr conspiracy, and the *Chesapeake* affair. But Jefferson did not limit the executive's prerogative to self-defense; he also approved actively seizing opportunity to advance the nation's interests. Jefferson believed that a President could act decisively, even without congressional approval, to acquire foreign territory like

Florida or Louisiana.

Jefferson did not make clear how the good officer was to "throw himself on the justice of his country and the rectitude of his motives" for approval of his actions. In some situations, Jefferson believed that seeking congressional ratification after the fact was enough. But with the Louisiana Purchase, he never introduced the constitutional amendments he believed necessary to expand the Union. If anything, he appeared to believe that the President and Congress were committing an illegal act, and that both had to appeal to the people as a whole for approval. Jefferson ultimately looked to public opinion as the judge of extraordinary uses of presidential power.

The last problem with Jefferson's prerogative is that its origins and justification remain unclear. One possibility is that an emergency power is inherent in the executive. This would be consistent with the line of thought begun by Machiavelli and, at the time, the view espoused by Hamilton. Another is that the power rests outside the Constitution entirely. This would be more akin to Locke's view. The former approach locates broad formal powers in the Presidency and might require the President to seek after-the-fact approval from Congress when he goes beyond the existing law, but for political rather than constitutional reasons. This view's virtue is that it does not bless presidential actions that are necessary but illegal. Viewing the prerogative as resting outside the Constitution relieves the executive of stretching the law so drastically to permit more freedom of action. Jefferson can be understood as favoring this approach. As Jeremy Bailey and Gary Schmitt have each argued, Jefferson's appeal to the prerogative allowed him to keep the formal powers of the Presidency limited.[42] Though extra-constitutional, public opinion would limit Jefferson's prerogative.

While it has the attraction of keeping a formal limit on presidential authority, Jefferson's prerogative requires us to accept that executive decisions can be both necessary and illegal. It forces Presidents to run the risk of violating the law in order to protect the nation from harm or seize outstanding opportunities. Only Presidents faced with the most imminent and serious emergencies or possessed of the surest feel for public opinion will survive. Throughout most of his Presidency, Jefferson could claim he had both. In Louisiana, he reached a bargain that secured the nation's prosperity and safety for generations. Until his second term, Jefferson seemed to act unerringly in line with popular wishes. He lost his touch at the end in his quest to maintain an embargo on the European powers, risking both the existence of the Union and its distance from foreign entanglements. Second term failure, however, was not the product of his constitutional powers, but rather ideological blinders combined with the political powers of the office, of which he continued to be a master.

PARTY GOVERNMENT

JEFFERSON'S POSITION THAT the President had an independent right to interpret and enforce the law was his greatest theoretical contribution to presidential power; his theory of the prerogative was his most practical contribution. But Jefferson's most striking addition to the political dimension of the office was his transformation of the President into a party leader. As head of the Republican Party (as it was then known), which held majorities in both the House and Senate throughout his Presidency, Jefferson could coordinate policy in both the executive and legislative branches. He never vetoed a bill on policy grounds, and never had to, because legislation inevitably reflected his wishes.

It was not obvious that party government should lead to a stronger President. During the contest over the 1800 election, John Marshall predicted that Jefferson would "embody himself in the House of Representatives." His status as leader of the majority party in Congress would "increase his personal power" but lead to the "weakening [of] the office of the President."[43] Jefferson enhanced presidential influence using his personal gifts and character, which when absent would lead to congressional dominance of government. Madison and Monroe owed their nominations to the party's congressional caucus, and John Quincy Adams would depend on its actual votes when the election of 1824 went to the House of Representatives. Jefferson, however, was able to maintain his control of the party without diminishing the power of the office in a way that would only be realized again under Woodrow Wilson.

Jefferson initially approached partisan politics with a measure of ambivalence. The Republican Party, in the words of Richard Hofstadter, was the "party to end party."[44] Jefferson thought of parties as a temporary measure to combat Hamilton's "monocrat" efforts to unbalance the Constitution and aggrandize the executive at the expense of Congress and the states. Once he won the 1800 election, the need for the Republican Party would disappear. Jefferson viewed it as unnecessary because the Constitution embodied different interests in each branch of government — the popular interest in the House of Representatives, the elites in the Presidency. With the Federalist Party destroyed, harmony and balance would return to the political system. He never intended to establish the stable political system we have today, with two permanent parties regularly competing for control of government by capturing a majority of the vote.[45]

Once in office, Jefferson found the uses of the political party irresistible. He accomplished effective party government through a combination of formal respect for Congress and informal political influence. Formally, Jefferson gave great deference to Congress's independence, and ended the practice of appearing in person to deliver the President's annual message to Congress. According to his great biographer, Dumas Malone, Jefferson rid the Presidency of any hints of monarchism, such as throwing grand parties, riding in a carriage, and declaring days of Thanksgiving.[46] He often sent legislative recommendations in a deferential tone and portrayed himself simply as the instrument of Congress. In a letter to Dr. Benjamin Rush, Jefferson called himself "but a machine erected by the constitution for the performance of certain acts according to the laws of action laid down for me."[47] Jefferson ended any Hamiltonian talk of using "corruption" to manage executive priorities through the legislature.

Informally, Jefferson experimented with his position as party chief to expand the Presidency's political influence. His first tool was social. Jefferson regularly entertained Congressmen at small dinners, at which he appeared wearing homespun cloth and sometimes slippers, with the dinner prepared by his French chef and accompanied by fine wines. While he performed terribly before large groups, Jefferson was dazzling in these small settings, in which he led discussions on topics ranging from art and architecture, to music, to science. During these dinners, Jefferson and his companions discussed public policy, and the President invariably steered them to his desired result.[48]

Jefferson's second tool was organizational. While Jefferson did not introduce the horse-trading, lobbying, and working of the press that are the stuff of the modern White House office of legislative affairs, he relied on Gallatin to manage his program in Congress. Congressmen did not resent Gallatin, who had been the Republican House floor leader, as they would have an executive official without legislative experience. Jefferson's involvement in legislation went as far as the selection of congressional leaders, who were responsible for carrying out the party agenda. Republicans created a congressional caucus that presented a unified front in the legislature which Jefferson also could more easily influence. They were aided by the steady deterioration of the Federalists, who proved unable to compete in political organization and campaigning and never again won the Presidency or majorities in Congress.

Political coordination between the executive and the congressional majority resulted in significant grants of authority to Jefferson. In the area of appropriations, for example, the Republicans soon adopted the same practices for which they had criticized the Federalists. Under the Articles of Confederation, Congress had proven incapable of managing the nation's finances, and under the new Constitution, Congress looked to the executive branch to gather information and develop expertise. Under Washington, the Treasury Department developed estimates for annual expenditures, and Congress responded by voting appropriations for the operations of the entire government in a few lump sums. The very first appropriations act, for example, provided for all civilian employees and military expenses in a single sentence, and Congress continued the practice for the following three years.[49] Executive branch officers exercised significant discretion in spending money, including the transfer of funds from one account to another. Sometimes, executive branch officials even entered into obligations before appropriations had been made, as Washington did to pay for the military costs of suppressing the Whiskey Rebellion. In 1793, Republicans launched a House investigation into Hamilton's alleged mixing of funds (proposals for his censure were defeated) and demanded specificity in appropriations.

Close coordination between the executive and legislative branch can lead to unity and harmony, but it can also lead to disaster. Such cooperation may lead the majority party to ignore dissenting opinions or to place excessive faith in its own judgment, render ideological blinders bigger and darker, or make it harder to change a doomed policy. The President's control of the majority party in Congress can make him more stubborn in the face of setbacks rather than more flexible. Single-party control of both branches of government makes Congress more likely to delegate broader powers to the President. Delegation expands the President's legal powers, but it also increases his political risks as he assumes more responsibility.

Jefferson's failure in his second term flowed from the successes of the first. The administration had kept the nation out of the European contest for supremacy without increasing defense spending or entering alliances, and it had solved the western issue by acquiring Louisiana. Jefferson could rest satisfied that he had assured America's future growth and security without incurring the heavy expenses and large bureaucracy needed for a more vigorous national defense. At the same time, Jefferson pursued the traditional national goals of territorial expansion and export markets. The Louisiana Purchase showed that he could have both, that he could follow the traditional interests of state, while rejecting the usual methods — force and coercion — that European nations had used to achieve them.[50] As Robert Tucker and David Hendrickson have observed, Jefferson attempted "to conquer without war."[51]

Jefferson's policies had succeeded because of a short lull in the struggle between Britain and France. Once war resumed, Jeffersonian policies could not survive. Napoleon's Continental System subjected to seizure any ships transporting goods with Great Britain; Britain retaliated with an order allowing the capture of any ships carrying goods between France and other countries. This threatened the booming trade that the United States had carried on not just with those countries directly, but between the European rivals and their colonies. Thanks to British naval warfare against France and Spain and the wartime diversion of Britain's own maritime fleet, the American merchant marine's registered tonnage grew from 558,000 tons in 1802 to 981,000 by 1810, a level it would not reach again for a century. Jefferson was quite clear on America's interest: for the United States to "become carriers for all parties as far as we can raise vessels" so that the New World could "fatten on the follies of the old."[52] Under Republican ideology, foreign markets would soak up the output of the virtuous yeoman farmers of the West.

Reversing these policies revealed a gap between Jefferson's ends and his means. If the United States wanted to coerce these nations into accepting free U.S. trade, it had no means available. The United States did not have the army or navy to coerce Britain or France, nor was Jefferson willing to alter his goal of free trade. If he were unwilling to build a military, Jefferson would have to pick sides. The choice that seems obvious today was Great Britain. The United States had close economic ties with Great Britain (50 percent of all U.S. exports went to the mother country), and the Royal Navy posed the only real military threat to the nation's territorial integrity. But Jefferson's worldview would not allow him to consider an alliance. Jefferson's love for all things French and his deep suspicions of Great Britain are well known. Even when the French had taken back Louisiana and put plans into action for its military occupation, Jefferson would not enter into a British alliance, though he entertained the idea at times. When his envoys had negotiated a peace treaty with Britain after the *Chesapeake* attack, Jefferson refused to send it to the Senate, even though it guaranteed favorable trade terms. British demands that the United States cease all trade with France and hand over alleged British deserters on American vessels were too much for the President to accept.

Jefferson instead chose the radical, untried tool of an economic embargo on both warring nations. Its object seems almost quixotic today — to use a cutoff of American raw materials to force the warring parties to accept the principle of free shipping by neutrals. Britain and France were locked in a decades-long contest to the death. It is difficult to believe that an American embargo would coerce either side to make a concession favorable to its enemy, or force either to accept free trade with neutrals. Meanwhile, government power ballooned as Jefferson engaged in one of the most significant exercises of government power in American history. His attempt to prevent all exports of American goods drove him to monitor all shipping and land transportation near the borders. It required the seizure of property upon mere suspicion that it was meant for export. The embargo was akin to Prohibition, and it met with the same success.

Jefferson's attempts to enforce the embargo made a ruin of his second term. Yet, the embargo does not support the spectacle of an executive run amok on its own constitutional power. At each step, Jefferson informally suggested and then received a delegation of power from Congress — each more draconian than the last. He took the plunge at a December 17, 1807, cabinet meeting, when he decided to send a message to Congress calling for the embargo. Displaying an uncanny prescience, Gallatin the next day told the President he "prefer[red] war to a permanent embargo" because of the "privations, sufferings, revenue, effect on the enemy, politics at home, etc."[53] Jefferson sent his special message to Congress that same day, requesting a ban on the ground that it would protect American ships and sailors from capture by Britain or France. Congress immediately passed the First Embargo Act, which prohibited any U.S. seagoing vessel from leaving a domestic port.[54] It allowed shipping between points within the United States, but only if the owner of the ship posted a bond equivalent to double the value of the goods and allowed the President to approve individual voyages abroad. Less than a month later, Congress passed the Second Embargo Act to expand the prohibition to coasting and fishing vessels, which apparently had picked up the trade with Canada and the West Indies.[55] In March 1808,

Congress followed with the Third Embargo Act, which required higher bonds, increased the penalties for violation, and extended the embargo beyond shipping, to any exports carried by sea or land.[56]

Resistance to the embargo was vigorous, but only in certain regions. While the middle states followed the law, New England — which depended on trade more than others — became a hotbed of disobedience. Ships left Boston Harbor at night in defiance of Treasury officials or moved to harbors with little official presence, and large rafts carrying goods traveled across the border to Canada. Smugglers evaded weak customs officers in Baltimore and Georgia. Defiance of the law caused Jefferson to seek a drastic solution — the First Enforcement Act — in April 1808. It required all vessels of any size in the nation to receive clearance to sail, and to load their cargo under the supervision of a Treasury official. No ship with cargo could leave a port near foreign territory, for any reason, without the permission of the President himself. Congress authorized naval vessels and smaller gunboats to stop and search any vessel suspected of intending to evade the ban. Federal officials could seize domestic goods in any area near foreign territory until a bond was posted to guarantee their delivery within the country. Congress did not require warrants or any judicial review for the search and seizure of ships or goods on land.[57]

Leonard Levy has charged the First Enforcement Act with approaching the "precipice of unlimited and arbitrary power as measured by any American standard then known." Putting to one side the Fourth Amendment problems, what remains surprising is the level of direct presidential involvement. Gallatin drafted each of the embargo and enforcement laws for Jefferson, who personally reviewed them and sent them on to congressional allies. The embargo allowed any shipper to appeal to the President for an exception, which Jefferson personally reviewed. Jefferson drafted and issued guidelines for federal port officials to use in administering the embargo, and he was as strict as possible in exercising his discretion, ordering executive officers "to consider every shipment of provisions, lumber, flaxseed, tar, cotton, tobacco…as sufficiently suspicious for detention." If doubt arose, Jefferson instructed, "consider me as voting for detention."[58]

As resistance to the embargo grew, the administration tightened its grip. Smugglers on Lake Champlain, along the New York-Canada border, began to use large rafts to carry goods with armed guards. Gunfire between smugglers and border guards broke out. In response, Jefferson issued an order declaring an insurrection and ordering the use of armed force to restore order. Jefferson used the same act that Washington had invoked during the Whiskey Rebellion, updated in 1807 to allow the President to call out the army and navy in addition to the militia.[59] Jefferson declared that the region was in insurrection, ordered the dispersal of those hostile to the laws, and ordered the use of armed force to restore order. Jefferson dispatched navy gunboats to patrol the lake, and the governors of New York and Vermont followed by sending the militia to the Champlain district. Armed conflict occurred between smugglers and the militiamen, with some loss of life. But the Jefferson administration found it difficult to win the cooperation of local populations in enforcing the embargo. Juries often refused to convict violators, while cargo owners brought suits in state court against federal officials for damages. When the Jefferson administration asked state governors to use their militias to enforce the law, they did so only reluctantly.

As smuggling spread, the administration relied more heavily upon the military. During the summer of 1808, Jefferson ordered the general use of the navy throughout the nation's seaboard and waterways to enforce the embargo. Navy vessels essentially blockaded American ports, and gunboats hunted down smugglers in rivers and

lakes. While the administration succeeded in keeping the vast majority of the merchant marine in port, significant amounts of exports
made it out of the country.[60] Gallatin wrote Jefferson to recommend
that the administration stop every vessel from moving anywhere in
the country, and affirmed that federal officials had the power to seize
or detain property anywhere. He even suggested that federal officials
remove the rudders of all ships in harbor, so they could not secretly
sail away. "Congress must either invest the Executive with the most
arbitrary powers and sufficient force to carry the embargo into effect,
or give it up altogether," the Treasury Secretary wrote the President.[61]
The only alternative, Gallatin observed, was war, "but with whom?"
Jefferson agreed, and proposed the Second Enforcement Act. Passed
by Congress in January 1809, it prohibited loading a vessel with the
intent to break the embargo, gave federal collectors the authority to
refuse permission to load cargo, delegated broad powers to detain
vessels, and allowed federal officials to seize cargoes from any ship,
wagon, or other vehicle upon suspicion they were heading abroad.[62]
For the first time, Congress vested the President with the authority
to call out the militia and the military to enforce the embargo laws.
Jefferson would no longer need to declare an insurrection or rely on
the courts to find that federal law was being blocked.

The administration soon made use of its new powers. As Leonard
Levy has observed, the systematic use of the military to enforce the
laws throughout the nation was and remains unprecedented. Aside
from the Civil War, the use of the military domestically has been
targeted at localized disturbances, temporary in nature, and deferential to the return of civilian government. During the embargo, Jefferson deployed military forces throughout the nation for long periods,
sometimes for more than a year. According to Levy, Jefferson "had
answered foreign attacks on American commerce by a steady siege
against American commerce and by quartering troops among the

American people."[63] Henry Adams claimed that "personal liberties and rights of property were more directly curtailed in the United States by embargo than in Great Britain by centuries of almost continuous foreign war." In light of these judgments, it should be no surprise that the embargo had a quick end. Within one month of the passage of the Second Enforcement Act, outright defiance of the embargo increased. Representatives from New England and New York rushed to overturn the embargo, which ended on Jefferson's last day in office. Jefferson did not try to stop them.

The embargo had succeeded in its immediate aims but failed in its grander objects. American exports to Europe were greatly reduced, but the larger end of forcing Britain and France to change their policies on neutral shipping was not achieved. Neither showed any intention of lifting its restrictions on American trade, and neither appeared to suffer much economic distress. Relations toward the competing European powers would continue to bedevil American leaders until they chose the disastrous course of intervention. The only thing the embargo brought was a reduction in the ability of American merchants and farmers to benefit from European disorder. Jefferson had expended significant resources, reduced civil liberties, and compromised his belief in government of limited powers. What should be clear is that this was not the product of an executive drunk on its own constitutional powers. Each expansion of the embargo, and the corresponding growth of government power to enforce it, was granted to the executive by legislative act. Rather than a cautionary tale about presidential power, the embargo disproves any direct link between executive power and reckless government policies. Jefferson showed that the President and Congress can agree, and still lead the nation down a path to failure and waste.

CONCLUSIONS

CONTRARY TO POPULAR belief, Jefferson believed in an independent Presidency with inherent powers, and he used them vigorously to the nation's great benefit. Jefferson did not hesitate to exert direct control over the entire executive branch, challenge the courts over the right to interpret the Constitution, and use the military to advance national interests abroad while keeping firm control over foreign policy. Jefferson believed that the President could act extra-constitutionally when the demands of necessity required, so long as he sought popular approval afterward. His belief in the prerogative allowed him to seize the great opportunity of his Presidency, the Louisiana Purchase, while also maintaining his strict construction of government powers. Domestically, Jefferson produced the innovation of the President as legislative leader, introduced a close coordination of the executive and legislative branches, and used the political party to overcome the constitutional separation of powers between the President and Congress.

Drawing the two closer together, however, did not prove an unadulterated blessing. With a conduit open between the two branches, power could flow in either direction. Once its founder left the Presidency, the Republican Party shifted its weight of gravity toward the legislature. Republicans in Congress assumed the right to select the party's presidential nominee, justifying the nickname "King Caucus." Indeed, it was unclear whether congressional Democrats would select Madison or Monroe for the 1808 elections until Jefferson made his wishes known. This broke the Framers' effort to forge a direct link between the Presidency and the people, and to give the Chief Executive independence from Congress. A candidate chosen by a congressional party caucus would make commitments to legislative leaders to get elected, and would remain keenly conscious of congressional wishes if he wanted to be renominated. A President chosen by Congress would be less likely to exercise his independent powers vigorously, nor stray far from the wishes of his party majority.

But a President's weak view of his powers need not result in poor performance. During periods of stability and peace, a quiescent President may be more predictable and less meddlesome, though an energetic President might at least prevent Congress from counter-productive interference with the economy and society. Presidential modesty, however, may very well lead to failure in the face of emergency and war, the critical moments for which the executive is designed. While the need for the executive's constitutional powers may not be compelling in times of peace, it would be a mistake to limit presidential power so as to prevent its exercise in times of emergency. The Presidency of James Madison, Jefferson's collaborator and handpicked successor, bears this out. Madison is one of the nation's great figures because of his role as the primary drafter of the Constitution and the Bill of Rights, one of the authors of *The Federalist*, and a founder of the Democratic Party. Yet, in polls of scholars, Madison ranks below Kennedy and Monroe, and just above Lyndon Johnson, as an average President, and would no doubt do far worse in popular opinion. In a recent short biography, Garry Wills judges Madison a "hapless" Commander-in-Chief and his Presidency a failed one.[64]

Madison's poor performance is attributable in part to his narrow view of his office. As President, Madison remained deferential to congressional wishes, which led the nation to the precipice of disaster and to its most humiliating military defeats. The source of these setbacks was Madison's failure to chart a successful course between Great Britain and France. Congress, rather than Madison, decided foreign economic policy, the primary tool used to coerce the belligerents. Madison played almost no role in the shaping of the 1809 Nonintercourse Act, and he took no part in the framing of the

1810 Macon's Bill Number 2, which triggered an embargo against the nation that failed to lift its anti-American trade laws. While the latter restored American exports, it effectively left U.S. international economic policy up to the decisions of Britain or France. Indeed, it allowed Napoleon to outmaneuver and embarrass the United States when he pretended to lift restrictions on American trade, causing Madison to cut off trade with Great Britain by mistake.[65] Neither bill caused either belligerent to change its ways. After the struggles of the 1790s, Madison believed that the President had to decide on foreign policy in concert with Congress, that he could not intervene in legislative deliberations, and that he had to accept Congress's embargo laws even though he wanted a different policy.[66]

Congress followed by driving the nation into an ill-conceived and disastrous war with Great Britain. The 1810 midterm elections sent a group of young Congressmen, including Henry Clay of Kentucky and John Calhoun of South Carolina, to Washington. Hailing from the growing Western and Southern states, they demonstrated their influence when the House elected Clay to be Speaker while only a freshman. Known as the "War Hawks," they welcomed a conflict with Great Britain, which they saw as the primary threat to American economic and territorial growth. They blamed the British for inciting an 1811 conflict between Indians led by Tecumseh and settlers of the Indiana Territory led by Governor William Henry Harrison. A war with Britain would remove the Indians, whose lines of support apparently led back to Canada, as an obstacle to Western settlement. The War Hawks also believed Canada to be lightly defended and ready for conquest. Finally, Britain's impressment policies and trade restrictions were an insult to American honor and an effort to fold the United States into the British mercantile system. "The independence of this nation is lost" if Britain's trade policies continued, said the young Calhoun. "[T]his is the second struggle for our liberty." A conflict with Britain would be nothing less than a second war of independence.[67]

At the same time, the United States was woefully unprepared for war. Madison displayed little leadership in convincing his own party to increase the army or navy, and he did not clearly urge Congress toward war or peace. In his November 1811 State of the Union message, Madison declared that Great Britain had made "war on our lawful commerce" and called upon Congress to put "the United States into an armor and an attitude demanded by the crisis."[68] Although the presidential message did not call for war, members of Congress pushed toward a conflict with Great Britain even though they were unwilling to take the steps necessary to adequately defend the Eastern seaboard. Between December 1811 and April 1812, Congress increased the size of the regular army to 35,000 troops and intended to rely on the state militias and short-term volunteers in the event of war. Even worse, Congress refused to authorize the construction of any new ships-of-the-line or naval drydocks. Instead, the Jeffersonians planned to rely on gunboats — the militia of the seas, in their view — to defend the coast. When war broke out, the British would have three ships-of-the-line for every American cannon. To fund the war preparations, Congress refused to enact any new taxes but instead passed legislation to borrow $11 million, a pitifully small amount with which to take on the world's leading naval power.[69]

When Britain refused to negotiate a change in its trade policies, the Madison administration kept its own counsel. Clay and his supporters stepped into the vacuum created by presidential caution and weakness. A more vigorous President would have prevented Congress from making such a disastrous mistake. War with Britain could not have been more ill-conceived. The United States could have pursued three policies: war with Britain, war with France, or neutrality.

Only war with Britain could directly threaten the nation's security, as she had the one navy in the world capable of reaching the United States in any strength. Britain had forces along America's northern border and Indian allies that could pressure the Western frontier. Britain also happened to be the largest trading partner of the United States, meaning that any conflict would eliminate the millions in trade between the two nations, and since Britain was likely to impose a naval blockade, would also end American trade with the rest of the world. Hopes of adding Canada to the Union were ill-founded, though they had obsessed Americans since the time of the Revolution. There was no real evidence beyond wishful thinking that a hodgepodge of American troops and militia could successfully invade and conquer Canada, and the United States had no serious defensive works or troops along the borders or the East Coast, leaving the nation open to attack. The United States would declare war just as the balance of power was to change in Europe, with Napoleon suffering from his 1812 invasion of Russia, eventually freeing up British veterans for service in the Americas.

With this balance of forces, the war went far better than the country could have realistically expected. Efforts to invade Canada were easily repulsed, with ill-prepared American armies surrendering, losing in battle to the British, or maneuvering fruitlessly in the Great Lakes region. State militias refused to leave their states, and the officer corps was, for the most part, inept. In the last year of the war, it was the British who would be invading the United States from Canada, but by the end neither side had made any progress. On the high seas, the United States won a few symbolic encounters, but for the most part the British kept a tight blockade on the East Coast. Success came only on the Great Lakes, where American sailors defeated their British counterparts (it was on Lake Erie where Oliver Hazard Perry declared, "We have met the enemy and they are ours"), and in the campaigns against the Indians by Harrison and Tennessee General Andrew Jackson.[70]

After Napoleon's abdication, Britain sent its veterans to the United States. Britain planned a three-prong assault: invasion from Canada to seize Maine and parts of New York, diversionary harassment in the capital area, and a strong force through the Mississippi to detach Louisiana. If the plans had succeeded, the United States would have been shrunk short of its 1783 borders and would have been permanently hemmed in by British colonies and allies. The diversions alone humiliated the young nation by capturing Washington, D.C., and burning the government's buildings, including the White House and the Capitol. Madison and his wife barely escaped the arrival of British troops, who were only turned back by a stiff defense at Baltimore. (The bombardment was described by Francis Scott Key in the "Star Spangled Banner."). The Canadian offensive went nowhere due to the lack of interest of the British commander and some well-timed American naval victories on his flank on Lake Champlain. At the Battle of New Orleans in December 1814, Jackson became a national hero by utterly defeating the redcoats at a cost of only 21 American lives. It is a sign of America's good fortune that the nation survived the war with a return to the status quo.[71]

A President who was independent of Congress could have resisted such a foolhardy war. Madison could have used his veto to block legislation increasing the military beyond the needs of defense, and he could have used his Commander-in-Chief power to conduct only a defensive strategy. Madison could have sought peace immediately, which was easily within his grasp. Britain had repealed its discriminatory trade policies almost at the very moment that Congress had declared war. From the very start, the public justification for war had evaporated. A peace agreement would have been little trouble.

Instead, Madison went along with what he viewed to be public sentiment, as represented by Congress, to wage a war that was not in the national interest. In his public messages, he left the question of war up to Congress. Madison surely presented a case against Great Britain in late 1811 and early 1812, but it was Congress that sought a war that would bring Canada within the United States and end British harassment of American trade and expansion.[72] Madison deferred to the judgment of Congress in the area where the President's power is at its maximum. He was even presented with the declaration of war and conceivably could have vetoed it, but he signed it instead. Madison compounded the mistake by exercising very little direct control of the war and allowing incompetent generals to guide national policy until, by the end, it seemed almost no one in Washington was in charge.

Just as Jefferson demonstrated the possibilities of vigorous and independent presidential leadership, Madison showed the dangers of modesty and deference. Madison seemed to shrink within his diminutive shell when he became President. Where Jefferson had used the party to control Congress, Congress used the party to control Madison. He deferred to Congress on the wisdom of a disastrous war, and could not exercise effective control over his cabinet or generals once war began. It is not always Presidents who harbor dreams of military adventures and Congresses who hold tight rein over the dogs of war. Under Madison, it was Congress who hoped to conquer and the President who went along. Because of it, the nation suffered its worst battlefield defeats and came within an inch of losing its future.

CHAPTER 5

Andrew Jackson

WHILE ANDREW JACKSON laid the foundations for what we can begin to recognize as the modern Presidency, he would have been out of place in the modern world. He fought duels, owned slaves, killed Indians (as well as spies), and carried a lifelong hatred of Great Britain because, as a captured boy soldier during the Revolutionary War, he had been struck in the face with a sword for refusing to clean an officer's boots. During the War of 1812, he won a resounding victory over the British at the Battle of New Orleans, but during the peace, Jackson invaded and occupied Spanish Florida without clear orders.[1]

When he lost the election of 1824 despite winning the most votes, Jackson did not graciously withdraw but spent the next four years attacking the "corrupt bargain" that had thrown the Presidency to John Quincy Adams. Jackson received a plurality of the popular vote, 153,000 out of 361,000, and of the electoral vote, 99 of the 131 needed to win. The Constitution sent the election into the House of Representatives, where Henry Clay, who had come in fourth, was Speaker of the House. Clay influenced the House to choose John Quincy Adams, who had received 84 electoral votes. Adams picked Clay to be Secretary of State, the position then seen as the stepping-stone to the Presidency. Jackson devoted the next four years to successfully undermining the legitimacy of the Adams administration. He became the symbol of a rising democracy, which he promoted as President.

Upon winning the election of 1828, Jackson embarked on a transformation of the political system and the Presidency. He sought to advance the cause of democracy and made an expanded executive power his tool in that great project. To Jackson, democracy meant that the will of the majority should prevail, regardless of existing governmental and social arrangements. Even Jefferson had not gone that far. The Framers designed the Senate, the Electoral College, and an independent judiciary to check and balance majority rule, but Jackson followed a different star. "[T]he first principle of our system," Jackson declared in his State of the Union Address, is *that the majority is to govern.*"[2] He called for a constitutional amendment to eliminate the Electoral College because "[t]o the people belongs the right of electing their Chief Magistrate."[3] The more elected representatives there were, he observed, the more likely the popular will would not be frustrated.[4] Jackson remains one of the greatest Presidents because he reconstructed the office into the direct representative of the American people.[5]

The two causes — democratization and expanding the Presidency — were linked, though they need not have been. Democracy was on the rise before Jackson reached office, and by the election of 1824, all but three states had granted the franchise to all white adult males. Many states directly elected their governors, judges, and other officials, and though large segments of the population, such as women and minorities, could not vote, the United States had achieved a high level of democracy for its time.

The Presidency, by contrast, had declined sharply. Beginning with James Madison in 1808, the Republican members of Congress selected their party's presidential nominee. When the Federalists disappeared after the War of 1812, "King Caucus" effectively selected the nation's President — the very result the Framers wanted to avoid. Cabinet agencies and their secretaries felt the pull of competing allegiances with the emergence of congressional committees. Cabinet members began to pursue their own agendas, in cooperation with Congress, and Presidents began to see themselves more as prime ministers holding together a coalition.

Presidential weakness was evident in the two great challenges of this "Era of Good Feelings." The central issue of the early Republic, the struggle for dominance between Britain and France, ended with the War of 1812. The other great antebellum issue was slavery. Jackson's victory at New Orleans guaranteed that American expansion would continue without interference from Great Britain, but the added territory called upon the national government to decide whether to permit slavery in the new territories. North and South proceeded to play a delicate balancing game over the admission of new states. Monroe played no significant role in setting a national agenda on the slavery question, and instead, congressional leaders took the initiative. Their 1820 Missouri Compromise prohibited slavery in all of the Louisiana Purchase north of the southern border of Missouri, except Missouri itself. The Great Triumvirate of Clay, Calhoun, and Daniel Webster exercised commanding leadership over the Jeffersonians. Presidents like Madison, Monroe, and Adams, who owed their nominations to the congressional caucus, had little leverage to influence the slavery debate.

As presidential power came into doubt, so too did the authority of the national government. Signs of regional separatism had first begun to emerge during Jefferson's embargo and Madison's

War. Although the disappearance of the Federalists led to a single dominant political party, regional divisions emerged over tariff levels and "internal improvements," such as roads and canals. The South, for example, exported raw materials and agricultural products and imported finished goods; high tariffs appeared to benefit Northern manufacturers while raising the South's costs. Internal improvements, which included the Erie Canal and interstate roads, created a different set of regional alliances between Westerners who favored expansion and Eastern states that benefited from increasing links to the West. Slavery exacerbated these centrifugal forces, as did democratization, which broke down social and political hierarchies.

Jackson swam against the tide of decentralization and a weak executive. He reinvigorated the Presidency and is generally considered by historians to have been one of the nation's most powerful Chief Executives. He advanced a new vision of the President as the direct representative of the people, and put theory to practice — interpreting the Constitution and enforcing the law independently, wielding the veto power for policy as well as constitutional reasons, and reestablishing control over the executive branch. In the first of two great political conflicts of his time, the Bank War, Jackson vetoed a law that the Supreme Court and Congress both thought constitutional, removed federal deposits from the Bank of the United States, and fired cabinet secretaries who would not carry out his orders. In the second, the Nullification Crisis, Jackson interpreted the Constitution and the meaning of the Union on behalf of the people, and made clear his authority to carry out federal law against resisting states. Although he was a staunch defender of limited government, Jackson confronted head-on the forces of disunion. His achievement would be to restore and expand the Presidency within a permanent Union. His leadership would spark resistance so strong that it would coalesce into a new political party, the Whigs, devoted to opposing concentrated executive power.

THE INVASION OF FLORIDA

AN ENDURING IMAGE of Andrew Jackson is the cartoon of "King Andrew the First," as his critics called him, sitting on a throne after his veto of the Bank,[6] but his war against the Bank produced more than caricatures. Both his critics and supporters understood that Jackson was exercising the powers of the Presidency in unprecedented ways, triggering congressional investigations, legislative proposals to rein in the executive — even censure by the Senate. Jackson, however, persevered and eventually prevailed. He similarly turned presidential powers to new directions when he overcame South Carolina's threats to nullify federal tariff laws. Throughout, Jackson's belief that he represented the will of the majority infused his conduct of the Presidency. He re-energized the office by wedding its constitutional powers to a theory of the executive as the focal point for national majority rule, a role that was at best implicit in the constitutional text.

Jackson's attitude was clear even before he became President. As a general, Jackson was not above interpreting his orders loosely, nor did he think he had to wait on congressional approval before taking offensive military action. In the wake of the War of 1812, Jackson concluded that the Spanish had to be expelled from the Southwest to make way for American expansion.[7] The first step in his strategy was to eliminate any possibility of an Indian buffer zone between the United States and Spain. After initial setbacks, Jackson defeated several Creek Indian tribes that had allied with the British during the War — in these battles, Jackson won the nickname "Old Hickory." During the peace, Jackson refused to follow the provisions of the Treaty of Ghent that restored the tribes to the status quo and removed them from the area of the Louisiana Purchase to lands on the Western frontier. In about 16 months, Jackson acquired about one-third of Tennessee, three-fourths of Florida and Alabama, one-fifth of Georgia and Mississippi, and about one-tenth of Kentucky and North Carolina. Jackson made no secret of his desire to drive the Spanish out of Florida, Texas, and even Mexico.[8]

The Treaty of Ghent and several U.S.-British treaties after the war formalized an implicit understanding between the mother country and her former colonies. Great Britain would no longer oppose American expansion into the South and West. In return, the United States demilitarized the northern frontier and relinquished any ambitions for Canada. This left Spain in an untenable position in Florida, where it had few military and administrative resources. Americans had wanted Florida since the days of Jefferson, if not before, but Congress never authorized any military action against the Spanish. Under prevailing practice at the time, a full offensive mission of conquest would have called for a declaration of war.

Seminole attacks on American territory in 1817 supplied Jackson with a pretext. The Seminoles had operated out of Spanish Florida and had refused to vacate lands under previous treaties, launching retaliatory attacks when American troops sought to relocate them. American settlers conveniently engaged in a separate raid into Florida, "liberated" Amelia Island, and then pled for help when Spanish forces moved to evict them. The Monroe administration authorized local commanders to pursue the Seminole raiders across the Florida line, but to stop short and await further orders should the raiders seek shelter in a Spanish outpost. Monroe placed Jackson in command of a broader expedition and ordered him to "[a]dopt the necessary measure to terminate a conflict" that the President claimed he wanted to avoid.[9] Jackson concluded that the best way to end tensions was to seize all of Spain's territory in Florida. He sent a letter to Monroe seeking authorization, which Monroe subsequently claimed he did not read until a year later.[10] Monroe independently sent Jackson a letter giving him command of the expedition against the Seminoles, the intervention at Amelia Island, and unspecified "other services."[11] Monroe urged Jackson that "[t]his is not a time for you to think of repose," declared that "[g]reat interests are at issue," and asked that "every species of danger" be "settled on the most solid foundation."[12]

Jackson took this as presidential authorization to invade Florida. He did not question that the President had the authority to send him; in fact, he had promised Monroe that he would conquer the whole territory within 60 days. In the First Seminole War of 1818, Jackson led a force of 3,000 regulars and volunteers that destroyed the main Indian settlement near present-day Tallahassee, and captured two British citizens — Alexander Arbuthnot and Robert Ambrister — who had been advising the Seminole. He convened a military commission to try the two as outlaws under his authority as the commander in the field, and after a guilty verdict, he sentenced both to death. Jackson then marched his troops to Pensacola, the seat of Spanish rule in Florida, and quickly seized it on the ground that hostile Indians were massed inside. None were found. A small Spanish force surrendered after a short battle nearby, with no casualties on either side. In June, Jackson issued a proclamation declaring Florida ceded to the United States and established a provisional government.[13]

Jackson's battlefield successes sparked a political firestorm. After the fighting ended, Secretary of War John Calhoun and Treasury Secretary William Crawford argued that Jackson had violated the Constitution and demanded his punishment. Secretary of State John Quincy Adams defended Jackson on the ground that the seizure of Pensacola was justified by military necessity.[14] Instead, Monroe sent Jackson a letter maintaining that the general had exceeded his orders, but that circumstances justified pursuit of the Indians into Spanish territory — even though under the Constitution the attack on Pensacola required a declaration of war from Congress.[15] Monroe was not about to admit that the conquest of Florida was illegal and return it to Spain.

Jackson took full responsibility for the invasion but continued to claim that Monroe had authorized it. Congress initiated an investigation, and Henry Clay sought Jackson's censure, along with legislation prohibiting the executive from invading foreign territory without congressional permission.[16] As Jackson journeyed to Washington to manage his defense personally, public opinion turned strongly in his favor.[17] Clay's proposals were resoundingly defeated in the House by 2–1 margins,[18] and in the Adams-Onis Treaty Spain ceded Florida in exchange for American assumption of claims against Spain of up to $5 million.[19]

As President, Jackson had no occasion to lead the nation into war, yet he never lost his belief that the Spanish, and their Mexican successors, should give ground to their more enterprising neighbors. Jackson pursued the acquisition of Texas throughout his Presidency because he believed it erroneously to be part of the Louisiana Purchase. He blamed the Adams-Onis treaty for giving up Texas and "dismember[ing]" the American empire.[20] Upon assuming the Presidency, he sent envoys to Mexico City to negotiate for Texas; they made matters worse by reporting on the Mexicans' susceptibility to bribery and corruption in letters leaked to the press.[21] About 35,000 Americans, some with slaves, had settled in Texas at the open invitation of the Mexican government between 1821 and 1835. When Jackson's efforts to buy Texas failed, Americans in Texas took matters into their own hands.

In November 1835, Texans established a provisional government, and in the spring of 1836, declared independence. General Santa Anna, who had established a military government over Mexico, sought to quell the rebellion with 6,000 troops. After he reduced the Alamo and executed the survivors, he met defeat at the hands of Sam Houston, the former governor of Tennessee and Jackson's close friend, on April 21, 1836, at the Battle of San Jacinto. A captured Santa Anna ordered Mexican troops out of Texas and signed treaties recognizing the withdrawal. Although news of the victory thrilled the American public, it also reopened the question of slavery in the territories. Texas sent delegations seeking annexation, but abolitionists and Northern leaders worried that its addition would give the slave states an advantage in the Senate.[22] Jackson was unwilling to move forward with annexation because he worried that sectional division over slavery would complicate the election of his chosen successor, Martin Van Buren; nor did he want to shift world opinion against the United States.[23] He left the matter to Congress, which controlled the acquisition of new territory and the admission of states under the Constitution. After both the House and Senate appropriated funds and confirmed an envoy to Texas, Jackson decided (on his penultimate day) to recognize Texan independence, which paved the way for the incorporation of Texas in 1845.[24] The Constitution nowhere granted the executive the explicit power to recognize foreign nations, but Presidents and Congresses had long considered it part of the executive power over foreign relations.

A second pillar of Jackson's support for western expansion was removal of the Indians to the frontier.[25] Federal treaties guaranteed millions of acres in the Southwest to the Indian tribes; federal policy recognized them as self-governing sovereigns and encouraged missionaries to civilize them.[26] The Cherokee, who had their own constitution and laws and held more than six million acres in Georgia, tried to force them to leave by imposing state law and prohibiting white Americans from assisting them.[27] Jackson saw removal of the Indians as advancing America's economic development and enhancing its strategic position in the Southwest. Without the Indians, fertile lands in the West would open to white settlement, and an anomaly would be eliminated from America's sovereignty.[28] In his mind, whites and Indians could not live together, and the best solution was to keep them apart.[29]

In his first State of the Union Address, Jackson announced his support for Georgia. To allow the Cherokee to administer their own laws, he declared, would create an independent state within the borders of Georgia.[30] He told Congress that he had "informed the Indians that their attempt to establish an independent government would not be countenanced by the Executive of the United States."[31] He "advised them to emigrate beyond the Mississippi or submit" to state law.[32] Jackson knew that the Indians would have little option but to emigrate.[33] Jackson's interpretation of the Constitution represented a 180-degree change in federal policy, but he showed little hesitation in announcing an independent opinion on the Constitution's meaning. The Supreme Court would not clearly identify the constitutional status of the Indian tribes until 1831.[34]

On the merits, Jackson's interpretation was mistaken. Presidents have generally controlled the recognition of foreign nations through their constitutional authority to receive foreign ambassadors, and Jackson could have claimed that his decision rested on the de-recognition of the Indian tribes as foreign nations. That, however, did not give the tribes the status of states, nor were the tribes transformed into states when the federal government granted them the right to enforce their own laws. If the tribes were states, the Constitution would have guaranteed them two Senators, the right to elect members to the House, and the right to send electors to the Electoral College. Nothing in the Constitution prohibited the exercise of sovereignty by a tribe within a state, just as nothing prevented the federal government from enjoying exclusive control of territory within a state.

Jackson placed the Indian Removal Bill, which set aside land west of the Mississippi for the Cherokee should they voluntarily leave Georgia, at the top of the legislative agenda for his first year in office.[35] To force the issue, the bill rejected Cherokee claims to sovereignty and subjected them to state laws. It was consistent with Jackson's general view of allowing the states to regulate all matters not specifically given to the federal government. Northern Christian groups accused Georgia of violating federal treaties and attacked the administration for racism. Fierce public opposition to the bill mobilized a permanent anti-Jackson movement throughout the country and led to a split between free and slave states. It passed handily in the Senate, but by only 102–97 in the House in 1830.[36]

Indians and their allies challenged Jackson in the courts. The Supreme Court threw out their first attempt to prevent Georgia from enforcing its laws because they were not a "foreign nation" that could appear in federal court.[37] Georgia had already declared that it would not obey the Supreme Court, and Jackson's supporters in Congress introduced a bill to repeal Section 25 of the Judiciary Act of 1789, which had given the Court jurisdiction over state court judgments.[38] The Cherokee secured a partial victory, however, because the Court declared that Indians were not simply citizens of Georgia, but instead were "domestic dependent nations" in a "state of pupilage," in which "their relations to the United States resemble that of a ward to his guardian."[39] The right case arose when Georgia arrested and jailed Christian missionaries who refused to leave Cherokee lands. Two missionaries, Samuel Worcester and Elizur Butler, challenged their imprisonment before the Supreme Court. In *Worcester v. Georgia*, Chief Justice Marshall struck down Georgia's

Cherokee laws, not because they violated treaties with the Indians, but because they violated the Constitution.[40] According to Marshall, the "Indian nations had always been considered as distinct, independent political communities, retaining their original natural rights, as the undisputed possessors of the soil, from time immemorial."[41] The Constitution, the Court held, gave exclusive control over all relations with the Indians to the federal government.

Georgia refused to appear before the Court and took no steps to obey the Court's ruling, and Jackson made no effort to enforce the Supreme Court's judgment. "Well, John Marshall has made his decision, now let him enforce it," Jackson was reported to have said.[42] Historians have disputed whether Jackson actually uttered those words, which were reported secondhand in a book long after he left office, but according to Daniel Howe's recent work, the comments were "consistent with Jackson's behavior and quite in character."[43] They illustrate Jackson's pugnacity, his Indian policy, and his view of the President's position in the constitutional system. Jackson followed Jefferson's belief that the executive had an equal right to interpret and enforce his own vision of the Constitution — a path he would pursue to great effect in his battle with the Bank of the United States. As he had made clear in his State of the Union Address, Jackson believed that the federal government did not enjoy the sole prerogative to regulate the Indian tribes, nor did he feel a constitutional obligation to obey the interpretation of the Constitution held by another branch. Because the federal government itself was not a party to the case, Jackson did not need to respond to the Court's decision.

Rather than defy the Supreme Court outright, the Georgia courts simply refused to acknowledge it. Without any formal acceptance or rejection of *Worcester* by the state, the Supreme Court had no formal legal authority to order Georgia to obey the decision.[44]

The Supreme Court, moreover, recessed for nine months and would have been unable to reverse any Georgia court decision.[45] Jackson commented that "the decision of the supreme court has fell still born, and they find they cannot coerce Georgia to yield to its mandate."[46] The confrontation generated political trouble for the administration. Newspapers widely reprinted *Worcester*, which served as ammunition against Jackson's reelection campaign. Jackson and Van Buren worked through the party machinery to convince the governor to commute the missionaries' sentences in exchange for their promise to drop the case.[47] Indian issues factored into the election of 1832, and Jackson took his reelection as a validation of his policy.

In Jackson's second term, the United States moved swiftly to remove the Indians. In 1835, a rump Cherokee government agreed to a treaty that traded their Georgia lands for $5 million and land in Oklahoma.[48] After the Senate ratified the agreement by only one vote, the U.S. Army forced the Cherokee to leave without any preparations for the long journey and hard winter. In 1838, 12,000 Cherokee migrated on the "Trail of Tears" to the West; it is estimated that 4,000 died.[49] By today's standards, American treatment of the Indians is shocking.[50] But under the standards of his time, Jackson's actions appear to have represented the views of the voting public.

Jackson may have honestly believed that the lot of the Indians would be improved by distance from whites, and his actions may have even prevented their wholesale destruction, which could have occurred had they attempted to remain in Georgia and other Western states. He achieved what he had wanted — the removal of a perceived obstacle to the growth of the American republic. Jackson opened up 100 million acres to white settlers in exchange for 30 million acres in Oklahoma and Kansas and $70 million.[51] Although he believed himself to be protecting the Indians by keeping them apart from whites, he also wanted to open the best farmland to white settlers and impose state law so as to drive out the Indians. While the Trail of Tears occurred after Jackson had left office, he surely bears great responsibility for the tragedy, and he used the power of the Presidency to bring it about.

THE BANK WAR

JACKSON'S USE OF executive powers domestically surpassed his actions in foreign affairs. He placed the constitutional powers of the office — removal, the veto, and the power to execute and interpret the law — in the service of a new constitutional theory of the office. For Jackson, the Presidency did not just rest on the same plateau with the other branches. It was the *primus inter pares*. Jackson conceptualized the Presidency as the direct representative of the American people, the only official in the federal government elected by the majority. He proceeded to exercise a broad interpretation of his constitutional powers, sometimes in conflict with Congress and the courts, because he believed he was promoting the wishes of the people. Jackson's vision came through in the symbolic — as in his first inaugural, when he opened the White House to any and all, who then proceeded to storm through the building destroying furniture, carpets, and fine china[52] — and the real, as when he took his reelection as a mandate to destroy the Bank of the United States.

At first, Jackson resorted to his constitutional authority just to keep his administration from imploding. As he entered office, Jackson made the basic mistake of appointing cabinet members who turned out to be at odds with one another — a mistake made by Washington, too. This problem was compounded by the presence of Vice President Calhoun, who had accused an unsuspecting Jackson of waging an illegal war in Florida while in the Monroe administration and who would become one of Jackson's fiercest political opponents. Dissension began, however, not over policy but a marriage. Tennessee Senator and Jackson friend John Eaton, the new Secretary of War, had allegedly carried on an affair with Peggy Timberlake, the daughter of his landlord.[53] Not only was Ms. Timberlake much younger than the Senator, but she was married to a Navy purser who then allegedly killed himself because of her behavior.[54] Eaton then married Timberlake, setting off a social scandal that rocked the administration. The wives of administration officials, such as Vice President Calhoun and the Secretaries of the Treasury and Navy, as well as the Attorney General and Jackson's close friends and aides openly snubbed the new Mrs. Eaton at social events.[55] Her supporters included Secretary of State Van Buren, the Postmaster General, and two of Jackson's presidential advisors.[56]

As Donald Cole has observed, the issue dominated Jackson's first years in office and led to Calhoun's downfall.[57] Because of the social division, the members of Jackson's cabinet were barely on speaking terms, and the first term ground to a halt. Jackson, who took the insults to heart and personally conducted research in Mrs. Eaton's defense, came to see the whole affair as an effort by Calhoun to succeed him in office.[58] By the end of 1829, Jackson switched his favor from Calhoun to Van Buren, who was known as "the Little Magician" for his political and organizational skills in New York.[59]

Jackson found his solution in his power of removal. He believed that his popular election gave him the right, in the name of reform, to replace those "unfaithful or incompetent hands" who held power, as he said in his First Inaugural Address, with officers of "diligence and talent" who would be promoted based on their "integrity and zeal."[60] He also believed that the concentration of power in the hands of long-serving public officials threatened American liberty,[61] and praised "rotation" in office as "a leading principle of the republican creed."[62] For Jackson, "as few impediments as possible should exist to the free operation of the public will."[63]

In his first year in office, Jackson moved quickly to put his words into effect. Of about 11,000 federal officials, Jackson removed somewhere between 10 and 20 percent in his first year.[64] Of those directly appointed by the President, he removed fully 45 percent, more than all of his predecessors combined.[65] Jackson believed he should have a bureaucracy that would support his program, but historians ever since have blamed him for introducing the "spoils system" into American politics and ruining a relatively honest and efficient federal bureaucracy.[66]

Removal became the answer to the Eaton affair. By 1831, Jackson obtained documents showing that Calhoun had attacked him over the invasion of Florida.[67] In a letter to Calhoun, accusing him of "endeavoring to destroy" his reputation, Jackson wrote "in the language of Caesar, *Et tu Brute*," and declared that "[n]o further communication" between the two would be necessary.[68] Calhoun published his correspondence with the President on the Seminole Wars in an effort to show that others — particularly Van Buren — were attempting to destroy him.[69] Jackson and the nation were shocked by the public airing of political dirty laundry. He could not remove the Vice President, but he could fire his quarrelsome cabinet *en masse* — especially its Calhoun supporters. The first President to demand the resignation of his entire cabinet at once,[70] Jackson made clear that he would use his power of removal vigorously, and that cabinet members had no constitutional right to autonomy. It struck the nation like a thunderclap, but it allowed Jackson to end the political infighting within his administration and to refocus on his policy goals. Jackson's control over the executive branch and the party would become even clearer when he decided in 1832 to replace Calhoun on the Democratic ticket with Van Buren.

The firings would provide the space for Roger Taney — who

would play a central part in Jackson's next great constitutional fight — to enter the cabinet as Attorney General. It is difficult today to understand why the Bank of the United States would spark a titanic political fight. Who would oppose the idea of keeping the money supply and interest rates out of the hands of politicians? Yet, Jackson made a point of mentioning the Bank at the end of his First Annual Message to Congress. He observed that "[b]oth the constitutionality and the expediency of the law creating this bank are well questioned by a large portion of our fellow-citizens," and he declared that "it has failed in the great end of establishing a uniform and sound currency."[71] Jackson recommended that if Congress were to keep the Bank, significant changes in its charter would be necessary.[72] Jackson disliked the Bank of the United States, and banks in general, because they were thought to be responsible for economic overexpansion and the resulting crashes, the source of corruption by a wealthy elite, and the generator of unreliable paper money and easy credit. "The connection of banks and government was fraught with financial and political peril, especially in a young republic whose citizens craved riches and yet resented every hint of aristocratic privilege," writes a historian of the period. "Banking was poorly understood, not yet professionalized, and its amateur practitioners sometimes wreaked disaster on their customers."[73]

Many Americans shared Jackson's hostility toward the Bank, which was a wholly different creature from today's Federal Reserve. The legislation establishing the first Bank of the United States, the one signed by George Washington and over which Hamilton and Jefferson had fought, expired just before the War of 1812.[74] Part of the responsibility for the Madison administration's setbacks fell on its difficulties in financing the war without a national bank.[75] Lesson learned, Congress established the Second Bank of the United States in 1816.[76] Madison, who had argued against the constitutionality of the first Bank while a Congressman, signed the legislation as President. In a veto of an earlier version of the bill, he had "[waived] the question of the constitutional authority of the Legislature" because of "repeated recognitions under varied circumstances of the validity of such an institution in acts of the legislative, executive, and judicial branches."[77] Madison conceded that the Bank's legality had been established by additional "indications, in difference modes, of a concurrence of the general will of the nation."[78] Chief Justice Marshall's 1819 opinion in *McCulloch v. Maryland* echoed Madison's statement and sustained the Bank along lines similar to those of Alexander Hamilton: although unmentioned in the constitutional text, a national bank fell within Congress's Necessary and Proper Clause power because it allowed the government to exercise its tax, spending, commerce, and war powers.[79]

As he suggested in his First Annual Message, Jackson did not feel bound by Madison's view or that of the Supreme Court. Jackson's objections to the Bank were not just constitutional; he believed that its concentration of power threatened individual liberties. The Second Bank had come to dominate the American economy and finance in a way unmatched by any other company or institution since.

The Second Bank was a private corporation chartered by the federal government, which held one-fifth of its stock and appointed one-fifth of the directors. By law, only the Second Bank could keep and transfer government funds, help in the collection of taxes, lend money to the government, and issue federal bank notes. Its $13 million in notes, which served as a form of paper currency, made up almost 40 percent of all notes in circulation, and its $35 million in capital was more than double the annual federal budget.[80] It made 20 percent of the nation's loans and held more than one-quarter of its deposits.[81] States could also charter banks, whose notes often came into the possession of the Second Bank during the course of normal business.[82] Because it could call in those notes for repayment at any time, the Second Bank effectively dictated the credit reserves of the state banks, and thus of the entire national banking system.[83] As with the Federal Reserve Bank today, the Second Bank's control over the supply of money allowed it to influence, if not control, the nation's lending activities, interest rates, and economic growth. Its stock was held by 4,000 shareholders, 500 of them foreigners, who enjoyed profits of 8 to 10 percent per year.[84]

Jackson decided to rein in, and then destroy, the Second Bank. He viewed it as an institution that benefited a small financial elite. Its first president, a former Navy and Treasury Secretary appointed by Madison, speculated in the Bank's stock, benefited from corrupt branch operations, and almost drove it into bankruptcy.[85] He resigned after a congressional investigation.[86]

During the Monroe administration, the Bank was widely blamed for the Panic of 1819, which closed several state banks, bankrupted many farmers and businesses, and sparked a sharp increase in unemployment.[87] The years after the War of 1812 witnessed a dramatic increase in land speculation fueled by bank notes. During the Panic, the Second Bank demanded that state banks redeem their notes in hard currency, which caused a sharp contraction of credit, a run of bankruptcies, and a rapid increase in unemployment.[88] Jackson was elected to the Senate by the Tennessee legislature in 1823 in part because of his public stance against the Bank. Political movements rose to oppose the Bank, with states enacting laws heavily taxing the Bank or trying to drive branches out of their territory.[89]

Ironically, by the time Jackson became President, the Bank had changed its ways and had become a powerful aid to the striking economic expansion of the 1820s and 1830s. Under Bank President Nicholas Biddle, the scion of a patrician Philadelphia family, the

Second Bank cleaned up its finances.[90] It ended internal corruption and kept a reserve of hard currency worth roughly half the amount of notes outstanding to prevent the speculative practices that had produced the Panic. Through its special relationship with the federal government and its holdings of specie and state bank notes, it effectively controlled the national money supply and had a profound effect on the amount of credit and growth in the economy.[91] Biddle believed that government oversight and public involvement in the Bank's operations were unwelcome and unnecessary,[92] and he made sure his influence was felt by paying newspaper editors and legislators to defend the Bank. Biddle was not a corrupt speculator, as were some of his predecessors, but a highly educated, intelligent man who brought great ability and energy to the job of administration. Neither Biddle nor his Bank would go quietly.[93]

The approach of the 1832 presidential elections prompted the first round in the fight between Jackson and Biddle's Bank. In his Second Annual Message to Congress, Jackson proposed folding the Bank into the Treasury Department, but the legislation establishing the Bank itself was not up for reauthorization until 1836.[94] As the elections neared, Jackson agreed not to seek any changes in the Bank's charter until after the elections.[95] A convention of National Republicans — the group that had split off from the Democratic Party to oppose Jackson — nominated Henry Clay as their presidential candidate.[96] Sensing a political opportunity, Clay convinced Biddle to seek renewal of the Bank's charter four years early.[97] Both the House Ways and Means Committee and the Senate Finance Committee had issued reports the previous year, finding the Bank constitutional and praising its operations (Biddle had personally drafted the Senate report). The Bank paid to distribute both reports throughout the country.[98] Jackson chose Senator Thomas Hart Benson, with whom he had once fought a duel that ended with a bullet in Jackson's shoulder, to lead the fight against the Bank.[99] Clay's supporters in the House and Senate passed the bill in the summer of 1832 by 28–20 in the Senate and 107–85 in the House.[100] In pushing the Bank Bill and working with Clay, Biddle had lived up to the charges that the Bank was a politicized institution, and had thrown down the gauntlet before a man who had never shrunk from a fight.

The initial setbacks steeled Jackson's determination. Van Buren came to see Jackson at midnight shortly after the votes. Jackson was stretched out on a sofa, his health suffering. Upon greeting his visitor, he declared, "The bank, Mr. Van Buren, is trying to kill me, *but I will kill it.*"[101] And he did. Jackson issued a thundering veto on July 10, 1832. For the first time in presidential history, a veto message extensively discussed political, social, and economic as well as constitutional objections to legislation.[102] Jackson portrayed the bill as a "gratuity" and a "present" transferred from the American people to the Bank's shareholders.[103] The Bank occupied the position of a monopoly that benefited "a privileged order, clothed both with great political power and enjoying immense pecuniary advantages from their connection with the Government," at the expense of "merchant, mechanic, or other private citizen[s]" who are not allowed to pay their debts with notes, rather than hard currency.[104] Such wealth, Jackson argued, ought to give "cause to tremble for the purity of our elections in peace and for the independence of our country in war," because the Bank would use its wealth to "influence elections or control the affairs of the nation."[105] Foreign shareholders, Jackson feared, might cause the financial system to collapse during a war — "[c]ontrolling our currency, receiving our public moneys, and holding thousands of our citizens in dependence" would pose a greater threat to national security than an enemy's armies and navies.[106]

Although the message broke from practice by introducing his policy views, the lasting impact of Jackson's veto remains his thinking on the President's independent authority to interpret and enforce the Constitution. He conceded that the precedents of the Supreme Court and previous Congresses had upheld the Bank;[107] however, Jackson declared that the Constitution established the executive as an independent and coordinate branch whose decisions could not be dictated by the Court. "The Congress, the Executive, and the Court must each for itself be guided by its own opinion of the Constitution," Jackson wrote.[108] In fulfilling its constitutional functions, each branch has an equal and independent duty to decide upon the constitutionality of legislation, whether in passing, enforcing, or adjudicating it. "The opinion of the judges has no more authority over Congress than the opinion of Congress has over the judges," Jackson declared.[109] And, he emphasized, "on that point the President is independent of both."[110] He concluded that "[t]he authority of the Supreme Court must not, therefore, be permitted to control the Congress or the Executive when acting in their legislative capacities..."[111] Jackson would only grant the courts "such influence as the force of their reasoning may deserve."[112]

Jackson remained convinced that Jefferson had been right in 1791. A national bank was not necessary and proper to execute the government's constitutional powers, because it was not truly indispensable. Congress, for example, has the power to coin money. It had already established a mint; therefore, a national bank could not truly be necessary and proper to execute that power. Jackson closed by linking his constitutional and policy objections to the higher goal of democracy and liberty:

> It is to be regretted that the rich and powerful too often bend the acts of government to their selfish purposes. Distinctions in society will always exist under every just government. Equality of talents, of education, or of wealth

can not be produced by human institutions. In the full enjoyment of the gifts of Heaven and the fruits of superior industry, economy, and virtue, every man is equally entitled to protection by law; but when the laws undertake to add to these natural and just advantages artificial distinctions, to grant titles, gratuities, and exclusive privileges, to make the rich richer and the potent more powerful, the humble members of society — the farmers, mechanics, and laborers — who have neither the time nor the means of securing like favors to themselves, have a right to complain of the injustice of their Government. There are no necessary evils in government. Its evils exist only in its abuses. If it would confine itself to equal protection, and, as Heaven does its rains, shower its favors alike on the high and the low, the rich and the poor, it would be an unqualified blessing. In the act before me there seems to be a wide and unnecessary departure from these just principles.[113]

Jackson's call to freedom does not fit modern conceptions of either liberal or conservative policy, but seems more libertarian. He wanted to support the common man by reducing, rather than expanding, the role of government in society. Jackson believed that government regulation entrenched the rich in power; getting the government out of the way would allow individual talents and merit to come to the fore.

Presidents from Washington to John Quincy Adams had vetoed 9 pieces of legislation; Jackson vetoed 12. He was the first President to make use of the "pocket veto," in which the executive vetoes bills enacted just before Congress goes into recess, without the possibility of override. Washington set the precedent for using the veto purely on policy grounds, but it was Jackson who transformed the power into one that gave the President significant leverage in the legislative process itself. The President would not use the veto only to protect the Constitution against encroachment by the legislature. Jackson's veto of the Bank presented a striking declaration of independence from the other branches of government. He gave no deference to the views of Congress, the Supreme Court, or even past Presidents. Jackson believed that the President should use his power affirmatively to prevent the other branches from violating his view of the Constitution, even if their policy did not infringe on executive branch prerogatives. The implication was that the other branches were also free to use their authority to advance their constitutional views, and they were in no way bound by the President.

Jackson made the President a permanent player in the legislative process, one whose power far exceeded any individual member of Congress. As Leonard White has observed, Jackson endowed the Presidency with the political force of two-thirds of Congress.[114] Because of Jackson, any modern President with the support of 34 Senators can stall any legislation. Not only does the veto give the President blocking power, but the mere threat of a veto provides him with a political advantage in influencing legislation.[115] Forceful Presidents have combined the veto power with the right to propose bills to ensure that Congress begins with the administration's proposals first.

Jackson's veto was greeted with howls of protest. Biddle wrote to Clay that Jackson was a demagogue calling for anarchy.[116] Daniel Webster told the Senate the President was grabbing for "despotic power."[117] "[A]lthough Congress may have passed a law, and although the Supreme Court may have pronounced it constitutional," Webster said, "yet it is, nevertheless, no law at all, if he, in his good pleasure, sees fit to deny it effect; in other words, to repeal and annul it."[118] Webster foresaw that Jackson's example would lead to today's presidential influence over legislation. His veto message "claims for the President, not the power of approval, but the primary power, the power of originating laws."[119] Clay followed with the claim that the veto was reserved for extraordinary moments when Congress had acted rashly.[120] Now, Clay observed, the President's veto had become a threat used to influence legislation, which was "hardly reconcilable with the genius of representative government."[121]

Jackson obviously aimed his message over the heads of Congress to the American people, and it was reproduced in newspapers and pamphlets by the tens of thousands, some at the expense of Biddle, who thought the arguments so specious that they made for good propaganda. More importantly, with the presidential elections approaching, Jackson was asking the people to decide the Bank issue by voting for him. As Remini writes, "[N]ever before had a chief executive taken a strong stand on an important issue, couched his position in provocative language, and challenged the American people to do something about it if they did not approve."[122] Jackson transformed the presidential election into a plebiscite; victory in the 1832 election would give the President a popular mandate to pursue the destruction of the Bank.

Jefferson, too, had turned the election of 1800 into a referendum, but it was not so much on a single issue as it was a struggle between the Federalists and Republicans for power. The first nominating conventions, held by the two parties in 1832, strengthened the link between popular wishes and his reelection. There was no mistake about the issues involved — Jackson's exercise of his constitutional powers stayed at the center of the election. National Republicans, who nominated Clay and counted Webster and Calhoun among their leaders, argued that Jackson had seized unconstitutional powers and was bent on tyranny.[123] A National Republican newspaper, for example, accused Jackson of annulling "two houses of Congress, the Supreme Court, and the Constitution of the United States."[124] Another asked, regarding Jackson and his veto, "Could it have any effect but to swell the power and augment the influence of the Executive...?"[125] A third declared that the Constitution was "a dead letter, and the will of a DICTATOR is the Supreme Law!"[126]

Democrats responded that Jackson represented the wishes of the common man against the concentrated power of the Bank and a wealthy aristocracy.[127] They had the luck to fight against a Bank determined to make itself a bigger target by interfering in the election. Biddle paid to reprint Webster's and Clay's speeches against the veto, and poured roughly $100,000 into the campaign.[128] Democrats used this as ammunition against Clay, claiming he fronted for a Bank that was trying to buy the election and bribe public officials.[129] Rather than run from Jackson's use of presidential power, Democrats welcomed the focus on their leader and used mass rallies, parades, and campaign events to make him the center of the campaign.[130]

Jackson won reelection overwhelmingly. He gained 219 electoral votes to Clay's 49, with a third-party candidate receiving seven.[131] Jackson won all of the South and the West except for Clay's home state of Kentucky and South Carolina, which gave its votes to someone who was not running. He lost only four other states, all in the Northeast. He won about 55 percent of the popular vote, with 687,502 in his favor against 530,189 for his opponents, only a slight decline from his percentage of the vote in the first election.[132] The election vindicated Jackson's decision to gamble on his opposition to the Bank. It transformed the nature of the Presidency by grounding his political support on the majority, rather than the states, the Electoral College, or his political party. Jackson would use this broad base to claim that his views on policy were those of the American people, and to lay an equal, if not superior, claim to that of Congress for the mantle of representative of the democracy.

The second term began with a renewed offensive against the Bank. Old Hickory was not going to wait four years for "the Monster" to go quietly. In spring 1833, Jackson decided to transfer all federal funds from the Second Bank to state banks.[133] Withdrawal would drain about half of the deposits from the Bank, effectively crippling it. Jackson believed that this would prevent Biddle from pushing a recharter bill through Congress.[134] It also placed the general in his favorite position, that of dictating events. On March 19, Jackson read a paper to his cabinet, laying out his policy toward the Bank.[135] He would not suffer its recharter and he would manage federal funds through state banks or possibly a new federal bank limited to doing business only in Washington, D.C. (which would not run afoul of Jackson's constitutional objections).[136] With only Taney in agreement, the rest of the cabinet thought it best to keep the government's business with the Bank.[137] Treasury Secretary Louis McLane argued in a lengthy letter to Jackson against withdrawal because of the effect on the economy and worries about mismanagement by the state banks.[138] The 1816 statute establishing the Second Bank authorized only the Treasury Secretary to withdraw federal funds from the Bank and required him to explain his reasons to Congress.[139]

Congress opposed any withdrawal. Calhoun, Clay, and Webster continued to dominate in the Senate, where the Jacksonians had failed to win a majority in the 1832 elections. Even the Democratic House overwhelmingly declared that federal deposits were safe in the Bank.[140] The President responded by drawing on his full constitutional powers to get the Bank out of the business of holding the government's money, and sparked a political and constitutional controversy of a kind that has rarely been repeated in the nation's history. Jackson first rearranged his cabinet to get McLane out of Treasury — he was moved to State — replacing him with William

Duane, a known opponent of the Bank.[141] Once in office, however, Duane got cold feet and delayed any decision.[142]

Jackson took the extraordinary steps of convening a cabinet meeting on September 17, 1833, to notify them of his decision to withdraw the funds, and the next day had Taney read the cabinet a lengthy "exposé" of the Bank in his name.[143] Jackson blamed the Bank for making the recharter an issue in the presidential election and trying to use its financial influence to defeat him. He alleged that it controlled major newspapers, delayed the retirement of the national debt, and charged the government unjustly high fees. Jackson interpreted "his reelection as a decision of the people against the bank," which he called "an irresponsible power which has attempted to control the Government,"[144] and declared that "the people have sustained the President, notwithstanding the array of influence and power which was brought to bear upon him."[145] The issue was whether the President or the Bank would govern.

Duane resisted and asked for a delay, but Jackson had the government announce the withdrawal on September 20.[146] Duane refused to carry out the order. Jackson informed him that as a member of the executive branch, Duane worked for him. "A secretary, sir,…is merely an executive agent, a subordinate, and you may say so in self-defense," the President told Duane.[147] Duane claimed that Congress had given him, not the President, the discretion to decide where to deposit federal funds, and asked for another delay. "Not a day," Jackson exclaimed, "not an hour."[148]

Jackson fired Duane in a letter on September 23 and replaced him with Taney. "I surely caught a tarter in disguise," Jackson explained to Van Buren, "but I have got rid of him."[149] Taney began carrying out the withdrawal immediately. Jackson had given form to the ideas of Washington and Jefferson. As Chief Executive, Jackson believed it was his constitutional right to decide how to carry out federal law, such as the statute on the deposit of federal funds. In order to execute the law, he had to control subordinate officials in the executive branch. If they did not follow his constitutional views and policy priorities, he exercised his constitutional authority of removal and replaced officials who refused to follow his orders.

Biddle fired back with everything he had. His Bank began a rapid restriction on credit and called in loans to state banks.[150] State banks responded by calling in their own loans, producing a contraction of lending throughout the national economy.[151] Shrinking credit sparked a financial panic, which Biddle hoped would pressure Congress to recharter the bank and override Jackson.[152] Opposition took political form, too. Critics of Jackson coalesced in the winter of 1833 into a new political party, the Whigs, which took as its main platform (as suggested by its name) opposition to Jackson's expansion of executive power.[153] As head of the new party, Clay convinced the Senate to launch an investigation into the withdrawal of the deposits and issued a demand for an official copy of the September 18 exposé widely reprinted in the papers.[154]

Having used his powers to veto, to fire officials, and to interpret and enforce the law, Jackson next turned to executive privilege. In a message to the Senate on December 12, 1833, Jackson wrote that "[t]he executive is a coordinate and independent branch of the Government equally with the Senate."[155] He had "yet to learn under what constitutional authority" the Senate could "require of me an account of any communication, either verbally or in writing, made to the heads of Departments acting as a Cabinet council."[156] If he had to produce the document, he might as well "be required to detail to the Senate the free and private conversations I have held with those officers on any subject relating to their duties and my own."[157] Jackson saw no reason why the document was needed for the performance of any legislative duty, and he believed production would interfere with the proper operation of his own branch. Although Jackson did not use the words "executive privilege," his explanation followed the same constitutional basis set out by Washington's message on the Jay Treaty and Jefferson's refusal to obey the Burr subpoena.

Clay responded with an idea that would make an encore appearance during the Clinton years — censuring the President. Although the Jacksonians held a majority of the House, taking impeachment out of the equation, the Whigs still had sufficient support in the Senate. Clay chose to make Jackson's usurpation of constitutional authority the grounds for censure. In his speech on the resolution, Clay exclaimed that "[w]e are...in the midst of a revolution," because of the veto and the removal of the funds, which was "tending towards a total change of the pure republican character of the Government, and the concentration of all power in the hands of one man."[158] The Great Compromiser repudiated Jackson's claim that the President represented the wishes of the democracy. "I am surprised and alarmed at the new source of executive power which is found in the result of a presidential election."[159] The President's sole authority came from the Constitution and the laws, not "loose opinions, in virtue of the election," which allegedly "incorporate themselves with the constitution, and afterwards are to be regarded and expounded as parts of the instrument!"[160] Clay urged that no one should doubt that Jackson had violated those duties entrusted to him by the laws — he had vetoed a bill on grounds not permitted by constitutional practice, and he had seized from the Secretary of the Treasury the duties entrusted to him by Congress. "The premonitory symptoms of despotism are upon us," Clay declared, "and if Congress do[es] not apply an instantaneous and effective remedy, the fatal collapse will soon come on, and we shall die — ignobly die — base, mean, and abject slaves; the scorn and contempt of mankind; unpitied, unwept, unmourned!"[161]

Clay's rhetoric may go unmatched in the history of attacks on the Presidency, and it had a profound effect upon the Senate. Webster and Calhoun followed with speeches that stretched for days.[162] The Senate eventually responded, enacting a resolution, without any legal effect, rejecting Taney's report of the reasons for withdrawal of the funds by 28–18. On March 28, 1834, it passed the censure of Jackson by 26–20.[163]

Jackson cared above all about his honor, but he did not shrink away nor seek compromise. A few days after the censure, he responded with his "Protest," which remains one of the most forceful declarations of presidential power in American history.[164] Jackson claimed the right as Chief Executive to use his powers to attack threats to the health of the nation. "So glaring were the abuses and corruptions of the bank," Jackson wrote, "so palpable its design by its money and power to control the Government and change its character, that I deemed it the imperative duty of the Executive authority" to check the bank.[165] He attacked the Senate for acting without power because it had neither enacted legislation nor initiated impeachment proceedings; the Constitution spoke nowhere of censure. Censure was no less than an effort by the Senate to interfere with, and even seize, his executive authority. Each branch was equal to and independent of the other and could not interfere with the allocation of powers by the Constitution.

Jackson argued that he was entitled to use his constitutional authorities to defeat the threat to democracy posed by the Bank.[166] He could order and, if necessary, fire subordinates such as Duane. The Constitution's grant of the executive power to the President, and his duty to execute the laws, made him "responsible for the entire action of the executive department."[167] Therefore, "the power of appointing, overseeing, and controlling those who execute the laws — a power in its nature executive — should remain in his hands."[168] If a subordinate would not obey the President's orders, the President had every constitutional right to fire the subordinate and replace him with someone who would. These subordinates included the Secretary of the Treasury, regardless of what duties Congress had delegated to him.

The third leg of Jackson's theory of the Presidency was to link his duty to protect and his constitutional power to enforce the law with his role as representative of the people. Jackson declared, not for the first nor last time: "The President is the direct representative of the American people."[169] Through their selection of a President, the American people held the executive branch accountable. This required that Jackson have full control over every executive branch official and the enforcement of all federal law. Otherwise, there is "no direct responsibility to the people in that important branch of this Government."[170] If the Treasury Secretary could reject a presidential order, it would allow him to defy "the Chief Magistrate elected by the people and responsible to them."[171] An independent Treasury Secretary, followed to its logical conclusion, "will be found effectually to destroy one coordinate department of the Government, to concentrate in the hands of the Senate the whole executive power, and to leave the President as powerless as he would be useless — the shadow of authority after the substance had departed."[172]

Jackson effectively claimed a role not unlike that of the ancient Roman tribunes, implying that the President had a superior tie to the people. In perhaps the first example of a now common presidential practice, Jackson directed his message over the heads of Congress to the people. He claimed that he was only carrying out the wishes of democracy against the conspiracies of an aristocracy to hoard power. In this, Jackson went beyond the vision of the Presidency held by Washington and Jefferson. Washington thought of himself as a republicanized monarch, and Jefferson as a prime minister. The

President remained independent of Congress, but the Presidency relied upon a symbiotic relationship with the legislature for progress.

Jackson's Protest was the Presidency's declaration of independence. Although each branch was independent of the other, the executive was no longer just an equal. He was superior in his direct ties to the American people. Rather than seek legislation from Congress, Jackson's Presidency would speak for the people and force Congress to cooperate with *his* agenda. The President, not Congress, would dictate the tempo of politics and the focus for legislation.

Whigs in the Senate understood what Jackson was about, and they reacted with anger. Webster argued that the President did not hold all of the executive power, did not enjoy a removal authority, and did not control the cabinet secretaries. But he reserved his strongest attack for the theory of a plebiscitary Presidency. Jackson believed his claims of presidential power were "enough for a limited, restrained, republican government! An undefined, undefinable, ideal responsibility to the public judgment!"[173] "The Constitution," Webster declared, "nowhere calls him the representative of the American people; still less their direct representative."[174] Why else, Webster asked, was the President chosen by the Electoral College rather than by direct ballot?[175] If Jackson were right, Webster exclaimed, "then I say, Sir, that the government (I will not say the people) has already a master."[176]

Calhoun spoke even more strongly, exclaiming, "What effrontery" and "boldness of assertion" from Jackson.[177] "Why, he never received a vote from the American people," but only from electors.[178] Calhoun predicted that Jackson would appeal to the people again to wage "hostilities" against the Senate.[179] Urging the Senate to repudiate the Protest, Clay again predicted the coming of dictatorship. Under Jackson, "everything concentrates in the president. He is the sole Executive; all other officers are his agents, and their duties are his duties."[180] This claim, Clay declared, "is altogether a military idea, wholly incompatible with free government."[181] The Senate voted 27–16 to reject Jackson's Protest, and then used its confirmation power over appointments to fight back.[182] It refused to confirm Jackson's nominees to the Bank's board of directors and, to put the icing on the cake, refused to confirm Taney as Treasury Secretary.[183]

Jackson, however, would not be beaten. Do what they might, Biddle, the Great Triumvirate, and the Whig Party could not overcome the fact that they lacked the two-thirds majority to force a recharter or a return of the deposits over Jackson's veto. Jackson used his leadership of the Democratic Party to name anti-Bank men to important congressional positions and to focus state organizations on the war with the Bank. Biddle's decision to instigate a financial panic backfired and turned public opinion against him. In January 1834, Jackson terminated the Bank's role in paying federal pensions to Revolutionary War veterans.[184] When Biddle refused to return the funds to the government, Jackson blamed the suspension of pensions on Biddle, a story the public was only too eager to believe.

By spring, the President's political work bore its fruit, with the governor, legislature, and two Senators from Pennsylvania — the home state of the Bank — publicly condemning Biddle and the Bank for the panic. Other state executives quickly followed suit. Led by Polk, the House passed a resolution against recharter and return of federal deposits, and launched an investigation into the Bank's role in causing the panic. Biddle made matters worse by refusing to testify or provide documents to the House investigation.

Within the year, Jackson's victory was complete: Democrats beat the Whigs badly in the 1834 midterm elections, his administration retired the entire federal debt (reducing the need for a federal bank) in January 1835, the Senate voted to remove the censure resolution from its books, and Roger Taney was confirmed as Chief

Justice upon John Marshall's death in 1835.[185] Jackson reveled in his victory. "I have obtained a glorious triumph," he wrote to a friend. The House's support "put to death, that mamouth [sic] of corruption and power, the Bank of the United States."[186]

There is a good case to be made that Jackson's campaign against the Bank contributed to the boom-and-bust swings of the American economy in the following decades. There is little doubt that a sophisticated market economy needs an independent central bank to prevent politicians from manipulating the money supply for political reasons. The problem for many developing economies is keeping politics out of the bank. The problem for Jackson, however, was to keep the Bank out of politics. He took on the Bank because it had become a renegade institution using its special economic position to interfere in political elections. Jackson's greatness did not come from destroying a crucial part of America's financial architecture, but in fighting an agency of the federal government that was trying to control the political process for its own benefit. It would have been impossible for Jackson to prevail had he not exercised his constitutional powers of the veto, removal, and law enforcement against the wishes of Congress.

THE TARIFF

JACKSON'S FINAL GREAT achievement again drew upon the power of his office to protect the Union. Early indications would not have placed Jackson in the camp of nationalists. Jackson had ended plenary federal control over Indian policy. In his veto of the Bank, as well as several improvements bills, Jackson adopted a limited view of federal powers that outdid even Jefferson in its devotion to strict construction. But when Jackson saw the rising threat of secession, he did not hesitate to stretch the powers of his office to preserve the Union.[187]

The threat came from South Carolina over national tariff rates. Like the national bank, the political importance of the tariff may be difficult to grasp today. The contemporary tariff is most noticeable for its absence — the success of the American-supported GATT, NAFTA, and WTO agreements has rendered the tariff a rather trivial matter. In antebellum America, however, the tariff was an issue over which some were willing to die, and others to break up the Union.

Clay's economic program, the "American System," deployed the tariff to protect domestic manufactures and promote road and canal construction, while Southerners deeply opposed the Tariff of 1824, which enacted steep duties on manufactured imports.[188] The tariff hit the South's economic interests hard; planters had to export raw material, primarily cotton, into the competitive world market, but had to purchase finished products in the home market. Some Southerners believed the Constitution prohibited taxation for purposes other than raising revenue and that one part of the nation — the North — could not benefit from taxes at the expense of another. In 1828, a bill that raised rates became known in the South as the "tariff of abominations" and sparked secessionist rallies in several Southern cities.[189]

South Carolinians rallied around the idea of "nullification." Developed by Calhoun, nullification maintained that the Constitution was only an agreement among the states, which retained their independent sovereignty.[190] No *single* American people had created the Constitution as their governing document. If a majority imposed an unconstitutional law on a single region, a state could nullify the federal law within its borders, and its officials could block federal officers from carrying out national laws.

Historians argue about the origins of nullification, but there can be little doubt that it more than echoes Jefferson's claim, made in the

Kentucky Resolves, that a state could oppose the implementation of the Alien and Sedition Acts. Calhoun similarly believed that South Carolina could refuse to enforce an unconstitutional tariff while it sought redress through the national political process. If those efforts failed, a state could consider secession. South Carolina adopted a legal brief defending nullification, secretly drafted by Calhoun and published as the "South Carolina Exposition and Protest," which concluded that the states possessed the sovereignty to veto actions of the federal government.[191]

The real issue behind nullification was slavery. A popular majority that could enact a tariff, Southerners worried, could eradicate slavery, too. This question prompted one of the greatest debates ever to occur in the Senate, between Webster and South Carolinian Robert Hayne.[192] After Hayne defended state sovereignty independent of the Constitution, Webster gave his well-known speech on the Union that ended with the famous words, "Liberty *and* Union, now and forever, one and inseparable."[193]

Jackson made his own views on nullification clear at a political banquet in honor of Jefferson in April 1830, held by Southern and Western Congressmen opposed to the tariff. With Calhoun in the audience, Jackson had come ready to take on nullification. Several preselected speakers gave increasingly inflammatory toasts in favor of state sovereignty, and when the President's turn came, all became silent to see what position he would take. As always, Jackson left no doubt about where he stood. "Our Union," he declared, "it *must* be preserved."[194] Calhoun followed. In the midst of a rambling toast, the Vice President responded, "The Union, next to our liberty the most dear. May we all remember that it can only be preserved by respecting the rights of the States, and distributing equally the benefit and burden of the Union."[195]

Jackson had declared war on nullification. Although perhaps in conflict with his views on the Bank and internal improvements, his view followed his guiding principle of democracy. If the majority of the people spoke through their elected representatives, a state had no right to frustrate their will. The Union had been the product of the Revolution, in which Jackson had risked his life as a young boy, and to which he had lost his mother and brother. He was not about to see it broken by a state, even the state of his birth. "There is nothing I shudder at more than the idea of the separation of the Union," he wrote in 1828.[196] Although he firmly believed that the powers of the federal government were limited and that the states were to exercise all others not granted, Jackson believed even more in the permanency of the Union. State sovereignty could not justify secession.

Jackson hoped to reach a compromise as the election of 1832 neared. Without admitting the legitimacy of the South's grievances, he successfully urged Congress to enact a new bill that reduced tariffs. The national debt was being steadily reduced, and soon the revenue from the tariff would no longer be needed. A mere month after Jackson won reelection, South Carolina responded by holding a convention that declared the 1832 law void and threatened secession.

Jackson responded with a two-front strategy, one political and one constitutional. In his December 4, 1832, Annual Message to Congress, Jackson offered a political compromise. Tariff protections "should not exceed what may be necessary to counteract the regulations of foreign nations and to secure a supply of those articles of manufacture essential to the national independence and safety in time of war."[197] There was "no reason to doubt" that domestic industry was "beneficial to our country," and he acknowledged that "large capital" had been invested in reliance on the tariff. Nonetheless, investors and producers had no right to expect "that the people will continue permanently to pay high taxes for their benefit, when the money is not required for any legitimate purpose…" In a nod to South Carolina, Jackson criticized a high tariff as tending "to beget in the minds of a large portion of our countrymen a spirit of discontent and jealously dangerous to the stability of the Union." He proposed that Congress study a gradual reduction of rates. To Jackson, the policy issue — how high tariff rates should be — was always open for bargaining.

The Union, however, was nonnegotiable. Six days later, Jackson issued an extraordinary proclamation that drew on his constitutional powers "for preserving the peace of the Union and for the execution of the laws."[198] The American people, he said, spoke as one in electing the President; on behalf of the nation, Jackson left no doubts about his position on nullification. Nullification was *incompatible with the existence of the Union, contradicted expressly by the letter of the Constitution, unauthorized by its spirit, inconsistent with every principle on which it was founded, and destructive of the great object for which it was formed.*[199] He made short work of South Carolina's criticism of the tariff laws and denied that a state could pick and choose which federal laws to enforce. Even if the Supremacy Clause had not expressly provided for the superiority of federal law, it was inherent in the creation of the federal system. "Our Constitution does not contain the absurdity of giving power to make laws and another to resist them."[200] If a single state could block federal law, the Constitution was useless. "Vain provisions! ineffectual restrictions! vile profanation of oaths! miserable mockery of legislation!"[201]

For Jackson, the question boiled down to what came first, the states or the nation. Only if the Constitution was merely a league, and the nation just an agreement of the states, could a state choose to withdraw or change the terms of the contract. But if the United States were a nation, representing the people directly, no state could set itself apart. Even before the Declaration of Independence,

Jackson observed, "we were known in our aggregate character as *the United Colonies of America*," and "[w]e declared ourselves a nation by a joint, not by several acts..."[202] The states have transferred parts of their sovereignty over issues such as war and peace to the federal government, and the allegiance of their citizens to the nation. No state could place itself above that act of union. Nullification was merely a "[m]etaphysical subtlety, in pursuit of an impracticable theory," designed to destroy the Union by forcing it to depend on the goodwill of individual states.[203]

It was no defense to claim that the tariff affected one region more than another. Every law impacts states and regions differently. On a point dear to him, Jackson suggested that the War of 1812 would have had a different outcome had states nullified laws that impacted them unequally—a veiled reference to the talk of secession that had swept New England.[204] It did not matter that Congress wanted to spend the money on unconstitutional projects, such as internal improvements, which Jackson himself had vetoed. What mattered was whether Congress's *act* in passing the tariff was constitutional, not whether its *motive* was.

It could not have been lost on observers that Jackson was arguing that states could not nullify a federal law, even though he had claimed almost the same power during the Bank fight. Nullification, however, did not undermine his claim of presidential power because the former represented the effort of a regional minority to block the authority of a national majority, while the latter (in his mind) represented the will of the people as a whole. Nullification struck at the very heart of Jackson's program, the expansion of majoritarian democracy. "The Constitution of the United States," he wrote in the proclamation, "forms a *government*, not a league..."[205] In that government, "all the people are represented," and it "operates directly on the people individually, not upon the States..."[206] Because of this

direct link between the people and the Union, the national government and its leaders could not arbitrarily choose to ignore the Constitution and give up powers to the states, nor could it allow a state
to fence itself off from federal law. "[S]uch secession does not break
a league, but destroys the unity of a nation; and any injury to that
unity is not only a breach which would result from the contravention
of a compact, but it is an offense against the whole Union."[207]

Secession, which Jackson believed was the real motivation
behind nullification, directly contradicted American nationhood.
"To say that any State may at pleasure secede from the Union is to
say that the United States are not a nation," Jackson wrote.[208] Robert
Remini observes that Jackson was the first major American statesman to argue that the Union was a perpetual entity.[209] Although
there were antecedents, such as the Articles of Confederation, the
Declaration of Independence, and Washington's Farewell Address,
Jackson's proclamation represents one of the most compelling statements of the theory of American nationhood. Lincoln would owe
much to Jackson's theory of the Constitution, the Presidency, and
the Union.

Jackson's conclusion followed his strategy of seeking political
accommodation while preparing for legal and even military confrontation. He appealed to South Carolina's citizens to put aside
thoughts of disunion. Jackson addressed them as "[f]ellow-citizens
of my native State." Their leaders had deluded them, and he warned
them as "a father would over his children whom he saw rushing to
certain ruin."[210] He appealed to their patriotism: "Carolina is one
of these proud States; her arms have defended, her best blood has
cemented, this happy Union."[211]

But Jackson left no doubts about what would happen if South
Carolina did not compromise. "Disunion by armed force is *treason*."[212] No one needed a refresher on what Jackson had done to the

enemies of the United States. "The laws of the United States must be executed," Jackson declared.[213] "I have no discretionary power on the subject; my duty is emphatically pronounced in the Constitution."[214] The President left little doubt that he would resort to military force if need be. "On your unhappy State will inevitably fall all the evils of the conflict you force upon the Government of your country."[215] Jackson promised that their defeat would be certain.

> [The Constitution's] destroyers you can not be. You may disturb its peace, you may interrupt the course of its prosperity, you may cloud its reputation for stability; but its tranquility will be restored, its prosperity will return, and the stain upon its national character will be transferred and remain an eternal blot on the memory of those who caused the disorder.[216]

South Carolina remained unmoved by the proclamation, which was greeted with widespread support throughout much of the country. Three days later, South Carolina's governor resigned to lead the state's militia; Senator Hayne became governor, and Calhoun became Senator. Twenty-five thousand South Carolinians volunteered to fight. The legislature authorized the governor to call out the militia and to begin a draft and appropriated $250,000 for arms.[217] Jackson sent military troops and a naval vessel to reinforce the federal bases in Charleston Harbor. He ordered the War Department to prepare three divisions of artillery to move against the state the moment it resorted to force.[218] In a letter to a Union supporter in the state, Jackson promised that if South Carolina attacked, he would "call into the field, such a force as will overaw[e] resistance, put treason and rebellion down without blood," and arrest those guilty of treason and rebellion.[219] Jackson planned for 10,000–15,000 federal troops to occupy Charleston within two weeks of an outbreak of violence, and drafted an order calling the militia to defend the Union.[220]

Jackson turned to Congress for a peaceful solution. Congressional action would slow the rush to confrontation and serve as a forum to further isolate South Carolina. Jackson recognized that if he acted unilaterally, he "would be branded with the epithet, *tyrant*."[221] He extended an olive branch by proposing to return tariffs to their 1818 levels.

At the same time, Jackson responded to South Carolina's military preparations by requesting a "Force Bill." Jackson informed Congress that he would continue the collection of federal customs in the port of Charleston and would move the location of the Customs House to a more defensible fort. South Carolina would have to fire the first shot, as it would in 1861. He wanted Congress to delegate broad authority to relocate these federal offices, make some technical changes to expand the jurisdiction of the federal courts in the area, and amend the Militia Acts to allow him to immediately call federal forces into action when federal law was obstructed. He labeled South Carolina's actions as "revolutionary in their character and tendency, and subversive of the supremacy of the laws and of the integrity of the Union," a "usurpation of power," and a threat to the "liberties and happiness of the millions composing this Union."[222] He closed by making clear, once again, that the Union represented the people, that he acted on behalf of that people, and that a small minority could not secede from it. The Framers "bequeathed to us a Government of laws and a Federal Union founded upon the great principle of popular representation."[223] Jackson was called upon to discharge the duty of protecting the Union. Congress must act to "solemnly proclaim that the Constitution and the laws are supreme and the *Union indissoluble*."[224]

While the Force Bill conveyed no new authority, it called for political support from Congress should military action become necessary. Congress remained the only national forum where different regional interests could negotiate a bargain, and it held the constitutional authority over tariff rates. Jackson's willingness to make a deal on the tariff, combined with his display of indomitable will on the constitutional issue, produced a political resolution. South Carolina postponed nullification while the Senate debated the force and tariff bills.

With the rare spectacle of Clay supporting the administration, the Senate passed the Force Bill after the few supporters of nullification left the Senate chamber in protest.[225] Clay reached a bargain with Calhoun, in which the former supported a reduction in tariffs in exchange for South Carolina's repeal of its nullification law. Jackson's "promise" of war had convinced South Carolina's representatives to give way.[226] The Clay-Calhoun tariff passed quickly at the same time as the Force Bill, which received an overwhelming 100-vote majority in the House — a demonstration of Jackson's success in politically isolating South Carolina, not just in the North and West, but also in the South.

Historians consider Jackson's victory in the nullification fight his greatest achievement as President. He stopped a movement to undermine the supremacy of federal law that could have brought secession three decades early. Although he threatened military force, he kept pushing for a political solution that would avoid conflict and preserve the Union. Jackson could not have reached this result without a broad vision of his duty to enforce the law, his power as Chief Executive and Commander-in-Chief, and his role as representative of American democracy. He used this robust understanding of the Presidency to pursue his understanding of the United States as a Union of one people. A President with a smaller conception of the office, like some of his successors, might have disclaimed any role in settling the issue of secession — after all, there is no enumerated power in the Constitution giving the President the authority to settle political disputes between the regions — and allowed South Carolina to go its own way. Jackson's genius was to harness the theory of one Union and one American people to the rising forces of democracy, but he could not have succeeded without a broad understanding of his constitutional powers and the willingness to use them.

CONCLUSIONS

JACKSON RECONSTRUCTED the Presidency. His tenure in the office was every bit as revolutionary as that of Washington or Jefferson. He did not restore the office by breaking its constitutional limits, as critics claimed, but by fulfilling the broadest visions of its Framers. They wanted the office to rest on the choice of a national electorate, bringing accountability and responsibility, but with enough distance to avoid the whims of temporary public passion. They wanted the President to be independent of Congress and exercise his own constitutional powers.

Jackson broke Congress's control over the office and established the Presidency as a coequal, competing voice of the people's wishes. The people, not Congress, would select the President. It would be the people, not Congress, whom Jackson represented. Critical to reasserting the Presidency's independence was Jackson's declaration of the right to interpret the Constitution for himself, rather than defer to the Supreme Court or Congress. In making the Presidency the *primus inter pares* of the national government, Jackson drew upon the other powers of his office, including control over the execution of the law, removal of subordinates, and of course, the veto pen.

Jackson's exercise of the Presidency's powers produced results that many would not agree with today. Jackson almost single-handedly conquered Florida for the United States, and set the stage for Texas's annexation, without legislative approval and support. While removing the Bank from politics, Jackson's war against Biddle destroyed the benefits of an independent central bank. A national bank, properly managed, could have helped smooth the boom-and-bust cycles of the American economy in the decades to come. Removal of the Indians allowed for broader settlement of the Southwest, but it visited untold suffering on the Cherokee and other tribes. Jackson's strong faith in American expansionism did not include a place for Indians, and the results of his policies remain one of the terrible examples of the nation's mistreatment of its own people.

Jackson's exercise of the powers of his office did not go without criticism and opposition. Like other Presidents who have made broad claims of executive authority, Jackson was attacked as a tyrant or dictator. Congress attempted to use its own powers to oppose Jackson, going so far as the only censure of a President in American history, but the people sent Jacksonian majorities to Congress that reversed these efforts. Nonetheless, Jackson's use of presidential power sparked a seismic political response, the creation of the Whig Party whose platform centered on executive restraint. Opposition to Jackson's use of presidential power restored the two-party political system to America.

Despite these negative aspects to his time in office, scholars continue to regard Jackson as one of the ten greatest Presidents. His foreign policy expanded the frontiers of the nation and opened land to economic development. Expansion did not trigger the centrifugal forces of nullification, and Jackson exercised the full powers of his office to protect the Union and the supremacy of federal law against the birth of secessionism. He democratized the political system by ending the corruption of the Bank, turning out long-time officeholders, and opening up the rising South and West. He reestablished the Presidency as an independent center of power that could pursue policies in the national interest, even if at odds with congressional wishes. He could not have achieved any of these goals without a reinvigorated understanding of the constitutional powers of the office. He bequeathed to a future President, Abraham Lincoln, an understanding of the office that allowed him to save the Union when secession came.

Jackson's restoration of the constitutional powers of the Presidency reached its apogee under his protégé, James K. Polk. Scholars consider Polk to be another of America's ten greatest Presidents, and today he is ranked even above his former mentor. Polk had served as Speaker of the House during the Jackson administration and was later elected governor of Tennessee. When the leading candidates for the 1844 election, Van Buren for the Democrats and Clay for the Whigs, both announced they would not support the annexation of Texas, Polk went the other way with the blessing of Jackson. Supporters of expansion at the Democratic convention blocked Van Buren's nomination, and Polk emerged as the dark horse candidate. He sought to unify the Democratic Party by promising to serve only one term. Whigs campaigned on his relative obscurity by asking, "Who is James K. Polk?" They received their answer when Polk won on the platform of annexing Texas, occupying all of the disputed Oregon territory (which would have included parts of Canada between the contemporary borders of Washington State and Alaska), and acquiring California. Polk prevailed in a close election with 1,337,000 votes to Clay's 1,299,000, but by a larger Electoral College advantage, 170–105.[227]

Like his mentor, Polk interpreted his election as a popular mandate. Polk coveted, in particular, California's fine harbors at San Francisco and San Diego for American merchants and the U.S.

Navy. The popular mandate for expansion was so clear that his predecessor, John Tyler, used his lame-duck months in office to engineer the annexation of Texas—and in a manner that further enhanced presidential power. Anti-slavery Democrats and Whigs in the North had successfully blocked proposals to annex Texas by treaty. With Polk's support, Tyler simply asked Congress to incorporate Texas by statute, which required a simple majority in both houses. The use of a statute, rather than a treaty, would set a precedent for future Presidents, who used what would become known as congressional-executive agreements to adopt the Bretton Woods agreement and the GATT in the wake of World War II.

Annexation of Texas almost guaranteed a confrontation with Mexico, with which it shared an uncertain border. Attempting diplomacy first, Polk sent John Slidell to purchase California and the Southwest Territories. Even though Mexico was bankrupt and had few settlers or troops in the territories, its leaders uniformly viewed a sale as dishonorable and refused to negotiate. Polk turned to military means, especially after rumors arrived that Mexican forces were reinforcing California with British financial support.

In early 1846, the President ordered General Zachary Taylor to move his force of 2,500 troops into the disputed territory between Mexico and Texas. Texas claimed that its territory reached as far south as the Rio Grande River, though as a Mexican province and an independent state it had never extended beyond the Nueces River (about 150 miles farther north of the Rio Grande). Most historians agree that Texas had little claim to the Rio Grande border, but Polk was determined to defend it with military force. He paired his efforts to create a provocation in Texas with preparations to seize California. Polk ordered naval units to be ready to seize San Francisco in the event of war, while Captain John Fremont, already in California, began to encourage American settlers to revolt.

Polk and his cabinet had decided to go to war even before these plans bore fruit. On April 25, 1846, the desired skirmish occurred between Taylor's patrols and Mexican forces. Taylor had moved all the way to the Rio Grande and surrounded the larger Mexican units in the area. The Mexican troops tried to fight their way out, with the loss of 11 Americans, but Taylor defeated them in two battles on May 8 and 9. Two days after the first news of the fighting arrived in Washington, Polk sent a war message to Congress. It misrepresented the facts to guarantee the majorities for war.

Polk claimed that he had deployed troops on the U.S. side of the disputed territory and had ordered them to assume a purely defensive posture. He asserted that Mexican forces had fired the first shot. "Mexico has passed the boundary of the United States, has invaded our territory, and shed American blood on American soil," Polk told Congress. In fact, "war exists, and, notwithstanding all our efforts to it, exists by the act of Mexico herself." He called upon Congress "to recognize the existence of the war, and to place at the disposal of the Executive the means of prosecuting the war with vigor, and thus hastening the restoration of peace."[228]

Polk used his authority over the military to create a situation that had triggered war, but could not conduct significant offensive operations against another nation without congressional authorization of a new army of 50,000 and $10 million in funding. Polk's demand for support opened a sectional divide in Congress that organized itself along partisan lines. Whigs in the North opposed the war, which they viewed as an effort to expand the territory open for slavery. It had become an article of faith in both the North and South that slavery would perish if it could not expand. Democratic leaders in the South and West overwhelmingly supported the war, except Calhoun, who worried that the entry of California and New Mexico as free states outweighed the benefits of adding Texas.

Approval for the recognition of a state of war with Mexico prevailed in test votes by 123–67 in the House, and 26–20 in the Senate. After heavy political pressure from the White House, the final declaration of war was attached to the funding and army bills and approved with only 14 votes against in the House and 2 in the Senate. Public opinion showed a strong majority in favor of territorial expansion, convincing Whigs to make no serious effort to stop the war. They continued to vote supplies for the troops, while denouncing Polk for starting the conflict.[229]

Once war began, Polk took firm command of operations. California fell quickly to a remarkably small group of American settlers and regular troops. Polk dispatched another small force to the New Mexico territory, which quickly capitulated. Taylor's army of 4,500 won a series of battles in northern Mexico, capturing Monterey in late 1846. His campaign culminated in the January 1847 battle of Buena Vista, where he defeated Santa Anna's army of 20,000.

Despite these military successes, the war was not as easy and swift as Polk and his advisors had anticipated. Mexico rejected peace overtures, and her forces put up stiff resistance in the north. Polk realized that Mexican politics would not permit a negotiated settlement, which drove him to seek a compelling victory. A drive to Mexico City from the north was impractical because of inhospitable terrain.

Polk decided on a risky amphibious landing at Veracruz on the Gulf of Mexico, to be followed by a land advance to the Mexican capital. He had the good sense to place in command Winfield Scott, who executed one of the most successful American military campaigns in history. With 10,000 troops, he captured the heavily defended Veracruz in March 1847, twice defeated larger armies led by Santa Anna, and took Mexico City on September 14. The Mexican government surrendered, and General Scott imposed an occupation government on the capital. Officers such as Grant, Lee,

Jackson, Meade, Pickett, and McClellan would all serve in this "dress rehearsal" for the Civil War.[230]

Even as his war plans succeeded, Polk came under increasing opposition at home. The 1846 elections returned a narrow Whig majority, which doubted Polk's claim that Mexico had started the war and the United States had only acted in self-defense. In a message to Congress, Polk argued that Mexico's past wrongs against the United States and its provocation of war required an "indemnity" — namely the Southwest and California. Congress had approved the war, and once declared, "it became my duty under the Constitution and the laws to conduct and prosecute it." To Whigs who argued against seizing new territory, Polk responded that "the doctrine of no territory is the doctrine of no indemnity." If adopted, he warned, it "would be a public acknowledgement that our country was wrong and that the war declared by Congress with extraordinary unanimity was unjust and should be abandoned."

A young freshman Congressman, Abraham Lincoln, rose to challenge Polk's accounting of events. He introduced a series of resolutions questioning whether the Rio Grande had ever been understood as the border of Texas and whether Mexico had started the war, and he demanded that Polk provide information to Congress on "the spot" where the first skirmish had occurred. In a speech on January 12, 1848, Lincoln accused Polk of starting the war and "trusting to escape scrutiny, by fixing the public gaze upon the exceeding brightness of military glory." Neither the House nor the President seems to have paid much attention to Lincoln, though the House passed a resolution praising General Taylor and declaring that Polk had started the war "unnecessarily and unconstitutionally," which the Senate rejected.[231]

An anti-war Congress could not prevent the Commander-in-Chief from continuing to dictate wartime strategy and operations.

Even before the war had started, Polk had decided how American forces would be deployed and defined their objectives. After the capture of Mexico City, the President unilaterally set occupation policy, which included holding the capital and the major ports and collecting tax revenues to offset the cost of military operations. While Polk had hoped to squeeze the Mexicans until they agreed to a favorable peace, he began to hope for broader territorial concessions. With Mexico's government weak, its military almost nonexistent, and its people unruly, Polk now wanted Baja California, all of Mexico as far south as Tampico (another 500 kilometers south of the Rio Grande), and control of the isthmus of Tehuantepec for the construction of a transcontinental canal.

Polk unilaterally governed the process for making peace. He chose peace envoys without Senate advice and consent, set the goals for the negotiations, and ultimately decided to send to the Senate the 1848 Treaty of Guadalupe Hidalgo (even though his negotiator, Nicholas Trist, had only won Polk's minimum terms). While it did not fulfill all of Polk's territorial ambitions, it transferred California, the future states of Arizona, New Mexico, Nevada, and Utah, and the disputed territory on the Texas border, in exchange for the paltry sum of $15 million. Mexico lost 40 percent of her territory, while the United States gained the land that would be the base for its future world power.[232] The treaty ended the Mexican-American War on acceptable terms, without a long-term occupation or a descent into chaos along the southern border.

Political opposition during the Mexican-American War demonstrates the checks that Congress always has available against the executive, even at the height of his wartime powers. Polk agreed to the terms of the Treaty of Guadalupe Hidalgo for a reason — Congress would not support the actions needed to conquer more land. Polk had wanted to pressure the Mexicans by continuing military operations. Even after the fall of Mexico City, he had ordered American troops to invade Baja California and had proposed sending forces to annex the Yucatán peninsula.

To expand military operations beyond occupation duty, the President needed more troops and money. American forces had suffered 10 percent casualties, with seven out of every eight being lost to disease rather than battle, and the costs of the war were reaching $100 million. The Whig-dominated Congress rejected Polk's requests for more military funding and increases in the size of the army, and the Senate ratified the terms of the peace treaty by 36–14. While some Southerners wanted more land, the majority of Whigs wanted no territory other than San Francisco.[233]

Like Jackson before him, Polk's energetic executive encouraged a partisan counterattack. Just as Jackson's war with the Bank led his opponents to organize a new opposition party, Polk's war sparked a Whig victory in the next presidential elections. Polk's success, in fact, provoked an even more dangerous reaction. Support for the war resided primarily in the South and among Democrats, while opposition centered in the Northeast among Whigs. By opening a huge territory to settlement and statehood, the Mexican-American War made the future of slavery the central issue of national politics. The war aligned North and South antagonism over slavery with the political parties, which would undermine their ability to ameliorate sectional tensions. The volatile mixture of new territory and political inflexibility would set the conditions for the coming of the Civil War.

Even though the treaty did not recognize even broader American gains, it cemented Polk's place among the nation's greatest Presidents. Polk secured Texas and added the land between the Louisiana Purchase and the Pacific Ocean to the United States. He increased the size of the nation more than any President before or since. While these lands had been sparsely settled under their previous owners, they would someday rank among the more populous and dynamic states in the Union. Polk's vision gave the United States a continent-wide breadth, and it neutralized any natural enemies along the northern or southern borders. With the addition of California and the Northwest, the United States would be protected on both flanks by wide oceans, and by the end of the century it would become a great power. The expansion of the United States was anything but inevitable, propaganda for "Manifest Destiny" notwithstanding. Polk pursued a high-risk strategy that prevailed thanks to Mexico's military weakness and the superior fighting abilities of the U.S. armed forces.[234]

A President with a modest view of his constitutional powers would have shrunk from provoking war over the Texas border, not to mention invading Mexico. Only by fully exercising the powers of the Presidency, as laid down by Jackson, could Polk have realized his dream of reaching the Pacific. Lincoln and other Whigs criticized Polk's exercise of his constitutional rights, just as future Congresses would challenge Presidents who claimed the authority to take the nation into war. And they had much to complain of. As Commander-in-Chief, Polk manipulated events to produce a war, maneuvered Congress into funding it, and held sole control over its goals and strategies. In the words of the leading historian of the period, Daniel Howe, Polk "probably did as much as anyone to expand the powers of the Presidency — certainly at least as much as Jackson, who is more remembered for doing it." Overcoming the errors of Madison's ways, the vigor and energy of his leadership set the model for other Presidents in wartime. Polk's success was inextricably intertwined with the Jacksonian understanding of a constitutionally energetic executive, and it worked to the nation's incalculable benefit.[235]

CHAPTER 6

Abraham Lincoln

NO ONE STANDS HIGHER in our nation's pantheon than Abraham Lincoln. Washington founded the nation — Lincoln saved it. Without him, the United States might have lost 11 of its 36 states, and 10 of its 30 million people. He freed the slaves, ended the planter society, and ushered in a dynamic political system and market economy throughout the nation. Building on Jackson's arguments against nullification, he interpreted the Constitution as serving a single nation, rather than existing to protect slavery. The Civil War transformed the United States from a plural word into a singular noun. That nation no longer withheld citizenship because of race, and guaranteed to all men the right to vote and to the equal protection of the laws. Where once the Constitution was seen as a limit on effective government, Lincoln transformed it into a charter that empowered popular democracy.

Part of Lincoln's greatness stems from his confrontation of tragic choices. As he famously wrote in 1864, "I claim not to have controlled events, but confess plainly that events have controlled me."[1]

He did not seek the war, but understood that there were worse things than war. Victory over the South came at an enormous cost to the nation. About 600,000 Americans lost their lives out of a population of 31 million — about equal to American battle deaths in all of its other wars combined. One-quarter of the South's white male population of military age were killed or injured. While the total value of Northern wealth rose 50 percent during the 1860s, Southern wealth declined by 60 percent.[2]

The human cost weighed heavily upon Lincoln, but it was necessary to atone for the wrong of slavery. "Fondly do we hope, fervently do we pray, that this mighty scourge of war may speedily pass away," Lincoln wrote in his Second Inaugural Address. "Yet, if God wills that it continue until all the wealth piled by the bondsman's two hundred and fifty years of unrequited toil shall be sunk, and until every drop of blood drawn with the lash shall be paid by another drawn with the sword," he continued, "as was said three thousand years ago, so still it must be said 'the judgments of the Lord are true and righteous altogether.'"[3] One of the lives lost would be Lincoln's — the first President to be assassinated.

Lincoln's greatness is inextricably linked to his broad vision of presidential power. He invoked his authority as Commander-in-Chief and Chief Executive to conduct war, initially without congressional permission, when many were unsure whether secession meant war. He considered the entire South the field of battle, and read his powers to attack anything that helped the Confederate war effort. While he depended on congressional support for the men and material to win the conflict, Lincoln made critical decisions on tactics, strategy, and policy without input from the legislature. The most controversial was the Emancipation Proclamation. Only Lincoln's broad interpretation of his Commander-in-Chief authority made that sweeping step of freeing the slaves possible.

Some have argued that part of Lincoln's tragedy is that he had to exercise unconstitutional powers in order to save the Union. In their classic studies of the Presidency, Arthur M. Schlesinger called Lincoln a "despot," and both Edward Corwin and Clinton Rossiter considered Lincoln to have assumed a "dictatorship."[4] These views echo arguments made during the Civil War itself, even by Republicans who believed that the Constitution could not address such an unprecedented conflict. Lincoln surely claimed that he could draw on power beyond the Constitution in order to preserve the nation. As he wrote to a Kentucky newspaper editor in 1864, "Was it possible to lose the nation, and yet preserve the Constitution?" To Lincoln, common sense supplied the answer: "By general law life and limb must be protected; yet often a limb must be amputated to save a life; but a life is never wisely given to save a limb." Necessity could justify unconstitutional acts. "I felt that measures, otherwise unconstitutional, might become lawful, by becoming indispensable to the preservation of the constitution, through the preservation of the nation."[5]

Lincoln, however, was no dictator. While he used his powers more broadly than any previous President, he was responding to a crisis that threatened the very life of the nation. He flirted with the idea of a Lockean prerogative, but his actions drew upon the same mix of executive authorities that had supported Washington, Jefferson, and Jackson. He relied on his power as Commander-in-Chief to give him control over decisions ranging from tactics and strategy to Reconstruction policy. Like his predecessors, Lincoln interpreted his constitutional duty to execute the laws, his role as Chief Executive, and his presidential oath as grants of power to use force, if necessary, against those who opposed the authority of the United States. Lincoln understood "my oath to preserve the constitution to the best of my ability, imposed upon me the duty of preserving, by every indispensable means, that government — that nation — of which that constitution was the organic law."[6] It seems clear that Lincoln believed that the Constitution vested him with sufficient authority to handle secession and Civil War without the need to resort to Jefferson's prerogative.

Lincoln refused to believe that the Constitution withheld the power for its own self-preservation. Rather than seek a greater power outside the law to protect the nation, he found it in the Chief Executive Clause. That gave Lincoln the authority to decide that secession justified military coercion, and the wide range of measures he took in response: raising an army, invasion and blockade of the South, military government of captured territory, suspension of the writ of habeas corpus, and tough internal security measures. Lincoln consistently maintained that he had not sought the prerogative, but that the Constitution gave him unique war powers to respond to the threat to the nation's security. Lincoln's political rhetoric invoked Jefferson, but his constitutional logic followed Hamilton.

Perhaps the most important defense to the charge of dictatorship is that the normal political process operated in the North throughout the war. An opposition party continued to challenge Lincoln's wartime policies, and regular elections were held in the states and national governments, with the crucial 1864 election giving voters a choice between more of Lincoln's war or a cessation of hostilities. While the administration took vigorous, sometimes extreme, steps to prevent assistance to the Confederacy from behind the lines, it refused to interfere with the normal workings of politics at home. Full-throated competition for elections and debate over the war continued between Republicans and Democrats, to the point where Lincoln worried that he would have to hand over the Presidency to his opponent, retired General George McClellan.

Throughout the war, the institutions of government kept their

characteristic features. Congress controlled the power of the purse
and initiated most domestic policies, such as the Homestead Act, a
protective tariff, land grant colleges, and subsidies for railroad construction. Lincoln followed a hands-off approach on domestic priorities and disclaimed any right to veto laws because of disagreements
on policy. He rarely interfered with legislation, often consulted with
members of Congress in making important appointments, and displayed little interest in the work of agencies with domestic responsibilities.[7] He was profoundly aware that members of Congress and
his cabinet enjoyed many more years of public service and experience
than he. Initially, he spoke in the language of deference to Congress
and sought its ex post approval of his actions at the start of the war.

Nonetheless, Lincoln was not reluctant to disturb relations with
the other branches of government in pursuit of his war aims. From
the very beginning, he had set the stage to make it difficult, if not
impossible, for Congress to reverse his initial military decisions. He
excluded Congress from important war policies and vetoed early
congressional efforts to dictate the course of Reconstruction. But
Lincoln could not rule out all congressional participation in the war.
Congress's cooperation was critical to any sustained war effort, for it
alone controlled taxing and spending, the size and shape of the military, economic mobilization, and the regulation of domestic society.
Lincoln did not refuse to obey any congressional laws, but he maintained his independent right to act in areas of executive competence,
such as the management of the war, and to act concurrently with
Congress in areas that might usually be thought to rest within the
legislature's purview. Lincoln, not Congress, decided the goals of the
war, the terms of the peace, and the means to win both.

Lincoln's attitude toward the judiciary is even more at odds with
today's conventional wisdom. He lost confidence in the courts after
Dred Scott v. Sanford, which recognized slave ownership as a prop-

erty right and made it unconstitutional for Congress to restrict slavery's spread in the territories.[8] Challenging the legitimacy of *Dred
Scott* defined the young Republican Party. In his famous, losing
debates with Stephen Douglas, Lincoln rose to national prominence
by arguing that *Dred Scott* applied only to the parties in the case.
In other words, the Supreme Court's decisions could not bind the
President or Congress, who had the right to interpret the Constitution too, or most importantly, the people. "I do not deny that such
decisions may be binding in any case, upon the parties to a suit, as
to the object of that suit," Lincoln explained in his First Inaugural
Address. Decisions of the Court should receive "very high respect
and consideration in all parallel cases by all other departments of
government." It might even be worth following erroneous decisions
at times because the costs of reversing them might be high. But "if
the policy of the government, upon vital questions, affecting the
whole people, is to be irrevocably fixed by decisions of the Supreme
Court," Lincoln argued, "the people will have ceased to be their own
rulers, having to that extent practically resigned their government
into the hands of that eminent tribunal."[9]

Lincoln laid the foundations of his Presidency on a vigorous
and dynamic view of his right to advance an alternative vision of
the Constitution. If Lincoln and the Republican Party had accepted
the supremacy of the judiciary's interpretation of the Constitution,
Dred Scott would have foreclosed their core position that the federal
government should stop the spread of slavery. Likewise, Lincoln's
Presidency could not have achieved its successes without a proac-
tive exercise of his constitutional powers. A passive attitude that
conceded to Congress the leading role in setting policy, or one that
waited on the Supreme Court to decide matters, would have led to a
sundered nation or military disaster. Lincoln became America's sav-
ior because he preserved the Union, freed the slaves, and launched a

new birth of freedom. He set in motion a political, social, and economic revolution, but one that had the conservative goal of restoring the nation's constitutional system of government. He could have achieved none of this without a broad vision of his office.

Waging War

ONE OF LINCOLN'S most remarkable exercises of presidential authority often goes unremarked. His decision that secession was unconstitutional and that the Union could oppose it by force was fundamental to the beginning of the Civil War. Today, most accept Lincoln's view, but they forget that the Constitution does not explicitly address the question, nor does it spell out who has the right to decide it. In today's environment of judicial supremacy, we have grown accustomed to the idea that constitutional questions are for the Supreme Court to decide. The Court, however, would not reach the question of secession until the Civil War had ended.[10]

One need only contrast Lincoln's approach to that of his predecessor, James Buchanan, usually thought to be the nation's worst President. The South had ensured Lincoln's election by walking out of the Democratic convention and nominating its own candidate for the Presidency, sitting Vice President John Breckinridge. Senator Douglas, who became the nominee of the Democratic Party in the North, took the position that the people of each territory should decide the slavery question for themselves — the doctrine of popular sovereignty. This was not good enough for Southern Democrats, who wanted Congress to enact a code making slavery sacrosanct throughout the territories. When it became clear that Lincoln had won, South Carolina led the Deep South toward secession.

Buchanan believed that secession was illegal but that he lacked the constitutional authority to stop it. In the waning days of his administration, his Attorney General concluded that the executive only had authority to defend federal property, and that he could not call in the militia to enforce federal law because no federal law enforcement officials remained in the South. The Constitution gave neither the President nor Congress, the Attorney General's opinion reasoned, the power to "make war" against the seceding states to restore the Union.[11] In his December 1860 annual message to Congress, Buchanan blamed the crisis on Northern agitation to overturn slavery. Even though the South could not secede, he could not "make war against a State," leaving the federal government powerless.[12] After the rest of the Deep South seceded and formed the Confederate States of America, Buchanan again declared that the executive power did not include the use of force against a state, and humbly requested that Congress, "the only human tribunal under Providence possessing the power to meet the existing emergency," do something.[13] Buchanan's narrow understanding of the constitutional powers of the office meant that the federal government was helpless before the greatest threat to the nation in its history.

Lincoln understood that the Constitution empowered him to do much more than issue a polite invitation that the South return home. The Confederacy made his case easier by seizing federal property and attacking Fort Sumter first. He had no need to address Calhoun's nullification arguments, or even those of Jefferson and Madison against the Alien and Sedition Acts, that states had a right to resist obviously unconstitutional actions by the federal government. The Confederate States were frustrating the constitutional system and denying the results of nationwide democratic elections. They had seceded from a national government that had yet to pass any law prohibiting slavery in the territories or the South itself. In his First Inaugural Address, Lincoln promised not to interfere with the bargain reached in the Constitution that the Southern states could decide on slavery as a matter of their own "domestic institutions." He construed his constitutional duty to execute the law to require him to enforce the Fugitive Slave Clause and refrain from any interference "with the institution of slavery in the States where it exists."[14]

Secession, however, was an unconstitutional response to his election by the democratic process. Echoing Jackson, Lincoln declared that the Union, as a nation, was perpetual. It preexisted the Constitution; it preexisted the Articles of Confederation. Even the Constitution recognized this fact by providing, in its Preamble, for a more perfect Union. Because secession was illegal, Lincoln reasoned, the Southern states were still part of the nation, and "the Union [was] unbroken."

Resistance to federal law and institutions was the work not of the states themselves, but a conspiracy of rebels who were illegally obstructing the normal operations of the national government. The Constitution called upon Lincoln to use force, if necessary, against these rebels in order to see "that the laws of the Union be faithfully executed in all the States." Though on a much greater scale, the Civil War triggered the same presidential power invoked by Washington during the Whiskey Rebellion and Jefferson during the Embargo. Lincoln did not believe he had any choice; the Constitution required him to put down the rebellion. "You have no oath registered in Heaven to destroy the government," Lincoln told the South, "while I shall have the most solemn one to 'preserve, protect and defend' it."[15]

Where Buchanan and previous Presidents found only constitutional weakness, Lincoln discovered constitutional strength. He patiently maneuvered circumstances so that Jefferson Davis's troops would fire the first shot. Federal officials who sympathized with the Confederacy handed over armories, treasuries, and property, but federal installations in several ports remained in Union hands. Fort

Sumter in Charleston Harbor held symbolic importance as a flash-point again, just as it did during the nullification crisis.

On April 4, 1861, exactly one month into his term, Lincoln ordered the navy to resupply the Union fort and to use force only if fired upon. Jefferson Davis ordered bombing to begin before the ships could arrive, and Union forces surrendered on April 14. Lincoln did not consult Congress, which was not in session, nor did he call Congress into session, as he could "on extraordinary Occasions" under the Constitution. He did not launch offensive operations against the South, but he placed American forces in harm's way, which carried a strong risk of starting a war between the states.

The North was woefully unprepared. Its small army was deployed primarily along the Western frontiers; its navy had only a few warships ready for action in American waters.[16] After the fall of Fort Sumter, Lincoln sprung to action. On April 16, he declared a state of rebellion and called forth 75,000 state troops under the Militia Act. He proclaimed that groups in the South were obstructing the execution of federal law beyond the ability of courts and federal officials to overcome.

Lincoln's proclamation prompted the upper Southern states to secede, led by Virginia. The President issued a call for volunteers, increased the size of the regular army, and ordered the navy to enlist more sailors and purchase additional warships. He also removed millions from the Treasury for military recruitment and pay. Article I, Section 8 of the Constitution expressly vests in Congress the power to raise an army and navy and to fund them; the President has no authority to exercise either power.

Lincoln put the army and navy to immediate use. He ordered a blockade of Southern ports and dispatched troops against rebel-held territory. Lincoln called Congress into special session but, significantly, not until July 4. While of obvious symbolic importance, the

July 4 date ensured that the executive branch, not Congress, would set initial war policy. Lincoln had three months to establish a status quo that would be difficult for Congress to change. This was remarkable leadership for a President who had been the underdog to win his party's nomination, who had not won a majority of the popular vote, whose cabinet was filled with men with far more distinguished records of public service, and who did not have close relationships with the congressional leaders of his party.

Rapid events forced Lincoln to exercise broad authorities on defense as well as offense. Maryland was a slaveholding state, and the state legislature and most city officers were pro-Confederacy. If it seceded the nation's capital would be utterly isolated. Mobs in Baltimore attacked the first military units from Massachusetts and Pennsylvania to reinforce the capital, and rebel sympathizers cut the telegraph and railroad lines to Washington.

Lincoln interpreted his constitutional powers to give him the initiative in responding to the emergency. On April 27, 1861, he unilaterally suspended the writ of habeas corpus on the route from Philadelphia to Washington and replaced civilian law enforcement with military detention without trial. Suspension prevented rebel spies and operatives detained by the military from petitioning the civilian courts for release. The Constitution surely describes this power in the passive tense: "The privilege of the writ of habeas corpus shall not be suspended, unless when in cases of rebellion or invasion the public safety may require it." But it is located in Article I, which enumerates Congress's powers and its limits. But Congress would not meet until July 4. Had Lincoln seized the powers of another branch?

A case presented Chief Justice Roger Taney, Jackson's Attorney General and author of *Dred Scott*, with the perfect opportunity to answer this question. Union officers arrested John Merryman, an officer in a secessionist Maryland militia, for participating in the destruction of the railroads near Baltimore. Upon the petition of Merryman's lawyer, Taney issued a writ of habeas corpus ordering the commander of Union forces in Maryland to produce Merryman in court.[17] The general refused to appear and instead sent an aide to notify Taney that Merryman had been detained under the President's suspension of habeas. Taney held the general in contempt, but the marshal serving the order could not gain entry to Fort McHenry.

Taney was left to issue an opinion, which sought to pull the heart out of Lincoln's energetic response to secession. He held that the Suspension Clause's placement in Article I, and judicial commentary since ratification, recognized that only Congress could suspend the writ. If military detention without trial were permitted to continue, Taney wrote, "the people of the United States are no longer living under a government of laws." Under presidential suspension, "every citizen holds life, liberty and property at the will and pleasure of the army officer in whose military district he may happen to be found."[18] Taney's opinion clearly questioned the legal bases for Lincoln's other responses to secession. Beyond suspending habeas corpus, he wrote, the Lincoln administration "has, by force of arms, thrust aside the judicial authorities and officers to whom the constitution has confided the power and duty of interpreting and administering the laws, and substituted a military government in its place, to be administered and executed by military officers."[19]

Merryman was not just an attack on Lincoln's suspension of the writ, but upon the President's right to interpret the Constitution. Taney declared that it was the responsibility of "that high officer, in fulfillment of his constitutional obligation" under the Take Care Clause to enforce the Court's orders. It was another declaration of judicial supremacy in interpreting the Constitution, to be expected of the Justice who had written *Dred Scott*, though perhaps not from Jackson's Attorney General. Taney wanted to dramatize the conflict

between the President and the judiciary. He appeared before a crowd
of 2,000 on the Baltimore courthouse steps to receive the commanding general's response, and declared that the officer was defying the law
and that even the Chief Justice might soon be under military arrest.[20]

Lincoln answered Taney, and the widespread claims of executive dictatorship, in his message to the July 4 session of Congress.
Lincoln stressed that the Confederacy had fired the first shot before
the national government had taken any action that might threaten
slavery. Secession attacked only the process of "time, discussion, and
the ballot box." In response, "no choice was left but to call out the
war power of the Government; and so to resist force, employed for
its destruction, by force, for its preservation." He recited the litany
of actions that followed: calling out the militia, the blockade, the
call for volunteers, the expansion of military spending. Lincoln
claimed that he had moved forcefully with the support of public
opinion. "These measures, whether strictly legal or not, were ventured upon, under what appeared to be a popular demand, and a
public necessity; trusting, then as now, that Congress would readily
ratify them."

Lincoln avoided the question of whether he had acted unconstitutionally. He sought justification from Congress's political support,
after the fact. "It is believed that nothing has been done beyond the
constitutional competency of Congress." Congress enacted a statute
that did not explicitly authorize war against the South, but declared
that Lincoln's actions "respecting the army and navy of the United
States, and calling out or relating to the militia or volunteers from
the States, are hereby approved and in all respects legalized and made
valid," as if "they had been issued and done" by Congress.[21] Congress
gave approval through its explicit control over the size and funding
of the military but did not seek to direct Lincoln's war aims or the
conduct of hostilities.

It would be a year and a half before the Supreme Court considered the constitutionality of Lincoln's immediate actions. *The Prize Cases* presented a demand for damages by the owners of several vessels seized by the Union blockade in the summer of 1861. They argued that international law limited blockades only to wars between nations, which conflicted directly with Lincoln's theory that the Confederacy was only a conspiracy of lawbreakers. If the Civil War were a war, the plaintiffs continued, Lincoln could not act without a declaration of war from Congress first.

A 5–4 majority of the Court upheld Lincoln's actions, with or without congressional authorization. It began by endorsing Lincoln's initial judgment that secession had begun an insurrection, not a war with a separate nation. They also agreed that the scope of the insurrection nevertheless granted the United States the rights and powers of war against a belligerent nation. "[I]t is not necessary to constitute war, that both parties should be acknowledged as independent nations or sovereign States. A war may exist where one of the belligerents claims sovereign rights as against the other."[22] Even though the South would never be recognized as a nation by the United States, the very nature of the conflict required that it be recognized as war, rather than as a matter for the criminal justice system. "When the party in rebellion occupy and hold in a hostile manner a certain portion of territory; have declared their independence; have cast off their allegiance; have organized armies; have commenced hostilities against their former sovereign, the world acknowledges them as belligerents, and the contest a *war*."[23] Lincoln's imposition of a blockade on Southern ports, though legal under international law only against another nation, was a legitimate exercise of war power under the Constitution.

The Court found that Lincoln did not need a declaration of war to respond to the attack on Fort Sumter. "If a war be made by invasion of a foreign nation, the President is not only authorized but bound to resist force by force. He does not initiate the war, but is bound to accept the challenge without waiting for any special legislative authority."[24] It did not matter whether the attacker was a foreign nation or a seceding state. The firing on Fort Sumter constituted an act of war against which the President automatically had authority to use force. "And whether the hostile party be a foreign invader, or States organized in rebellion, it is none the less a war, although the declaration of it be '*unilateral*.'" The Court expressly declared that the scope and nature of the military response rested within the hands of the executive. "Whether the President in fulfilling his duties, as Commander-in-Chief, in suppressing an insurrection, has met with such armed hostile resistance, and a civil war of such alarming proportions as will compel him to accord to them the character of belligerents, is a question to be decided *by him*."

Judicial review would not extend to the President's decisions on whether to consider the Civil War a war, and what type of military response to undertake. Justice Grier wrote for the majority, "this Court must be governed by the decisions and acts of the political department of the Government to which this power was entrusted." The Justices only entertained the need for legislative approval as a hypothetical to buttress its conclusion, and never held that Congress's approval was necessary as a constitutional matter. "If it were necessary to the technical existence of a war, that it should have a legislative sanction, we find it in almost every act passed at the extraordinary session of the Legislature of 1861, which was wholly employed in enacting laws to enable the Government to prosecute the war with vigor and efficiency."[25] Both the courts and Congress vindicated Lincoln's constitutional position of the early days of the war.

We tend to focus on these early presidential acts because they raise questions of the gravest moment — presidential power to act even in areas of clear congressional authority during emergency.

What is sometimes forgotten is how quickly Lincoln took direction of the Union's response. In addition to deciding the fundamental question that secession was illegal, Lincoln managed the events following his election to put the South in a difficult position. He made the decision, announced in his First Inaugural Address, that the Union would keep all federal installations and bases, and he made the call that Fort Sumter would be resupplied.

Lincoln did not consult with Congress whether to seek a political compromise, or whether to let the South go its own way. This is striking not just in light of Buchanan's narrow view of presidential power, but also the history of negotiations between the North and South over slavery. Congress had passed the Missouri Compromise of 1820; the Compromise of 1850, which admitted California as a free state, allowed slavery in the other territory conquered from Mexico, and enacted the Fugitive Slave Law; and the Kansas-Nebraska Act of 1854, which allowed "popular sovereignty" to decide on slavery in the Kansas and Nebraska territories. Henry Clay, Daniel Webster, and Stephen Douglas crafted the agreements; Presidents played bystanders with little influence. Congress's superior role turned on its sole constitutional powers to regulate the territories and to admit new states to the Union, but it also took advantage of presidential weakness during much of the antebellum period.

Imagine what might have happened had Congress assumed the lead in the period between Lincoln's election and his inauguration. In early December, the House of Representatives established a committee of 33, with one member for each state, while the Senate named Senators Stephen Douglas, Jefferson Davis, John Crittenden, and William Seward to a committee of 13, to reach a deal on slavery. The Crittenden Compromise, as it became known, would have revived the Missouri Compromise line and absolutely protected slavery where it existed. The House committee proposed an unamendable constitutional amendment that would prohibit federal interference with slavery in the states.

Although he seemed aloof from the political horse-trading, Lincoln scuttled the whole affair. While still in Springfield, Illinois, he wrote to Republican legislators: "Let there be no compromise on the question of *extending* slavery. If there be, all our labor is lost." Lincoln welcomed a split sooner rather than later: "The tug has to come, & better now, than any time hereafter."[26] It is true, as historians have concluded, that the North went to war in 1861 with conservative goals in mind: the restoration of the Union as it was, which allowed slavery to exist in the South. At the same time, that system contained the mechanism — control over slavery in the territories — that allowed Lincoln to keep faith with his moral commitment to end slavery. Lincoln was unwilling to give up the fruits of electoral victory, and the workings of constitutional democracy, to reach a settlement between North and South.[27]

Lincoln displayed presidential initiative not just when the war came, but after. He exercised clear command over the generals and often urged Union forces to attack while his subordinates preferred more time for training and organization. After the defeat at the first Battle of Bull Run in July 1861, Lincoln began to intervene in military decisions. He replaced General McDowell with General McClellan, and in November 1861 he removed General John Fremont for his conduct in the Department of the West.[28]

The burdens of the command fell heavily on Lincoln, especially as Union casualties soared. Nonetheless, he urged the overcautious McClellan to use his growing Army of the Potomac to move south, and he removed and reinstated generals until he found the ones — Ulysses S. Grant and William Tecumseh Sherman — who agreed with his strategy of going on the offensive. Lincoln's frustrations with his generals fill history books. It was Lincoln who approved the broader strategy to control the Mississippi River and divide the Confederacy in two, and it was Lincoln who saw, earlier than most generals, that the war would become a war of attrition where Northern resources would overwhelm a South with no industrial base and a small population.

Lincoln did not seek congressional involvement in the strategic decisions about the war. Congress's main job was to supply the resources needed to win on the battlefield, a task it performed far more effectively than its Southern counterpart. Taxes were raised, bonds were sold, a federal bank reestablished, paper currency introduced, and money spent (the federal budget increased by 700 percent in the first year of the war).[29] Hundreds of thousands of soldiers were trained, equipped, and organized into units, and once on the front they were fed and supplied far better than the enemy.

The Senate established a Committee on the Conduct of the War that became a forum for investigation and criticism of Lincoln's commanders, especially those perceived to be too cautious, and for praise of those willing to take aggressive measures. Lincoln and his second Secretary of War, Edwin Stanton, did nothing to shield the generals from congressional criticism, but instead seemed to see it as a welcome prod to McClellan and his fellow West Pointers.[30] Beyond its oversight function, however, Congress played little significant role in setting war policy or strategy. As Phillip Paludan has written, "Congress left most decisions on the fighting to the generals, the secretary of war, and the president."[31] Military strategist Eliot Cohen has shown that the development of Civil War strategy was largely a process of civilian struggle for control of the military, which boiled down to a contest between Lincoln and his generals.[32]

Throughout the war, Lincoln stayed in close contact with Grant and Sherman, reviewed their movements, and continued to suggest different strategies. He asked Francis Lieber, an expert on the laws of war at Columbia University, to draft the first modern code on the rules of warfare, and he issued it as General Orders No. 100 in April 1863. He did not ask Congress to enact it by statute. Upon learning that Confederate troops had executed surrendering black soldiers and their white officers, he threatened retaliatory action.[33] But perhaps no military policy was as far-reaching as the decision to emancipate the slaves, a measure he executed solely under his authority as Commander-in-Chief.[34]

In the first years of the war, Radical Republicans in Congress had kept up a drumbeat of criticism against Lincoln for not immediately ending slavery. In 1861, Lincoln reversed General Fremont's emancipation order in Missouri, and the following year he overturned General Hunter's freeing of slaves in Georgia, Florida, and South Carolina. Lincoln was concerned about keeping the loyalty of the slaveholding border states, especially Kentucky, the third most populous slave state and occupant of a strategic position in the Western theatre.[35] Lincoln reportedly said that he hoped for God's support, but he needed Kentucky's.[36]

Whether the federal government even had the power to abolish slavery remained unresolved. As he had proclaimed in his First Inaugural Address, Lincoln believed that slavery's preservation was a matter of state law and that the federal government had no power to touch it where it already existed. Emancipation might qualify as the largest taking of private property in American history, for which the government would owe just compensation under the Fifth Amendment. Another question that remained unclear was whether the United States had the right as a belligerent, under the laws of war, to free slaves. A nation at war generally had the right to seize enemy property when necessary to achieve its military goals, but it also could not, as an occupying power, simply take all property held by private citizens.[37]

As the conflict deepened, Lincoln's view on whether to order emancipation as a military measure underwent significant change. He had overturned Generals Fremont and Butler because their proclamations were essentially political — they sought to free all slaves in their territories, even those unconnected to the fighting. When General Benjamin Butler in Virginia declared that slaves that escaped to Union lines were "contraband" property that could be kept by the Union, Lincoln let the order stand.[38] Congress urged a more radical approach by enacting two Confiscation Acts: the first deprived rebels of ownership of their slaves put to work in the war; the second freed the slaves encountered by Union forces. Because both laws required an individual hearing before a federal judge before a slave could be freed, neither had much practical effect.[39]

Of greater impact was the July 1862 Militia Act, which freed the slave of any rebel, if that slave joined the U.S. armed forces.[40] On August 25, 1862, Secretary of War Stanton authorized the raising of the first 5,000 black troops for the Union army. As the war grew increasingly difficult, Lincoln became convinced that emancipation would be a valuable weapon for the Union cause. It would undermine the Confederacy's labor force and economy while providing a much-needed pool of recruits for the Union armies.

As the cost of the war in blood and treasure became ever dearer, demands for an end to slavery grew louder in the North. At the same time, the border states rejected proposals for gradual emancipation paid for by the federal government. By late July 1862, Lincoln had a draft proclamation of emancipation ready and had notified his cabinet, which advised him to wait for a Union victory. Antietam provided Lincoln the moment.

While Union casualties were steep (6,000 dead and 17,000 wounded — up to that point the most American casualties ever suffered in a single day), the Army of the Potomac had forced the Confederate army from the field. On September 22, 1862, five days after the battle, Lincoln issued the Emancipation Proclamation as President and Commander-in-Chief. It declared that all slaves in areas under rebellion as of January 1, 1863, "shall be then, thenceforward, and forever free; and the executive government of the United States, including the military and naval authority thereof, will recognize and maintain the freedom of such persons."[41] Lincoln stated his intention to ask Congress for compensation for the loyal slave states that voluntarily adopted emancipation and for Southerners who lost slaves but remained loyal to the Union.

The President remained clear that the war was not about slavery, but "for the object of practically restoring the constitutional relation between" the United States and the rebel states. Nevertheless, his proclamation freed 2.9 million slaves, 75 percent of all slaves in the United States and 82 percent of the slaves in the Confederacy.[42] On January 1, 1863, Lincoln issued the final Emancipation Proclamation, "by virtue of the power in me vested as Commander-in-Chief, of the Army and Navy of the United States in time of actual armed rebellion against the authority and government of the United States." The President rooted the constitutional justification for the Emancipation Proclamation as "a fit and necessary war measure for suppressing said rebellion."[43]

Lincoln's dependence on his constitutional authority explains the Proclamation's careful boundaries. He did not free any slaves in the loyal states, nor did he seek to remake the economic and political order of Southern society. Lincoln never claimed a broad right to end slavery. Rather, the Emancipation Proclamation was an exercise of the President's war power to undertake measures necessary to defeat the enemy.

With the cost of war in both men and money rising steeply, emancipation became a means to the end of restoring the Union. Shortly before issuing the preliminary Proclamation, Lincoln wrote

to Republican newspaper editor Horace Greeley, and through him
to a broad readership, that his goal was to restore "the Union as it
was." Emancipation was justified only so far as it helped achieve victory. "My paramount object in this struggle *is* to save the Union, and
is *not* either to save or to destroy slavery," Lincoln wrote. "If I could
save the Union without freeing *any* slave I would do it, and if I could
save it by freeing *all* the slaves I would do it; and if I could save it by
freeing some and leaving others alone I would also do that."[44]

After he issued the Proclamation, Lincoln made clear that the
Commander-in-Chief Clause allows measures based on military
necessity that would not be legal in peacetime. Responding to critics of the Proclamation's constitutionality from his home state, he
admitted that "I certainly wish that all men could be free, while I
suppose you do not." Still, emancipation was a valid war measure.
"I think the constitution invests its Commander-in-Chief, with the
law of war, in time of war," he wrote. Anything that belligerents
could lawfully do in wartime, therefore, fell within the President's
authority.

There was no question in Lincoln's mind that taking the enemy's property was a legitimate policy in war. "Armies, the world over,
destroy enemies' property when they cannot use it; and even destroy
their own to keep it from the enemy." "Civilized belligerents do all
in their power to help themselves, or hurt the enemy, except a few
things regarded as barbarous or cruel," such as the massacre of prisoners or noncombatants. Lincoln would consider anything permitted by the laws of war.

Emancipation did not just deny the South a vital resource, but
it also provided black soldiers for the war effort. Lincoln claimed
that Union generals "believe the emancipation policy, and the use
of colored troops, constitute the heaviest blow yet dealt to the rebellion."[45] Black soldiers saved the lives and energies of white soldiers,

and indeed, the lives and rights of white civilians. "You say you will not fight to free negroes," Lincoln wrote. "Some of them seem willing to fight for you." But he closed by emphasizing again that emancipation was not the goal, but the means. When the war ended, "it will have been proved that, among free men, there can be no successful appeal from the ballot to the bullet; and that they who take such appeal are sure to lose their case, and pay the cost." When that day comes, Lincoln promised, "there will be some black men who can remember that, with silent tongue, and clenched teeth, and steady eye, and well-poised bayonet," they helped achieve victory.

The Emancipation Proclamation is usually studied as a question of the war powers of the national government, though it has also been studied as a question of whether it amounted to a taking of property requiring compensation.[46] What is sometimes neglected is that the Proclamation was a startling demonstration of the constitutional powers of the Presidency. Lincoln decided that military necessity justified emancipation. The Supreme Court did not reach the question of the wartime confiscation of property until after the war, when it upheld the seizure, transfer, and destruction of private property that supported the enemy's ability to carry on hostilities.[47] While Congress passed the two Confiscation Acts, it required individual hearings proving that a slave's owner was engaged in the rebellion or that a slave was being used in the Confederacy's war effort. Lincoln freed the slaves en masse and bypassed the painstaking judicial procedures established by Congress. The legislature authorized the acceptance of escaped slaves into the Union armed forces, but it remained for the President to organize and deploy in combat the more than 130,000 freedmen who joined the Union armies.

While the Proclamation had a broad scope, it also recognized the limits of presidential power. It only touched those areas, the Southern states, where slaves helped the enemy. It did not reach into the institution of slavery in the loyal states. Emancipation would no longer be a justifiable war measure once the fighting ceased, and it could even be frustrated by the other branches while war continued. Congress might use its own constitutional powers to establish a different regime — a reasonable concern with Democratic successes in the 1862 midterm elections — and allow the states to restore slavery once the war ended.

Lincoln understood that to ensure slavery's permanent end, the states would have to adopt a constitutional amendment making emancipation permanent. Toward the end of the war, he pressed for adoption of a complete prohibition of slavery in what eventually became the Thirteenth Amendment. Ratification made the link between emancipation and democratic rule clear. In June 1864, Congress rejected the amendment, which would be the first since the changes to the Electoral College after the Jefferson-Burr deadlock in 1800.

After resounding Republican victories in the November elections, Lincoln called upon the same lame-duck Congress to ratify the Thirteenth Amendment. "It is the voice of the people now, for the first time, heard upon the question." In a time of "great national crisis," Lincoln said "unanimity of action" was needed, and that required "some deference to the will of the majority, simply because it is the will of the majority."[48] Congress promptly agreed to ratify the amendment even before the new Republican majorities took over.

Lincoln's great political achievement was to meld the original purpose of the war with the new goal of ending slavery. Emancipation of the slaves and restoration of the Union both drew upon Lincoln's belief, expressed in his First Inaugural Address, that the Constitution enshrined a democratic process in which the fundamental decisions were up to the people, as expressed in the ballot box. He tied together the concepts of popular sovereignty and liberty in the Gettysburg Address, reconciling the political structure of the Constitution with the values of the Declaration of Independence.[49]

Lincoln justified the carnage of the battle with the prospect of preserving the "new nation," created by "our fathers," that was "conceived in Liberty, and dedicated to the proposition that all men are created equal." The equality of all men, of course, was not an explicit goal of the Union as established in the Constitution, but instead was recognized by the Declaration. Lincoln called on "us the living" to dedicate themselves "to the great task remaining before us," to ensure "that this nation, under God, shall have a new birth of freedom," and "that government of the people, by the people, for the people, shall not perish from the earth."[50] Restoring the Union now stood for two propositions: the working of popular democracy *and* freedom and equality for all men. Emancipation may have been a policy justified by military necessity, but it became an end of the war as well as a means.

Lincoln's words at Gettysburg illustrated, as perhaps nothing else could, the President's control over national strategy in wartime. When the war began, Lincoln established the limited goal of restoring the Union, and Congress agreed in the Crittenden-Johnson resolutions, which declared that the goal of the war was preservation of the Union, while leaving alone the "established institutions" of slavery in the existing states. Initial military strategy focused on blockading the Confederacy in the East while dividing it in the West through capture of the Mississippi. This "Anaconda" strategy would slowly strangle the South until it came back to its senses and returned to the Union.[51]

By the middle of 1862, stiff Southern resistance had convinced Lincoln that only unconditional surrender could end the war. National goals became both restoration of the Union and, after the Emancipation Proclamation, freedom for all. Strategy shifted to the destruction of Confederate armies in the field and the end of the government in Richmond. Lincoln's declaration that the war sought a new birth of freedom, he believed, would encourage "the army to strike more vigorous blows" by setting an example of the administration "strik[ing] at the heart of the rebellion."[52]

Lincoln rejected Southern peace feelers that only sought a restoration of the Union without emancipation. In response to one Southern effort to open negotiations, which Lincoln suspected were false anyway, the President sent emissaries with instructions that negotiations could only begin after the South accepted the Union and the permanent abandonment of slavery. This "surprise" term went beyond the Emancipation Proclamation, which was limited only to Confederate territory in wartime, and even Lincoln's understanding of the powers of Congress.[53] Jefferson Davis spurned the Northern representatives with the words that "we are not fighting for slavery. We are fighting for Independence — and that, or extermination, we will have."[54] Describing the exchanges later, Lincoln wrote that "between him and us the issue is distinct, simple, and inflexible. It is an issue which can only be tried by war, and decided by victory."[55] Lincoln's control over the conduct of the war had transformed the political goals of the conflict into Union and Liberty, and made the means no longer limited war, but a drive for total victory.

CIVIL LIBERTIES IN WARTIME

THE UNIQUE NATURE of the Civil War forced the Lincoln administration to reduce civil liberties in favor of greater internal security. Unlike a war against a foreign nation, the rebellion was fought against other Americans, and events in Maryland and Missouri showed that parts of Union territory would have to be placed under military rule. The common heritage of the North and South increased the likelihood of irregular guerilla fighting, espionage, and sabotage. Southerners could operate easily behind Union lines and find supporters of their cause. Significant political dissent from Democrats and anti-war opponents worried the administration, which tried to walk a fine line between respecting free speech and the political process and preventing the disloyal from undermining the war effort. Congress did not give its immediate approval to all of Lincoln's actions; it did not enact any law regarding habeas corpus until 1863.

Lincoln initially gave Secretary of State Seward the job of operating an internal security service responsible for detaining those suspected of aiding the Confederacy. His special agents either arrested suspects themselves or asked the military or local police to do so at strategic points in cities, ports, and transportation hubs. Seward even had newspaper editors and state politicians suspected of disloyalty thrown in detention and had the mails opened to search for espionage.[56] Seward boasted to a foreign diplomat that he could "ring a little bell" and have anyone in the country arrested.

Lincoln's domestic policies on detention logically followed those applied to combat. More than 400,000 prisoners were captured in the war by both sides. Under Lincoln's theory that the Southern states were still part of the Union, all of the members of the Confederacy were still American citizens. In war, however, the United States used force to kill and capture Confederate soldiers, destroy Confederate property, and impose martial law on occupied Confederate territory. Prisoners had no right to a jury trial, and Confederate civilians had neither a right to sue for damages for destroyed property nor a right to immediately govern themselves. Occupied Confederate states would have no right to send Senators and Representatives to Congress once Union control had returned.

The normal process of law could not handle the unique nature of the rebellion. Confederate leaders, for example, were being detained not because they were guilty of a crime, but because their release would pose a future threat to the safety of the country. What if federal authorities, Lincoln wrote in a letter published in June 1863, could have arrested the military leaders of the Confederacy, such as Generals Breckinridge, Lee, and Johnston, at the start of the war? "Unquestionably, if we had seized and held them, the insurgent cause would be much weaker," Lincoln argued. "But no one of them had then committed any crime defined in the law. Every one of them, if arrested, would have been discharged on *habeas corpus* were the writ allowed to operate."[57] Suspension of the writ made clear that captured Confederates could not seek the benefits of the very civilian legal system that they sought to overthrow.

Lincoln's July 4, 1861, message to the special session of Congress mounted a powerful defense of his suspension of the writ. He argued that his presidential duty called upon him to protect the Constitution first before the decisions of the Supreme Court. "The whole of the laws which were required to be faithfully executed, were being resisted, and failing of execution, in nearly one-third of the States." Saving the Union from a mortal threat, Lincoln suggested, could justify a violation of the Constitution and the laws, and certainly a single provision of them. "Must they be allowed to finally fail of execution, even had it been perfectly clear, that by the use of the means necessary to their execution, some single law, made in such extreme tenderness of the citizen's liberty, that practically, it relieves more of the guilty, than of the innocent, should, to a very limited extent, be violated?" In a famous passage, Lincoln asked, "Are all the laws, *but one*, to go unexecuted, and the government itself go to pieces, lest that one be violated?" He suggested that painstaking attention to the habeas corpus provision would come at the expense of his ultimate constitutional duty — saving the Union. "Even in such a case, would not the official oath be broken, if the government should be overthrown, when it was believed that disregarding the single law, would tend to preserve it?"[58]

Lincoln performed some acrobatics to pull back from a constitutional conflict. It was obvious that the nation indeed was confronted with "rebellion or invasion." Written in the passive voice, the Constitution's habeas corpus provision did not specify which branch had the right to suspend it. Lincoln quickly returned to the need for prompt executive action to address the crisis. "As the provision was plainly made for a dangerous emergency," he wrote, "it cannot be believed the framers of the instrument intended, that in every case, the danger should run its course, until Congress could be called together." A rebellion might even prevent Congress from meeting.

In an opinion issued the next day, Attorney General Edward Bates agreed that the President's duty to execute the laws and uphold the Constitution required him to suppress the rebellion, using the most effective means available. If the rebels sent an army, the President had the discretion to respond with an army. "If they employ spies and emissaries, to gather information, to forward rebellion, he may find it both prudent and humane to arrest and imprison them," Bates wrote. A President must have the ability to suspend habeas in case of an emergency that required him to call out the military, the vagueness of the Suspension Clause notwithstanding. In times of emergency, "the President must, of necessity, be the sole judge, both of the exigency which requires him to act, and of the manner in which it is most prudent for him to employ the powers entrusted to him."[59]

Bates's legal opinion launched a frontal assault on Taney's claim to judicial supremacy in *Merryman*. "To say that the departments of our government are coordinate, is to say that the judgment of one of them is not binding upon the other two, as to the arguments and principles involved in the judgment." Independence required that no

branch could compel another. No court could issue a writ requiring compliance by the President, just as no President could order a
court how to decide a case. Bates's opinion ventured even further
than Lincoln's view on *Dred Scott*, which he agreed to enforce at
least as to the parties in the case. Bates's claim of the independent
status of each branch implied that the President had no obligation to
obey a court judgment even in that narrow case — a position that the
administration had to adopt because Lincoln had already ignored
Taney's order releasing Merryman.

Bates questioned whether the courts had any competence to
decide questions relating to the war. "[T]he whole subject-matter is
political and not judicial. The insurrection itself is purely political.
Its object is to destroy the political government of this nation and to
establish another political government upon its ruins," the Attorney
General reasoned. "And the President, as the chief civil magistrate
of the nation, and the most active department of the Government,
is eminently and exclusively political, in all his principal functions."
A court, Bates concluded, had no authority to review these political decisions of the President. The Attorney General suggested that
something like the modern political question doctrine applied to
judicial review of the President's wartime decisions. Almost as an
aside, Bates addressed the merits of the constitutional question. He
observed that the Suspension Clause was vague and did not specify
whether Congress alone, or the President too could suspend habeas.
He argued that it was absurd to allow habeas to benefit enemies in
wartime, as it would imply that the enemy could sue for damages
when the Union destroyed their arms and munitions.

In September 1862, the President turned to more aggressive
measures. Military rule had displaced civilian government in areas
touched by the battlefield, in the border states where confederate
irregulars conducted guerilla operations, and in recaptured terri-

tory. Martial law went unmentioned in the Constitution but had been used during the Revolution and the War of 1812, and had even been upheld by Chief Justice Taney in a case involving civil unrest in Rhode Island.[60] Lincoln drew upon his Commander-in-Chief power to impose military rule in areas where fighting or occupation were ongoing.

In a September 24, 1862, proclamation, Lincoln extended military jurisdiction beyond the battlefield to those giving assistance to the enemy behind the lines. He ordered the military to detain anyone within the United States who gave aid or comfort to the rebels, and anyone who resisted the draft or discouraged volunteers from enlisting. Detainees would have no right to seek a writ of habeas corpus and would be tried by courts-martial or military commission, a form of military court used to try the enemy or civilians for violations of the laws of war and to administer justice in occupied territory.[61] Under Lincoln's order, the jurisdiction of the military commissions extended to those suspected of assisting the rebellion or disrupting the war effort well behind the front lines.

Union officials primarily deployed these authorities in or near active hostilities to detain spies and saboteurs. A common use was to capture irregular Confederate forces that were killing Union soldiers and attacking supply trains in states such as Missouri, or to maintain order in recaptured territory such as New Orleans. Civilian processes of justice simply could not handle cases of widespread violence by guerillas and Confederate soldiers in the areas around the front lines. According to existing Union records, the army conducted 4,271 military commission trials during the Civil War. About 55 percent took place in Missouri, Kentucky, and Maryland, border states that saw significant disorder and unrest, with Missouri alone accounting for about 46 percent. Almost all of these cases involved guerrilla activity, horse-stealing, and bridge-burning.[62]

Lincoln ordered the use of military detention and trial in the North, not because it was under direct threat of attack, but because "agitators" were interfering with the North's war effort. Although recent historical work has shown that Union officials did not exercise these authorities as broadly against political activity as some have thought, they did detain and try newspaper editors and politicians who urged disloyalty or opposition to the administration's war measures.[63] The most well-known case was that of Clement Vallandigham, a former member of Congress and Ohio Democrat who was seeking his party's nomination for governor on a peace platform. Union authorities arrested Vallandigham for a speech attacking the war as "wicked, cruel, and unnecessary" because it sought to abolish slavery rather than restore the Union. He made a particular point of attacking "King Lincoln" for depriving Northerners of their civil liberties. A military commission convicted Vallandigham and sentenced him to prison for the rest of the war, but Lincoln altered the sentence to banishment to the Confederacy.

Vallandigham's case became a cause célèbre to Lincoln's opponents in the North, who accused him of wielding dictatorial powers ever since the start of the war. Unlike Merryman, the Ohio Democrat had refrained from any overtly hostile actions against the United States, other than using his right to free speech to criticize the administration's wartime policies. The Supreme Court refused to hear Vallandigham's petition for a writ of habeas corpus because a military commission was not a "court" over which it could exercise review.[64] Its decision effectively removed the federal courts as a check on executive detention while hostilities were ongoing. As political protests erupted, Ohio Democrats nominated Vallandigham for governor on a platform of opposition to executive tyranny.

In a June 12, 1863, public letter to New York Democrats, Lincoln responded that his administration had properly held Vallandigham because the Constitution recognized that military rule was appropriate "when, in cases of rebellion or invasion, the public safety may require." "Under cover of 'liberty of speech,' 'liberty of the press,' and 'habeas corpus,'" Lincoln claimed, the Confederacy "hoped to keep on foot among us a most efficient corps of spies, informers, suppliers, and aiders and abettors of their cause in a thousand ways." Enemies were not just those who took up arms against the Union, but those who attempted to prevent the mobilization of its men and industry. Words could be just as deadly as bullets. "He who dissuades one man from volunteering, or induces one soldier to desert, weakens the Union cause as much as he who kills a Union soldier in battle." In one of his memorable turns of phrase, Lincoln asked: "Must I shoot a simple-minded soldier boy who deserts, while I must not touch a hair of a wily agitator who induces him to desert?"[65]

Arresting civilians for crimes and detaining the enemy in war achieved different goals in different circumstances. "The former is directed at the small percentage of ordinary and continuous perpetration of crime," Lincoln argued, "while the latter is directed at sudden and extensive uprisings against the Government." During war, detention "is more for the preventive and less for the vindictive." He rejected the Democrats' argument that military detention could run only on the battlefield or in occupied territory. Lincoln interpreted the Constitution as allowing suspension of the writ "whenever the public safety" requires, not just in areas of actual combat. Lincoln remained conscious that political speech should not be suppressed. Vallandigham "was not arrested because he was damaging the political prospects of the administration, or the personal interests of the Commanding General, but because he was damaging the Army, upon the existence and vigor of which the life of the Nation depends." Lincoln closed by invoking Andrew Jackson, who, as military governor in New Orleans, arrested a newspaper editor and judge for endangering public order while the city was under threat of British invasion.[66]

Even as Lee's armies marched north toward Pennsylvania, Ohio Democrats sent a letter to Lincoln criticizing his domestic security policies. They claimed that the President treated the Constitution as if it were different during war than peace, and that he had trampled on individual liberties. Lincoln defended his suspension of the writ on the ground that the Constitution did not specify which branch held the authority to suspend. He turned to the basic difference between crime and war. The nature of war required detentions without trial, which "have been for *prevention*, and not for *punishment* — as injunctions to stay injury, as proceedings to keep the peace."

Turning to the rhetorical offensive, Lincoln accused the Ohio Democrats of encouraging resistance to lawful authority by rejecting the legitimacy of military force to restore the Union. "Your own attitude, therefore, encourages desertion, resistance to the draft and the like," Lincoln claimed, "because it teaches those who incline to desert, and to escape the draft, to believe it is your purpose to protect them." Lincoln challenged the Ohio Democrats to agree that a military response to secession was valid, that they should not hinder the efficient operation of the army or navy, and that they should support the troops. They refused, but Lincoln had won the battle (but not the war) for public opinion. He had appealed to more than just military necessity, and he had carefully argued that his exercise of extraordinary powers remained within the Constitution.[67]

Congress waited until March 1863 to approve the President's suspension of habeas corpus.[68] Although some leading Republican and Democratic members of Congress had severe misgivings over the policy, some historians have read Congress's silence as implicit approval of Lincoln's actions. And indeed, the Habeas Corpus Act recognized Lincoln's suspension of the writ, immunized federal officers who detained prisoners, and left untouched executive policy on the detention of prisoners of war and the operations of military commissions.

Others have argued that the Act rebuked Lincoln, because it required the military to provide the courts with lists of prisoners and to allow for their release if they were not indicted by a grand jury. As J. G. Randall has pointed out, these arguments ignore the fact that the Lincoln administration did not change its detention policies in any meaningful way. The military did not interpret the Act to apply to anyone triable by military commission or places where martial law held sway. Vallandigham himself, for example, would not have benefited from the Act. The Secretary of War or the military sometimes simply refused to provide complete lists of prisoners to the federal courts, and it appears that there was no measurable difference in the numbers of civilians arrested or released because of the Act.[69] Randall estimates that the Lincoln administration detained approximately 13,500. Mark Neely puts the number at about 12,600, though the records are incomplete.

Not until the end of the war did the other branches of government truly push back. In *Ex parte Milligan*, the Supreme Court took up the case of an Indiana Peace Democrat who had conspired to raid federal arsenals and prisoner-of-war camps. In December 1864, a military commission convicted Milligan and sentenced him to death, later commuted to life imprisonment.[70] Milligan and his co-conspirators filed for a writ of habeas corpus. In 1866, the Supreme Court overturned the military commission and ordered the release of Milligan.[71] It held that he could not be tried by the military because he was not a resident of a Confederate state, not a prisoner of war, and never a member of the enemy's armed force. He had been captured in Indiana, where the normal civilian courts were open, and there was no showing of a military necessity to try him outside of that system. Only if Indiana had been under attack, and the normal judicial system closed, the Court found, could Milligan be subject to military courts.

Four Justices concurred. They did not take issue with the majority's argument that the military commission lacked jurisdiction, but focused instead on the claim that Congress could have, if it had wanted to, authorized the use of military commissions. Since Congress had not authorized the use of military commissions, they agreed with the Court's outcome. Implicitly, five Justices of the *Milligan* majority rejected Lincoln's argument that military detention could extend to those well behind the front lines who aided the rebellion or sought to interfere with the war effort, and any claim that the Constitution did not operate during the Civil War. The Constitution, the majority declared, "is a law for rulers and people, equally in war and in peace, and covers with the shield of its protection all classes of men, at all times, and under all circumstances."

While *Milligan* is cited today as a ringing endorsement of civil liberties in wartime, it was heavily criticized at the time and sparked a remarkable political response. Congress's authority was not presented in the *Milligan* case, but the majority's desire to reach it, and to answer it in such broad terms, plunged the Court into the maelstrom of Reconstruction politics. *Milligan* suggested that any continuation of military occupation in the South was unconstitutional, and signaled that Republicans would have to count the judiciary among their opponents. "In the conflict of principle thus evoked, the States which sustained the cause of the Union will recognize an old foe with a new face," wrote the *New York Times*. "The Supreme Court, we regret to find, throws the great weight of its influence into the scale of those who assailed the Union and step after step impugned the constitutionality of nearly everything that was done to uphold it."[72] Comparing *Milligan* to *Dred Scott*, *Harper's Weekly* declared that "the decision is not a judicial opinion; it is a political act." The *New York Herald* raised the idea of reforming the Court: "[A] reconstruction of the Supreme Court, adapted to the paramount decisions of the war, looms up into bold relief, on a question of vital importance."[73]

Congress was determined to prevent the Court from ending Reconstruction prematurely. Radical Republicans were already at war with President Johnson, who wanted a quick readmission of the Southern states into the Union. Johnson vetoed bills to deepen Reconstruction policies, citing in part that continued occupation of the South violated *Milligan*. Colonel William McCardle, a Vicksburg newspaper editor held in military detention for virulent denunciation of Union authorities, challenged the constitutionality of Reconstruction. In 1868, to forestall McCardle's challenge, Congress enacted legislation eliminating the Court's jurisdiction to hear appeals from military courts in the South.[74] Only after Johnson's acquittal on impeachment charges, and Grant's election to the Presidency, did the Court announce in 1869 that it accepted the reduction of its jurisdiction and would not reach the merits of the *McCardle* petition. Thus, *Milligan* became the motivating factor that led to the only clear example of congressional jurisdiction-stripping in the Court's history.[75] *Milligan* may be remembered as the Court's resistance to Lincoln's wartime measures, but it also embroiled the Court in national politics of the highest order, and ultimately it led to a severe counterstroke against judicial review.

While Lincoln claimed extraordinary authority over civil liberties during the Civil War, he exercised it in a restrained manner. After examining the records of detentions and military trials, Neely concludes that more were detained than was commonly thought, but that most came from border states near the scene of fighting or

were citizens of the Confederacy. Only a small number of the overall figures could be considered political prisoners.[76] While hostilities
were ongoing, no branch of government opposed Lincoln's internal security program. His administration cooperated at times with
Congress's suspension of the writ, but at times it continued to follow
military policy. Even in its decision after the war, the Supreme Court
did not reverse President Lincoln's suspension of habeas corpus or
the extension of martial law to the areas under occupation or threat
of attack. Its decision left unclear whether its demands for the protection of citizens detained beyond the battlefield would apply to
those actively associated with the enemy.

Historians and political scientists have long criticized Lincoln
for going too far in limiting civil liberties, but no one doubts that he
did so with the best of intentions, in unprecedented circumstances.
Americans were fighting Americans and the mobilization of the
home front held the key to victory. It is easy today, with the benefit of hindsight, to argue that Lincoln went too far.[77] But it is also
impossible to know, either at the time or even now, whether his policies kept the North committed and prevented Southern successes
behind the lines. Lincoln's approach to civil liberties may well have
been an indispensable part of his overall strategy to win the Civil
War, though one that came with a high price.

RECONSTRUCTION

THE CIVIL WAR's hybrid nature as a rebellion on American territory and as a traditional war colored a third major arena of
presidential action — Reconstruction. If the Confederacy were considered an enemy nation, the laws of war permitted the occupation
of recaptured territory. But if the states had never left the Union, as
Lincoln had argued from the beginning, they could have claimed

an immediate restoration of their authority. They could again pass their own laws and run their own courts and police. If the defeated states were automatically restored to the Union, they could exercise their rights in the federal government, including the election of Senators and Representatives. In the unprecedented circumstances of the Civil War, there were no rules for the readmission of rebellious states to the Union or how much authority the national government could exercise in occupied territory.[78]

Lincoln did not hesitate to take the initiative in setting occupation and Reconstruction policy. He believed that the Constitution concentrated in the Commander-in-Chief the rights of a nation at war, and one aspect of the nation's powers under the laws of war was the right to occupy captured territory. The conflict's nature as an insurrection gave him even greater powers. The key feature of the laws of war is to retain as much of the normal civilian governmental structure as is consistent with military necessity. An occupying military may take measures to prevent attacks on its soldiers, but it generally cannot change civil or criminal laws wholesale, and it generally leaves civilian government and its officials in place.[79] But since the United States was waging war to restore its authority over rebellious authority, occupation of Southern territory inevitably involved change not just of local officials, but of the institutions of government.

When territory in Tennessee and Louisiana fell under Northern control in 1862, Lincoln appointed military governors to establish occupation governments. As military governor of Tennessee, Andrew Johnson appointed the Secretary of State, Comptroller General, and Attorney General, as well as Nashville's mayor and city council. Elections were not held, and Tennessee did not exercise the political rights of a state within the federal system. In New Orleans, General Benjamin Butler delivered justice by military commissions, which included executing a man who had torn down the Union flag, and ran the city by decree, such as the infamous "Women's Order," which declared that any woman who showed disrespect to a Union soldier would be considered "as a woman of the town plying her avocation."[80]

Military commanders ordered arrests without warrant or criminal trial; the seizure of land and property for military use; the closure of banks, churches, and businesses; and the suppression of newspapers or political meetings deemed to be disloyal.[81] Military courts were established that enforced law and order among civilians, without effective appeal to federal courts — an arrangement upheld by the Supreme Court after the war, as was the whole system of occupation government.[82] The basic rule of occupation government was the will of the military commander, checked only by his superior officers and ultimately the President. As the Supreme Court observed when it reached cases challenging military government, the occupation was "a military duty, to be performed by the President as Commander-in-Chief, and instructed as such with the direction of the military force by which the occupation was held."[83]

Congress never played a successful role in the operation of the military governments. In 1862, out of discontent with Lincoln's reversal of General Hunter's emancipation order, it considered legislation to treat the Southern states as territories subject to its regulation, but Congress eventually chose to accept Lincoln's policies and put the legislation aside.[84] On the question of the readmission of recaptured states, however, it held a critical constitutional power — that of judging whether to seat members of Congress. Congress, not Lincoln, would control whether any reconstituted Southern state could send Senators and Representatives.

As the war wore on, Radical Republicans in Congress were determined to set a high bar before restoring rebel states to the Union. Lincoln wanted an easier path to peace. His initial promise of returning the "Union as it was" suggested that he would be open to allowing states to return with slavery intact, and for a time, he pursued a similar policy in the loyal border states. Congressional leaders wanted a greater role in Reconstruction and a more radical reshaping of Southern society which included the abolition of slavery. Congress refused to seat representatives sent by Louisiana, but at the same time identified no clear path in the war's first years on the readmission of the states of the Confederacy.

Lincoln seized the initiative in his 1863 annual message, delivered less than a month after the Gettysburg Address. He rejected the idea that a Confederate state would be entitled to automatic readmission to the Union upon occupation. "An attempt to guaranty and protect a revived State government, constructed in whole, or in preponderant part, from the very element against whose hostility and violence it is to be protected," Lincoln observed, "is simply absurd."[85] While setting the terms of political debate, the President paid careful attention to constitutional details.

Lincoln based his right to set the terms for Reconstruction on his plenary power to grant pardons, and the Constitution's provision guaranteeing to every state a "republican form of government." He proposed a plan that required at least 10 percent of a state's voters in the 1860 election to take an oath of loyalty and obedience to the Emancipation Proclamation and Congress's laws against slavery. Lincoln excluded from chances of a pardon all ranking Confederate civilian and military officials, any federal Congressmen or officers who joined the rebellion, or any who had not treated black soldiers as prisoners of war. When a former Confederate state reached the 10 percent requirement, it would be permitted to form a government. In exchange, the reconstructed states would retain their pre-war names, boundaries, constitutions, and laws, so long as they accepted the end of slavery. While Lincoln set out the first plan for Reconstruction, he recognized that only Congress could decide whether to seat the elected Congressmen of the reconstructed states.[86]

Lincoln's plan set relatively easy terms because he wanted to get Louisiana back into the Union as quickly as possible. He hoped Louisiana's example would weaken the resolve of other Southern states and end the war. Republican Congressmen, however, worried that allowing the Southern states to return too soon would lead to the oppression of the black freedmen. They drafted an alternative, the Wade-Davis Bill, which required a state to write a new constitution ending slavery and providing protections to the former slaves.[87] Only those who took an oath of past and future loyalty — known as the "ironclad" oath — could elect delegates to the constitutional convention, and it required 50 percent, rather than Lincoln's 10 percent, of the 1860 voters to take the oath before the state could elect a government. Confederate officeholders and members of the Confederate armed forces could not vote. The bill gave federal officials and judges authority to override state laws that attempted to continue involuntary servitude. Reconstruction under Congress's plan would take longer and require the federal government to play a far more intrusive role in state politics.

As casualties increased in the summer of 1864, Republicans in Congress believed that more, rather than fewer, radical measures were needed. The Wade-Davis Bill passed by healthy majorities. Though he had taken the position that the veto should not be used over policy disagreements, Lincoln resorted to a pocket veto in July 1864 to reject the Wade-Davis Bill. Because Congress had submitted the bill at the end of its session, Lincoln's veto gave Congress no chance to override. Lincoln considered Wade-Davis to be at odds with his theory of the Civil War by treating the Confederate states as if they had left the Union during the rebellion. Wade-Davis, he wrote in an unusual veto message, would have set aside the new constitutions that had been adopted by Arkansas and Louisiana. Nor could Congress ban slavery in the states without a constitutional amendment. When Republican Senator Zachariah Chandler of Michigan responded, at the signing of the other bills passed during the congressional session, that Lincoln had already banned slavery, the President answered: "I conceive that I may in an emergency do things on military grounds which cannot be done constitutionally by Congress."[88] Above all, Lincoln sought flexibility in Reconstruction policy. He was willing to accept the restoration of any state that met Wade-Davis's standards, but he also kept his own approach, which allowed Southern states to reassume their political rights under more lenient standards.

Lincoln's fellow Republicans did not let his pocket veto go unchallenged. The authors of the bill, Senator Benjamin Wade and Congressman Henry Davis, issued a "manifesto" in the *New York Tribune* attacking Lincoln for his "grave Executive usurpation." Congress, not the President, controlled the restoration of the Union. The President's veto to protect his Reconstruction policies violated the separation of powers. "A more studied outrage on the legislative authority of the people has never been perpetrated," they claimed. In words not much different from those of the Democrats who had long accused Lincoln of dictatorship, they portrayed his veto as "a blow…at the principles of republican government" and declared that "the authority of Congress is paramount and must be respected." The President "must confine himself to his executive duties — to obey and execute, not make the laws."[89]

Coming a few months before the 1864 election, the Wade-Davis manifesto gave heart to Lincoln's opponents. Democrats praised the two Republicans "found willing at last to resent the encroachments of the executive on the authority of Congress." It also inspired Republicans who wanted to replace Lincoln. Their electoral fortunes that summer had waned with Union failures to capture Richmond and Atlanta. The future turned so bleak that Lincoln drafted a "Memorandum on Probable Failure of Re-election" for his files. Lincoln believed it "exceedingly probable that this administration will not be re-elected" and declared his duty to "cooperate with the President elect, as to save the Union between the election and the inauguration."[90]

Sherman's capture of Atlanta on September 4, 1864, marked a turnabout in Lincoln's fortunes. Democrats helped by nominating General McClellan as their presidential candidate on a platform that sought a "cessation of hostilities" because of "four years of failure to restore the Union by the experiment of war." Boosted by the fall of Atlanta, Lincoln unified his party by removing his Postmaster General, who was hated by the Radical Republicans, and announcing that he would appoint Chase, whom he had forced to resign as Treasury Secretary for leading the Republican opposition, to the position of Chief Justice.

While Lincoln exerted all his energies to ensure his reelection, he never questioned the importance of holding the elections themselves. "We cannot have free government without elections," he told serenaders after his reelection. "[I]f the rebellion could force us to forego, or postpone a national election, it might fairly claim to have already conquered and ruined us."[91] Lincoln won an overwhelming victory: 55 percent of the vote and 212 electoral votes to 21 for McClellan. His overall share of the popular vote had grown by more than 340,000 votes, and Republicans increased their control of the Senate to 42–10 and the House to 149–42.[92] To Lincoln, the election answered the "grave question whether any government, not *too* strong for the liberties of its people, can be strong *enough* to maintain its own existence, in great emergencies."[93]

Returned to office with a more secure electoral base, Lincoln pursued Reconstruction anew. As David Donald has observed, Lincoln and Congress had very different goals in mind. Lincoln wanted to use Reconstruction to end the fighting. He believed that quickly forming loyal governments in recaptured territory might encourage other Confederate states to rejoin the Union. Radical Republicans, by contrast, were concerned about a host of other issues, such as the continuing strength of the white elites and the economic and political rights of the black freedmen.[94] Reconstruction involved the intersection of executive and legislative powers: The President had the authority as Commander-in-Chief to govern occupied enemy territory and the executive power to pardon rebels; Congress controlled the seating of members of Congress, the rules governing the territories, and the admission of states. Lincoln wanted a quick restoration of the Union; Congress wanted to remake Southern society first.[95]

After his election, Lincoln threatened to veto any congressional effort to deny admission to Louisiana, which had been reconstructed according to his 10 percent plan. While congressional Republicans in 1864 had passed the Wade-Davis Bill, in 1865 they could not override Lincoln's approach. When he first came to the legislature, "this was a Government of law," Congressman Davis exclaimed. "I have lived to see it a Government of personal will."[96] Nevertheless, in a demonstration of the checks that Congress still possessed over executive war policy, Radical Republicans filibustered a Lincoln-supported proposal to admit Louisiana in the spring of 1865. Lincoln had recognized Congress's power in his December 1864 State of the Union message. Some Reconstruction questions, he admitted, "would be beyond the Executive power to adjust; as, for instance, the admission of members of Congress, and whatever might require the appropriation of money."[97]

It was in this political setting that Lincoln delivered one of his greatest speeches, the Second Inaugural Address. He would not venture a prediction for the end of the war, but held "high hope for the future." Lincoln's main purpose was to argue not just for Reconstruction, but reconciliation. It is true, he said, that insurgents had sought to dismember the Union to preserve slavery, which the government could not permit. "Both parties deprecated war; but one of them would *make* war rather than let the nation survive; and the other would *accept* war rather than let it perish. And the war came."

Lincoln avoided placing the blame on individuals or on states. "Neither party expected for the war, the magnitude, or the duration, which it has already attained. Neither anticipated that the *cause* of the conflict might cease with, or even before, the conflict itself should cease." Both sides were guilty of miscalculation. "Each looked for an easier triumph, and a result less fundamental and astounding." He emphasized their common heritage, too. "Both read the same Bible, and pray to the same God; and each invoked His aid against the other." While Lincoln remarked that owning slaves was not his idea of a good Christian — "it may seem strange that any men should dare to ask a just God's assistance in wringing their bread from the sweat of other men's faces" — even there he insisted, "let us judge not that we be not judged."[98]

Lincoln was not interested in assigning responsibility for the amazing costs of the war. He referred to the war almost as an act of God: "All dreaded it — all sought to avert it." He saw it as God's punishment of the nation as a whole for the sin of human slavery. "He gives to both North and South, this terrible war, as the woe due to those by whom the offence came." No one wanted the war to go on. "Fondly do we hope — fervently do we pray — that this mighty scourge of war may speedily pass away." But it would be God, not man, who would decide how long the war must continue to atone for slavery.[99]

If the Civil War was God's judgment upon a sinning nation, Reconstruction should have pursued healing, not retribution. Lincoln's final paragraph is among the most eloquent in American public speeches, and it is a plea for mercy and reconciliation. "With malice toward none; with charity for all; with firmness in the right, as God gives us to see the right," the North should "strive on to finish the work we are in." That work was "to bind up the nation's wounds; to care for him who shall have borne the battle, and for his widow, and his orphan." The goal was to "achieve and cherish a just, and a lasting peace, among ourselves, and with all nations." While the Second Inaugural Address is widely praised for its eloquence, it also explained Lincoln's reasons for a more lenient Reconstruction.

As the Union armies moved closer to victory, Lincoln continued to signal flexibility on his Reconstruction plans. Sherman had captured Savannah by Christmas, and Columbia and Charleston in early 1865, while Grant's steady pressure had forced the Confederate government to abandon Richmond. Lincoln held the upper hand. He was the first President since Andrew Jackson to be reelected, the head of a party that had just won stunning majorities in Congress, with a cabinet staffed with political allies. Nevertheless, as the end of the war approached, his constitutional authority would weaken because the reach of his Commander-in-Chief power would narrow.

After news of Lee's surrender reached Washington, Lincoln used the occasion of an impromptu celebration outside the White House to give a speech on Reconstruction. After giving thanks to God for General Grant's victory, Lincoln declared that the "re-inauguration of the national authority" in the South would be "fraught with great difficulty" and that there was great division in the North about the right policy. He pled again for the quick admission of Louisiana, but in a new sign of flexibility he declared that he would drop his public demands for it. "But as bad promises are better broken than kept," Lincoln said, "I shall treat this as a bad promise, and break it, whenever I shall be convinced that keeping it is adverse to the public interest." Lincoln said he had yet to be convinced, however.[100]

This time, Lincoln did not want to open up the difficult constitutional issues involved. He observed that he had "*purposely* forborne any public expression upon" the question of whether the Southern states had ever left the Union as a matter of constitutional law. Deciding that question, Lincoln now thought, would only distract from the more important goal of restoring those states "into that proper practical relation" with the Union. It would be easier to embark on a quick Reconstruction without deciding whether the Southern states had actually seceded. "Finding themselves safely at home, it would be utterly immaterial whether they had ever been abroad."

Louisiana had met Lincoln's terms and it had adopted a new constitution abolishing slavery. Lincoln admitted that he wished the reconstructed Southern governments had broader popular support and had extended the franchise to the "very intelligent" blacks or those who had served in the war; he clearly hoped that the states would grant the freedmen their political and civil rights without the use of federal power. But the question was whether Louisiana, and the states to follow her, would be restored to the Union "*sooner* by *sustaining*, or by *discarding* her new State Government." It would be better to get a start immediately by nurturing the new state governments into the Union than to ruin the loyal effort in Louisiana. Lincoln also observed that quickly readmitting Louisiana and other states might help the Thirteenth Amendment reach the three-quarters vote of the states required for ratification.

Lincoln closed with an offer of negotiation to the Radical Republicans. He declared that Reconstruction was so "new and unprecedented" that "no exclusive, and inflexible plan can safely be prescribed as to details and collaterals." Radicals in Congress reacted negatively to Lincoln's failure to protect the full political and civil rights of the freedman, even though his April 11 speech made him the first American President to call for black suffrage of any kind. Pressing forward with plans for a quick Reconstruction, Lincoln decided at a cabinet meeting on April 14 (with General Grant in attendance) to set in motion plans for military governors in the Southern states, who would exercise martial law until loyal civilian governments could be established. Lincoln planned to set Reconstruction on an inalterable course before Congress could act. "If we were wise and discreet," Lincoln said at the cabinet meeting, "we should re-animate the States and get their governments in successful operation, with order prevailing and the Union re-established, before Congress came together in December."[101] Lincoln believed that several members of Congress were simply so "impracticable" or full of "hate and vindictiveness" toward the South that the executive branch would accomplish more good without legislative participation.

John Wilkes Booth assassinated Lincoln at Ford's Theatre that very night. It is impossible to know whether Lincoln's second term would have brought about a different kind of Reconstruction than the one that followed, but it seems clear that Lincoln intended that the executive would take the lead through its constitutional powers over the making of war and peace. With hostilities winding down, Lincoln wanted to create a state of affairs in the South that Congress would be unable to undo. He was following the same strategy toward Congress at the end of the war that he had adopted at its start — he would take swift action under his Commander-in-Chief and Chief Executive powers while the legislature remained out of session.

Lincoln wanted Congress's cooperation, and he openly acknowledged that its power over the seating of its members exercised a check on a state's restoration to the Union. But he would not go as far as the Radicals, nor did he agree with Democrats who were content to allow the dominance of the Southern economic and political systems. The Civil War had not just restored the Union — it had ended slavery. Lincoln wanted the freedmen to have equal rights, but he sought to achieve them through a restoration of the state governments and the traditional principles of constitutional government.

CONCLUSIONS

LINCOLN WAS NEITHER a dictator nor an unprincipled partisan. His unprecedented action to preserve the Union exploited the broadest reaches of the Constitution's grant of the Chief Executive and Commander-in-Chief powers. Once war had begun, Lincoln took control of all measures necessary to subdue the enemy, including the definition of war aims and strategy, supervision of military operations, detention of enemy prisoners, and management of the occupation. He freed the slaves, but only those in the South, because his powers were limited to the battlefield. He took swift action, normally within Congress's domain, but only because of the pressure of emergency. After the first months of the war, Lincoln never again usurped Congress's powers over the raising or funding of the military. He was not afraid of a contest with Congress, particularly over Reconstruction, but the Civil War witnessed far more cooperation between the executive and legislative branches than is commonly thought. But when Lincoln believed Congress to be wrong, he did not hesitate to draw upon the constitutional powers of his own office to follow his best judgment.

Lincoln's administration provides valuable lessons on the nature of civil liberties in wartime. Lincoln undeniably took a tough posture toward citizens suspected of collaborating with the Confederacy and ordered the restriction of peacetime civil liberties, especially the rights of free speech and of habeas corpus. No reduction in constitutional rights is desirable, standing alone, but the measures were part of a systematic mobilization to win the most dangerous war in our nation's history. They had costs, but they also bore benefits for a war effort that eventually defeated the South and left behind no permanent diminution of individual liberties. If anything, the Civil War was followed by the passage of the Reconstruction Amendments and the freeing of the slaves, the expansion of the franchise, and the constitutional guarantee of due process and equal protection rights against the states. To demand that Lincoln should have been more sensitive to civil liberties is to impose the ex post standards of peacetime on decisions made under the pressures of wartime.

Lincoln's greatness in preserving the Union depended crucially on his discovery of the broad executive powers inherent in Article II for use during war or emergency. But not every President is a Lincoln, and not every crisis rises to the level of the Civil War. Once a crisis passes, presidential powers should recede, and if there is no real emergency in the first place, Congress should generally have the upper hand. While great Presidents have been ones who have held a broad vision of the independence and powers of their office, every President who uses his constitutional powers does not necessarily rise to greatness. Presidents may so overstep their political bounds in the use of their constitutional powers that they trigger a reaction by the other branches. Either the President or Congress can succeed in producing a stalemate, which may or may not yield the best result.

Lincoln's Vice President, Andrew Johnson, shows the perils of exercising constitutional powers to bring on, rather than resolve, a crisis. A Tennessee Democrat, Johnson held sharply different views on Reconstruction than the Radical Republicans. Like Lincoln, he favored a quick restoration of the South to its normal status as part of the political community. Southerners only had to pledge an oath

of loyalty to the Union, hold constitutional conventions, ratify the
Thirteenth Amendment, repudiate the public debts borrowed by
the Confederate government, and repeal secession. Under Johnson's
plan, many Republican Congressmen believed, the Southern social
and economic system would remain intact. Aside from former Confederate government officeholders and military officers, who could
not receive amnesty, the Southern elites would remain in charge.[102]

Congressional Republicans wanted a far more radical reordering
of the South. They wanted to grant to black freedmen, whose fate
did not figure in Johnson's scheme, equality with whites in the economy, government, and society. They passed the Freedmen Bureau
and Civil Rights Acts to continue economic assistance to the freed
slaves and to guarantee their equal legal rights, and proposed the
Fourteenth Amendment, which guaranteed the rights of due process and equal protection against the state governments. Congress
had constitutional powers at its disposal that were the equal, if not
greater, than those available to Johnson. While the President was the
Commander-in-Chief over the military forces occupying the South,
only Congress could determine whether Southern states could reassume their standing as political equals. If the Southern states had formally left the Union, the Constitution gave only Congress the right
to admit new states. If the Confederate states had simply been taken
over by disloyal conspiracies, but had never lost their status as states,
Congress could refuse to seat the Southern Representatives and Senators until the South properly reconstructed their governments.[103]

Fundamental disagreement over Reconstruction policy
prompted the battle between the executive and legislative branches
after Lincoln's death. Johnson vetoed the Freedman and Civil
Rights Bills for upsetting the proper balance between the powers of
the national and state governments and urged the Southern states
to reject the Fourteenth Amendment. He allowed rebel-dominated

governments to exercise civil authority in the South and assured their leaders that he would push for quick readmission to the Union. Congress was furious. Johnson, who had the unfortunate combination of a terrible temper, political inflexibility, and a zealot's fervor, responded by attacking the Republicans just as angrily as he had once attacked the rebels. Both, the President said in January 1866, were traitors. Southerners stood "for destroying the Government to preserve slavery," while Republicans wanted "to break up the Government to destroy slavery."

Johnson joined forces with his old party, the Democrats, in the 1866 midterm elections, but the Republicans prevailed. In 1867, Congress overrode the vetoes of the Freedman and Civil Rights Bills and passed a Reconstruction Act that required the Confederate states to ratify the Fourteenth Amendment and repeal all racially discriminatory laws. Congress further required the Southern states to extend to the freedmen the equal right to vote. A supplementary Reconstruction Act swept away Johnson's Reconstruction and ordered new elections and constitutional conventions.[104]

Just as Congress blocked Johnson's policies, Johnson used his constitutional powers to frustrate Congress. In 1865, he appointed former rebels as provisional governors in the South, freely granted pardons at their recommendation, and gave federal offices to other former rebels. His Attorney General ordered federal prosecutors to drop cases that transferred the lands of rebel officers to the Freedman Bureau for the use of freed slaves. On April 2, 1866, he issued a proclamation that the insurrection had ended, which implied an end to occupation government. As the split with Congress worsened, Johnson used his power of removal to fire federal officials, including 1,283 postmasters, to bind the executive branch to his policies.

Even implementation of the Reconstruction Acts was up to the military, which served under the command of the President.

Johnson declared the Reconstruction Acts to be "without precedent and without authority, in palpable conflict with the plainest provisions of the Constitution, and utterly destructive to those great principles of liberty and humanity for which our ancestors on both sides of the Atlantic have shed so much blood and expended so much treasure."[105] By summer 1867, he had adopted the legal position that the military governors could keep the peace and punish criminal acts, but not remove Southern officeholders nor enforce civilian laws such as the Civil Rights Act. Johnson had effectively declared that the military would not execute the Reconstruction Acts. He had set the nation toward his minimal Reconstruction policy solely by exercising his powers as Commander-in-Chief.

Angry Republicans believed Johnson was conducting a coup. They struck back in the February 1867 Tenure of Office Act. It prohibited the President from removing any appointed official while the Senate was in session until the Senate had confirmed his successor. It required the President to explain the reasons for any removal and required Senate approval before it became official. That summer, Congress enacted a third Reconstruction Act that restored the authority of the military governors to enforce civilian laws in the South. Johnson waited until the Senate went on recess and then replaced Stanton as Secretary of War with General Grant. He fired the military governors who had used their authority under the Reconstruction Acts to remove Southern officeholders. Johnson had completely blocked congressional Reconstruction. "Yet," observes Michael Les Benedict, "Johnson had broken no law; he had limited himself strictly to the exercise of his constitutional powers."[106]

A Congress determined to have its way had one tool left: impeachment. An initial drive to impeach Johnson in 1867 failed, even after his State of the Union message declared that he would not enforce the Reconstruction Acts. Congress tried again after Johnson

violated the Tenure of Office Act. On February 24, 1868, the House
overwhelmingly impeached Johnson for violating the Act, blocking implementation of the Reconstruction Acts, and publicly vilify-
ing Congress. House managers argued that the President could not
refuse to enforce an Act because he believed it to be unconstitutional.
Such power would give him, they claimed, an absolute veto over all
legislation. These legal grounds joined the unstated political motives
for impeachment. The Senate refused to convict by only one vote,
however, with seven Republican Senators voting in favor of Johnson
(dramatically retold in John F. Kennedy's *Profiles in Courage*).[107]

Both the President and Congress had exercised their legitimate
constitutional powers. Johnson had the duty not to enforce laws he
believed to be unconstitutional. He had only followed the example
of past Chief Executives by using his powers of appointment and
removal to promote his policies. Johnson was even correct on the
merits. The Tenure of Office Act violated the Constitution's grant of
the removal power to the President as part of its vesting of the executive power, the issue resolved in 1789 by the First Congress.[108] Still,
Congress had every right to pursue its own vision of the Constitution, and if it honestly disagreed with the President, it could remove
him through impeachment. While the Senate failed to convict Johnson, the impeachment process rendered his administration a sham-
bles and convinced him to end his confrontational ways. The 1868
elections soon replaced him with Grant, the hero of the Civil War.

Johnson's example modifies the lessons of the Lincoln Presidency in several important respects. Not all Presidents who press
their constitutional powers to the limits will prevail. Johnson today
is ranked as one of the worst Presidents because of his racist views
and his efforts to block a Reconstruction that sought to guarantee
equality for the black freedmen. Eric Foner views Reconstruction
as a shining moment when the South could have been remade into

a racially harmonious and egalitarian society.[109] Johnson set that vision back at least four years, and perhaps a century, but he could not have been so successful an obstacle without the same vigorous understanding of presidential power shared by his predecessor. When it came to the questions about the power of removal and non-enforcement of unconstitutional laws, Johnson even had the better of the constitutional arguments.

Johnson failed not because he misunderstood the scope of his constitutional powers, but because he misjudged when to use them. It could be argued that Johnson simply could not overcome congressional opposition, but what made Johnson's defeat profound was his effort to use his constitutional powers in a way that triggered his impeachment. Earlier Presidents had invoked their constitutional powers during times of great national challenge and opportunity: establishing a new government, charting a course between the Napoleonic wars, winning Louisiana and the Southwest. With Reconstruction, the great emergency that had forced Lincoln to draw on a robust vision of the Commander-in-Chief role was waning, not beginning. With complex questions about the nature of restoring the Union at hand, and with little need for swift and decisive action, the demand for the unique qualities of the executive was less evident. If Johnson had limited his opposition to political measures, without invoking his constitutional authority, Congress would have prevailed, but impeachment would have been unnecessary.

Reconstruction reaffirms another lesson about executive power: even at its greatest height, the other branches always have ample authority of their own to counter it. Johnson could block congressional policy, but he could get nowhere on his own. Congress could not choose the generals in charge of the occupation, but it could grant them broader powers over the Southern governments. Even if Johnson would not enforce the Reconstruction Acts, Congress could refuse to readmit the Southern states to the Union. If Congress disagreed so sharply over the executive branch's definition and use of its constitutional powers, it could resort to the ultimate remedy of impeachment.

Johnson failed to understand that Congress was just as wedded to its principles as he was to his. Instead of triggering a constitutional confrontation with no good outcome, he should have cooperated with Congress. The Reconstruction crisis was not an external one confronting the government, but one of his own making. The former demands that Presidents exercise their powers decisively for the benefit of the nation; the latter does not.

CHAPTER 7

Franklin D. Roosevelt

WITH WASHINGTON and Lincoln, Franklin D. Roosevelt is considered by most scholars to be one of our nation's greatest Presidents. Roosevelt confronted challenges simultaneously that his predecessors had faced individually. Washington guided the nation's founding when doubts arose as to whether Americans could establish an effective government. Roosevelt radically reengineered the government into the modern administrative state when Americans doubted whether their government could provide them with economic security. Lincoln saved the country from the greatest threat to its national security, leading it through a war that cost more American lives than any other. Roosevelt led a reluctant nation against perhaps its most dangerous foreign foe, an alliance of fascist powers that threatened to place Europe and Asia under totalitarian dictatorships. To bring the nation through both crises, FDR drew deeply upon the reservoir of executive power unlike any President before or since — as demonstrated by his unique status as the only Chief Executive to break the two-term tradition.[1]

Roosevelt came to the office in the midst of the gravest challenges to the nation since the Civil War. The most obvious and immediate crisis was the Great Depression. FDR placed the President in the role of legislative leader and produced a dramatic restructuring of the national government, even though the Depression, as a breakdown of the domestic (and global) economy, fell within the constitutional authority of Congress. Large Democratic majorities in Congress expanded federal regulation of the economy beyond anything before seen in peacetime. Regulation of prices and supply, product quality, wages and working conditions, the securities markets, and pensions became commonplace where they had once been rare. Social Security was not just one of the New Deal's most important planks, but the expression of the whole platform. The federal government would declare its responsibility to coordinate and regulate economic activity to provide stability. It had always exercised broad economic powers during wartime, but FDR made management of the economy by a bureaucracy of experts a permanent feature of American life. While the Republican Presidents who had dominated elections since the Civil War had left economic decisions to the market, FDR placed the federal government in the role of providing economic as well as national security.

Roosevelt's revolution radically shifted the balance of power among the three branches of government as well as between the nation and the states. Under the New Deal, Congress delegated to the executive branch the discretion to make the many decisions necessary to regulate the economy. Congress did not have the time, organization, or expertise to make the minute decisions required. The New Deal did not just produce a federal government of broad power — it gave birth to a President whose influence over domestic affairs would begin to match his role in foreign affairs. When the Supreme Court stood in the way of the new administrative state,

Roosevelt launched a campaign to increase the membership of the Court to change the meaning of the Constitution. When political parties challenged the New Deal, Roosevelt concentrated power in the executive branch, which undermined their ability to channel benefits to their members. The New Deal produced a Presidency that was more institutionally independent of Congress and more politically free of the parties than ever before.[2]

The Great Depression spawned foreign threats, too. Economic instability in Europe set the conditions for the rise of fascism first in Italy, then in Germany and Japan. Roosevelt realized early that American interests would be best served by supporting the democracies against the Axis powers, but he was confronted by a nation wary of another foreign war and a Congress determined to impose strict neutrality. FDR used every last inch of presidential power to bring the nation into the war on the side of the Allies, including secretly coordinating military activities with Britain, hoping to force an incident with Germany in the North Atlantic, and pressuring Japan until it lashed out in the Pacific. FDR's steady leadership in the face of stiff congressional resistance stands as one the greatest examples of presidential leadership in the last century, one that redounded to the benefit of the United States and the free world.

THE NEW DEAL AND THE COURTS

FDR ENTERED OFFICE in the midst of the worst economic contraction in American history. Between the summer of 1929 and the spring of 1933, nominal gross national product dropped by 50 percent. Prices for all goods fell by about a third; income from agriculture collapsed from $6 billion to $2 billion; industrial production declined by 37 percent; and business investment plummeted from $24 billion to $3 billion. About one-quarter of the workforce,

13 million Americans, remained consistently unemployed, and the unemployment rate would remain above 15 percent for the rest of the decade. More than 5,000 banks failed, with a loss of $7 billion in deposits. From the time of the crash in October 1929 to its low in July 1932, the Dow Jones Industrial Average fell more than 75 percent.[3] It was not a problem caused by famine or drought, dwindling natural resources, or crippled production; crops spoiled and livestock were destroyed because market prices were too low.

Americans were losing faith in their political institutions to solve the crisis. Though the causes of the Depression were complex, some, Roosevelt included, blamed "economic royalists," financiers and speculators, and the rich. Economists and historians have argued ever since over the causes of the Depression. Little evidence seems to support the claim that the stock market crash triggered the Depression — stock markets have sharply declined since then, most recently in 1987, with no underlying change in economic growth.

In their classic *Monetary History of the United States,* Milton Friedman and Anna Schwartz argued that a normal recession deepened into the Great Depression because the Federal Reserve mistakenly responded to the banking panic by restricting the money supply. A deflation in prices followed, which led to a steep drop in economic activity. Ben Bernanke, the current Chairman of the Federal Reserve, elaborated on this theme by arguing that the Fed's deflationary banking policies tightened the credit available to businesses and households, further suppressing economic activity.[4] Others argue that the Great Depression must be understood within the context of the international economy, which witnessed bank failures and recession in Germany and France, defaults on World War I loan and reparation payments, abandonment of the gold standard, and the dumping of agricultural products on world markets.

Our understanding of the causes of the Great Depression has

improved, thanks to the scholarship of the last 40 years, but even to this day there is no clear consensus. To the Americans who lived through it, the collapse of the economy was bewildering, confusing, and without historical precedent. The Hoover administration's policies did not help, and might have made matters even worse. As historians have realized, Hoover did not adopt the aloof, hands-off attitude claimed by his political opponents. During his administration, Congress doubled public works spending, and the federal budget deficit rose to $2.7 billion, at that time the largest in American peacetime history. He pressed business executives to maintain employment and wages, and experimented with policies, such as the Reconstruction Finance Corporation's emergency loans to businesses, which would set important examples for the New Dealers.[5]

But Hoover's initiatives were mere stopgaps that were swamped by other policy mistakes. Though he had initially asked for tariff reductions, Hoover signed the notorious Smoot-Hawley Act, which raised rates and killed international trade flows. Following the conventional economic wisdom of the day, Hoover sought to balance the budget with tax increases at a time when the economy needed fiscal stimulus. As Milton Friedman and Allan Meltzer have separately argued, the Federal Reserve pursued a deflationary strategy, cutting off the economy's oxygen, when increases in the money supply were called for.[6]

Some of Hoover's failure rests on his vision of the Presidency. He refused the role of the President as legislative leader, resisted the expansion of the federal agencies, and opposed national welfare legislation — all on constitutional grounds.[7] FDR's vision of the office could not have created a sharper contrast. FDR led the nation through a frenzy of experimentation in policies and government structure without parallel in American history. There appeared to be no overall philosophy behind the New Deal, which comes as little surprise, given the confusion that prevailed at the time over the causes of the Depression.

Without any true understanding of the reasons for the collapse, the New Dealers tried anything and everything. Thinking that over-production was the culprit, some recommended the cartelization of industries to reduce supply and increase prices. Others who blamed underconsumption advocated public jobs programs and welfare relief. Some believed that the budget deficit was the problem, and urged an increase in taxes and cuts in spending. Some thought international trade was a cause, and advocated both more flexibility in trade negotiations and the dumping of excess agricultural production overseas. Pragmatic and political (he had been a professional politician for most of his life), and unsure about the true causes of the Depression, Roosevelt flittered from idea to idea. Some had the effect of canceling each other out — public works projects sponsored by the National Recovery Administration had to buy raw materials at prices inflated by controls imposed by the Department of Agriculture.

Throughout all the experimentation and expansion of government, the one thing that did not change was the focus on the Presidency. FDR became the father of the modern Presidency by moving the Chief Executive to the center of the American political universe. FDR drafted the executive's wartime powers into peacetime service, but without calling for any formal change in the Constitution. In his First Inaugural Address, he declared that "our Constitution is so simple and practical that it is possible always to meet extraordinary needs by changes in emphasis and arrangement without loss of essential form." What FDR wanted was access to the constitutional powers granted to the President during time of emergency. He promised to seek from Congress "broad executive power to wage a war against the emergency, as great as the power that would be given me if we were in fact invaded by a foreign foe."[8] FDR's expansion of the powers of the Presidency, both political and constitutional, would grow from this basic theme — the economy and society would henceforth be regulated in ways that were once considered suitable only for war.

The nation got a taste of what FDR meant when, on his second day in office, he issued the second emergency proclamation in American history. During the period between FDR's election and his inauguration, a massive run on banks had forced many to close their doors or stop lending. Invoking the Trading with the Enemy Act, FDR imposed a national banking holiday and prohibited all gold transactions.[9] Roosevelt's use of the Act was questionable, to say the least. Congress had passed the Act in 1917 to give the President broad economic powers during wartime or national emergency, but not to regulate the domestic economy in the absence of a foreign threat. Without the statute, FDR was left to act under an unspecified presidential emergency power. At the end of the banking moratorium, Congress convened in special session and passed the Emergency Banking Act, which gave the federal government powers to control gold and currency transactions, to own stock in banks, and to regulate the reopening of the banks. Because the Roosevelt administration had only finished drafting the legislation the night before, a rolled-up newspaper substituted as a prop for an actual copy of the bill's text, and the House spent only 30 minutes discussing the legislation.

Roosevelt set a precedent for his successors by rushing a torrent of legislation through Congress in his first 100 days. The National Industrial Recovery Act (NIRA), the Agricultural Adjustment Act (AAA), the Banking Act, the Emergency Railroad Transportation Act (ERTA), and the Home Owners Loan Act (HOLA) all granted FDR extraordinary economic powers to fight the Depression. Their enactment witnessed the breakdown of the sharp distinction between the executive and legislative branches. The executive branch took the primary responsibility for drafting bills, Congress passed them quickly with a minimum of deliberation (sometimes sight unseen), and the laws themselves delegated broad authority to the President or the administrative agencies.[10]

Through the agencies, the executive branch would impose an unprecedented level of centralized planning over the peacetime economy. The AAA, for example, gave the executive the power to dictate which crops were to be planted. Under the NIRA, agencies enacted industry-wide codes of conduct, usually drafted by the industries themselves, to govern production and employment. New Dealers sought to address falling prices for commodities by setting higher prices, reducing competition, and limiting production.[11]

Little attention was given to constitutional problems with the legislation, which threatened to exceed the Supreme Court's limitations on federal power. Laws like the NIRA or the AAA pressed the Constitution's grant of authority to Congress to make laws "to regulate Commerce...among the several States." Other laws, such as the new public employment and unemployment relief programs, raised constitutional issues about the national government's taxing and spending authority, but again these were only problems of federalism, not of presidential power. They mirrored the steps that the national government had taken to mobilize the economy for military production while reducing domestic consumption — many of the early programs of the New Deal were modeled on World War I efforts. As William Leuchtenberg has observed, war became a metaphor for the calamity brought on by the Depression, and FDR and his advisers turned to the wartime experience for solutions. "Almost every New Deal act or agency derived, to some extent, from the experience of World War I."[12]

FDR's legislative whirlwind set in motion a series of events that culminated in confrontation with the Supreme Court. Even though the President would suffer politically and constitutionally, he would eventually prevail. The roots of the conflict stretched back to the Progressive Era, when the Justices had held that the Interstate Commerce Clause did not allow regulation of manufacturing or agriculture within a state. Under the theory of dual federalism, the Court had blocked antitrust enforcement against a sugar-refining monopoly in 1895 because the refining itself did not cross interstate lines.[13] In 1918, it had held unconstitutional a federal law that prohibited the interstate transportation of goods made with child labor. Even though the federal ban applied only when the product moved across state lines, the Court held that "the production of articles, intended for interstate commerce, is a matter of local regulation."[14] When Congress attacked child labor again with a 10 percent excise tax, the Court blocked that, too, on the ground that Congress could not use a tax to achieve a prohibited end.[15]

The Court matched its limits on federal authority to regulate the economy with similar restrictions on the states. Where Congress could only exercise the powers carefully enumerated in Article I, states enjoyed a general "police power" over all conduct within their borders. The courts, however, read the Fourteenth Amendment — which forbids states from depriving individuals of life, liberty, or property without due process — to block a great deal of state business regulation. In *Lochner v. New York* (1905), the Court struck down a state law that prohibited bakers from working more than 60 hours a week or 10 hours per day. According to the majority, the Constitution protected the bakers' individual right to contract to work as much as they liked.[16] The state could not adopt economic legislation to redistribute income within the industry (the law favored established bakeries at the expense of immigrant bakers), or infringe the rights of free labor. In dissent, Justice Oliver Wendell

Holmes famously accused the majority of following its preferences
rather than the law. "A Constitution is not intended to embody a
particular economic theory, whether of paternalism...or of laissez
faire," Holmes memorably wrote. "The Fourteenth Amendment
does not enact Mr. Herbert Spencer's *Social Statics*." From the time
of *Lochner* to the New Deal, the Court invalidated 184 state laws
governing working hours and wages, organized labor, commodity
prices, and entry into business.[17]

Legislation enacted during FDR's first 100 days in office virtually dared the Justices to block the New Deal. The NIRA did not
just attempt to ban a single product or manufacturing process — it
placed all industrial production in the nation under federal regulation. The AAA did the same with agriculture, and another law with
coal mining. Laws passed later in FDR's term, such as the National
Labor Relations Act (NLRA) and the Public Utility Holding Company Act (PUHCA), set nationwide rules on unions and utilities,
while the Social Security Act (SSA) created a universal system of
unemployment compensation and old age pension.

FDR was following in the footsteps of Presidents who dared to
interpret the Constitution at odds with the other branches. FDR
himself appears to have held few constitutional doubts. New Deal
theorists believed, for example, that the Interstate Commerce Clause
pertained to almost all economic activity in the nation because all
goods manufactured or grown within a state traveled through the
channels of interstate commerce to reach market. While the federal
government might usually defer to the states on many matters, the
Depression was so grave that the states were powerless to control a
nationwide problem.[18]

Roosevelt recognized early on that his program risked antago-
nizing the federal courts, which were filled with Republican judges.[19]
He could count on the opposition of Justices James McReynolds,

Willis Van Devanter, George Sutherland, and Pierce Butler, known as "The Four Horsemen" for their skepticism toward government regulation of the economy and their defense of individual economic rights. But FDR believed he could expect the general support of progressive Justices Louis Brandeis, Harlan Fiske Stone, and Benjamin Cardozo. Chief Justice Charles Evans Hughes and Justice Owen Roberts held the swing votes. FDR hoped that the Court would grant the political branches more constitutional leeway to respond to the national crisis of the Great Depression. In previous national security emergencies, the courts had allowed the federal government to mobilize the economy with little objection. FDR had reason for his hopes in early 1934, after 5–4 majorities of the Court upheld state laws setting milk prices and delaying mortgage payments.[20]

Those hopes were dashed with the opening of the Court's business in January 1935. In its first case examining a New Deal law, an 8–1 majority of the Court invalidated the NIRA's "hot oil" provision, which allowed the executive branch to prohibit the interstate transportation of petroleum produced in violation of quotas. Chief Justice Hughes wrote that the provision unconstitutionally delegated legislative power to the President.[21] That decision was only a preview to May 27, 1935 — known as "Black Monday" to New Dealers — when the Court struck down three New Deal laws. The centerpiece was the Court's unanimous rejection of the NIRA in the "Sick Chicken" case, *Schechter Poultry v. United States*, in which the owners of a chicken slaughterhouse were prosecuted for violating industrial codes of conduct.[22]

In finding the NIRA unconstitutional, the Justices threatened the two core features of the New Deal. *Schechter Poultry* held that the Constitution prohibited Congress from delegating legislative power to the President, especially when rule-making authority was then sub-delegated to private industry groups. The NIRA also violated the Constitution's limits on the reach of federal economic power. The owners of the slaughterhouse sold their chickens into a local market, which did not directly impact interstate commerce, even though a high percentage of chickens came from out of state. If the Court were to keep to its precedent that *intra*state manufacturing and agriculture lay outside federal authority, more pillars of the New Deal — perhaps even the whole program itself — might collapse. In pointed language, the Court specifically rejected the Roosevelt administration's overarching approach to the Great Depression: "Extraordinary conditions do not create or enlarge constitutional power."[23]

FDR responded with a political attack on the Court. In a 90-minute press conference, the President declared *Schechter Poultry* to be the most significant judicial decision since *Dred Scott*. While critical of the Court's ruling on executive power, he believed that those problems could be fixed by rewriting the statutes to give more direction and less delegation.[24] It was *Schechter*'s narrow view of the Commerce Clause that posed the real threat to the New Deal. If Congress could not regulate the activities of the butchers because they were local in nature, it would be unable to police most other manufacturing or agricultural enterprises. "The whole tendency over these years has been to view the interstate commerce clause in the light of present-day civilization," Roosevelt told the press. "We are interdependent — we are tied together." To Roosevelt, the Justices' way of thinking failed to take account of the national character of the economy. "We have been relegated to a horse-and-buggy definition of interstate commerce."[25]

FDR considered a variety of proposals if the Court were to continue ruling against the New Deal: increasing the number of Justices (giving the President enough new appointments to change the balance on the Court), reducing the Court's jurisdiction, or requiring a supermajority of Justices to declare a federal law unconstitutional. He rejected them all as premature, but he had been prepared to respond to a potential rejection of the prohibition on gold transactions with a declaration of national emergency, a fixed price for gold, and an attack on the Court for "imperil[ing] the economic and political security of this nation."[26] But the Court upheld the gold regulations, causing FDR to shelve his plans.[27]

The administration continued to work with Congress to expand federal intervention in the economy. Known as the Second New Deal, these laws went beyond the simple, sweeping delegations of authority to the President in the NIRA or the AAA. New laws such as the National Labor Relations Act and the Social Security Act created specialized bureaucracies to handle discrete areas of economic regulation. While the First New Deal vested the President with emergency powers to handle the Depression, the Second New Deal of 1935–36 promised permanent government intervention in the economy. One of FDR's political achievements was to transform the social contract so that government benefits became understood as rights, rights just as real to many Americans as those in the Constitution itself. But they did nothing to avoid the constitutional problems of the First New Deal: their very success depended on their ability to regulate all economic activity, rather than just trade that crossed interstate borders.

Rather than recede before this second outburst of lawmaking, the Court stuck to its guns. In the spring of 1936, it declared unconstitutional more elements of the New Deal. In *United States v. Butler,* the Court held unconstitutional the AAA's use of taxes and grants to regulate agricultural production, which lay within the reserved powers of the states.[28] *Butler* threatened the Social Security Act, which used a combination of taxes and spending to provide relief and pensions to the unemployed and elderly.

In *Carter v. Carter Coal Co.*, a 5–4 majority struck down a 1935 law that set prices, wages, hours, and collective bargaining rules for the coal industry.[29] The Court found that the production of coal did not amount to interstate commerce, but instead fell within the reserved powers of the states. "[T]he effect of the labor provisions…primarily falls upon production and not upon commerce," Justice Sutherland wrote for the majority. "Production is a purely local activity." *Carter* made clear that the sick chicken case was not a fluke; any federal regulation of intrastate industrial production or agriculture was now in constitutional doubt. In *Jones v. SEC*, the Justices attacked the proceedings of the Securities and Exchange Commission as "odious" and "pernicious" and compared them to the "intolerable abuses of the Star Chamber."[30] *Morehead v. Tipaldo* found that New York's minimum wage law violated the Due Process Clause, just as it had earlier found that such laws interfered with the right to contract.[31] As the Court had already found a federal minimum wage in the District of Columbia unconstitutional in the 1920s, it had made the regulation of wages, in FDR's words, a "no-man's land" forbidden to both the federal and state governments.

In the space of just two years, the Court had ripped apart the central features of the First New Deal and was promising the same for the Second. Roosevelt stopped discussing the Court's decisions publicly, and did not make any proposals about the Court during his reelection campaign. He attacked business and the rich as "economic royalists" and the "privileged princes of these new economic dynasties." Roosevelt proposed a new economic order that would provide stability and security through new forms of government-provided rights. FDR reconceived rights from the negative — preventing the state from intruding on an individual liberty — to the positive — a minimum wage, the right to organize, national working standards, and old-age pensions. Running against the lackluster Republican Alf

Landon, FDR secured one of the great electoral victories in American history: 523 electoral votes to Landon's 8 (the largest advantage ever recorded in a contested two-party election in American history), every state but Maine and Vermont, more than 60 percent of the popular vote, and a Democratic Congress with two-thirds majorities in both Houses, including 75 of the 96 seats in the Senate. Observers could legitimately question whether the Republican Party would shortly disappear as a political force.

Fresh off his victory, FDR proposed a restructuring of the Court that would eliminate it as an opponent of the New Deal. On February 5, 1937, he sent Congress a judiciary "reform" bill that would add a new Justice to the Court for every one over the age of 70. Because of the advanced age of several Justices, Roosevelt's proposal would have allowed him to appoint six new Court members. Rather than criticize the Court for its opposition to the New Deal, Roosevelt disingenuously claimed that the elderly Justices were delaying the efficient administration of justice. In his message to Congress, FDR pointed out that the Court had denied review in 695 out of 803 cases. How can it be "that full justice is achieved when a court is forced by the sheer necessity of keeping up with its business to decline, without even an explanation, to hear 87 percent of the cases presented to it by private litigants?"[32]

Only indirectly did FDR imply a link between the advanced age of the Justices and their opposition to the New Deal. "Modern complexities call also for a constant infusion of new blood in the courts," FDR wrote. "A lowered mental or physical vigor leads men to avoid an examination of complicated and changed conditions. Little by little, new facts become blurred through old glasses fitted, as it were, for the needs of another generation." FDR declared that the remedy would bring a "constant and systematic addition of younger blood" that would "vitalize the courts and better equip them to recognize and apply the essential concepts of justice in the light of the needs and the facts of an ever-changing world."[33] The President's purpose could not have been clearer. He submitted the plan on the Friday before the Court would hear Monday arguments challenging the constitutionality of the National Labor Relations Act, one of the pillars of the Second New Deal.

Despite his electoral success, FDR's court-packing plan — the first domestic initiative of his second term — suffered a humiliating defeat. Mail and telegrams to Congress went nine-to-one against the plan, and polling showed a majority of the country opposed.[34] Elements of the New Deal coalition, such as farmers and some unions, attacked the plan early. Senate Republicans unified in opposition shortly after the President announced his proposal, and conservative Senate Democrats came out against the plan within days. Several liberal supporters of the New Deal followed. Hatton Summers, the chairman of the House Judiciary Committee, organized a majority of his committee against the bill, saying "Boys,...here is where I cash in my chips."[35] Various college and university presidents, academics, and the American Bar Association opposed the plan. The *coup de grace* was delivered by none other than Chief Justice Hughes, in a letter made public during Senate Judiciary Committee hearings, who rebutted point by point FDR's claims that the Court was overworked and that the older Justices could not perform their duties. Both Brandeis and Van Devanter approved the letter, which most historians believe ended the court-packing plan for good. Upon its release, Vice President Garner called FDR in Georgia to tell him, "We're licked."[36]

Historians and political scientists have argued ever since over whether FDR still won the war. On March 29, 1937, a week after the release of the Hughes letter, the Court handed down a 5–4 decision upholding a Washington State minimum wage law for women. In

West Coast Hotel v. Parrish, the lineup of votes for and against New York's minimum wage, which had been struck down in *Tipaldo* the year before, remained the same — except for Justice Roberts, who switched sides to uphold the law.[37] Overruling the earlier bans on minimum wage laws, *Parrish* made clear that the Due Process Clause would no longer stand in the way of government regulation of wages or hours.

Two weeks later, the Court upheld the National Labor Relations Act, which had been challenged on the same grounds raised in the Sick Chicken and *Carter* cases.[38] In *NLRB v. Jones & Laughlin Steel Corp.*, Chief Justice Hughes led a 5–4 majority in rejecting the doctrine that manufacturing did not constitute interstate commerce. Jones & Laughlin Steel was the fourth-largest steel company in the nation, with operations in multiple states. As the Court observed, "the stoppage of those operations by industrial strife would have a most serious effect upon interstate commerce." "It is obvious," the Court found, that the effect "would be immediate and might be catastrophic." Henceforth, the Court would allow federal regulation of the economy, even of wholly intrastate activity, because of the interconnectedness of the national market. To do otherwise would be to "shut our eyes to the plainest facts of our national life" and to judge questions of interstate commerce "in an intellectual vacuum."[39] Justice Roberts again switched positions to make the 5–4 majority possible.

The Court's about-face sapped the strength from FDR's court-packing campaign. By May 1937, it appeared that an outright majority of the Senate opposed the proposal, and opinion polls showed that only 30 percent of the public supported it. At the end of the month, the Senate Judiciary Committee reported the bill out with an unfavorable recommendation.[40] Two more events finished things. Justice Van Devanter announced his retirement, timed for

the same day as the Judiciary Committee vote, giving Roosevelt his
first Supreme Court appointment. His departure would give the
New Deal a secure majority on the Court. The Court also upheld
the Social Security Act from attack as an unconstitutional spending
measure or an invasion of state sovereignty.[41] The court-packing bill
lost all momentum, never emerged from the House Judiciary Committee, and never reached a floor vote.

While FDR lost in Congress, he had won his larger objective.
The Court would not strike down another regulation of interstate
commerce for almost 60 years. Journalists and political scientists
immediately attributed the "switch in time that saved nine" to
FDR's threat to pack the Court.[42] Even today, a few creative scholars
like Bruce Ackerman defend the sweeping constitutional changes of
the New Deal — which, unlike Reconstruction, were never written
into a constitutional amendment — with the 1936 electoral landslide and the attack on the Court.[43] More recent work claims that
the Court's jurisprudence was evolving in a more generous direction toward federal power anyway.[44] The Court, this work points
out, had confidentially voted to uphold the minimum wage in *West
Coast Hotel* on December 19, 1936, six weeks before FDR sprung
his proposal on the nation. The court-packing legislation could not
have pressured the Court because it obviously had little chance of
passage. The argument that the 1936 elections prodded the Justices
to switch positions on the New Deal also suffers from the absence
of the Court as an issue during the campaign. If anything, FDR
suffered politically from his confrontation with the Court. A growing bipartisan coalition against the New Deal and another sharp
recession in 1938 stalled FDR's domestic agenda for the rest of his
Presidency.

Nonetheless, if FDR is considered a great President because of
the New Deal, critical to his success was his willingness to advance

his own understanding of the Constitution. FDR never accepted the Court's right to define the powers of the federal government to regulate the economy. While FDR did not join Lincoln in declining to obey a judicial order, his administration regularly proposed laws that ran counter to Supreme Court precedent, and FDR openly questioned the competence of the judiciary to review the New Deal. He sought to change the Court's composition and size as means to pressure it to change its rulings. With the retirement of the Four Horsemen, Roosevelt would appoint Hugo Black, Stanley Reed, Felix Frankfurter, and William O. Douglas to the Court, and by 1941, eight of the nine Justices were his appointees. While they would fight about the application of the Bill of Rights against the states, among other issues, they would unanimously agree that Congress's powers to regulate the economy were almost without limit.[45]

In its call for a peacetime state of emergency, the New Deal went beyond changes to the balance of powers between the federal and state governments. Wartime inevitably shifts power and responsibility to the President. FDR and the New Deal Congress created an administrative state that had the same effect, but which would be permanent rather than temporary. Laws enacted in the Hundred Days and in the years after vested sweeping legislative powers in the executive branch. The executive branch became the fount of legislative proposals. FDR's bills to cut federal spending and veterans' benefits to balance the budget passed with alacrity.

The effort to engage in rational administration made the executive branch the locus of regulation — issued through agency rule-making, rather than acts of Congress — as government took on the job of regulating the securities markets, banks, labor unions, industrial working conditions, and production standards. Victory was all the more difficult because war requires the rationing of scarce resources in favor of military production. Ending the Depression required stimulating demand and production of all manner of goods, essentially altering millions of market decisions made every day.

The New Deal's resemblance to mobilization relied upon a government bureaucracy more typical of wartime. America's administrative state had grown in ebbs and flows, with the early Hamiltonian vision of a state centered around the Treasury Department and the Bank, Jefferson's embargo machinery, and the massive departments of the Civil War representing the high-water marks. With the creation of the Interstate Commerce Commission in 1887, the American administrative state started to grow in earnest. Progressive-era efforts to create national administration to manage discrete economic and social issues culminated in the World War I mobilization effort, which included everything from production quotas to press censorship.[46] Between 1887 and 1932, Congress created a few new agencies to oversee aspects of the economy, such as railroad rates, business competition, and the money supply. These early examples set the precedent of delegating lawmaking authority to the executive branch to set the actual rules governing private conduct.

FDR supplemented the New Deal's delegation of legislative authority to the executive branch with a focus of the political system on the President. Even before his election, FDR had made clear that the candidate, not the party, would be the center of the campaign by renting a small plane to fly to Chicago to accept his nomination in person — the first nominee of either major party to do so. Once in office, he used new technology to reach over the heads of Congress and the media. Radio allowed the President to forge a direct relationship with the American electorate that went unfiltered by the newspapers. His famous "fireside chats," the first delivered on the day before the government reopened the banks on March 13, 1933, allowed FDR to campaign for his policies directly with the people. Roosevelt did not neglect the press either: He held twice-a-week off-the-record press conferences in the Oval Office, where report-ers could ask him any question they liked. He employed his ample charm to win over the reporters, who burst out in applause after the first press conference on March 8, 1933.

FDR used these tools to marshal support for his legislative pro-gram and to change the political culture. Under Roosevelt, the Presi-dent became the leading force for positive government, rather than the leader of a political system where power was dispersed among the branches of government, the states, and the political parties.[47] If the Presidency were to play this leading role, it had to strengthen its con-trol over the executive branch itself. In order to fulfill the promise of economic stability, the President wanted full command over the varied programs and policies of the government. This challenge was compounded by the New Deal's blizzard of new commissions and agencies, such as the National Recovery Administration, the Securi-ties and Exchange Commission, and the Federal Communications Commission, as well as the lack of a rational government structure that matched form to function. When Congress enacted New Deal legislation, it usually did not reduce the size or shape of federal agen-cies, often simply creating another agency or layer of bureaucracy on top of the existing ones.

Roosevelt sought to master the executive branch in various ways, with limited success. He expanded the use of aides attached to the White House to develop and implement policy instead of govern-ing through the cabinet. FDR brought in a "Brain Trust," many of them academics who had advised him during the 1932 campaign, to develop legislation, draft speeches, and manage policy. Some were located in the White House, and others were spread in appointed positions in the agencies, but they all worked for the President.

Cabinet meetings became primarily ceremonial occasions. Pol-icy development was evolving into the form that it has today, with meetings between the President and his White House staff and a cabinet officer and agency staff, or in special committees that include some cabinet members along with White House staff and other agency officials.[48] The cabinet as a whole no longer represented leaders of important factions within the President's party, nor did there seem to be a guiding principle behind their appointment. As James MacGregor Burns has observed, "[T]he real significance of the cabinet lay in Roosevelt's leadership role. He could count on loyalty from his associates; almost everyone was 'FRBC' — for Roosevelt before Chicago" (where the Democratic Party nominated FDR in 1932).[49] The declining importance of the cabinet, both in its corporeal form and in its individual members, naturally enhanced the control of the White House over the government.

FDR used his removal power to direct policy, following the examples set by Lincoln, Jackson, and Washington. He fired the head of the Federal Power Commission, whom Hoover had appointed, and replaced him with his own man, even though legislation appeared to give the Commission itself the authority to choose the chairman.[50] As the United States came closer to entry into World War II, he summarily dismissed his Secretaries of War and Navy and replaced them with internationalist Republicans without serious opposition from Congress or his own party.

FDR also used his removal power to seek control over the independent agencies. Unlike the core departments, such as State, War, Treasury, and Justice, independent agencies were designed by Congress to be less amenable to presidential direction.[51] Their organizing statutes usually create a multi-member commission at the top with a required balance between the political parties. In some cases, Congress shields the commission members from presidential removal except for cause (for malfeasance in office or for violating the law). Congress uses these devices to delegate the power to make legislative rules, while keeping the ability to influence its exercise and preventing its direct transfer to presidential control. Until FDR, according to Steven Calabresi and Christopher Yoo, Presidents were generally understood to have the constitutional ability to freely remove commissioners even in the presence of these "for cause" protections against removal, though it is unclear whether Presidents in fact used this authority.[52]

Upon taking office, FDR decided to replace the head of the Federal Trade Commission, William Humphrey, a Hoover administration appointee. The FTC had a potential role in overseeing important New Deal programs due to its responsibility to investigate "unfair methods of competition in commerce," a broad jurisdiction that allowed it to sue companies for monopolistic activity. The statute establishing the FTC allowed removal of a commissioner only in cases of "inefficiency, neglect of duty, or malfeasance in office."[53] FDR decided to remove Humphrey only because he wanted to have his own man in the job. FDR wrote Humphrey: "You will, I know, realize that I do not feel that your mind and my mind go along together on either the policies or the administering of the [FTC]." When Humphrey refused to leave, FDR fired him. Congress did not complain, and instead promptly confirmed FDR's nomination of a new FTC chairman. Humphrey, however, remained undaunted and sued to recover his pay for the rest of his term.

Four years later, Humphrey's estate eventually took his case to the Supreme Court, which dealt Roosevelt and the Presidency a serious blow. The Justice Department argued that the FTC statute was an unconstitutional infringement on the President's removal power and his constitutional duty to faithfully execute the laws.[54] Roosevelt's lawyers relied on *Myers v. United States*, a nine-year-old case that had struck down a law requiring Senate consent before a President could fire a postmaster. In *Myers*, Chief Justice (and former

President) William Howard Taft had written: "The vesting of the executive power in the President was essentially a grant of the power to execute the laws. But the President alone and unaided could not execute the laws. He must execute them by the assistance of subordinates."[55] Taft concluded that the President's duty to implement the laws required that "he should select those who were to act for him under his direction" and that he must also have the "power of removing those for whom he cannot continue to be responsible." Based on this precedent, FDR seemed on safe ground.

On the same day that it decided *Schechter Poultry*, May 27, 1935, the Court substantially revised its removal jurisprudence. With Justice Sutherland writing, the majority held that the FTC "cannot in any proper sense be characterized as an arm or an eye of the executive." Creating a wholly new category of government, Sutherland described the FTC's functions as "quasi legislative or quasi judicial" because it investigated and reported to Congress and conducted initial adjudications on claims of anti-competitive violations before a case went to federal court.[56] The FTC acted "as an agency of the legislative and judicial departments," and was "wholly disconnected from the executive department." *Myers*, and the President's discretionary removal authority, only applied to "purely executive officers" such as the Secretary of State or a postmaster.

The decision has long been puzzling, especially its recognition of a fourth branch of government that falls outside the three mentioned in the Constitution. *Humphrey's Executor*'s reasoning, however, has shriveled on the vine. Recent cases continue to recognize Congress's authority to shield certain government agents (such as the independent counsel) from removal but because of the importance of their independence to their functions, even when they fall within the executive branch, not because they perform quasi legislative or judicial functions.[57] Another oddity is that FDR lost at the hands of

Justice Sutherland and the conservatives on the Court, who were (as we shall see) strong supporters of executive power in foreign affairs.

As they demonstrated in other decisions, the Justices were concerned with the New Deal's great expansion of federal power. They may have believed that one way to blunt centralization in the national government was to force dispersion once at the federal level.[58] Not surprisingly, Congress found the Court's approach quite congenial. It could delegate authority to the executive branch while preventing the President from exercising direct control over the agency. This would naturally make the independent agencies more responsive to congressional wishes, which controlled their funding and held oversight hearings into their activities. And since the agencies were still within the executive branch, Congress could disclaim any formal responsibility for unpopular regulatory decisions. After *Humphrey's Executor*, Congress added "for cause" limitations on removal for members of the National Labor Relations Board, the Civil Aeronautics Board, and the Federal Reserve Board.[59]

Creation of the permanent administrative state strained the Presidency. With the Supreme Court and Congress limiting the main constitutional tool of executive control, independent agencies might be able to pursue policies at odds with the President's understanding of federal law. Or they might press policy mandates in a way that caused conflict with other agencies, created redundancies, or ran counter to other federal policies. A number of methods for taming the behemoth were possible. Presidents could impose order by forcing the menagerie of departments, commissions, and agencies to act according to a common plan, and thereby coordinate the activities of the government rationally; the administrative state could be freed of direct control by either the President or Congress, and instead be subject to a variety of checks and balances by all three branches; or the agencies could work closely with private business and interest groups, which would raise objections to agency action with the courts, Congress, and the White House.

FDR rejected the idea that the administrative state should float outside the Constitution's traditional structure, and he continued to fire the heads of agencies even when Congress had arguably limited his power of removal. FDR, for example, removed the chairman of the Tennessee Valley Authority in 1938, even though Congress had established that he could only be fired for applying political tests or any other standards but "merit and efficiency" in running the agency. The chairman had attacked his TVA colleagues and had declared that he took orders from Congress, not the President. FDR removed him on the ground that the Executive Power and Take Care Clauses of the Constitution required that he control his subordinates.[60] FDR established various super-cabinet entities with names like the Executive Council, the National Emergency Council, and the Industrial Emergency Committee, composed of cabinet officers, commission heads, and White House staff. None of these improvisations provided a structural solution to the challenge posed by the administrative state, as these various bodies proved a poor forum for rational planning and control over the varied arms of the federal government.

FDR's last thrust to control the administrative state required the cooperation of Congress. In 1936, the President asked a commission, headed by administration expert Louis Brownlow, to recommend institutional changes for the improved governance of the administrative state. A year later, it reported: "[T]he President needs help." Its bottom line was clear. "Managerial direction and control of all departments and agencies of the Executive Branch," Brownlow wrote, "should be centered in the President."

According to Brownlow, the President's political responsibilities did not match his formal authorities. "While he now has popular responsibility for this direction," the committee reported, "he is not equipped with adequate legal authority or administrative machinery to enable him to exercise it."[61] Brownlow and FDR, who approved the report, held the usual concern that the administrative state was wasteful, redundant, and contradictory, but more importantly, they worried that it would become so independent as to lose touch with the people. The administrative state suffered from a democracy deficit.

The Brownlow Committee concluded that Congress must give the President more management resources, while keeping the Chief Executive at the center of decision-making. It advised that to make "our Government an up-to-date, efficient, and effective instrument for carrying out the will of the Nation," presidential control must be enhanced. It recommended the creation of a new entity, the Executive Office of the President (which would house the Bureau of the Budget), six new White House assistants to the President, centralization of the government's budgets and planning, and the merger of independent agencies into the cabinet departments. Brownlow's report did not call for a professional secretariat that would supervise the activities of the government, as existed in Great Britain. Rather, the new assistants to the President and the Bureau of the Budget would provide information to the President and carry out his orders, with Roosevelt still making all critical policy decisions.[62] By centralizing the administrative state under the Presidency, it would become directly accountable to Congress and the American people. "Strong executive leadership is essential to democratic government today," the report concluded. "Our choice is not between power and no power, but between responsible but capable popular government and irresponsible autocracy."[63]

FDR had the report's recommendations distilled into a bill he presented to the congressional leadership in January 1937. In a four-hour presentation, FDR personally laid out the plan and declared: "The President's task has become impossible for me or any other man. A man in this position will not be able to survive White House service unless it is simplified. I need executive assistants with a 'passion for anonymity' to be my legs."[64] Even though the 75th Congress began with a two-thirds Democratic majority, it was wary of FDR's plans and less than thrilled at the prospect of greater presidential influence over the New Deal state. Roosevelt's plan undermined the benefits to Congress of delegation, because it would weaken Congress's influence over agency decisions while expanding the President's authority over what was essentially lawmaking.

Brownlow's report landed before Congress at the same time as FDR's court-packing plan. While the two plans addressed different problems, they both fed fears of presidential aggrandizement at the expense of the other branches. Key congressional leaders had not been consulted or briefed on the reorganization plan, which they proceeded to attack as another step toward despotism, or a power grab by the university intellectuals who no doubt would run the new agencies, all at a time when totalitarianism was raising its ugly head in Europe. In 1938, the bill failed in the House and was replaced by a more modest bill that gave FDR a limited ability to reorganize government.[65] Under that authority, FDR still managed to locate the Bureau of the Budget within a new Executive Office of the President. As the Office of Management and Budget, it today exercises central review over the economic costs and benefits of all federal regulation, one of the President's most powerful tools for rationalizing the activities of the administrative state.[66]

FDR also expanded the resources within the White House, an institution now separate from the Executive Office of the President, which enabled him to gain more information and control over the cabinet agencies. Still, the independent agencies remained outside the cabinet departments. FDR never successfully established any single entity to coordinate the activities of the entire administrative state, and his failed bill demonstrates the enduring constitutional checks on the Presidency. Only Congress could pass the laws needed to reorganize the cabinet departments, reshape the jurisdiction and structure of the independent agencies, and provide the funds and positions in a new, revitalized White House.[67]

While FDR suffered defeats at the hands of Congress, he continued to claim and exercise inherent executive authority that went beyond mere control of personnel. He signed statements to object to riders inserted into needed spending bills, which he believed to be unconstitutional. Congress, for example, attempted to force the President to fire three bureaucrats it believed were "subversives" by specifically barring any federal funds to pay their salaries. Roosevelt signed the bill but objected to its unconstitutional end run around the President's power over the removal of executive branch officials. Ultimately, the officials left within months, but they sued for their back pay all the way to the Supreme Court, which agreed that Congress had violated the Constitution.[68]

President Roosevelt also followed Lincoln's example in using his executive power to fight racial discrimination. Although Lincoln had relied on his power as Commander-in-Chief to free the slaves, the Southern states imposed racial segregation in the years after the Civil War, ultimately with the approval of the Supreme Court.[69] While FDR did not take segregation head on, he issued an executive order in 1941 to prohibit racial discrimination in employment on federal defense contracts.[70] Roosevelt had no statutory authority to order the federal government to provide fair treatment in employment to all, regardless of race. He could rely only upon his constitutional authority as President to oversee the management of federal programs. Once war began, President Roosevelt could clarify that his orders were taken under his power as both Chief Executive and Commander-in-Chief in wartime.[71] FDR's orders would not be the first, nor the last, time that the cause of racial equality would depend on a broad understanding of presidential power.

The New Deal depended upon broad theories of the Presidency and the role of the federal government in national life. What remains less clear is whether FDR's fundamental reorientation of the government into a positive, active instrument of national policy was worthwhile. Contemporary critics of the modern Presidency question whether Chief Executives, acting alone, have led the nation into disastrous wars. We need also ask, but rarely do, whether the expansion of executive power at home has benefited the nation. To the extent we debate the desirability of the administrative state, most American scholars today bemoan the fact that the New Deal did not go far enough. They argue that the New Deal failed because it did not achieve a full-fledged European welfare state, or that FDR's coalition fragmented and failed to follow through on the promise of liberal reform.[72] These critics, who usually are those most likely to criticize the President in foreign affairs, cry out for more executive power domestically.

Vesting the President with more authority to control the government's regulation of the economy may make sense during an emergency, but it did not work in solving the Great Depression. Economists recognize today that the New Deal neither put an end to high rates of unemployment nor restored consistent economic growth. FDR's monetary and fiscal policy often pursued the opposite of what was needed, and full employment would return only with American rearmament in the first years of World War II. Other New Deal policies were counterproductive, such as allowing industry to set production quotas, reduce production to raise prices, and restrict employment by raising minimum wages. Economists similarly doubt whether the creation of national regulation of the securities markets and other industries contributed to the eventual economic recovery, even though it was certainly valuable for postwar prosperity. If, as Milton Friedman argues, the Great Depression would have proven to be only a normal recession with some deft monetary policy from the Federal Reserve, it bears asking whether the permanent bureaucracy was needed at all.

Decades later, American Presidents would campaign against the excessive regulation set in place by the New Deal. The administrative state we have today failed to end the Great Depression. Was the administrative state worth the price? There is little doubt that the explosion in the size and power of the administrative state has transformed the nature of American politics.

The federal government has dramatically expanded the scope of regulation to include not just national economic activity, such as workplace conditions and minimum wages and hours, but also the environment and endangered species, educational standards, state and local corruption, consumer product safety, communications technology and ownership, illegal narcotics and gun crimes, and corporate governance. It has produced less deliberation in Congress, which now delegates sweeping powers to the agencies, and has placed the initial authority to issue federal law affecting private individuals in administrative agencies. Those agencies are not directly accountable to the people through elections, except for the thin layer of presidential appointees at the very top. Special-interest groups have come to play a significant role in influencing both congressional committees and agencies, gaining economic "rents" for their members at the expense of the broader public.

This is not a plea to return to the laissez-faire capitalism of the 19th-century variety. The administrative state no doubt has produced social benefits, and there are important areas where the greater information and expertise held by the executive agencies improves government policy, but it remains an open question whether the centralization of economic and social regulation in the national government has been, on balance, a success. It is undeniable that the requirement of minimum national standards, most especially in the area of civil rights, was a necessary and long-overdue change. Equality under law should not have been a matter of legislative or executive discretion, but a requirement of the Reconstruction Amendments to the Constitution. National control of other economic and social issues, however, may not have been worth the cost in increased government spending, larger budget deficits, a permanent government apparatus of unprecedented size (at least in the American experience), the rise of interest-group politics, and interference with efficient market mechanisms.

Federal agencies may impose uniform rules, but they may not impose the best rules. In the absence of broad national regulation, states could enact a diversity of policies on issues such as the economy, the environment, education, crime, and social policy. People could vote with their feet by moving to states that adopt their preferred package of policies, while experimentation could identify the most effective solutions to economic and social problems. The New Deal's concentration of regulatory authority in Washington, D.C., sapped the vitality of the states, whose powers are only a pale imitation of those they held in the 19th century.[73] FDR certainly deserves credit for restoring Americans' optimism and faith in government, and for alleviating the suffering inflicted by the Depression, but it remains doubtful whether the great wrenching in the fabric of our federal system of government and the expansion in the President's constitutional powers in the domestic realm can be justified by any limited advance in triggering a recovery. Despite its revolution in domestic presidential power and government structure, the New Deal appears to have had little impact on ending the worst economic collapse in American history.

THE GATHERING STORM

FDR'S CLAIM TO GREATNESS lies not in the New Deal, but his defeat of one of the greatest external threats our nation has faced, fascist Germany and Japan. FDR exercised farsighted vision in preparing the nation for a necessary war unwanted by a large minority, and arguably a majority, of Congress and the American people. In the process, the President skirted, stretched, and broke a series of neutrality laws designed to prevent American entry into World War II. Sometimes he went to Congress and the American people to seek support for his actions, sometimes he did not, but throughout the lead-up to war, FDR set national security policy within the executive branch.[74]

Debate has raged for decades over whether the Japanese attack on Pearl Harbor was a surprise, or whether FDR or the American government had advance knowledge of the attack. Some have suspected that FDR believed that the only way to rouse the American people to war was for the United States to be attacked first. In this respect, FDR had the same instincts as Lincoln. The conventional wisdom today attributes more of the blame for Pearl Harbor to incompetence by the field commanders and complacency in Washington, and has put to rest the idea that FDR actually knew that the Japanese would attack Pearl Harbor.[75]

Recent scholarly work suggests that FDR managed events to maneuver the Japanese into a corner, with a strong possibility that the Japanese would attack American interests somewhere in the Pacific, most likely the Philippines. Roosevelt's imposition of an arms, steel, and oil embargo against the Japanese Empire was designed to force Tokyo to either withdraw from China or attack American, British, and Dutch possessions in Asia for natural resources.[76] FDR pressed Japan in order to bring the United States to bear against the greater

threat of Germany.[77] FDR could not have walked the United States
to the brink of war without a broad understanding of the President's
constitutional powers and the willingness to exercise them.

Roosevelt had laid claim to sweeping executive authority in foreign affairs even before war with Germany and Japan looked certain.
One assist came from the hands of an unlikely source: Justice Sutherland. While Sutherland believed the New Deal state unconstitutionally trampled on the natural rights of individuals, as Hadley Arkes
has argued, he still strongly supported presidential power in foreign
affairs.[78] This became clear in the case *United States v. Curtiss-Wright
Export Corporation.*[79]

In 1934, Congress had delegated to the President the authority
to cut off all U.S. arms sales to Bolivia and Paraguay, which were
fighting a nasty border war, if he found the ban would advance peace
in the region. FDR proclaimed an arms embargo in effect on the
same day that Congress passed the law, and the next day the Justice Department prosecuted four executives of the Curtiss-Wright
Export Corporation for trying to sell 15 machine guns to Bolivia.
Curtiss-Wright, which traced its roots to the Wright brothers,
would supply the engines for the DC-3 air transport and the B-17
Flying Fortress and build the P-40 fighter.[80] Taking its case all the
way to the Supreme Court, the company argued that the law had
delegated unconstitutional authority over international commerce
to the President. If Congress wanted to impose an arms embargo, it
would have to do it itself, not just hand the authority to FDR.

In a remarkable and controversial opinion, Justice Sutherland
declared that the constitutional standards that ruled the government's actions domestically did not apply in the same way to foreign affairs. The Constitution's careful limitation of the national
government's powers, so as to preserve the general authority of the
states, did not extend beyond the water's edge. In the arena of for-

eign affairs, Sutherland maintained, the American Revolution had directly transferred the full powers of national sovereignty from Great Britain to the Union. "The powers to declare and wage war, to conclude peace, to make treaties, to maintain diplomatic relations with other sovereignties," Sutherland wrote, "if they had never been mentioned in the Constitution, would have vested in the federal government as necessary concomitants of nationality."[81] In words that could have been cribbed from Abraham Lincoln, the Court declared that the "Union existed before the Constitution," and therefore the Union could exercise the same powers over war and peace as any other nation.

An argument in favor of exclusive federal power over national security and international relations, however, does not dictate which branch should exercise it. Sutherland located that authority in the President because of the dangers posed by foreign nations and the executive branch's structural ability to act swiftly and secretly. "In this vast external realm, with its important, complicated, delicate and manifold problems, the President alone has the power to speak or listen as a representative of the nation." Echoing Hamilton and Jefferson, and quoting then-Congressman John Marshall, Sutherland declared, "The President is the sole organ of the nation in its external relations, and its sole representative with foreign nations."

It did not matter that, on the facts of *Curtiss-Wright*, FDR was acting pursuant to congressional delegation. "We are here dealing not alone with an authority vested in the President by an exertion of legislative power, but with such an authority plus the very delicate, plenary and exclusive power of the President," which does not "require as a basis for its exercise an act of Congress." Sutherland found great advantages to the United States in vesting these powers in the executive, rather than the legislature. The President, not Congress, "has the better opportunity of knowing the conditions which prevail in foreign countries, and especially is this true in time of war. He has confidential sources of information."

Another case gave Justice Sutherland the opportunity to deliver a second blessing to FDR's vigorous use of his presidential powers. In 1933, Roosevelt ended American efforts to isolate the Soviet Union and unilaterally recognized its communist government. As part of an executive agreement with the Soviets, the United States took on all rights and claims of the USSR against American citizens, such as those involving the expropriation of property. The federal government sued to recover money and property held by Russians in the United States, which were allegedly owed to the Soviet government. What made the recognition of the Soviet Union so remarkable was that FDR not only had set the policy of the United States and entered into an international agreement on his own, but the government used that agreement to set aside state property and contract rules — all without any action of Congress or the Senate.

Property owners resisted. Augustus Belmont, a New York City banker, refused to turn over deposits held on behalf of the Petrograd Metal Works after the nationalization of all Russian corporations in 1918. FDR's executive agreement with the Soviets required that legal ownership of the profits be transferred to the United States government. Belmont's estate refused to turn the money over because, it claimed, the property law of New York state protected it.[82]

In *United States v. Belmont*, the Supreme Court again sided with the executive. It found that the recognition of the USSR, the international agreement, and the preemption of state law all fell within the President's constitutional powers to the exclusion of the states. "In respect of all international negotiations and compacts, and in respect of our foreign relations generally, state lines disappear. As to such purposes the State of New York does not exist." Presidents since have used this power to make literally thousands of international agreements with other countries without the Senate's advice and consent — from 1939 to 1989, the United States entered into 11,698 executive agreements and only 702 treaties.[83] The courts have upheld sole executive agreements several times since, including an agreement ending the Iranian hostage crisis and another preempting the state law claims of Holocaust survivors against German companies.[84]

The Supreme Court did not grant the President these powers in foreign affairs. Only the Constitution could do that. Presidents from Washington onward had interpreted the Constitution's vesting of the Chief Executive and Commander-in-Chief authorities to give them the initiative to protect the national security, set foreign policy, and negotiate with other nations. Sutherland's opinions gave judicial recognition to decades of presidential practice; what had been the product of presidential enterprise and congressional acquiescence became formal constitutional law. Roosevelt would draw on these authorities as he maneuvered to send aid to the Allies and bring the United States into the war against the fascist powers.

FDR had to draw on his well of presidential powers because he faced both a looming external threat and vocal domestic isolationism. As early as 1935, Roosevelt had concluded that Hitler's Germany posed a threat to the United States.[85] As the Axis powers increased their militaries and launched offensives against their neighbors, the President became convinced that military force would be necessary to protect American interests. FDR's approach represented something of a revolution in American strategic thought. No longer would American national security depend on the safety provided by two oceans and control of the Western Hemisphere, where it had felt no reluctance to launch wars of its own.[86] German defeat of Great Britain would remove a valuable buffer that had prevented European nations from naval and air access to the Americas. And if Hitler succeeded in gaining complete control of the resources of the European continent, Germany would become a superpower with the means to threaten the United States.[87] A central objective of American strategy was to maintain a balance of power in Europe and Asia to contain expansionist Germany and Japan, but if war came, FDR and his advisors identified Hitler as the primary threat.[88]

By December 1940, FDR could be relatively open with the public about his broader goals. In his famous "Arsenal of Democracy" speech, he accused the fascist powers of conquering Europe as a prelude to larger aims that threatened the United States. Never since "Jamestown and Plymouth Rock has our American civilization been in such danger as now," FDR warned.[89] "The Nazi masters of Germany have made it clear that they intend not only to dominate all life and thought in their own country," FDR told the nation by radio, "but also to enslave the whole of Europe, and then to use the resources of Europe to dominate the rest of the world." He rejected the idea that the "broad expanse of the Atlantic and of the Pacific" would protect the United States. It was only the British navy that protected the oceans from the Nazis. The United States had to begin massive rearmament and provide arms and assistance to the free nations that were bearing the brunt of the fighting. FDR did not tell the public that he was already taking action to bring the nation closer to war, first against Europe to stop Hitler, while holding off Japanese expansion in Asia.

FDR's strategic vision required several elements to succeed. The United States had to send military and financial aid to Britain and France, help those supplies cross the Atlantic Ocean and build up the United States military (especially the navy and army air corps). If the Allies' fortunes fell far enough, the nation would have to be prepared to intervene. Resistance would come from the many Americans who believed that Wilson had erred in entering World War I and wanted to avoid American involvement in another internecine

squabble in Europe. Between 1939 and 1941, a majority of Americans
grew to support aid to the Allies, but that was as far as they would
go. By as late as May 1941, almost 80 percent of the public wanted
the United States to stay out of the conflict. Seventy percent felt that
FDR had gone too far or had helped Britain enough.[90] Isolationists
blamed American entry into World War I on President Wilson's use
of his executive powers to tilt American neutrality toward Britain
and France. Worried about a rerun, they pressed for strict limitations on presidential power to keep the United States out of the
European war.[91]

Opposition to American intervention took more concrete form
than public opinion polls. Congress enacted Neutrality Acts in
1935, 1936, 1937, and 1939 to prevent the United States from aiding
either side. Congress passed the 1935 Act after Germany repudiated
the disarmament requirements of the Treaty of Versailles and Italy
threatened to invade Ethiopia in defiance of the League of Nations.
It required the President to proclaim, after the outbreak of war
between two or more nations, an embargo of all arms, ammunition,
or "implements of war" against the belligerents.[92] It gave FDR the
authority to decide when to terminate the embargo, but it left him
little choice as to when to begin one.

The Act prohibited the United States from helping a victim
nation and punishing the aggressor, instead requiring a complete
cutoff for both. FDR had privately opposed the law's mandatory
terms, fought to keep his discretionary control over foreign affairs,
and in signing the bill predicted that its "inflexible provisions might
drag us into war instead of keeping us out."[93] Later acts prohibited the extension of loans or financial assistance to belligerents,[94]
extended the embargo to civil wars,[95] and allowed the ban to cover
only arms and munitions, but not raw materials. In 1939, Congress
enacted an even tougher prohibition that sought to prevent belliger-

ents from "cash-and-carry" transactions for raw materials by prohibiting American vessels from transporting anything to nations at war.

Domestic resistance required FDR to adopt an approach that
gave the appearance that the United States was being dragged into
the war. By 1941, with Hitler in control of Europe, and Japan occupying large parts of China, FDR wanted to find a way for the United
States to enter the war on the side of Britain. In August 1941, for
example, FDR told Prime Minister Winston Churchill that he
could not rely on Congress to declare war against Germany. Instead,
FDR "would wage war, but not declare it." According to Churchill's
account of their conversation at the Atlantic Conference, FDR said
"he would become more and more provocative" and promised that
"everything would be done to force an incident" that would "justify
him in opening hostilities."[96]

Roosevelt's plans to move the United States toward war
depended in part on Congress. The Constitution gives Congress
control over international and domestic interstate commerce, as well
as the money and property of the United States. FDR could lay little
claim to constitutional authority to dictate arms-export policies or
to provide financial and material aid to the Allies. FDR initially
hoped that the United States could provide enough assistance to
Britain and France — the United States would prove the "great Arsenal of Democracy," in his famous words — to postpone the need for
American military intervention in Europe. After the fall of France,
FDR realized that Great Britain could not hold off the Nazis on
its own, but he hoped to send enough aid to keep Britain independent while he prepared the American public for war. FDR pressed
Congress for several changes to the Neutrality Acts that would send
more help to the Allies. In the 1936 and 1937 Acts, for example, the
administration won more presidential discretion to determine when
a foreign war had broken out. By 1939, it succeeded in changing the

law to allow the President to put off a proclamation of neutrality if necessary to protect American peace and security.[97] This effectively allowed Britain and France, which controlled the sea routes to the Americas, to continue to receive aid.

FDR used this flexibility to continue supplying arms and money to China by not finding a war to exist there, even after Japan had attacked Beijing and Nanjing.[98] Similarly, Roosevelt refused to invoke the Neutrality Acts when Germany invaded Czechoslovakia in 1939, or Russia in 1941, because a blanket embargo would have prevented American aid from flowing to the Allies.[99] FDR was not living up to the spirit of the Neutrality Acts because by manipulating the embargo rules he was actually helping one side in various conflicts, but Congress would not allow him to go farther. FDR's proposals throughout 1939 and 1940 to reform the Neutrality Acts to allow for direct military aid to the Allies repeatedly failed.

As his efforts to get Congress to change the Neutrality Acts flagged, FDR became more aggressive in calling forth his constitutional powers. He asked Attorney General Robert Jackson, "How far do you think I can go in ignoring the existing act — even though I did sign it?" Vice President John Nance Garner and Secretary of the Interior Harold Ickes argued that the President's constitutional authority in foreign affairs allowed him to act beyond the Acts.[100] Instead of overriding them, however, Roosevelt simply became more creative in interpreting them. On May 22, 1940, as German armies swept through France, FDR ordered the sale of World War I–era equipment to the Allies; on June 3, he ordered the transfer of $38 million in weapons to U.S. Steel, which promptly sold them at no profit to the British and French. The administration argued that these sales did not violate the Neutrality Acts because the arms were "surplus."[101] Three days later (just after the British had evacuated 300,000 soldiers from the German noose around Dunkirk), the navy sold 50 Hell Diver bombers, which had been introduced to service only in 1938, and 93 obsolete army bombers to Britain because they were "temporarily in excess of requirements."[102] The sales occurred at a time when the United States Army could field only 80,000 combat troops in five divisions, while the German army in Western Europe deployed 2 million men in 140 divisions. The U.S. Army Air Corps had only 160 fighter planes and 52 heavy bombers.[103] Announcing the decision on June 8, FDR told a news conference that "a plane can get out of date darned fast." Two days later, in a speech at the University of Virginia, FDR declared isolationism an "obvious delusion" and called for an Allied victory over "the gods of force and hate" to prevent a world run by totalitarian governments.[104]

American aid came too little, too late; France requested an armistice on June 17, 1940. In the midst of a presidential campaign for an unprecedented third term, FDR sought bipartisan support for his policies and replaced isolationists in his cabinet with two internationalist Republicans: Henry Stimson as Secretary of War and Frank Knox as Secretary of the Navy. Both favored repealing the neutrality laws, boosting the U.S. military through a draft, and sending large amounts of aid to Great Britain.[105] Britain's destroyer fleet, which had suffered almost 50 percent losses, needed reinforcements to block a German invasion force and safeguard its trade lifelines.[106] Churchill wrote to Roosevelt that acquiring American destroyers was "a matter of life and death."[107] FDR reacted by planning to send two dozen PT boats immediately, and said that Navy lawyers who thought the sale illegal should follow orders or go on vacation.[108] After word of FDR's plans leaked, Congress enacted a law forbidding the sale of any military equipment "essential to the defense of the United States," as certified by the Chief of Naval Operations or the Army Chief of Staff, and reasserted a World War I law's ban on sending any "vessel of war" to a belligerent.[109]

Congress's tightening of neutrality delayed FDR for two months. While the Battle of Britain raged in the skies, Churchill begged FDR for additional destroyers. "The whole fate of the war," the Prime Minister wrote in July, "may be decided by this minor and easily remediable factor," and he urged that "this is the thing to do now."[110] FDR and his advisors planned a transfer to Britain of 50 World War I destroyers declared to be "surplus," even though similar warships from the same era were being activated for navy service. In exchange, Britain would provide basing rights in its Western Hemisphere territories to the United States. In August, the President concluded an executive agreement with Britain, kept secret at first and without congressional approval, to make the trade.

FDR's advisors divided over the deal's legality. One legal advisor believed it violated the June 28 statute and the Espionage Act of 1917, which forbade sending an armed vessel to any belligerent while the United States remained neutral; State Department and Justice Department lawyers agreed. But Dean Acheson, then Undersecretary of the Treasury, argued that the June 28 law implicitly recognized the President's constitutional power to transfer any military asset in order to improve national security, while others recommended that the government first sell the destroyers to private companies that could then resell them to the British.[111] Acheson even argued that the 1917 law applied only to ships that were built specifically on order for a belligerent and not to existing ships originally built or used for the navy.

Attorney General Jackson drew on these ideas in his legal opinion blessing the deal, but also relied on the President's Commander-in-Chief power. "Happily there has been little occasion in our history for the interpretation of the powers of the President as Commander-in-Chief," Jackson wrote to FDR. "I do not find it necessary to rest upon that power alone." Nevertheless, "it will hardly be open to controversy that the vesting of such a function in the President also places upon him a responsibility to use all constitutional authority which he may possess to provide adequate bases and stations" for the most effective use of the armed forces. The perilous circumstances facing the United States reinforced the Commander-in-Chief's power. "It seems equally beyond doubt that present world conditions forbid him to risk any delay that is constitutionally avoidable."[112] Any statutory effort by Congress to prevent the President from transferring military equipment to help American national security would be of "questionable constitutionality."

Jackson defended the exclusion of Congress. He thought that the deal could take the form of an executive agreement because it required neither the appropriation of funds nor an obligation to act in the future. Justice Sutherland's opinion in *Curtiss-Wright*, which the Attorney General extensively quoted, supported the argument. Jackson had a more difficult time with the Neutrality Acts. He read the June 28 law to recognize the President's authority to transfer naval vessels to Britain, subject only to the requirement that they be surplus or obsolete. It did not prohibit the transfer of property "merely because it is still used or usable or of possible value for future use," but only if the transfer weakened the national defense. The "overage" destroyers, as he called them, could be found to fall outside the statute and hence within the President's authority, which must have derived from the Commander-in-Chief power, to exchange them for valuable military bases. Jackson, however, advised that transferring brand-new mosquito boats would violate Congress's ban on sending ships to a belligerent.

Jackson issued an even broader reading of the Commander-in-Chief power in May 1941, when FDR allowed British pilots to train in American military schools. Under the Commander-in-Chief power, the President "has supreme command over the land and naval forces of the country and may order them to perform such military duties as, in his opinion, are necessary or appropriate for the defense of the United States."[113] The President could "command and direct the armed forces in their immediate movements and operations" and "dispose of troops and equipment" to promote the national security. Jackson read the passage of Lend-Lease as support for FDR's judgment that helping Britain was important to the national defense. If the President had full constitutional authority to use the armed forces, even to use military force, to protect the nation by helping Britain, then he must also have the lesser power to train British airmen. "I have no doubt of the President's lawful authority to utilize forces under his command to instruct others in matters of defense which are vital to the security of the United States." It "would be anomalous indeed," Jackson observed, if the military could provide Britain with arms but could not train the British how to use them.

Reaction to the destroyers-for-bases deal, announced in early August, attacked FDR's methods more than his goals. Roosevelt worried that his energetic use of executive power would feed fears that he was becoming an autocrat, worries punctuated by his nomination that summer for an unprecedented third term as President. Leaks of secret Anglo-American staff talks and announcement of a joint U.S.-Canadian defense board already had isolationists attacking FDR for taking the United States into war. FDR predicted that revelation of the executive agreement would "raise hell with Congress" and lead to accusations that he was a "warmonger" and "dictator," and might torpedo his reelection hopes.[114]

FDR's first two predictions quickly came true. His Republican opponent, Wendell Willkie, supported the policy but declared that FDR's unilateral action was "the most dictatorial and arbitrary act of any President in the history of the United States."[115] Edwin Borchard, a Yale professor of international law, argued that Roosevelt had assumed dictatorial powers, placed himself above the law, and threatened to "break down constitutional safeguards." The Constitution, Borchard wrote, "does not give the President *carte blanche* to do anything he pleases in foreign affairs."[116] The nation's leading scholar of constitutional law, Edward Corwin of Princeton, attacked Jackson's opinion as "an endorsement of unrestrained autocracy in the field of our foreign relations, neither more nor less." In the *New York Times*, Corwin asked "why may not any and all of Congress's specifically delegated powers be set aside by the President's 'executive power' and the country be put on a totalitarian basis without further ado?"[117]

Despite these ringing attacks on presidential power, the destroyers-for-bases deal proved remarkably popular — Gallup polls showed 62 percent in favor — encouraging even bolder steps.[118] By October 1940, FDR asked for and received appropriations of $17.7 billion for national defense — his administration's original estimate for the year had been $1.84 billion — and defense spending doubled the following year.[119] In June 1940, he called for the first peacetime draft in American history, which Congress enacted in September only after Willkie publicly agreed. A Wall Street lawyer and former Democrat, Willkie was a dark-horse candidate who had won the nomination without ever having occupied public office. His attacks on the New Deal had gained little traction during the campaign, so Willkie campaigned against a "warmonger" and dictator who had made "secret agreements" to enter a war that would kill thousands of young Americans. "If his promise to keep our boys out of foreign wars is no better than his promise to balance the budget," Willkie said on the stump, "they're already almost on the transports."[120] By the end of October, Willkie came within four points of the President, and Roosevelt went on a speaking tour to reassure mothers in a speech at Boston Garden on October 30, 1940, that "your boys are not going to be sent into any foreign wars."[121] Though the polls showed the election close, FDR prevailed by 27 million to Willkie's 22 million and an Electoral College majority of 449–82.

After the election, FDR redoubled his efforts to send aid to Britain. He authorized secret staff talks between American and British military planners, who recommended a grand strategy of defeating Germany first while holding Japan to a stalemate.[122] In November, FDR ordered the army to make B-17 bombers immediately available to the British, to be replaced by British planes on order in American factories, and he discussed making half of all American arms production available to the British. British finances collapsed in late November; the country could no longer pay for the material it needed to continue the war. Britain's ambassador to the United States, Lord Lothian, appealed to the American public on November 23 by saying to a group of journalists, "Well, boys," he said, "Britain's broke; it's your money we want."[123]

Lothian's report of Britain's functional bankruptcy shocked the White House into action. FDR approved the sale of $2.1 billion in weapons that the British could not pay for, as well as the diversion of $700 million in Reconstruction Finance Corporation funds to underwrite the factory expansions needed for the increased arms sales.[124] The President hit upon one of his most artful evasions of neutrality, Lend-Lease, which would "get away from the dollar sign," as he told reporters at a December 17, 1940, press conference. The United States would "lend" Britain weapons and munitions and, rather than demand immediate payment, would expect their return after the war's end. Of course, the idea was a complete fiction; war would consume the arms. FDR deployed a homey analogy: if a house were on fire, a neighbor would lend a garden hose with the expectation that it would be returned later, rather than demanding $15 for the cost of the hose.[125]

Lend-Lease required congressional action. In his famous "Arsenal of Democracy" speech on December 29, Roosevelt defended Lend-Lease and broader aid to the Allies with his most stirring language. FDR declared that the Nazis posed the most direct threat to the security of the United States since its founding. To avoid war, the United States would have to become the great "arsenal of democracy" for the free nations carrying on the fight. The United States would be less likely to get into war "if we do all we can now to support the nations defending themselves against attack by the Axis," rather than "if we acquiesce in their defeat."

Disclaiming any intention to send a new "American Expeditionary Force" outside the United States, FDR declared that "the people of Europe who are defending themselves do not ask us to do their fighting." All they seek are "the implements for war." Increasing national defense production and sending it to Britain would "keep war away from our country and our people."[126] It was one of the most popular speeches of FDR's Presidency: roughly 80 percent of the public agreed.[127] Congress waited until March 1941 to give its approval to Lend-Lease,[128] but FDR decided to move forward during that critical time anyway. He authorized British purchase of 23,000 airplanes in November 1940, and rifles and ammunition in February 1941. He ordered the U.S. military to purchase munitions factories but diverted the production to Britain.[129]

In spring 1941, FDR turned to the protection of the supplies that would begin to flow across the Atlantic, and took unilateral action that provoked the Nazis and drew the United States ever closer to war. In March, FDR moved to place Greenland under American military protection, and in April he gave orders to the navy to extend its security zone as far as Greenland and the Azores, and to begin locating German submarines and reporting their positions to the Royal Navy. In May, he transferred one-quarter of the Pacific fleet to the Atlantic to deter any German effort to seize Atlantic islands for bases. He declared an "unlimited national emergency" at the end of the month and told the nation that helping Britain win the battle of the Atlantic was critical to keeping the Nazis out of the Western Hemisphere. "It would be suicide to wait until they are in our front yard," Roosevelt argued.[130] He followed his speech with a June deployment of a Marine brigade to occupy Iceland (which is about 1,200 miles from London and 2,800 miles from Washington, D.C.), which freed up a British division and extended the American security zone even farther. In July, he announced that the navy would begin escorting ships between the United States and Iceland.

FDR did not seek or receive congressional approval for any of these deployments, which made clear, if earlier aid had not, that the United States was no longer a true neutral. Still, Congress retained ample checks on presidential power. FDR could send only 4,000 marines to Iceland because of the small size of the regular armed forces, and he could not send any of the new draftees because Congress had attached a provision to the Conscription Act forbidding their deployment outside the Western Hemisphere. Congress had also limited the terms of service of the 900,000 draftees to one year, requiring FDR to go to Congress to win an extension. Even with America occupying Iceland and Greenland and escorting ships in the North Atlantic, only 51 percent of Americans supported the draft extension, and Congress narrowly approved it.[131]

Meanwhile, FDR pursued measures to check Japan's expansion and perhaps provoke it into a conflict. Japan had been waging war in China since the 1931 Manchuria crisis and had launched an invasion to conquer the whole nation in 1937. Japanese military and civilian leaders sought to create a "Greater East Asia Co-Prosperity Sphere" that would supply the raw materials for the Japanese economy and the war in China. In 1940, Japan had intensified its attacks in China and had moved into Indochina. In September 1940, it entered into the Axis agreement with Germany and Italy.

Roosevelt launched a campaign of economic warfare, without any effort to rely on legal authority. In July 1940, for example, FDR blocked aviation gasoline exports to Japan. Chiang Kai-shek had sent an urgent message to Roosevelt that without more aid, the Nationalist Chinese resistance to Japan would fail. FDR responded by banning the export of iron and steel to Japan. In November, he sent $100 million and 100 warplanes to the Chinese Nationalist government, and in the spring he authorized volunteers — Colonel Chennault's Flying Tigers — to fly fighters for China. FDR had never found China and Japan to be at war under the 1939 Neutrality Act, so he had no statutory authority to impose the materials embargo on Japan or to send money and arms to China.[132] Roosevelt simply undertook the actions as President in order to protect the national security.

Japan's expansion south toward Indochina and Thailand raised the possibility of conflict. On August 1, 1941, FDR ordered a freeze of Japanese assets in the United States, reduced U.S. oil exports to pre-war levels, and prohibited the sale of high-octane aircraft gasoline to Japan. By mistake, administrators executed a complete oil embargo against Japan, which FDR did nothing to correct. FDR opened negotiations to reach a settlement with the Japanese government, though he knew because of American code-breaking success that Tokyo was considering an attack on American, British, and Dutch possessions in Asia.

Some historians believe that FDR's goal was to hold off Japan while resources could be devoted against the more dire challenge in Europe, a view held by many of his military and civilian advisors. Marc Trachtenberg, however, has convincingly argued that FDR deliberately painted the Japanese into a corner.[133] In the course of negotiations, Roosevelt demanded that Tokyo end its war in China in exchange for a resumption of U.S. oil and steel exports, yet FDR and his advisors knew that Japan would not willingly give up its territorial gains in China. "[T]he United States had been waging preventive economic warfare against Imperial Japan for at least 18 months prior to Pearl Harbor," Colin Gray writes. "U.S. measures of economic blockade left Japan with no alternative to war consistent with its sense of national honor. The oil embargo eventually would literally immobilize the Japanese Navy. So Washington confronted Tokyo with the unenviable choice between de facto complete political surrender of its ambitions in China, or war." [134]

As FDR squeezed Japan, he expanded political and military assistance to the British. On August 9, he met Churchill in Placentia Bay, off Newfoundland, where the two leaders issued the Atlantic Charter. It declared Anglo-American principles in the war to be: no Anglo-American aggrandizement, opposition to undemocratic changes in territory, self-government for all peoples, equal access to trade and natural resources, international economic cooperation, a guarantee of security and freedom to all nations, freedom of the seas, disarmament of aggressors and reduction in armaments, and plans for a collective system of international security.[135] During the discussions, FDR made clear to Churchill his desire to bring the United States into the war by forcing an incident with Germany,[136] and set out to make his wish come true by ordering full naval escorts for British convoys between the United States and Iceland, which put the Germans in the position of firing on U.S. warships or conceding the Battle of the Atlantic. Without input from Congress, FDR had joined together the fates of the United States and Britain.

An undeclared shooting war soon broke out. On September 4, a German submarine fired on the destroyer USS *Greer*, which FDR used to publicly justify "shoot-on-sight" orders for naval escorts in the Atlantic. Only later did Congress learn that the *Greer* had been hunting the submarine with British airplanes and had dropped depth charges on the Germans. FDR declared the Nazis to be the equivalent of modern-day pirates and compared German subs and commerce raiders to "rattlesnakes of the Atlantic." As he put it, "[W]hen you see a rattlesnake poised to strike, you do not wait until he has struck before you crush him."[137]

FDR won broad support for the navy's new rules of engagement in the Atlantic, but at the price of deliberately deceiving the public about the facts.[138] He followed with an October speech claiming that captured Nazi plans envisioned the division of North and South America into five dependent states and the abolition of the freedom of religion.[139] The shooting war led to German submarine attacks on two American destroyers, the USS *Kearny* and the USS *Reuben James*, with the deaths of 11 and 115 sailors, respectively. FDR responded by seeking amendment of the neutrality laws to allow merchantmen to arm and carry goods directly to British ports.

The changes passed Congress by small majorities because 70 percent of the public told pollsters they opposed American entry into the war. FDR concluded that the public, influenced by the memory of the way Wilson had led the country into World War I, would not rally behind a war waged in response to these isolated incidents. Rising tensions with Japan, however, provided other opportunities. After the Atlantic Conference, FDR informed the Japanese ambassador that any further expansion in Southeast Asia would force him to take any and all measures necessary "toward insuring the safety and security of the United States."[140] He offered to undertake formal negotiations with Prince Konoye, the Japanese Prime Minister, only if Japan suspended its "expansionist activities" and openly declared its intentions in the Pacific. FDR asked that Japan terminate the Axis alliance, withdraw from China, and open up its trading system. He consciously demanded terms he knew that the Japanese were unlikely to accept.

Japanese cabinet meetings on September 3–6 concluded that unless the government reached a settlement with the United States by October, its military would attack American, British, and Dutch possessions in Asia. Tokyo decided its terms must include the freedom to conclude matters in China, an end to Anglo-American military action in the Pacific, and secure access to raw materials for the economy. FDR refused to negotiate on these conditions and instead ordered the reinforcement of the Philippines. By October 15, FDR and his advisors believed that they needed more "diplomatic fencing" to create the image "that Japan was put into the wrong and made the first bad move — overt move."[141]

Thanks to electronic intercepts of Japanese communications, FDR knew that the Japanese would attack if no settlement were reached, and he tried to string out negotiations to give the armed forces time to strengthen the Philippines. On Thanksgiving Day, FDR discussed with his advisors the chances of a Japanese sneak attack and asked "how we should maneuver them into the position of firing the first shot without allowing too much danger to ourselves."[142] He also told the British that he would respond to any attack on their possessions in Asia. Still, FDR realized that without an enemy attack on the United States, his other measures would not convince the American people to support entry into World War II.

On December 7, 1941, the Japanese solved FDR's conundrum. No evidence supports the theories that FDR knew that Pearl Harbor was the target, nor that he willfully ignored the possibility of devastating losses to the Pacific Fleet. FDR did not consciously know about any attack on the United States — rather, he placed the Japanese in the position of choosing between war and giving up their imperial ambitions in China and the rest of the Pacific. The most that can be said is that if war were to come, FDR had tried for more than a year to maneuver the Axis powers into firing a first shot. Pearl Harbor guaranteed the unity of the American people, just as Fort Sumter had eight decades before. As FDR told the American people the next day, December 7 was a "day that would live in infamy," and he asked Congress for a declaration of war, which it promptly granted.

Hitler further obliged by declaring war on the United States three days later. FDR exercised foresighted leadership in recognizing the Axis threat to the United States and the free nations of the West. But faced with a recalcitrant Congress and a reluctant public, FDR had to use his constitutional powers to move the nation into a war that he knew, as perhaps no one else did, was in the country's best interests. If he had faithfully obeyed the Neutrality Acts, American entry into the war might have been delayed by months, if not years. A President who viewed his constitutional authorities as narrowed to executing the will of Congress might well have lost World War II.

WARTIME CIVIL LIBERTIES

IT IS COMMONPLACE today to read the argument that war reduces civil liberties too much. We can gain a useful perspective on the question by examining Roosevelt's wartime measures. FDR responded to the devastating Pearl Harbor attack with domestic policies, such as the use of military commissions, the internment of Japanese-Americans, and the widespread use of electronic surveillance. As in the Civil War, the federal courts deferred to the political branches until the war ended, and Congress went along with the President for the most part.

MILITARY COMMISSIONS

MILITARY COMMISSIONS are a form of tribunal used to try captured members of the enemy for violations of the laws of war. American generals have used them from the Revolutionary War through World War II, and as we have seen, the Lincoln administration deployed them during the Civil War to try Confederate spies, irregular guerrillas, and sympathizers. Military commissions are neither created nor regulated by the Uniform Code of Military Justice, which is enacted by Congress and governs courts-martial; instead, they were established by Presidents as Commander-in-Chief and by military commanders in the field.[143]

World War II witnessed the use of military commissions on a par with the Civil War, but primarily for the administration of postwar justice. While the Nuremburg trials were the most well-known, military commissions heard charges of war crimes against many former German and Japanese leaders at the end of the war. But the first commission was set up well before those to hear the case of "The Nazi Saboteurs." In June 1942, eight German agents covertly landed in Long Island and Florida with plans to attack factories, transportation facilities, and utility plants. All had lived in the United States before the war, and two were American citizens. One of them turned informer; after initially dismissing his story, the FBI arrested the plotters and revealed their capture by the end of June. Members of Congress and the media demanded the death penalty, even though no statutory provision established capital punishment for non-U.S. citizens.[144]

Roosevelt wanted a trial outside the civilian judicial system. On June 30, he wrote to his Attorney General, Francis Biddle (Jackson having been elevated to the Supreme Court), supporting the idea of using military courts because "[t]he death penalty is called for by

usage and by the extreme gravity of the war aim and the very existence of our American government." Roosevelt already thought they
were guilty, and the punishment was not in doubt: "Surely they are
just as guilty as it is possible to be...and it seems to me that the death
penalty is almost obligatory." Two days earlier, Biddle and Secretary
of War Henry Stimson had worried that the plot was not far enough
along to win a conviction with a significant sentence — perhaps two
years at most. Stimson was surprised that Biddle was "quite ready
to turn them over to a military court" and learned that Justice Felix
Frankfurter also believed a military court preferable.[145]

On June 30, Biddle wrote to Roosevelt summarizing the advantages of a military commission. Proceedings would be speedier, it
would be easier to prove violations of the laws of war, and the death
penalty would be available. Biddle also believed that using a military
commission would prevent the defendants from seeking a writ of
habeas corpus. "All the prisoners can thus be denied access to our
courts." He did not commit to writing another important consideration: secrecy. According to Stimson, Biddle favored a military commission because the evidence would not become public, particularly
that the Nazis had infiltrated U.S. lines with ease and had been captured only with the help of an informant. Biddle recommended that
FDR issue executive orders establishing the commission, defining
the crimes, appointing its members, and excluding judicial review.[146]

On July 2, 1942, Roosevelt issued two executive orders. The first
created the commission and gave it the authority to try any "subjects,
citizens, or residents of any nation at war with the United States"
who attempt to "enter the United States or any territory or possession thereof, through coastal or boundary defenses," with an effort
to "commit sabotage, espionage, hostile or warlike acts, or violations
of the law or war." The commission would try the defendants for violations of the laws of war, which mostly took the form of unwritten

custom. FDR prohibited any appeals to the civilian courts, unless the Secretary of War and the Attorney General consented.[147] His second order, in one paragraph, established the rules of procedure. The military judges were to hold a "full and fair trial" and could admit any evidence that would "have probative value to a reasonable man." The concurrence of two-thirds of the judges was required for sentencing, and any appeals had to run directly to the President himself.[148]

As structured by FDR, the commissions subjected the Nazi saboteurs to a form of justice very different from that normally applied in civilian courts. The most striking departure was the absence of a jury, as guaranteed by the Sixth Amendment to the Constitution. Neither civilian criminal procedure nor the normal rules of evidence applied, and FDR made no allowances for a right to legal counsel, a right to remain silent, or a right of appeal. Another important difference was that the laws of war, which at that time remained mostly unwritten, would define the crimes. This was radically different from the civilian system, which requires that the government prosecute defendants for crimes that are clearly defined and written.

FDR's order was of uncertain constitutionality under the law of the day. At that time, the governing case was still *Ex parte Milligan*. *Milligan* held that the government had to use civilian courts when the defendant was not a member of the enemy armed forces, and the courts were "open to hear criminal accusations and redress grievances."[149] FDR created military commissions to avoid *Milligan*, to charge the defendants with violations of the laws of war, and to preclude any form of judicial review. Military counsel for the Nazi saboteurs challenged the constitutionality of the trial on the ground that courts were open, the defendants were not in a war zone, violations of the laws of war were not subject to prosecution under federal law, and military commissions violated the Articles of War enacted by Congress.[150]

FDR was not deterred when the Supreme Court agreed to hear the defendants' case. As the Justices gathered in conference before oral argument, Justice Roberts reported that Biddle was worried that FDR would order the execution of the saboteurs regardless of the Court's decision. Chief Justice Stone, whose son was working on the defense team, said, "That would be a dreadful thing."[151] While Stone did not recuse himself, Justice Murphy — who was in uniform as a member of the army reserve — did. Justice Byrnes, who had been serving as an informal advisor to the administration, did not. Biddle himself argued the case and urged the Court to overrule *Milligan*, but after two days of oral argument, the Justices decided to uphold the military commission. The great pressure on the Court is reflected in its decision to deliver a brief *per curiam* opinion the day after oral argument, with an opinion to follow months later.

Commission proceedings began the day after the Supreme Court issued its order. The commission convicted and sentenced the defendants to death in three days. Five days later, FDR approved the verdict but commuted the sentences of two defendants. Roosevelt's two executive orders remained the only guidance for the commission on the rules of procedures and the definition of the substantive crimes. There was no written explanation, for example, of the elements of the violations of the laws of war, nor were procedures given, aside from the votes required for conviction and the admission of evidence.

When the Supreme Court finally issued its opinion, it carefully distinguished *Milligan*. Chief Justice Stone's unanimous opinion for the Court found that *Milligan* applied to a civilian who had never associated himself with the enemy. The Nazi saboteurs, by contrast, had clearly joined the German armed forces. Neither the Bill of Rights nor the separation of powers barred FDR from using military courts during wartime to try enemy combatants. Congressional creation of the court-martial system and the absence of any criminal provisions to punish violations of the laws of war presented no serious obstacle. Stone read the Article of War recognizing the concurrent jurisdiction of military commissions as congressional blessing for them. The Justices decided not to address the issue that had divided them behind the scenes — whether Congress could require the President to provide the saboteurs with any trial at all, civilian or military — because they did not read any congressional enactment as prohibiting military commissions. If the United States were at war, and it captured members of the enemy armed forces, it could try the prisoners for war crimes outside the civilian or courts-martial systems.

DETENTION

IN THE WAKE OF Pearl Harbor, President Roosevelt ordered sweeping military detentions that in absolute numbers went well past Lincoln's policies in the Civil War. After the Japanese attack and the German and Italian declarations of war, FDR authorized the Departments of War and Justice to intern German, Japanese, and Italian citizens in the United States. In February 1942, for example, the government detained approximately 3,000 Japanese aliens.[152] Detention of the citizens of an enemy nation had long been a normal aspect of the rules of war, and was authorized by the Alien Enemies Act (on the books since 1798). That same month, FDR went even farther and authorized the detention of American citizens suspected of disloyalty. On February 19, 1942, FDR signed Executive Order 9066, allowing the Secretary of War to designate parts of the country as military zones "from which any or all persons may be excluded."[153] By the end of 1942, the government moved 110,000 Japanese-Americans to ten internment camps because they might provide aid to the enemy. Recent historical work suggests that Roosevelt took a far more active role in the detention decision than has been commonly understood.[154]

There was substantial disagreement within the military and the administration on the internments.[155] General John DeWitt, commander of the Fourth Army on the West Coast, initially opposed the mass evacuations of Japanese-Americans, as did officials in the Justice Department and several prominent White House aides, but by late January 1942, thinking had changed. A popular movement on the West Coast demanded removal of the Japanese-Americans to the nation's interior. It gathered momentum as the United States suffered a string of military defeats in the Pacific. It appears that the precipitating factor was the release of the Roberts Commission report on the Pearl Harbor attacks. While the commission only briefly mentioned that Japanese in the Hawaiian Islands, along with Japanese consular officials, had sent intelligence on military installations before the attacks, it "attracted national attention and transformed public opinion on Japanese Americans."[156] Newspapers, California political leaders, and military officials demanded that the Roosevelt administration intern Japanese-Americans out of fear of further sabotage and espionage. Some in the War Department discounted the effect of espionage on the West Coast, and FBI Director J. Edgar Hoover dismissed claims of disloyalty.

Cabinet members raised the issue twice with the President before the final executive order. Biddle met FDR for lunch in early February 1942 to express doubts about the need for internment, and while FDR did not make a decision at that time, he concluded the lunch by saying he was "fully aware of the dreadful risk of Fifth Column retaliation in case of a raid."[157] A few days later, Stimson called President Roosevelt after learning that General DeWitt would recommend removal of Japanese-Americans on the West Coast. News that Singapore had fallen arrived the day before Stimson's call, making it unlikely that FDR would second-guess claims of military necessity. Nonetheless, Stimson — who had his own doubts about the necessity and legality of the evacuations — proposed three options: massive evacuation, evacuation from major cities, or evacuation from areas surrounding military facilities. Roosevelt responded that Stimson should do what he thought best, and that he would sign an executive order giving the War Department the authority to carry out the removals. DeWitt soon found the evacuations necessary on security grounds, and Stimson and Biddle agreed on a draft of the executive order, which was based on Roosevelt's constitutional authorities as Chief Executive and Commander-in-Chief. It appears that FDR based his decision solely on the military's claim of wartime necessity.

Several scholars have observed that Roosevelt was not vigilant in protecting civil liberties, and in this case, according to one biographer, the decision was easy for him. FDR believed that the military "had primary direct responsibility for the achievement of war victory, the achievement of war victory had top priority, and 'victory'" had for him "a single simple meaning" of defeating Germany and Japan. Victory, for Roosevelt, "was prerequisite to all else."[158] There was no great outcry from liberal leaders, there was no cabinet meeting or forum for debate within the administration, and the Attorney General came to agree with the War Department that the measure was legal. Recent historical work argues that the internment decision did not arise solely because of misinformation about Japanese-Americans or the pressure of events early in the war. The internments happened in part because FDR was ready to believe the worst about the potential disloyalty of Japanese-Americans.[159]

Presidential consultation with Congress did not improve national security decision-making. Both Congress and the Court approved FDR's actions. In March 1942, Congress passed a bill establishing criminal penalties for those who refused to obey the evacuation orders.[160] Support for the law was so broad that it was approved in both the House and Senate by voice vote with only a single speech, by Republican Senator Robert Taft of Ohio, in opposition.

The Supreme Court did not directly address the constitutionality of the detentions until *Korematsu v. United States*, decided on December 18, 1944. According to the Court, the mass evacuation triggered "strict" scrutiny under the Equal Protection Clause because it discriminated on the basis of race.[161] Nonetheless, the Court agreed that these wartime security measures advanced a compelling government interest, and the Court deferred to the military's judgment of necessity. According to Justice Black's 6–3 majority opinion, "[W]e are unable to conclude that it was beyond the war power of Congress and the Executive to exclude those of Japanese ancestry from the West Coast war area at the time they did."[162] While not disputing the deprivation of individual liberty involved, the majority recognized that "the military authorities, charged with the primary responsibility of defending our shores, concluded that the curfew provided inadequate protection and ordered exclusion." As with an earlier case upholding a nighttime curfew on Japanese-Americans in the Western military region, the Court concluded, "[W]e cannot reject as unfounded the judgment of the military authorities and of Congress that there were disloyal members of that population, whose number and strength could not be precisely and quickly ascertained."[163]

The Court majority stressed that the Constitution afforded leeway to the executive branch during time of emergency. Justice Black agreed that the government generally could not detain citizens based solely on their race, but that was not this case. The exclusion order was necessary, Black wrote, because "the properly constituted military authorities feared an invasion of our West Coast," and their judgment was that "the military urgency of the situation demanded that all citizens of Japanese ancestry be segregated from the West Coast temporarily." Although it observed that Congress supported the military's power "as inevitably it must" during wartime, the Court attached no special importance to the authorization.

The press of circumstances required deference to military judgment. "There was evidence of disloyalty on the part of some, the military authorities considered that the need for action was great, and time was short." Perhaps most important, Justice Black concluded that decisions taken during the emergency itself had to be understood in light of the information known at the time. "We cannot — by availing ourselves of the calm perspective of hindsight — now say that at that time these actions were unjustified."[164]

Korematsu remains one of the most criticized decisions in American history, considered second only to *Dred Scott* on the list of the Court's biggest mistakes. The three dissenters believed that the Constitution clearly protected Japanese-American citizens from what we today would call racial profiling. The government, Justice Roberts wrote, was "convicting a citizen as a punishment for not submitting to imprisonment in a concentration camp, based on his ancestry, and solely because of his ancestry, without evidence or inquiry concerning his loyalty and good disposition toward the United States."[165] The dissenters did not challenge the proposition that "sudden danger" might require the suspension of a citizen's right to free movement, or that the Court owed the military broad deference during wartime, but a hypothetical did not represent the true facts of the case. Any "immediate, imminent, and impending" threat to public safety was absent.[166] Justice Murphy wrote in dissent that "this forced exclusion was the result in good measure of [an] erroneous assumption of racial guilt rather than bona fide military necessity."[167] The dissenters pointed out that the government presented no reliable evidence that Japanese-Americans were generally disloyal or had done anything that made them a threat to the national defense. The exclusion order relied simply on unproven racial and sociological stereotypes.

Justice Jackson used his dissent to harmonize the role of the executive and the courts during wartime. "It would be an impracticable and dangerous idealism to expect or insist that each specific military command in an area of probable operations will conform to conventional tests of constitutionality."[168] For a Commander-in-Chief and the military, "the paramount consideration is that its measures be successful, rather than legal." In words that echoed Lincoln and Jefferson, Jackson declared that the "armed services must protect a society, not merely its Constitution," and observed that "defense measures will not, and often should not, be held within the limits that bind civil authority in peace." That said, Jackson did not want to provide constitutional legitimacy to the exclusion order. There might be no limit to what military necessity would allow when courts are institutionally incapable of second-guessing the decisions of military authorities. "If we cannot confine military expedients by the Constitution, neither would I distort the Constitution to approve all that the military may deem expedient." Upholding the Japanese-American internment would create a dangerous precedent for the future. "The principle then lies about like a loaded weapon ready for the hand of any authority that can bring forward a plausible claim of an urgent need." A one-time-only action is only an "incident," but once upheld by the Court, it becomes "the doctrine of the Constitution." In a solution many have found unsatisfying, Jackson wanted the Court neither to bless nor block the military's enforcement of the exclusion.

Historical research has revealed that some government officials doubted whether any real security threat justified the exclusion order. Nonetheless, the Justice Department chose in *Korematsu* to assert that military authorities believed the evacuations necessary because of an alleged threat against the West Coast. A companion case, *Ex parte Endo*, however, found that the government could not detain a Japanese-American citizen whom the government had conceded was "loyal and law abiding."[169] To this day, the debate over the necessity of the measures continues, but regardless of which side one falls on in that debate, it seems clear that the internment of the Japanese-Americans in *Korematsu* represents a far more serious infringement of civil liberties than that which occurred in the Civil War. The first and most obvious difference is one of magnitude. FDR interned — without trial — about 110,000 Japanese-Americans on suspicion of disloyalty to the United States. Lincoln ordered the detention of about 12,600.

The second difference is one of justification. FDR ordered the detention of the Japanese-Americans not because any had been found to be enemy combatants. They were interned because of their *potential* threat due to loyalty to an enemy nation imputed to them from their ethnic ancestry. FDR could have pursued a narrower policy that detained individuals based on their individual ties to a nation with which the United States was at war. The citizens of Japan, Germany, and Italy could be interned as a matter of course, and anyone fighting or working for the enemy, regardless of citizenship, could be detained. With regard to aliens, FDR could have relied upon the Alien Enemies Act to detain natives or citizens of a hostile nation during wartime.[170] FDR's internment policy did neither — instead, it tried to sweep in people who were presumed to have loyalty to the enemy based solely on their ethnicity.

ELECTRONIC SURVEILLANCE

ROOSEVELT HAS BEEN described by one historian as the President most interested in covert activity other than Washington, who personally managed spies and directed the interception of

British communications. During World War I, Roosevelt had served as assistant secretary of the navy, with responsibility for intelligence. During World War II, his interest in covert operations led to the establishment of the Office of Strategic Services, the forerunner of the Central Intelligence Agency.[171]

Less well known are Roosevelt's actions with regard to the interception of electronic communications. The administration initially had not engaged in any wiretapping for national security purposes, as Attorney General Jackson believed that electronic surveillance without a warrant violated the Federal Communications Act of 1934. In March 1940, he issued an order prohibiting the FBI from intercepting electronic communications without a warrant. As Europe plunged into war, however, J. Edgar Hoover grew increasingly concerned about the possibility of Axis spies within the United States. Aware of Jackson's order, Hoover went to Treasury Secretary Henry Morgenthau and asked him to speak to Roosevelt to authorize the interception of the communications of potential foreign agents who might sympathize with Germany.

Roosevelt had long been concerned with the potential threat of a "fifth column" inside the United States. The spectacular 1916 sabotage of an American munitions plant remained vivid in his memory. As early as 1936, Roosevelt authorized the FBI to investigate "subversive activities in this country, including communism and fascism."[172] When World War II broke out, Roosevelt ordered the Bureau to "take charge of investigative work in matters relating to espionage, sabotage, and violations of neutrality regulations," and commanded state and local law enforcement officers to "promptly turn over" to the FBI any information "relating to espionage, counterespionage, sabotage, subversive activities and violations of the neutrality laws." FDR did not define what "subversive activities" meant.

France's collapse in May 1940 had a profound effect. At the time,

Germany's smashing victory seemed inexplicable as a feat of arms alone, so the idea grew that collaborators and spies were also responsible. Roosevelt increasingly spoke of his concern that the United States, too, might suffer from Axis sympathizers or covert agents intent on undermining its war preparations. Even before Hoover came to make his request, FDR had already encouraged amateurish surveillance efforts. His friend, publisher and real estate developer Vincent Astor, had set up a private group he had called "the Room," which included leading figures in New York City. As a director of the Western Union Telegraph Company, Astor ordered the covert interception of telegrams. He and his friends also arranged for the monitoring of radio transmissions in New York. Using its connections, the group gathered the private banking records of companies connected to foreign nations to determine whether they were supporting espionage within the United States. While there is no direct record of a presidential order authorizing this surveillance, historical evidence suggests that the group was acting in response to a request by Roosevelt.[173]

Given his suspicions, Roosevelt quickly agreed with Morgenthau and Hoover that the wiretapping of suspected Axis agents or collaborators was necessary to protect national security. The next day, he issued a memorandum to Jackson to allow the FBI to wiretap individuals who posed a potential threat to the national security.[174] And after Pearl Harbor, FDR authorized the interception of *all* international communications. Even though some Justices had criticized wiretapping, the Court had held in 1928, in *Olmstead v. United States,* that the Fourth Amendment did not require a warrant to intercept electronic communications.[175] It would not be until 1967, in *Katz v. United States*, that the Supreme Court would hold that electronic communications were entitled to Fourth Amendment privacy protections.[176]

Congress, however, appeared to have prohibited the interception of electronic communications in the Federal Communications Act of 1934. It declared that "no person" who receives or transmits "any interstate or foreign communication by wire or radio" can "divulge or publish" its contents except through "authorized channels of transmission" or to the recipient. In *United States v. Nardone*, decided in 1937, the Supreme Court interpreted this language to prohibit wiretapping by the government as well as by private individuals.[177] In a second *Nardone* case, the Court made clear that the government could not introduce in court any evidence gathered from wiretapping.[178]

FDR recognized that his wiretapping order of May 1940 violated the text of the statute, or at least the Supreme Court's reading of it, but the President claimed that the Supreme Court could not have intended "any dictum in the particular case which it decided to apply to grave matters involving the defense of the nation."[179] Administration supporters in Congress introduced legislation to legalize wiretapping, but the House rejected the bill 156–147. FDR continued the interception program throughout the war despite the Federal Communications Act and *Nardone*. FDR's pre-war interception order applied to anyone "suspected of subversive activities" against the U.S. government, which included individuals who might be sympathetic to, or even working for, Germany and Japan.[180] At that time, however, the United States was not yet at war. While FDR wanted the FBI to limit the interceptions to the calls of aliens, his order did not exclude citizens. Most importantly, it was not limited only to international calls or telegrams, but included communications that took place wholly within the United States.

CONCLUSIONS

WAR AND EMERGENCY demand that Presidents exercise their constitutional powers far more broadly than in peacetime. That was nowhere more true than under President Franklin Roosevelt. FDR tackled the Great Depression by treating it as a domestic emergency that called for the centralization of power in the federal government and the Presidency. But he could not act alone, because the Constitution gives Congress the authority to regulate the economy and create the federal agencies. Under Roosevelt's direction, Congress enacted sweeping legislation vesting almost complete power over industry and agriculture in the executive branch, which repeatedly sought to centralize power over the plethora of New Deal agencies in the Presidency.

Roosevelt responded to the looming threat of fascism by bringing the United States into World War II, and he made all the significant decisions of foreign and domestic policy once the war began. Histories rarely, if ever, mention any role for Congress in the prosecution of the war against Germany and Japan, aside from the provision of money and arms. It was the President, for example, who decided that the United States would allocate its resources to seek victory in Europe first, and Roosevelt alone declared that the Allies would demand unconditional surrender as the only way to end the war.

FDR, not Congress, made the critical decisions about the shape of the postwar world. He wanted a world policed by four major countries, the United States, Great Britain, China, and the Soviet Union. He agreed with Great Britain and the Soviet Union to divide Germany—the "German question" was the fundamental strategic problem at the root of both World Wars. At Yalta, FDR agreed that the Soviet Union would control a sphere of influence extending over

Eastern Europe, and in return, those nations would be allowed to hold democratic elections.

While some believe that Stalin had hoodwinked him, FDR may have recognized the reality of the balance of power in Europe after the war. He may have hoped that his reasonableness in agreeing to Stalin's demands would win, in exchange, Soviet support of the United Nations. Roosevelt also demanded that Britain and France give up their colonies. FDR wanted to forestall a return to both the isolationism and the international disorder of the interwar period. Historians argue today whether Roosevelt truly believed in collective security, or whether he was a realist who accepted the balance of power at the end of World War II. Either way, it was the President who took the initiative to set the policy, although it was one where he could not act alone. Without the Senate's approval, the United Nations would have gone the way of the League of Nations.

Too often, we focus on mistakes of commission — a decision to go to war gone bad, or a law that has unintended consequences — known as *Type I* errors. FDR showed that the Presidency may be far more effective than the other branches in preventing a failure to take action — errors of omission, or *Type II* errors. Left to its own devices, Congress would have blocked aid to the Allies and delayed American entry into World War II by several months, if not years. This may be a result of the internal structure of Congress, which suffers from serious collective action problems. The passage of legislation through both Houses with many members is so difficult that the Constitution can be understood to favor inaction and, therefore, the status quo. The status quo may be best for a nation when it enjoys peace and prosperity, and threats come more often from ill-advised efforts at reform or revolutionary change, but maintaining the status quo may harm the nation when long-term threats are approaching, or unanticipated chances to benefit present themselves during a small window of opportunity.

In the area of domestic affairs, whether the New Deal or internal security programs, Roosevelt worked with Congress. He had to: the Great Depression's economic nature brought it squarely within the enumerated powers of Congress. Nevertheless, the emergency of the Depression brought home the advantages of presidential leadership in the legislative process. A complex economy beset by a mysterious, but dangerous, ailment required administrative expertise for a cure, and Congress willingly cooperated by transferring massive legislative authority to the agencies.

FDR ought to be praised for trying every reasonable idea, including this transformation of executive-legislative relations, to reverse the sickening drop in economic activity, but no one knew how to end the Depression. Only now do we know that the New Deal, combined with the Federal Reserve's tight monetary policy and the government's restrictive fiscal policies, made the Great Depression worse. World War II, not the New Deal, ended the persistent unemployment levels of the 1930s, which left behind bloated, independent bureaucracies that future Presidents would struggle to control. The mistakes in these areas show that presidential cooperation with Congress provides no guarantee of success, and in fact, can produce quite the opposite.

Throughout FDR's astounding Presidency, a theme unites both his success in foreign policy and his appearance of progress in domestic policy. FDR believed deeply in the independence of the Presidency and a vigorous use of its constitutional authorities. He did not shrink from constitutional confrontations with the other branches in order to pursue policies he believed to be in the national interest. He openly disagreed with the Supreme Court's limitations on the New Deal and publicly sought to manipulate its membership. He pushed his powers as Commander-in-Chief to the fullest, refusing to abide by the spirit, and sometimes the letter, of the Neutrality Acts in order to involve the United States in a war that neither Congress nor a clear majority of Americans favored. FDR correctly judged the threat to the nation's existence posed by the rise of fascism, and the nation and the world are better off today because he led a reluctant nation into war. His broad understanding of his executive powers created the foundation for policies that secured freedom in the twentieth century.

CHAPTER 8

The Cold War Presidents

P RESIDENTS FROM Harry Truman to Ronald Reagan inherited the world that FDR made. Conservative Republicans and liberal Democrats alike accepted the permanence of the administrative state. Even Reagan, whose First Inaugural Address declared that "in this present crisis, government is not the solution to our problem, government is the problem," did not shrink the bureaucracy or roll back the New Deal. FDR's apparent success in addressing the Great Depression made Presidents responsible in the public mind for economic growth. Demands on the Presidency rose in tandem with the people's expectations of the national government, and Chief Executives responded by continuing the centralization of their authority over the government. If they were going to rise or fall for everything from unemployment to pollution, Presidents wanted control over the administrative state that made the real policy decisions.

FDR's second challenge became another constant of the postwar world. The Soviet Union replaced Germany and Japan as the central national security threat — its nuclear weapons could have destroyed the United States in minutes, it enjoyed superiority in conventional forces, and it could project its influence globally. FDR's successors did not have to worry about isolationism. Truman convinced Congress to cooperate in placing the United States in a permanent state of mobilization, unprecedented in American history, to counter the Soviet threat. His successors kept the United States committed to the strategy of containment over a period far longer — 45 years — than any "hot" war. While they sometimes turned to Congress for support, Presidents continued to dispatch the military into hostilities abroad on their authority, a prospect with even more dangerous consequences in the nuclear age. During the Cold War, the United States transformed its role from the arsenal of democracy to the guardian of the free world. Without recognizing broad constitutional powers in the Presidency, the United States could not have prevailed, and without Congress's consistent provision of resources for the military and security agencies, the Presidents could not have succeeded.

For guiding the nation safely through an existential threat unlike any the United States had ever faced, Presidents Truman, Eisenhower, and Reagan rank among our ten greatest Presidents. This pattern has mistakenly led some to believe that war produces great Presidents. Not all Presidents, however, were up to the challenge of the Cold War. President Kennedy found his moment in the Cuban Missile Crisis but led the nation into Vietnam, where Lyndon Johnson's ambitions foundered.

But it was Richard Nixon who showed that a broad exercise of presidential power could produce disaster. His efforts to cover up Watergate made heavy use of executive privilege, control of law enforcement, and authority over the agencies. Watergate spurred a series of "reforms" that sought to constrain executive power, but they aimed at the wrong target — the Presidency, rather than Nixon. Subsequent Presidents defied the post-Watergate limits, and without their restoration of executive powers it is doubtful that they could have brought the Cold War to a successful and unexpected conclusion.

PRESIDENTS AND NATIONAL SECURITY

AFTER EARLIER CONFLICTS, the United States had usually demobilized its armed forces and brought defense spending down to minimal levels, but the Cold War changed that. Defeat of Germany gave birth to a powerful totalitarian empire that would threaten American national security for a half-century. The Soviets had a large and well-educated population, ample natural resources, and an ideology that presented an alternative to democracy and capitalism. They ended the war with their troops in possession of Eastern Europe and half of Germany, and would soon gain allies in China and parts of Africa, Asia, and Latin America. The possibility of war was the gravest challenge to the United States in its history — by the end of the 1940s, Moscow had developed nuclear weapons; in the 1950s, it could reach the United States with bombers and missiles; by the end of the 1960s, it achieved nuclear parity; in the 1970s, its conventional and nuclear forces arguably outmatched those of the West.

Presidents of different parties and personalities kept to a strategy of containment. Defeating the Soviet Union required the patience to act in multiple dimensions, including military alliances, limited wars, foreign aid, covert action, and economic coercion. It called for a permanent, standing military to project power abroad, and intelligence agencies to secretly gather and analyze information. It demanded the ability to act swiftly and decisively as in the Cuban Missile Crisis. It required long-term guarantees for the security of other nations, as with the North Atlantic Treaty Organization (NATO), a permanent alliance unprecedented in American history. As the United States entered a semipermanent state of national emergency, marked by multiple wars and boosts in defense spending, power naturally flowed to the Presidency. It was not the extent of the President's powers that was extraordinary; rather, it was the duration and magnitude of the Soviet threat that was remarkable.

The Cold War demanded significant changes in the size and shape of the military. In peacetime, the United States had been content to maintain a small army and navy and keep its overseas commitments to a minimum. Between the end of Reconstruction and the Spanish-American War, American force levels stayed within a narrow range of 34,000 to 43,000 troops. This was small given the large size of the nation, but unsurprising given the absence of any natural enemies on the northern and southern borders and the protection provided by the oceans. Between the end of the Spanish-American War and World War I, the armed forces numbered between 100,000 and 175,000 troops; in the interwar years, 243,000 and 380,000. In 1932, at the start of FDR's Presidency, the armed forces numbered only 244,902 officers and enlisted men. The armed forces dropped from 12 million at the end of World War II to 1.4 million in 1948, but moved upward to 3.2 million during the Korean War. The military fluctuated between two and three million soldiers for the rest of the Cold War, about the same size as the World War I military.[1] The Cold War brought forth one of the Framers' great fears, a large, standing army in peacetime far more powerful than the citizenry or its militia.

One cannot argue that this growth was a function of population or economic growth; America's military simply expanded to carry out the nation's new international strategy. To be sure, the United States had never been as "isolationist" as commonly thought. As historians John Lewis Gaddis and Walter McDougall separately observe, the United States has engaged in numerous wars to expand its territories and neutralize competitors on its borders.[2] But World War II proved that direct threats to American national security could now come from across the oceans. Intervention overseas could prevent these threats from maturing. Containment assumed that a certain international order, maintained by a large permanent military, would prevent foreign threats from reaching the point of open conflict. It was thought that preventing the Soviets from expanding their territory and power, and defending the critical industrial and population centers of the Free World, would eventually force the communist bloc to collapse.[3]

Under containment, the United States implicitly accepted spheres of influence for the West and the Soviet bloc. While the United States would protect the Free World by limiting communist expansion of its sphere, different Presidents played variations on the theme. The Truman, Kennedy, and Johnson administrations followed a strategy of "Flexible Response" that treated Soviet threats throughout the world as equally dangerous and relied on all available conventional and nuclear options to match them. While this "symmetric" approach had the virtue of meeting Communist expansion at all points and giving the President more options, it required a larger military, placed greater demands on the economy, and gave the opponent the initiative.

By contrast, the Eisenhower administration's "New Look" strategy and Nixon's détente were asymmetric. They abstained from direct competition with the Soviets in conventional weapons and did not try to meet every threat, but instead sought to apply American strengths against Soviet weaknesses. Asymmetry reduced the demand on economic resources, but at the price of yielding peripheral interests or leaving incremental threats unanswered.[4] President Reagan's victory in the Cold War arose from a reinvigorated across-the-board challenge to the Soviets, won by dramatic increases in military spending and financed by a large Keynesian stimulus to the economy.

For bringing the nation safely through the Cold War without a nuclear exchange or even a conventional armed conflict with the Soviet Union, several of the Presidents during the postwar period are considered to be among our best Chief Executives. Presidents Truman (seventh), Eisenhower (eighth), and Reagan (sixth) all rank today among the top Presidents, and their efforts to meet the Soviet threat demanded the broad and vigorous exercise of their constitutional power. Sometimes this involved going to war, as in Korea or Libya, without the authorization of Congress; at other times, it involved the threat of force, as in the Suez or Taiwan. Some of those conflicts turned out worse than others, though there is no reason to think that congressional approval or the lack thereof produces success on the battlefield. The conflict in Korea, which reversed the Communist invasion but ended in a stalemate, received no congressional authorization. The war in Vietnam, which ended in defeat, did. Other limited interventions, often taken by Presidents alone, produced success and failure equally.

To begin with grand strategy, Truman continued FDR's practice of making commitments at summit meetings with foreign leaders with little or no congressional approval. The postwar world took its initial shape in the summer of 1945 at the Potsdam conference, where the Truman administration had concluded, unlike Roosevelt, that the Soviets were not interested in genuine cooperation. Truman agreed to a division of Germany, in which the U.S., USSR, Britain, and France would occupy individual sectors of the country and run them with a free hand. Each could take reparations from their own sectors, as the Soviets were already doing and the United States never did. Truman accepted a new border between Germany and Poland along the Oder-Neisse line, which moved the eastern border of Germany farther west away from the Soviet Union, and accepted a Soviet sphere of influence over Eastern Europe.[5]

The invention of containment itself was almost wholly the product of the Truman administration. It was the President, not Congress, who developed and announced the 1947 "Truman Doctrine" that the United States would support Greece and Turkey, and any other governments in the future, with economic and military aid to prevent them from falling into the Soviet orbit. Truman ordered covert action to prevent Communist parties from winning elections in Italy and France, and he followed with policies designed to increase the ability of the West to resist Communism: creating NATO and the Marshall Plan, incorporating the Allied-occupied sectors of Germany into the West, restoring the Japanese government and economy, and building the hydrogen bomb. He did not seek a negotiated settlement with the Soviets.[6] While several of these actions, such as the NATO treaty and the Marshall Plan, required congressional cooperation, several were taken unilaterally, and all were decisions made by Truman first.

The executive branch alone defined the national means and ends in the struggle with the Soviets. The first comprehensive statement of containment was outlined in a memorandum known as NSC-68, developed in secret by an ad hoc group of Defense and State Department officials. In the wake of the fall of China to the Communists, and the Soviet explosion of an atomic bomb in 1949, NSC-68 established a policy of almost universal opposition to Communist threats worldwide. In doing so, the new strategy discarded earlier policies, drafted primarily by State Department official George Kennan, to focus on the more limited protection of valuable strongpoints. The United States henceforth would mount a perimeter defense that would seek to keep all territory then within the orbit of the United States and its allies out of Communist hands.

Allowing the Soviets to advance in even a peripheral area would question American credibility to defend more vital regions. This bold commitment to maintain international peace and security, primarily through the buildup of conventional and nuclear forces, would be financed by using deficit spending to stimulate the economy. Approving NSC-68 in April 1950, Truman set the United States down the path of containment for the next four decades, with no input from Congress. Though the outlines of containment would be made known in congressional hearings, NSC-68 itself would not be declassified until 1975.[7]

Implementation also came almost solely at Truman's hands. The first deadly move was the response to the invasion of South Korea on June 25, 1950, which seemed to fulfill NSC-68's prediction of worldwide Soviet aggression. After the UN Security Council issued a resolution authorizing member states to resist the attack (though Truman did not believe that the UN's approval was necessary), the President immediately ordered the U.S. military into action. The war would last three years, result in 33,000 American combat deaths and 103,000 wounded, and trigger an expansion of the armed forces to 5.7 million.[8]

Truman made the initial decision to intervene on his own, and briefed congressional leaders after the fact. According to Secretary of State Dean Acheson, seeking legislative approval would have set a "precedent in derogation of presidential power to send our forces into battle."[9] Led by Senator Tom Connally, chairman of the Senate Foreign Relations Committee, influential members of Congress told Truman that he had the constitutional authority to order the use of force as Commander-in-Chief.[10] Only Senator Robert Taft protested that the President's actions violated Congress's authority to declare war. Even Arthur Schlesinger, Jr., who would later write *The Imperial Presidency*, publicly opined that American Presidents "have repeatedly committed American armed forces abroad without prior congressional consultation or approval."[11]

Truman had earlier demonstrated little reluctance to make strategic and tactical decisions of the greatest import, such as the decision to drop the atomic bomb on Hiroshima and Nagasaki. He readily approved General MacArthur's plan to mount a daring amphibious landing at Inchon and to pursue the fleeing North Korean forces across the thirty-eighth parallel. At that point, American actions changed from pure defense of an ally into offensive military operations to unify the peninsula. It never crossed Truman's mind that the switch to offensive operations required congressional approval, even though it risked Chinese intervention.

Truman also used his power of removal to dramatic effect to reinforce his authority over the conduct of the war. After Chinese troops attacked and drove American forces back below the thirty-eighth parallel, Truman decided that the United States would no longer pursue reunification. General MacArthur publicly criticized the decision and called for a widening of the war into China itself, one of the most direct challenges to civilian control of the military since the Civil War. On April 11, 1951, Truman fired him. MacArthur had the support of 69 percent of the public and of the Congress, in which Republican gains in the 1950 midterm elections had reduced the Democratic majority in the Senate from 12 to 2. Truman later denied that he had demonstrated steadfastness in the face of public criticism. "Courage didn't have anything to do with it," he said. "General MacArthur was insubordinate, and I fired him. That's all there was to it."[12]

More critical to America's long-term security than the Korean conflict was the defense of Europe. Even before containment had become official U.S. policy, Truman had taken steps to resist Soviet moves in Germany. In June 1948, the Russians closed off all ground and water transportation into and out of Berlin. Stalin wanted to apply pressure to the United States and its allies, who had decided to unify their sectors of Germany into a sovereign state. While he rejected proposals to send an armed convoy through Russian-occupied East Germany, Truman approved an air bridge that would lift supplies to the beleaguered city. The flights of military transports through East German airspace could have triggered a direct superpower conflict if the Russians had decided to force them down.

Truman signaled his determination by deploying two squadrons of B-29 bombers to Germany, the planes that had dropped the atomic bombs on Japan (though unbeknownst to the Russians, they were not equipped with nuclear weapons). After a year and a half, the Soviets backed down and restored access to West Berlin. Truman never sought congressional approval for the airlift, nor for the fundamental political decision that gave rise to the dispute in the first place: to turn the Allied sectors of Germany into a new sovereign state firmly attached to the West. Truman gave further guarantees, again without congressional consent, to Western Europe by announcing that American occupation troops would remain in Germany — effectively creating a trip wire that would trigger an American defense of any Russian invasion.[13]

Once the Korean War began, Truman followed the logic of NSC-68 in Europe. Korea was just the manifestation, in American planners' eyes, of a general Communist effort to test the West after the loss of the U.S. monopoly on nuclear weapons. Truman and his advisors decided that the West would have to balance the Soviet advantage in conventional forces, and quickly. Western Europe would no longer be defended by a small force backed up with the implicit threat of nuclear retaliation for a Soviet invasion. In 1951, Truman deployed four combat divisions to Europe to signal American commitment and to reassure Europeans that the restoration of sovereignty to West Germany would be carefully watched. He also approved the rearming of Germany within the framework of NATO under the command of an American general. Military spending increased dramatically to support the new strategy. At the outset of the Korean War, military spending amounted to 4.4 percent of gross national product, but by the end of the Truman administration, the defense budget reached 13.2 percent of GNP, with only a small part devoted to the Korean fighting.[14]

Republican members of Congress loudly attacked Truman's unilateral deployment of troops to Europe. In January 1951, a member of the House introduced a resolution that prohibited sending troops abroad without prior congressional authorization. Senator Taft declared that Truman's decision to defend Korea without a declaration of war had "simply usurped authority" in violation of the Constitution, and his European deployment similarly lacked authority. Truman defended his decision "under the President's constitutional powers as Commander-in-Chief of the Armed Forces" and declared that he did not legally need the approval of Congress. "Not only has the President the authority to use the Armed Forces in carrying out the broad foreign policy of the United States and implementing treaties," Acheson testified before Congress, "but it is equally clear that this authority may not be interfered with by the Congress in the exercise of powers which it has under the Constitution."[15] Scholars such as Henry Steele Commager and Arthur M. Schlesinger attacked Taft, while Edward Corwin criticized Truman. The Senate, however, passed nothing more than a non-binding resolution demanding congressional approval before any additional troops were sent abroad. The deployments went forward, and Presidents since have decided the location of American forces in Europe without any specific congressional authorization.

Truman made the fundamental decisions that gave American strategy its basic shape for decades to come. To say, as some scholars do, that Truman ruled as an imperial President is to confuse politics and constitutional law. Congress could have blocked many of Truman's initiatives if only it had chosen to exercise the powers at its disposal. If it had disagreed with the Truman Doctrine's assistance to Greece and Turkey, it could have refused to appropriate any aid. If Congress had wanted to withdraw from Europe, as it had during the interwar years, the Senate could have rejected the NATO treaty and Congress could have refused to fund the Marshall Plan. Even if Truman had based troops in Western Europe, Congress could have cut off their funding and reduced the size of the military. Truman may have been able to send the first troops to Korea, but Congress could have ended the conflict by refusing to pay for the war. Congress could even have blocked the containment policy, which called for active American engagement throughout the world. Truman's symmetric version of containment depended on large, permanent increases in military spending as a share of a fast-growing economy. Only Congress could appropriate the funds needed to make containment a reality.

The Supreme Court imposed limits on the scope of presidential power in wartime, but in a way that has been dramatically overread in the decades since. In the spring of 1951, at the height of the Korean War, a labor strike threatened to close production at most of the nation's steel mills. Following a similar action by FDR in World War II to end a strike at a critical aviation plant, Truman ordered the Department of Commerce to take possession of the mills because of their importance for arms production. The owners sued on the ground that the President was exercising lawmaking authority without delegation from Congress. Truman argued that the President's Commander-in-Chief and Chief Executive powers allowed him to take action to avert a national catastrophe during wartime. It would be "unthinkable," he said in a press conference, to allow a strike to undermine "our efforts to support our armed forces and to protect our national security."

In a 6–3 decision, the Supreme Court found that seizure of the mills fell within Congress's power over interstate commerce. Congress's only law in the area delegated no power to the President to seize property to prevent work stoppages; Congress had rejected a proposal for such authority when it enacted the 1947 Taft-Hartley labor law. Writing for the majority, Justice Black concluded that the Commander-in-Chief power did not apply because even though "theatre of war be an expanding concept," it did not extend to the legislative authority to settle domestic labor disputes. "This is a job for the Nation's lawmakers, not for its military authorities."[16]

Youngstown Sheet & Tube Co. v. Sawyer has become more influential due to Justice Jackson's concurrence rather than Justice Black's majority opinion. Jackson proposed a three-part test for presidential power: (i) in cases where the President acted pursuant to congressional authorization, "his authority is at its maximum"; (ii) when the President acts in the absence of any authorization in an area concurrently regulated by Congress, "there is a zone of twilight" where the outcome is uncertain, and the "actual test of power is likely to depend on the imperatives of events and contemporary imponderables rather than on abstract theories of law"; and (iii) when the President acts contrary to congressional wishes, "his power is at its lowest ebb, for then he can rely only upon his own constitutional powers minus any constitutional powers of Congress over the matter."[17] Critics of the Presidency ever since have converted Justice Jackson's framework into a broad test for all exercises of executive power. Scholars such as Louis Henkin, Harold Koh, and Michael Glennon have generally relied on *Youngstown* to argue that Presidents must receive congressional authorization before making war, and that congressional policy takes precedence in foreign affairs.[18]

Youngstown, however, stands for less. The majority reached the right outcome because the Constitution gives Congress, not the President, exclusive power over managing the domestic economy. Congress's power over raising and supporting the Army and Navy makes clear that the existence of a war does not give the President the constitutional authority to control the domestic activities to supply the military. As Commanders-in-Chief, Presidents have historically exercised sweeping powers on the battlefield to seize and destroy property, a principle that the Supreme Court did not challenge, nor did it question President Truman's decision to begin the Korean War in the first place. Rather, the Court held that the President's control of battlefield operations in Korea did not reach all the way back to the home front.

This conclusion respects the control each branch has over its own constitutional turf. Justice Black's approach is just as likely to support the opposite proposition that Congress cannot direct the President as to the conduct of battlefield operations. Justice Jackson's opinion even recognizes that at its lowest ebb, the President might still prevail if his actions fall within his constitutional powers. "I should indulge the widest latitude of interpretation to sustain his exclusive function to command the instruments of national force," Jackson wrote, "at least when turned against the outside world for the security of our society." It was only when those powers were exercised upon "a lawful economic struggle between industry and labor" that the President could not act without congressional authorization.[19]

President Dwight Eisenhower never had occasion to test *Youngstown* because, unlike his predecessor and successors, he never sent the American military into combat. That did not reflect any reluctance to exercise his powers in the realm of foreign affairs and national security. Using his enormous prestige gained from World War II, Ike had campaigned that he would go to Korea and end the war. He rejected the advice of his military commanders in the field, Secretary of State John Foster Dulles, and Republican congressional leaders to expand the war and fight for reunification. Instead, Eisenhower decided to force China to accept a basic return to the status quo by threatening the use of nuclear weapons.

In a February 1953 NSC meeting, Eisenhower raised the possibility of a nuclear attack on North Korean and Chinese forces.[20] In a cabinet meeting that month, the President said that he would let the Chinese know "discreetly" that if progress toward a peace agreement were not made, the United States would "move decisively without inhibition in our use of weapons." The United States "would not be limited by any world-wide gentleman's agreement" on nonuse.[21] Eisenhower threatened a serious escalation, just as Truman had taken the fateful step of using the atomic bomb to end World War II, on his own. An armistice was reached in July; it was never sent to Congress for approval.

Like Truman, Eisenhower embarked on a wholesale reconsideration of American grand strategy, and like Truman, it was carried out in secret without congressional consultation or input. Eisenhower had campaigned on the rhetoric of liberating "the enslaved nations of the world," which everyone understood as referring to the Communist-controlled nations in Eastern Europe. Dulles attacked containment as a failed policy that would "keep us in the same place until we drop exhausted." The Republican platform rejected containment as "negative, futile and immoral" because it abandoned "countless human beings to a despotism and Godless terrorism."[22]

Once in office, however, Eisenhower pulled back from the campaign rhetoric and kept the fundamental goal of containment in place, but with different means. The United States would remain the protector of the free nations in Europe and Asia, but it would leave behind the universal opposition to any and all Communist offensives. Eisenhower and his advisors were concerned that NSC-68 placed too much strain on the economy, which would ultimately result in reduced standards of living, inflation, and excessive government regulation. The United States would not attempt to match Soviet conventional force advantages, but instead would play to its strengths — nuclear weapons, naval and air superiority, covert action, economic and political alliances, and negotiations — a strategy that came to be known as the "New Look."

Reliance on nuclear weapons rather than conventional ground troops allowed the Eisenhower administration to reduce defense spending from roughly 12–13 percent of GNP at the close of the Korean War to 9 percent when he left office. Approved by Eisenhower in October 1953 in the secret NSC 162/2, the New Look required that in a war with the Soviets or Chinese, "the United States will consider nuclear weapons to be as available for use as other munitions." Or, as Ike said privately to congressional leaders in late 1954, the plan was "to blow hell out of them in a hurry if they start anything."[23]

Eisenhower's brand of containment required the United States to take the initiative to keep the Soviets off balance. If the Truman administration's symmetric strategy emphasized a certain American response to every Soviet action, the key to Ike's asymmetric strategy was that the United States would act in ways and in places that the Soviets could not predict. Eisenhower emphasized covert action by the CIA, which had been created by the 1947 National Security Act, but whose operations the President directed with little congressional oversight. Under Truman, the CIA had focused primarily on intelligence collection; Eisenhower expanded its central mission to include covert action.

As the United States and the Soviet Union reached equilibrium in Western Europe and East Asia, superpower competition moved to the Third World, where covert action offered a cheap option to prevent the spread of communism. In 1953, the CIA overthrew the regime of Iranian prime minister Mohammed Mossadegh, who had nationalized Western-owned oil companies, and restored the Shah to the throne at minimal cost. In 1954, the CIA overthrew the socialist government of Jacobo Arbenz Guzman in Guatemala, but other attempts in Indonesia in 1958 and Cuba at the end of Ike's second term failed. Congress played no role in authorizing any of these operations and would not generally know of them until congressional investigations after Watergate.

An important element of the New Look was to expand the participants in the struggle against the Soviet Union. In addition to Truman's NATO and ANZUS (Australia, the U.S., and New Zealand) treaties, the Eisenhower administration reached security agreements in Southeast Asia (SEATO), Turkey, Iran, and Pakistan (CENTO), and bilateral agreements with South Korea and Taiwan. Dulles hoped to encircle the Soviets with a ring of American allies; Eisenhower thought that alliances could complement American military strength. Those nations could provide ground troops for any communist expansion in their regions, while the United States could provide naval, air, and strategic forces. Congress played little role in the initiation and negotiation of these security arrangements, but they could not become treaties without the Senate's advice and consent.

In those moments when American involvement called for military action, Eisenhower sometimes turned to Congress and sometimes did not. In two cases, Ike asked for congressional support for the use of force overseas. The first arose in August 1954, when Communist China shelled the tiny islands of Quemoy and Matsu, which were occupied by Chiang Kai-shek's nationalist army. Both Chiang's and Eisenhower's military advisors worried that the shelling was a prelude to an attack on Taiwan itself. In one NSC meeting,

Eisenhower stated his belief that an offensive attack on China would require congressional authorization "since it would be a war. If congressional authorization were not obtained there would be logical grounds for impeachment." But when Eisenhower decided to seek support from Congress for the use of military force, he publicly left vague whether the Constitution required any legislation.

"Authority for some of the actions which might be required would be inherent in the Commander-in-Chief," Eisenhower told Congress in January 1955. "Until Congress can act, I would not hesitate, so far as my Constitutional powers extend, to take whatever emergency action might be forced upon us in order to protect the rights and security of the United States." So far, this was a traditional claim for inherent executive authority to use force abroad. Eisenhower had to make a nod toward the congressional wing of his party, which had criticized Truman for exactly the same claim. "However," he said, "a suitable Congressional resolution would clearly and publicly establish the authority of the President as Commander-in-Chief to employ the armed forces of this nation promptly and effectively." In describing the resolution, Eisenhower focused on its political effects, not its constitutional ones. "It would make clear the unified and serious intentions of our Government, our Congress, and our people."[24] Eisenhower wanted to consult with Congress, but the primary purpose was political, rather than legal — he wanted a show of unity against China and to avoid claims that he had shut Congress out.[25] Congress passed the resolution overwhelmingly four days later.

The administration came close to using nuclear weapons to end the crisis. In March 1955, Eisenhower sent Dulles to publicly threaten the use of nuclear weapons in case of a war in the Taiwan straits. On March 16, Eisenhower used a press conference to confirm publicly that the United States would use tactical nuclear weapons in the event of war. "Yes, of course they would be used," he said. "I see no reason why they shouldn't be used just exactly as you would use a bullet or anything else." The Chairman of the Joint Chiefs of Staff and Dulles both recommended the bombing of the Chinese mainland with both conventional and nuclear weapons. In April, Chinese leaders publicly announced their desire for a negotiated settlement, and by August talks had begun.[26] While the display of national unity may have had some effect, it is likely that the administration's threat of a nuclear attack made the deeper impression on the minds of China's leaders.

Eisenhower went to Congress again two years later, this time during a crisis in the Middle East. After Egyptian leader Gamal Nasser's nationalization of the Suez Canal, Britain, France, and Israel launched a plan to seize the Sinai Peninsula and the Canal in October 1956. Eisenhower immediately opposed their attack as a foolish effort to reestablish colonialism in the Middle East. The United States introduced a UN resolution calling for a cease-fire and imposed an oil embargo on Britain and France.

Khrushchev threatened Russian intervention, and Eisenhower had American forces mobilized in response; he wanted the British and French out, but not because of Russian arms. He asked Congress in January 1957 for a resolution of support for possible military force in the region. Again, Eisenhower sought the resolution more for political than constitutional reasons. "I deem it necessary to seek the cooperation of the Congress. Only with that cooperation can we give the reassurance needed to deter aggression," he told a joint session.

In a private session with congressional leaders, Eisenhower would only go so far as to say that the Constitution wanted the branches to work together, but he did not specify how. "Greater effect could be had from a consensus of Executive and Legislative opinion," he told them. "The Constitution assumes that our two branches of government should get along together."[27] Congress obliged and passed the authorization.[28] The following year, after Egypt and Syria joined to form the United Arab Republic, and pro-Nasser forces overthrew the government of Iraq, the President dispatched 14,000 troops to protect the pro-Western government of Lebanon.

Eisenhower spent his last years in office seeking an accommodation with the Soviet Union. Despite his rhetorical call for the liberation of the "captive nations," Ike did little when the Soviets brutally put down Hungary's 1956 revolution. He acted on his own to ascertain the Soviet Union's real strength while at the same time seeking negotiations for a settlement of outstanding issues. Eisenhower secretly ordered U-2 spy flights over the Soviet Union and approved the planning for what would become the failed Bay of Pigs operation against Castro. Secret flyovers discovered that despite Democrat claims of a "missile gap," the United States held an overwhelming superiority over the Soviet Union in strategic nuclear weapons. But the May 1960 downing of Gary Powers's U-2 sank the Paris summit meeting with Khrushchev, and the Bay of Pigs operation would fail miserably early in Kennedy's Presidency.

Despite these setbacks, Eisenhower's management of foreign policy and national security has won him high marks. In the years immediately after he left office, scholars ranked him as a below-average President, struck as they were by the contrast between Kennedy's image of energy and youth and Eisenhower's bumbling public performances and moderate policies. History has since revised its opinion. With the opening of his papers, the image of Eisenhower as a detached, grandfatherly chairman of the board has given way to a "hidden-hand" Presidency in the words of Fred Greenstein.[29] Eisenhower was a shrewd politician who was fully in command of his administration and made almost all of the important policy decisions himself. Strategists credit Ike with pursuing the most sensible version of containment, one that matched the nation's ends with limited means. He achieved deterrence without actually going to war.

The exercise of presidential power did not become necessary only in crises, nor did it exert an inevitable pressure toward conflict. Eisenhower rejected the traditional isolationism of the Republican Party, but he also overruled the advice of his military and civilian advisers to seek a nuclear confrontation with the Soviet Union and China. Only the executive branch could successfully develop and pursue a coherent strategic policy that avoided sharp swings between isolationism and unnecessary war. Eisenhower presided over a stabilization of the Cold War that contained the Soviet Union, deterred incursions against core allies in Europe and Asia, and limited the defense burden on the economy.

Even Cold War Presidents who do not rank highly today found their greatest moments during times that demanded the exercise of constitutional power. While John F. Kennedy's glamorous public image and premature death have won him a popularity that persists to this day, his historical reputation has steadily declined. Kennedy oversaw the Bay of Pigs fiasco, first sent American troops to Vietnam, risked nuclear war over Berlin and Cuba, engaged the United States in counterinsurgency wars, and failed in his efforts to reach an understanding with the Soviets. Kennedy pursued a strategy of "flexible response" that paralleled NSC-68's call for almost unlimited resources to pursue a more activist foreign policy.[330]But JFK's finest hour did come in foreign affairs. He ordered a naval blockade of Cuba to prevent Soviet construction of intermediate-range nuclear ballistic missiles, which had the ability to reach most of the continental United States. Although styled a "quarantine," the blockade was an act of war under international law — it required the use of naval force to block shipping from reaching Cuban ports.

Kennedy could not justify the quarantine under any theory of self-defense or authorization by the United Nations. The Soviets and Cubans had not attacked the United States, and the nuclear missiles themselves were incomplete. Even if the missiles had been finished, a Soviet attack could not have been said to be imminent — the traditional test under international law for the pre-emptive use of force.[331]Rather, Kennedy used force and the threat of a wider conflict to prevent a dramatic shift in the balance of power toward the Soviet Union, which at the time had only a limited force of intercontinental ballistic missiles.

As we now know, American forces came perilously close to a military conflict with Soviet and Cuban units, which could have escalated into a nuclear exchange — the President had earlier served notice that any missile launch from Cuba would trigger a full retaliatory response on the Soviet Union. Kennedy never sought any formal authorization from Congress for his actions, though he did meet with congressional leaders to inform them. Several of the leaders recommended that Kennedy invade Cuba, advice he did not take. Rather, JFK carefully maintained the blockade until the Soviets agreed to dismantle the missiles, in exchange for U.S. removal of medium-range nuclear missiles from Turkey and a pledge not to invade Cuba.[332]Critics of presidential power believe that the Constitution must be read to require congressional approval of the use of force. They believe that a more difficult process will "'clog' the road to combat," in John Hart Ely's words, and so keep the United States out of war.[333]World War II shows that this go-slow approach can have a steep cost — congressional delay can keep the United States out of wars that are in the national interest. Madison's acceptance of the War of 1812 demonstrates the opposite as well: Congress can force the nation into senseless wars. American involvement in Vietnam reveals a third dimension. Congressional participation is no guarantee against poor judgment, ineffective tactics, or just bad luck.

President Lyndon Johnson sought and received the approval of Congress for the Vietnam War in the Tonkin Gulf Resolution, passed in August 1964 after an alleged attack by North Vietnamese gunboats on U.S. Navy destroyers in international waters. Controversy continues over whether North Vietnamese forces truly attacked the warships and whether the vessels invited the attacks by supporting covert operations in northern territory. LBJ ordered retaliatory strikes and asked Congress for support, but informed the public only that the North's attacks represented deliberate and unprovoked aggression. In a resolution enacted unanimously in the House and by 88–2 in the Senate, Congress declared that it "approves and supports the determination of the President, as Commander-in-Chief, to take all necessary measures to repel any armed attack against the forces of the United States and to prevent further aggression." The United States was prepared, "as the President determines, to take all necessary steps, including the use of armed force," to defend any SEATO nation "requesting assistance in defense of its freedom."[34]

Presidents received consistent support from Congress throughout most of the Vietnam War. Congress approved LBJ's 1965 decision to increase dramatically American military involvement with full financial support. The escalation began in the spring of 1965 with Operation Rolling Thunder, which launched a three-year bombing campaign of North Vietnamese targets. Ground deployments began with 4,000 marines in March but quickly reached 200,000 by the end of the year, and 500,000 within two years. Congress overwhelmingly approved the appropriations for the 1965 escalation and the expansion of the draft. Congressional and popular opinion did not fully turn against Johnson and the war until the Tet Offensive in January 1968, which turned a military defeat into a media victory for the North. Even so, Congress continued to provide the men and material for Nixon's new strategy of "Vietnamization" to take hold.[35]

Richard Nixon ranks among the below-average Presidents in American history, stuck between Herbert Hoover and Zachary Taylor. To the extent Nixon's Presidency benefited the United States, it came in foreign affairs. His administration introduced détente toward the Soviet Union and the historic opening to China, which created new fissures in the communist bloc. Henry Kissinger's surprise trip to China was carried out in secrecy, even from the State Department, and Nixon extricated the United States from Vietnam, albeit at a high cost (one-third of all American casualties in Vietnam occurred under his Presidency).

To force the North Vietnamese to the bargaining table, Nixon secretly ordered U.S. ground and air intervention into neutral Cambodia, which the North Vietnamese had been using to transport reinforcements into the South. When announced to the public, protests erupted domestically, but efforts in Congress to cut off funds failed. In December 1972, Nixon ordered bombings of Hanoi and other North Vietnamese cities to press for a peace agreement, which was reached in Paris the following month. The Justice Department, relying on a speech by then–Assistant Attorney General William Rehnquist, defended Nixon's Cambodian bombings and his other Vietnam War decisions as an exercise of the Commander-in-Chief power.[36] On a different front, the United States threatened the use of force in the Middle East during the 1973 Yom Kippur War in order to ensure the survival of Israel and prevent the conflict from escalating beyond the region.

Watergate weakened the Presidency to the point where Congress changed the balance of powers in its favor. In the 1973 War Powers Resolution (WPR), Congress authorized the President to introduce the American military into hostilities, whether actual or

imminent, only with a declaration of war, specific statutory authorization, or an attack on the United States or its forces. The WPR
requires that the President "in every possible instant shall consult
with Congress" before sending the armed forces into hostilities (or
imminent hostilities) and that he must report to Congress within
48 hours afterward. It requires the President to terminate the intervention 60 days after the report unless Congress authorizes the use
of force. Nixon vetoed the act on the ground that it violated the
President's war authorities, but two-thirds of Congress overrode
him. Every President since has refused to acknowledge the WPR's
constitutionality, and several have undertaken action in violation of
its terms. In these conflicts, Congress chose to allow the President
to take the initiative in war-making but also to suffer the political
consequences alone.[37]

Like Eisenhower, President Reagan received little respect from
scholars and pundits, who had always dismissed him as little more
than an actor, and when he left office, Reagan was considered a
below-average President. The passage of time has given scholars a
newfound appreciation, and he now ranks along with Truman and
Eisenhower, among the top Presidents in our history. Reagan came
to office when the United States seemed to be in retreat on the world
stage, and left it with the Soviet Union on its way to collapse under
the weight of its economic inefficiencies and military spending. Critics have suggested that Reagan turned out to be lucky, as he had been
all his life, and just happened to be in the Oval Office when internal
problems caused the Soviet Union to crumble. Yet, the United States
was back on its heels when he took office in 1981. Watergate had led
to congressional restrictions on executive power in foreign affairs,
the Soviets had achieved superiority in nuclear as well as conventional arms, and the aftermath of Vietnam and the Iranian hostage
crisis had given rise to the idea that America was an over-muscled

Gulliver whose great military strength was of little use.[38]

No one would have predicted in 1981 that eight years later the Soviet Union would disappear, and the Warsaw Pact along with it. Few scholars thought that the West's liberal constitutionalism and market economics would prevail, and our nation's preeminent Cold War historian, John Lewis Gaddis, concludes that Reagan contributed to the victory of the United States and its allies in the Cold War. Reagan adopted a national security strategy that would place high demands on the economy for resources and a large buildup of the military. Unlike NSC-68 and Flexible Response, however, the Reagan Doctrine did not aim to react in the same manner and place to block the Soviets. It built up forces in order to challenge the Soviets to a competitive arms race that would bankrupt their economy, while pursuing rollback in the Third World.

Reagan also introduced a strong element of moral values into containment. Under détente, as practiced by Nixon, Ford, and Carter, the superpower struggle had lost its moral content. Reagan, however, had no difficulty declaring the Soviet Union an "evil empire," one that would be consigned to the "ash heap of history." In 1987, Reagan gave a speech in front of the Berlin Wall, demanding, "Mr. Gorbachev, open this gate! Mr. Gorbachev, tear down this wall!" Historians today believe that Reagan's decision to challenge the legitimacy of the Soviet Union, which was heavily criticized by congressional leaders, was an essential element of America's victory in the Cold War.[39]

In the developed world, the Reagan administration pursued a strategy of expanding American conventional and nuclear forces to force the Soviets to strain their economy to keep pace. Central to his plan was the Strategic Defense Initiative (SDI), announced in March 1983, which aimed to develop a space-based weapons system that could shoot down Soviet missiles in flight. Despite opposition from many congressional leaders, the legislature eventually provided $60 billion for SDI research. Reagan supplemented SDI with an upgrade of America's nuclear forces, including the B-1 bomber, the MX nuclear missile, and the Pershing II medium-range nuclear missile in Europe.

Congress cooperated by voting for substantial increases in American military spending. Under the Carter administration, defense-related spending ranged between $244–247 billion, about 4.6 percent of GNP. By the end of Reagan's first term, Congress approved a buildup that reached $358 billion annually. Defense spending would peak at $380 billion in 1986 and level out to $374 billion by the end of the second term. Under Reagan, the military spent more in constant dollars than it did during the Vietnam or Korean Wars, though as a portion of GNP it was on a par with spending between 1972 and 1974.[40]

Despite the large buildup, Reagan's approach to containment bore more resemblance to Eisenhower's New Look than to Kennedy's Flexible Response. Rejecting détente, the Reagan Doctrine supported anti-communist insurgents in the Third World with the goal of reversing Soviet gains. In National Security Decision Directive 75, the administration declared its policy "to contain and over time reverse Soviet expansionism." As approved by President Reagan, American national security policy declared: "The U.S. must rebuild the credibility of its commitment to resist Soviet encroachment on U.S. interests and those of its Allies and friends, and to support effectively those Third World states that are willing to resist Soviet pressures or oppose Soviet initiatives hostile to the United States." The Reagan administration sent covert assistance to the contras in Nicaragua, to the mujahedeen in Afghanistan, and to rebels in Angola. While these projects met with success in pressuring Soviet military and economic resources, they involved no U.S. ground troops. American involvement was limited to intelligence support, covert operations, and military and technical aid, while the local forces conducted the fighting on the ground.[41]

While the Reagan administration's policies helped end the greatest national security threat of the twentieth century, they were marked by constitutional struggles between the executive and legislative branches. Reagan, for one, clearly rejected the constitutionality of the War Powers Resolution and believed that he held the authority to commit troops abroad. In 1983, he launched a quick invasion of the Caribbean island of Grenada to remove a Cuban-supported Marxist regime, an operation that required only 1,900 combat troops. In 1986, Reagan ordered the aerial bombing of military and civilian targets in Libya, including the headquarters of leader Muammar Gaddafi, in response to an attack on American servicemen in Germany. In 1987, Reagan directed the U.S. Navy to protect Kuwaiti oil tankers traveling through the Persian Gulf from Iranian threats. In all of these cases, Reagan claimed the authority to deploy troops under the President's "constitutional authority with respect to the conduct of foreign relations and as Commander-in-Chief of the United States Armed Forces." He did not seek congressional approval, though he usually notified Congress in a manner consistent with the War Power Resolution's reporting requirements.[42]

Neither Congress nor the courts acted to counter Reagan's interventions. The closest Congress came to enforcing the War Powers Resolution was in 1983 in Lebanon, when the United States and its allies sent troops to Beirut to end a civil war. Congress passed a law requiring the withdrawal of troops 18 months later, and Reagan signed the bill in order to gain funding for the operation, though he refused to concede the constitutional point. No confrontation over the Lebanon deployment occurred after the killing of 241 Marines in a terrorist bombing of their Beirut barracks, which caused the administration to withdraw the troops well before the deadline.[43]

Instead of cutting off funds, some Congressmen sued the President in federal court. They sued Reagan twice to block aid to the contras and once to stop the escort of Kuwaiti tankers. In all three cases, the federal courts refused to hear the cases because they presented political questions outside the scope of judicial review.[44] Disputes over war powers, the courts suggested, were to be resolved politically between the President and Congress. Since Congress took no action as a body, the Reagan administration was left with the initiative and the responsibility for success or failure.

When Congress chose to flex its own institutional muscles, it could effectively bring the executive branch to a virtual standstill. This truth was vividly displayed during the Iran-Contra affair, which began with congressional efforts to stop U.S. covert activities against Nicaragua. In 1982, Congress prohibited funds for the aid of groups seeking to overthrow the government of Nicaragua. In 1984, news of the CIA's mining of Nicaragua's harbors became public, leading to a funding ban on such operations. Later in the year, Congress enacted the "Boland amendment," which cut off all defense and intelligence funds, for one year, to support any covert or insurgent activity in Nicaragua. National security advisors Robert McFarlane and John Poindexter, and NSC staffer Colonel Oliver North, sought to evade the Boland amendment and also achieve the goal of freeing American hostages held in Lebanon. Using shady arms dealers, they sold weapons to Iran, which controlled the terrorist groups in Lebanon, in exchange for the hostages. They then transferred the proceeds of the arms sales (about $4 million) to the contras, without the money ever reaching the U.S. Treasury.[45]

What started out as a dispute over foreign affairs turned into yet another Washington, D.C., scandal. Congress conducted lengthy, nationally televised hearings, and an independent counsel undertook criminal investigations. Reagan's public defense — that he did not remember approving any arms-for-hostages deal — undermined his image as a Chief Executive in full control of his administration. The independent counsel convicted several of the players in the controversy, including McFarlane, North, and Poindexter for withholding information or making false statements to Congress, but an appeals court overturned the convictions of the latter two. After losing the 1992 election, President George H. W. Bush pardoned five others, including former Secretary of Defense Caspar Weinberger and McFarlane.

Congress had the Constitution on its side. While the President controls foreign affairs and the use of military force abroad, only Congress appropriates federal funds and governs federal property. The legislature should not use criminal law to get its way in a struggle with the President over foreign affairs and national security, but there is no doubt that it can, just as there is no doubt that the President can use his control over the enforcement of the law to preclude any prosecutions — as Jefferson had with the Alien and Sedition Acts. If Congress believed that the President or his subordinates had violated the Constitution, it should have placed pressure on the executive branch to fire the officials, cut off funds and held oversight hearings, refused to confirm nominees, and even considered impeachment. Using independent counsels transforms policy disputes into criminal cases, which undermines the very flexibility and initiative in government for which the executive branch exists.

At the start of the Iran-contra affair, Reagan's approval ratings fell from 67 to 46 percent in a single month, but by the time he left office, Reagan's popularity had recovered to reach the highest approval ratings of any Cold War President (68 percent).[46] Much of this was due to the rise of Mikhail Gorbachev as the leader of the Soviet Union. Gorbachev sought to prop up the Soviet economy by introducing Western-style market reforms (perestroika), and opening up the government (glasnost). Needing to reduce the huge Soviet military budget, Gorbachev was willing to reach deals to freeze or cut conventional and nuclear arms. Two summit meetings in 1985 and 1986 failed to produce any results, but the next conference produced the first-ever reduction in nuclear arms, the Inter-mediate-Nuclear Forces Treaty banning short- and medium-range nuclear missiles in Europe. Negotiations began for the Strategic Arms Reduction Treaties and the Conventional Forces in Europe Treaty. When completed under the administration of George H.W. Bush, the agreements sharply reduced the nuclear arsenals of the two superpowers and their conventional weapons in the European theater. While he controlled policy toward the Soviet Union and arms control, Reagan needed the cooperation of the Senate to ratify the treaties and the House to fund the destruction of weapons systems. Nonetheless, it was presidential initiative in foreign affairs, supported by the executive's constitutional primacy in the area that was critical to Reagan's success.

A similar story holds true for the more average Presidents of the Cold War. Scholars consider George H. W. Bush's defining moment to be the 1991 Persian Gulf War. After Saddam Hussein's forces invaded Kuwait on August 2, 1990, President Bush ordered a buildup of American forces along the border of Saudi Arabia with more than 400,000 troops deployed over the course of four months. The administration ultimately sought congressional authorization for the use of force in January 1991 and prevailed in the Senate by a mere five votes. The administration made clear it wanted legislative approval only for political, not constitutional, reasons. Secretary of Defense Dick Cheney testified before Congress, and the Department of Justice argued in court, that the President could order an invasion without congressional approval. After the war, President

Bush said, "I felt after studying the question that I had the inherent power to commit our forces to battle."[47]

Bush made his more lasting, though less noticed, contribution to the national security in managing the peaceful end of the Soviet empire. Bush successfully pressed for the reunification of Germany, the enlargement of NATO to include former Warsaw Pact nations, and the recognition of Russia and the former Soviet republics. These diplomatic initiatives were conceived and executed by the executive branch. Treaties requiring Senate consent eventually formalized German reunification and NATO expansion, but the underlying changes were achieved by the Bush administration's control over foreign policy.[48]

What did not happen in the Cold War is even more important than what did. For the three centuries after the recognition of the nation-state system in the Peace of Westphalia, great power wars were commonplace. Just as the twentieth century had its World Wars I and II, the nineteenth had the Napoleonic Wars, and the seventeenth had the Thirty Years' War, to name but a few. These wars took an enormous toll on humanity — military deaths in World War I reached about 10 million for all nations, and 25 million in World War II, with estimates ranging from double to triple those numbers in civilian deaths.

By the twentieth century, the United States could no longer isolate itself from the struggles in Europe. World War I cost the United States 116,000 soldiers and sailors killed and 204,000 wounded. In World War II, the U.S. armed forces had 405,000 killed and 672,000 wounded. In World War I, the Wilson administration spent about $310 billion on the military. In World War II, the military consumed about $3.5 trillion (both figures in 2008 dollars). With the development of tactical and strategic nuclear weapons, military conflict between the United States and the Soviet Union would have been far worse in terms of casualties and financial costs than both World Wars — and probably all U.S. wars — put together.

That the United States avoided another great power conflict from 1945–92 is a testament to the stewardship of Presidents from Truman through George H. W. Bush. Nine American Presidents from different parties, over half a century, patiently pursued a policy that contained, and ultimately exhausted, an enemy that outmatched the United States in land power. They had to follow a moderate course that sometimes required active challenges to the Soviets, at other times, restraint. It was not produced by a system where Congress generally controls foreign and national security policy.

Many academics assume that congressional dominance would lead to less war, because Congress is slower to move at home and less adventuresome abroad. In effect, this approach finds a virtue in the internal transaction costs within Congress, which make it difficult for a large number of people to reach agreement.[49] But there is no historical reason why Congress should be less warlike than Presidents. It was the war hawks in Congress, not President Madison, who pushed the United States into the War of 1812, for example. A Congress eager for territorial expansion sought war in 1846 and 1898.

Putting aside whether their assumptions about Congress are accurate, the critics' reading of the Constitution could have placed the nation in a straitjacket as it rose to confront the challenges of the Cold War. It is true that a high level of cooperation among the branches was necessary to prevail, but containing the Soviet Union called for a wide range of instruments of national power, ranging from covert action, to crisis management, to shorter conflicts, to long-term national security planning. Congress could not have conducted successful policy along these dimensions. The unpredictability, suddenness, and high stakes of foreign affairs were the very reasons for the Framers' creation of an independent executive branch.

Presidential leadership during the Cold War did not just advance American interests in the short term, but benefited human welfare in the West and Asia. At the end of World War II, the economies and populations of the Axis powers were ruined. Germany's population had fallen to its 1910 level, 68 million, and its economy had collapsed. Japan was similarly devastated; its population in 1950 was estimated to be roughly 84 million, and the war destroyed about 40 percent of its industrial capacity. Today, Germany's population is 82 million, and its GDP is $2.9 trillion, third in the world. Japan's population today is 127 million, and its GDP is $4.34 trillion, second in the world. Italy's GNP today is $1.84 trillion, seventh in the world. Although Presidents had demanded unconditional surrender, once the war was over they reintegrated our former enemies into the political and economic systems of the West. Presidents supported a system of market-based economies and constitutional democracy — with the financial support of Congress at times — primarily through their control over foreign policy.[50]

We can also see the effects in the countries that witnessed the most direct American intervention. South Korea, a small agrarian nation with a population of 21 million in 1955, today has a population of 48 million and is the 13th largest economy in the world with a GNP of $888 billion. (Nominal GNP in 1962 was only $2.3 billion.) North Korea's population, by contrast, has stagnated for the past decade at around 21–22 million, with annual economic growth of less than half of one percent; its economy is barely functional, with a GNP of no more than $40 billion (which ranks it at the very bottom in the world), and its society is governed by the most extreme Communist dictatorship left on earth.

Vietnam, too, took its toll on the lives and treasury of the

United States and arguably destroyed two Presidencies, but the effects of American withdrawal may have been even steeper — millions of Vietnamese were killed or sent to concentration camps, or fled as boat people. Wars in both Korea and Vietnam sent important signals to the Soviet Union and China that the United States would continue to resist Communist expansion forcefully. It is impossible to answer counterfactual questions, but if Congress had held the upper constitutional hand in war and had refused to send troops to Korea and Vietnam, the Cold War may have ended very differently. The costs of congressional paralysis during the Cold War could well have been higher than the costs of executive action, even taking into account these setbacks.

PRESIDENTS AND THE ADMINISTRATIVE STATE

PRESIDENTS DURING the Cold War period complemented their activist foreign policy with consistent efforts to establish tighter control over the administrative state. This was a natural response to fundamental changes in American government. The Court's removal of the limits on federal power allowed economic regulation on a truly national scale. In the 20 years after the New Deal, Congress — often at the behest of Presidents — enacted laws setting national standards for working conditions, labor unions, and wages and hours, among other subjects. Another burst of federal regulation followed in the 1960s and 1970s; federal rules spread to cover crime, voting, housing, race, consumer rights, and the environment. The New Deal had taught Americans to expect their national government to do more to cure everyday problems, and Presidents and Congresses together responded with a mixture of direct rules, criminal laws, tax benefits, and spending. Even Republican Presidents like Eisenhower, Nixon, and Reagan never seriously tried to undo the New Deal's paradigm shift in the role of the federal government.

Congress delegated sweeping powers over these new objects of federal attention to the agencies. It is fair to say that the administrative state, rather than Congress, makes the majority of the federal rules that affect individual citizens today. Delegation gives Presidents more power, but at a price. It allows Congress to escape responsibility for difficult public policy choices, usually ones that will spark high levels of opposition no matter what option is chosen. Congress can avoid decisions that are risky or unpredictable, or that require scientific or technical judgment. Better to have the executive branch, for example, balance safety, air quality, industrial growth, and fuel costs in setting minimum mileage requirements for automobiles. Individual legislators can criticize almost any agency decision without having to face the difficult trade-offs themselves. They can focus instead on funneling benefits to discrete groups that will support them with votes or campaign contributions.[51]

FDR set the example of the Presidency, not Congress, as the energetic force responsible for solving the nation's domestic problems. Presidents are now held accountable for the nation's economic performance, over which they have little real power (in contrast to the Chairman of the Federal Reserve Board). They are expected to submit annual budgets to Congress, even though it is the legislature that commands the power of the purse. They launch comprehensive reform proposals to deal with every imaginable national problem, even though the Constitution gives Congress almost all of the national government's powers over domestic affairs.

Presidents today are expected to have solutions at hand for problems big and small: natural disasters (Hurricane Katrina relief), local crime (midnight basketball for teens), and poor borrowing decisions (lowering mortgage rates). As Richard Neustadt wrote five decades ago, "everybody now expects the man inside the White House to do something about everything." Presidential proposals for legislation, managed by White House lobbyists and backed up by the veto, are now a central feature of national politics. As a constitutional matter, the President can only block (assuming he has one-third of the Senate or House with him) Congress's initiatives, not force it to pass his own. This gap between high public expectations and weak constitutional powers is one of the sharpest paradoxes of the American Presidency today.[52]

While these developments had their historical antecedents, they emerged during the New Deal on a massive scale. Like FDR, the Cold War Presidents responded by seeking to impose order and rationality over the executive branch. Originally, delegation was driven by the idea that the executive branch would bring greater technical expertise. Rules would come from neutral administrators, rather than the political process and its susceptibility for temporary passions or interest-group biases.

During the later New Deal and postwar period, however, it became evident that politics were inseparable from administration, especially as the delegations became broader. The Clean Air Act, for example, orders the Environmental Protection Agency to set air-quality standards the attainment of which "are requisite to protect the public health." Deciding how much air pollutant to allow goes beyond technical expertise and requires trade-offs among competing values, such as economic growth, improved health, and feasibility of reductions. As an original matter, it is doubtful that the Framers believed the legislature could grant such sweeping power absent the necessities of wartime emergency. But after losing the New Deal confrontations, the courts no longer policed the amount of delegation from Congress to the executive branch.[53]

All of the Cold War Presidents struggled to increase their control over the vast swaths of bureaucracy inside the Beltway — both to inject more expertise into decisions and to make themselves the voice of electoral accountability within the administrative state. They wanted to make sure that the thousands of decisions made by the agencies every day were moving in the same direction. If the President had just been elected in the midst of a recession, for example, his White House could press each major agency decision to strike its regulatory balance toward pro-growth policies and private-market ordering. The primary method became direct presidential control over agencies' decisions through a larger and more specialized White House staff.

The Bureau of the Budget, located inside the Executive Office of the President, became "OMB," the Office of Management and Budget, and its authority expanded beyond supervision of the agency budget process to include the review of proposed legislation and congressional testimony by executive branch officials. Under the Nixon, Ford, Carter, and Reagan administrations, OMB imposed cost-benefit analysis on executive rule-making without any clear statutory mandate. Under Director George Shultz, OMB began to review environmental regulations to determine whether their economic benefits outweighed their costs. Presidents Ford and Carter gradually expanded the scope of cost-benefit review until President Reagan, in Executive Order 12291, broadened it to all executive branch regulations and allowed OMB to stall any regulation for failing cost-benefit review.

Cost-benefit analysis put in sharp relief the President's powers of management and administration. Critics of Executive Order 12291 correctly noted that many statutes did not impose a standard that a regulation's economic benefits exceed its costs. Congress had codified the basic procedures for agency rule-making in the 1946 Administrative Procedure Act, which left White House review unmentioned.

Most statutes place the duty to issue the regulation with the head of an agency, rather than the President. Nonetheless, President Reagan claimed the authority to require cost-benefit standards and to oversee all regulations issued by any executive branch agency as part of his constitutional authority to execute the laws. He even requested that the independent agencies voluntarily comply with E.O. 12291, but none did so.[54] Congress attempted to defund the OMB office in charge of the review, but failed, and no court has issued an order attempting to shut it down. Presidents seem to have prevailed, with cost-benefit review continuing as a central function of the White House today.[55]

The National Security Council, established in the National Security Act of 1947, sets the basic model for White House coordination and control. It brings together the State and Defense Departments and the CIA and is staffed by dozens of officials on loan from the agencies, who help run a policy-making process that attempts to set policies so as to produce a uniform approach throughout the administration. A Domestic Policy Council attempts to perform the same function for the operations of the domestic agencies, and a National Economic Council, headed by the President's economic advisor, seeks to coordinate government policy on domestic and international economic issues. The most recent addition was the Homeland Security Council, which coordinates policies to protect against terrorist attacks and other emergencies.[56]

All of these entities transmit as well as receive. White House aides handle the daily business between the President and the cabinet agencies and coordinate the overall operations of the executive branch. While White House staff have no legal authority to command cabinet members or agency heads, they have implicit presidential backing behind them. Looming behind command is the constitutional authority of removal. Executive orders as well as sign-

ing statements became the tools for the communication of instructions to the administrative state. With executive orders, Presidents
announced and implemented their policy preferences using delegated or constitutional powers. Signing statements instructed the
agencies how Presidents wanted the laws to be read when it came
time for implementation. It should come as no surprise that the use
of both has leaped since FDR. The dramatic expansion of the scope
of federal power and its sweeping delegation to the President has
broadened the subjects that fall within the presidential ambit.[57]

A prominent example of presidential leadership in domestic
policy, using the constitutional powers of the office, can be found in
the area of race relations. President Truman invoked his authority as
Commander-in-Chief to desegregate the military and as Chief Executive prohibited racial discrimination in federal employment. Presidents Eisenhower, Kennedy, and Johnson continued those orders
and — the latter two devising the term "affirmative action" — added
a ban on racial discrimination in government contracts. There was
no statutory authority for these policies. Southerners in the Senate
had prevented Congress from enacting any civil rights laws from
the end of Reconstruction to 1957, and it was only after Kennedy's
assassination that the political momentum existed for passage of the
1964 Civil Rights Act and the 1965 Voting Rights Act. Before then,
the national government eliminated racial discrimination in its own
operations through presidential, not congressional, action.

Perhaps the most dramatic example was the reaction to *Brown
v. Board of Education*. *Brown* declared that segregation in the public schools violated the Constitution's guarantee of equal protection
of the laws to all citizens regardless of race. Eisenhower generally
attempted to avoid the race question, and he privately said that he
wished the Court had upheld *Plessy v. Ferguson*.[58] Throughout his
administration, he sought to escape political responsibility by defer-

ring to the courts, and he never publicly said whether he agreed with the merits of *Brown* or whether he thought segregation was morally wrong. But once the courts spoke in *Brown*, Eisenhower listened.

Two days after the Court announced its decision, Eisenhower declared at a press conference that "the Supreme Court has spoken, and I am sworn to uphold the constitutional processes in this country; and I will obey."[59] He did not have to live up to his promise for three years. In September 1957, Arkansas Governor Orval Faubus defied a federal court order and called out the state national guard to block a dozen black students from entering Central High School in Little Rock. Eisenhower ordered the 101st Airborne Division and federalized units of the national guard to escort the black students to school. Federal troops had not entered the South to enforce the law since Reconstruction, and Eisenhower's orders, contrary to his own views on segregation, signaled to the South that armed resistance to *Brown* would be futile. He had acted under his constitutional authority to see that the laws were faithfully executed, and he defined "the laws" to include *Brown* and the decisions of the Supreme Court.[60]

When it came to delegated powers, however, Congress attempted to place numerous obstacles in the way of presidential action. While Congress wants to shift political responsibility to the President by delegation, it still seeks to retain as much influence over the agency as possible. In Congress's ideal world, the President would take all of the downside for politically unpopular decisions, while Congress could continue to dictate to the agencies. During the Cold War, Congress tried to achieve something close to this arrangement in several ways. One was to expand the practice of insulating agencies from presidential control.

Congress cannot prevent the President from appointing the heads of the agencies, and all of the Cold War Presidents generally chose nominees who agreed with administration policies, but Congress could condition the President's ability to fire them. Without the threat of removal, Presidents would have little formal authority to compel independent agencies to obey their orders. Agency leaders would become more susceptible to control by Congress, which would continue to control their funding and legislative mandates, and potentially embarrass them (or praise them) in oversight hearings. Several Presidents, such as Truman, Kennedy, and Reagan, sought to place the independent agencies under their control, but Congress always refused to make the necessary legal changes.[61]

Another method of congressional influence was the "legislative veto." In delegating authority to the executive branch, Congress often would include a provision that allowed one or both Houses to overrule the agency's decision. In an extreme form, a legislative veto would give the power to a single committee of the House or Senate to block executive branch action. Under the Eisenhower administration, for example, Congress passed a law allowing either the House or Senate appropriations committees to block any Defense Department decision to privatize work on a military base. Even though Eisenhower ordered the Defense Department to ignore any committee veto as an intrusion on his constitutional authority to execute the law, subordinate officials would not issue the checks without the approval of the Comptroller General, who decided to obey the committees.[62] Thousands of legislative veto provisions entered the law and became almost standard boilerplate in delegation statutes. They make perfect sense from the congressional perspective, as they allow Congress to delegate authority, but with strings attached.

A third method, which came to prominence in the wake of Watergate, was to create independent officials who could investigate the executive branch. The centerpiece of this effort was the 1978 Ethics in Government Act, which established the independent counsel in response to perceived conflicts of interests revealed by Watergate.

Special Justice Department prosecutors had the task of investigating President Nixon and his closest aides for the break-in of Democratic Party headquarters at the Watergate Building on June 17, 1972. "Watergate" would come to refer to a host of scandals that included the electronic surveillance of Nixon's political opponents, "dirty tricks" to sow confusion in the Democratic primaries, IRS audits to harass critics, misuse of campaign finances, and the cover-up. Congress and the Justice Department conducted investigations that followed the trail from the Watergate burglars to Nixon's reelection campaign to White House counsel John Dean to Nixon's closest aides, Bob Haldeman and John Ehrlichman. Watergate reached the level of a major constitutional crisis when testimony revealed that Nixon had taped his conversations in the Oval Office, which might contain proof that Nixon had ordered the break-in or interfered with the investigation. Nixon ordered the Attorney General, Elliot Richardson, to fire special prosecutor Archibald Cox, who had subpoenaed the tapes. Richardson and the deputy attorney general resigned instead, and it fell to Solicitor General Robert Bork to fire Cox.

Known as the "Saturday Night Massacre," the October 20, 1973, firing created a conflict between the President's authority to supervise the enforcement of the laws and his status as a potential subject of investigation. Although Jimmy Carter campaigned on the idea of making the Justice Department an independent agency, and several members of Congress introduced legislation, the proposals went nowhere, and they would almost certainly have presented an unconstitutional invasion of a core power of the President. Treating prosecution as a neutral act of administration ignores the fundamental policy choices made in law enforcement, such as where to place resources, what crimes to prioritize, and where to ameliorate the harshness of the laws. The only way that the people can affect these judgments is through their election of the President; making the Justice Department independent would have left these critical choices in the hands of unaccountable bureaucrats. It would have been akin to making the Joint Chiefs of Staff and the military independent of the Commander-in-Chief.

Congress and President Carter decided to create an independent prosecutor instead. Under the Ethics in Government Act of 1978, the Attorney General must conduct a preliminary investigation upon receiving information "sufficient to constitute grounds to investigate" whether high-level executive branch officials, including the President, Vice President, top White House aides, and cabinet officers, have violated federal law. If the Attorney General concludes that there are "reasonable grounds" for further investigation, he must ask a special division of the federal appeals court in Washington for the appointment of an independent prosecutor. The court selects the independent counsel, who exercises the "full power and independent authority" of the Justice Department, and defines his jurisdiction. The Attorney General can only remove the prosecutor for "good cause," which can be challenged in court. The Act produced a plethora of investigations, ranging from the important (Iran-contra under Reagan, Whitewater under Clinton), to the insignificant (cabinet officials accepting free event tickets). By 1999, when the law lapsed, more than 25 independent counsels had conducted investigations at a cost of about $175 million. Operating without any superiors, independent counsels used every available resource to leave no stone unturned.[63]

Congress also inserted a mini-independent counsel into each agency. The 1978 Inspector General Act centralized investigations and auditing within each agency into an Inspector General. The statute required IGs to be confirmed by the Senate and to report regularly to Congress and prohibited the President from removing them unless he explained his reasons to the legislature.[64] While not an attempt, like the independent prosecutors, to make the inspectors totally free from presidential control, the Act tried to weaken executive control by creating offices within each agency that would feel more loyalty toward Congress.

Watergate gave birth to yet another method of congressional control, the introduction of "framework statutes" that attempted to restrict the exercise of delegated authority or the operations of the Presidency itself. These laws only permitted the President to exercise certain powers after making a series of findings, accompanied by requirements of consultation and reporting to Congress. The War Powers Resolution was but one example. After the Church Committee hearings into the CIA's activities, Congress enacted the 1980 Intelligence Oversight Act to regulate the President's control of covert operations. It required the CIA to keep the House and Senate Intelligence Committees fully informed of all intelligence activities, including covert action as well as intelligence gathering and counter-intelligence. No funding would be available for covert actions unless the President made a finding that an operation was necessary to advance the national security.

The National Emergencies Act of 1976 terminated existing national emergencies and required the President to make certain findings to declare a new one. The International Emergency Economic Powers Act of 1977 (IEEPA) allowed the President to impose economic sanctions only after a finding that a grave foreign threat to the national security existed. Presidents from FDR through Nixon had authorized wiretaps for foreign intelligence purposes on their executive authority, rather than through the courts. While the Supreme Court had held that surveillance of domestic threats required a warrant as required by the Fourth Amendment, it expressly left open whether the President would need one to protect against foreign threats. In the Foreign Intelligence Surveillance Act of 1978, Congress required a warrant from a special federal court before electronic surveillance of foreign spies or terrorists could occur domestically. The Case-Zablocki Act required the President to send Congress any international agreement that did not rise to the level of a treaty.[65]

Other Watergate reforms aimed at the operation and activities of the Presidency at home. Congress amended the Federal Election Campaign Act (FECA) in 1974 to limit individual contributions to candidates, political action committees, and political parties, and it placed a ceiling on campaign expenditures for presidential elections in exchange for public financing. In creating a Federal Election Commission for enforcement, the FECA eroded the President's appointment powers by allowing the leaders of Congress to choose some of its members, though the Supreme Court would hold this provision unconstitutional.[66] Presidents had long considered White House papers to be their personal property, which allowed them to control the access of researchers. In the Presidential Records Act, Congress made Nixon's papers and those of all future Presidents public property and opened them to the public 12 years after the President leaves office.

Congress pressed openness in government to general executive branch operations as well. It overhauled the Freedom of Information Act to expand the right of access to government records, subject only to narrow exceptions with review by the courts. In the Privacy Act, Congress gave private citizens the right to sue if their own government records were disclosed, and the right to see those records for themselves. The Sunshine Act required that meetings of government commissions and boards be made public, and the Federal Advisory Committee Act extended the same rule to meetings between the executive branch and private groups.[67]

All of these laws had the intent to bind the executive branch, to narrow its discretion, to slow its decisions, to force it to act within congressional preferences, and to allow public inspection of its operations. These acts undermined the very character of executive power. Forcing the President to act solely through framework statutes, turning the executive branch into a Swiss cheese of insulated agencies and unremovable officers, and subjecting White House decisions to easy congressional override ignored the reasons for an independent executive in the first place. The President is at his best when responding swiftly and decisively to unforeseen events, when rising to a challenge that is too difficult or dangerous for the legislature. While subjecting the executive to legislative control might alleviate concerns about an unchecked President, it would disrupt the Constitution's creation of three independent branches with the power to balance each other through the political process. Legislative supremacy would threaten liberty just as surely as unchecked executive power would.

Presidents naturally resisted these efforts to dilute their authority. Aside from Carter's approval (and Reagan's extension) of the Ethics in Government Act, it does not appear that any Cold War President accepted congressional efforts to regulate their core executive functions.[68] Efforts to reclaim executive power reached their climax as President Reagan sought most aggressively to expand OMB's powers. The Carter administration had shown in high resolution that national policy would lose its coherence under a President with weak powers. Reagan consciously sought to unify law enforcement in the executive branch, and ultimately the White House, to reduce the burdens of regulation on the economy, and to return decisions to the private markets.

Presidents in the post-Watergate era used the framework laws to enhance, rather than limit, their power and interpreted any congressional failure to prohibit past presidential practice as implicit congressional acquiescence. With the War Powers Resolution, for example, Presidents acted quickly within the 60-day window, which they claimed recognized their constitutional powers to use force without congressional consent. Statutory procedures for approval of covert actions were interpreted to recognize presidential authority to undertake covert actions in the first place. Presidents often treated consultation with Congress before a decision as a mere act of notification, and often delayed filing reports with Congress that triggered restrictions on their powers. Members of Congress usually showed no desire to challenge presidential actions, especially in foreign affairs, that claimed new power under a framework statute. Any legislation to overrule presidential action would be subject to a veto.

The courts used a variety of procedural doctrines to stay out of conflicts between the executive and legislative branches, or even blessed presidential claims to broad powers.[69] A case in point was the resolution of the Iranian hostage crisis. In 1979, Iranian students seized the American embassy in Teheran and held the diplomatic personnel hostage for the next 444 days. In April 1980, President Carter launched a military rescue operation that failed miserably in the Iranian desert. Carter did not follow the War Powers Resolution in carrying it out. In early January 1981, a deal was finally reached to release the hostages in exchange for the lifting of a freeze on Iranian assets in the United States. Companies owed money by Iran sued to prevent the transfer of the assets, which federal courts had attached to satisfy the outstanding claims.

Carter issued an executive order under IEEPA suspending the claims, nullifying the judicial orders, and transferring the funds out of the country. In an emergency lawsuit, the Supreme Court unanimously rejected the corporations' claims that the government had taken their property without just compensation. They further rejected a separation-of-powers challenge that the President had acted without legal authority. Although IEEPA gave the President the power to nullify orders and transfer assets, the companies correctly argued, it was silent on any power to suspend legal claims. Borrowing Justice Jackson's *Youngstown* framework, Justice Rehnquist wrote that a long, unbroken practice of presidential settlement of claims with foreign nations, combined with Congress's failure to oppose the practice, amounted to acquiescence. As a sign of Carter's bad luck, even though he had negotiated the agreement with Iran, the hostages did not return until Reagan took office.[70]

The Reagan administration sought further judicial ratification for its reassertion of presidential power. Its first step was to cut the ties that allowed Congress to pull formal strings over the exercise of delegated power. In *INS v. Chadha* (1983), the Reagan administration challenged the legislative veto. Acting under the Immigration and Naturalization Act (INA), the Attorney General suspended the deportation of Chadha, an alien, because he would suffer "extreme hardship." Using the INA's legislative veto provision, the House overruled the Attorney General and placed Chadha back on the deportation list.

In Chief Justice Burger's majority opinion, the Court found that the House's action amounted to legislation because it changed the legal rights and duties of a private individual. Congress could establish national rules only by enacting a law — passing a bill by a majority of both Houses (bicameralism), which is signed by the President (presentment). Otherwise, it would have to live with the results of the executive branch's exercise of its delegated power. "Congress must abide by its delegation of authority until that delegation is legislatively altered or revoked."

More was at stake than just the Presidency. The Framers, according to the Court, had lived with unchecked legislative power and wanted to make the passage of legislation difficult in order to protect private liberty. Bicameralism and presentment "were intended to erect enduring checks on each Branch and to protect the people from the improvident exercise of power." To be sure, the elimination of the legislative veto might make Congress less likely to delegate power to the executive branch in the future. But *Chadha* clarified the lines of accountability and returned Congress to the regular methods of legislation, oversight and confirmation hearings, or funding cut-offs.[71]

Step two was to reverse Congress's efforts to shift law enforcement authority away from presidential control. In 1986, the Reagan administration sued to block the Balanced Budget and Emergency Deficit (Gramm-Rudman-Hollings) Act of 1985. Unable to overcome the collective action problem in agreeing to reduce the budget deficit, Congress set spending reduction targets for a five-year period. If the deficit did not hit the target, the Act required automatic across-the-board spending reductions to be calculated by the Comptroller General and implemented by the President.

A strange hybrid, the Comptroller General serves as head of the General Accountability Office and can be removed only by Congress. According to the Court, granting the Comptroller General a role in the Gramm-Rudman-Hollings scheme violated Article II of the Constitution. "To permit the execution of the laws to be vested in an officer answerable only to Congress would, in practical terms, reserve in Congress control over the execution of the laws." This violated the Framers' intent to create "a vigorous Legislative Branch and a separate and wholly independent Executive Branch, with each branch responsible ultimately to the people." Again, the Court emphasized that the Framers were worried that "the Legislative Branch of the National Government will aggrandize itself at the expense of the other two branches."[72]

Reagan's campaign before the Supreme Court rested on the

independent agencies. The administration challenged the constitutionality of the independent counsel, who received the same protections from presidential removal as agency commissioners. *Morrison
v. Olson* (1988) addressed the investigation of Theodore Olson for his
advice, while assistant attorney general for the Office of Legal Counsel, that the President invoke executive privilege before a congressional investigation. The committee claimed that Olson had misled
Congress in providing the advice. Upon the referral of the chairman
of the congressional committee, the Attorney General asked for an
independent counsel. Olson challenged the constitutionality of the
counsel's appointment and removal provisions while the Iran-contra
affair was unfolding, and prevailed in the U.S. Court of Appeals
for the D.C. Circuit.[73] The Reagan Justice Department supported
Olson before the Supreme Court.[74]

No doubt worried about the public criticism that would follow an end to the Iran-contra investigation, the Court jumped off
the Reagan revolution train. Rejecting *Humphrey's Executor*'s creation of quasi functions, the Court returned to a cleaner division
among the executive, legislative, and judicial branches. Congress
cannot interfere with the President's executive power or his constitutional responsibility to execute the laws, and according to Chief
Justice Rehnquist's majority opinion, there was no doubt that the
independent counsel's functions were executive. Unlike *Bowsher v.
Synar*, however, Congress had not retained control over the independent counsel but had only restricted the prosecutor's removal.
While there was some reduction in the President's authority, the
Court believed it was outweighed by the importance of establishing
independence for those who would investigate the highest-ranking
executive branch officials.[75]

"Frequently an issue of this sort will come before the Court clad,
so to speak, in sheep's clothing," Justice Antonin Scalia declared in

his *Morrison* dissent. "But this wolf comes as a wolf." The independent counsel, in his view, violated the Constitution's vesting of *all* of the executive power in the President. It upset the political functioning of the separation of powers by releasing a politically unaccountable and unrestrained prosecutor whose sole job was to pursue selected executive branch officials. The following decade fulfilled Scalia's prophecy.

At least five independent counsel investigations targeted Clinton administration cabinet members, including the Secretaries of Commerce, Housing, and Agriculture, but the most serious and damaging to the Presidency focused on the web of scandals known as "Whitewater." At its center was an allegation that then-Governor Clinton and his wife had protected a failed federal savings and loan in exchange for favorable real estate investments and financial support. Eventually led by former judge Kenneth Starr, the investigation grew to include the firing of the staff of the White House Travel Office, the death of Vince Foster, the misuse of White House security files, and allegations of a cover-up of the sexual harassment of Paula Jones and an affair with intern Monica Lewinsky. Clinton partisans launched personal attacks on Starr because of his long Republican ties, including service in the Reagan and Bush Justice Departments. Undaunted, Starr reported to Congress that Clinton had likely committed perjury about his relations with Lewinsky. A sharply divided House voted to impeach Clinton, but the Senate acquitted. After eight years on the receiving end of investigations, Democrats joined Republicans in allowing the independent counsel law to lapse in 1999.[76]

Presidents did not neglect methods outside the courts to reassert their constitutional authority. Executive privilege remained an important method for presidential control, but one that continued to spark controversy over the right balance between democratic accountability and effective administration of government. It is important to recognize that executive privilege has only taken on the taint of cover-up since Watergate. Presidents have long resisted congressional and judicial inquiries for information, though not consistently, when the release of the information could harm the national interest. Presidents have sought to protect the confidentiality of diplomatic and national security information for obvious reasons: a failure to keep secret negotiations, intelligence, or military planning could lead to setbacks for national policy or discourage other nations from cooperating. Domestically, the harm from disclosure of executive branch information is less dramatic but perhaps more systematic. Confidentiality preserves the benefit of candid advice and open argument and discussion among advisors and reduces the amount of outside political pressure on government decisions. The Framers, after all, conducted the Constitutional Convention in secret for that very purpose. Some information, such as the subject of criminal investigations, might prove highly prejudicial if prematurely released to the public.[77]

Truman and Eisenhower illustrate the exercise of executive privilege for good purposes. Probably the most corrosive development in domestic politics during the Cold War was the Red Scare. In 1947, the House Un-American Activities Committee (HUAC) began investigations into the loyalties of members of the Truman administration. The Soviet acquisition of nuclear weapons and the fall of China led to even stronger Republican claims of traitors within the executive branch. Truman issued an executive order establishing a loyalty and security program, but it did little to slow the political juggernaut, and Whittaker Chambers's testimony before the HUAC that Alger Hiss, a former top State Department official under FDR and Truman, was a member of the Communist Party drove investigations to even greater lengths. In 1950, an obscure Republican Senator from Wisconsin, Joe McCarthy, began to make his sensational and unsubstantiated claims of Communists in the State Department. McCarthy even went so far as to attack the loyalty and patriotism of General George Marshall. In 1953, from his perch as chairman of the Senate Committee on Government Operations, McCarthy launched the hearings into the army which would eventually destroy him.

Presidents responded by invoking executive privilege to protect government officials. In 1948, Truman refused to transfer to HUAC any files on the loyalty of employees. Two years later, he directed the Secretary of State and Attorney General to decline a Senate subpoena for information on the loyalty of State Department employees. The following year, he prohibited General Omar Bradley from testifying before the Senate Armed Services Committee about the MacArthur firing, a claim of privilege that the committee accepted.

In 1954, McCarthy's committee demanded communications between the army counsel, top White House aides, and Justice Department officials, provoking perhaps the most sweeping invocation of privilege by any President. In a public letter on May 17, 1954, Eisenhower ordered the Secretary of Defense that no DOD employees were to testify or provide information to McCarthy's committee. Eisenhower declared that it was "essential to efficient and effective administration" that executive branch officials "be in a position to be completely candid in advising with each other on official matters" and that it was "not in the public interest that any of their conversations or communications" or documents containing their advice be disclosed to Congress. Eisenhower observed that the executive branch had an obligation to furnish information to congressional committees to assist in their legislative activities, but that Presidents were responsible for the conduct of the executive branch and could withhold information that was "confidential or its disclosure would be incompatible with the public interest or jeopardize the safety of the Nation."[78] Summarizing his order for top Republican lawmakers, he declared that "any man who testifies as to the advice he gave me won't be working for me that night." Eisenhower's invocation of privilege effectively, though indirectly, put an end to the McCarthy hearings.[79]

Executive privilege protects the President's control over the executive branch, just as the confidentiality of advice between members of Congress and their legislative directors, or judges and their law clerks, is central to the effective operation of the other branches. Its utility depends on the function and the relative positions of the Presidents and Congresses on the issue at hand. Just as McCarthyism showed the potential for good in executive privilege, Watergate showed the bad. In the Watergate crisis, Nixon would not allow his staff to testify before the Senate Watergate Committee on national security matters or written and oral communications with the President. But the conduct under investigation was not part of their official duties. Ordering the burglary of the offices of the Democratic Party, or covering up the President's involvement, does not fall within the definition of the official duties of the Chief Executive. Nixon's invocation of the privilege was the most damaging politically, and on the weakest grounds constitutionally, in response to subpoenas from the Senate Watergate Committee and the special prosecutor for the White House tapes. The end began when tapes turned over to the federal district court revealed an 18.5-minute gap in a conversation between Nixon and Chief of Staff H. R. Haldeman three days after the break-in. In March 1974, the second special counsel, Leon Jaworski, indicted Haldeman, Ehrlichman, and former Attorney General John Mitchell.[80]

Nixon went to the Supreme Court to resist further subpoenas. He agreed only to hand over written transcripts of the tapes, but with significant redactions. The redactions were revealed to cover important exchanges, such as the President encouraging aides to take the Fifth Amendment before the grand jury. In *United States v. Nixon*, the Supreme Court unanimously rejected Nixon's claim. Executive privilege, Chief Justice Burger wrote, protects the right of the President to expect confidentiality in his writings and discussions. "A President and those who assist him must be free to explore alternatives in the process of shaping policies and making decisions," Burger wrote, "and to do so in a way many would be unwilling to express except privately."

Executive privilege derived from the separation of powers itself, and would be almost absolute where diplomatic and military information is involved, because the right to keep internal deliberations confidential is part of the "supremacy of each branch within its own assigned area of constitutional duties." But when the claim includes only an "undifferentiated claim of public interest" in confidentiality, the President's right must be balanced against the constitutional need for the information by the other branches. In *Nixon* itself, privilege gave way before the judicial system's need to gather information contained in the Watergate tapes to conduct a fair trial.[81] While the Court failed to explain adequately why these rights were at stake in a case brought by the special prosecutor, nevertheless, on July 24, 1974, the Supreme Court ordered Nixon to hand over the tapes.

After briefly hesitating, Nixon obeyed but could not head off the political momentum for impeachment. The following week, in a bipartisan vote, the House Judiciary Committee reported out articles of impeachment for obstruction of justice. Released to the public on August 5, 1974, the tapes revealed that Nixon had ordered the CIA to block the FBI's investigation only six days after the Watergate break-in. With significant numbers of House and Senate Republicans supporting impeachment, party leaders and high-ranking administration officials urged Nixon to resign. He left office on

August 8, 1974, the only President to leave office voluntarily before the end of his term. Along with the impeachment and near conviction of Andrew Johnson, Nixon's resignation represents the nadir of presidential power.

Watergate is widely and rightly understood as a heavy blow to executive privilege. While it made executive privilege more difficult to claim politically, Watergate oddly set it on more secure constitutional foundations. *Nixon* affirmed the existence of the privilege and rooted it in the President's supremacy over the constitutional activities of the executive branch. It ratified, for the first time, the claims of Presidents from Washington forward that effective control of the executive branch required confidentiality in receiving and discussing advice. *Nixon* demonstrates that the Constitution provides effective checks and balances on each of the branches through the political process, rather than through legal decisions in court. It was not the Watergate tapes case that ultimately drove Nixon from office, nor was it arguments that his exercise of executive power in foreign or domestic policy was unconstitutional. Impeachment, rather than court tests or judgments about constitutional right and wrong, was the ultimate check on a President who abused executive power to protect his personal interests, rather than those of his office.

PRESIDENTS AND THE COURTS

I F THE COLD WAR witnessed a dramatic expansion in executive power, it was not because of a fundamental change in the Presidency. The change came in the expectations of the federal government's responsibilities for national affairs, and of America's role in the world. Congress wanted the President to run a government that guaranteed economic security at home, and it was willing to allow Presidents to take their traditional initiative in advancing American interests abroad. The President's constitutional powers remained fundamentally the same, but in the postwar period they played on a broader field. A President from an earlier time would have recognized the control of the military, the appointment and removal of executive officials, or policy-making through the interpretation and enforcement of the law. The daily struggle for supremacy between the executive and legislative branches would not have seemed foreign to the writers of *The Federalist* or the great Presidents who followed.

What would have seemed strange to them was the executive's relationship with the third branch, the courts. There is a reason why the landmarks in the development of presidential powers during the Cold War often involve Supreme Court cases. During the Cold War, the courts rebuilt the standing that they had lost in the New Deal. The Justices turned their backs on the enforcement of economic liberties and instead expanded judicial authority over the states, and as their popular approval grew, they intervened more directly in the central social issues of the day. Presidents confronted with the challenges of preserving domestic stability and national security deferred more often to the Supreme Court's interpretation of the Constitution. They joined Congresses in leaving the field of controversial issues to judges, who would suffer no electoral consequences for making difficult choices. One result of this dynamic is that presidential nominations to the Supreme Court and even lower courts assumed the trappings of political campaigns.

Opponents used unprecedented tactics against Supreme Court nominees Robert Bork, Clarence Thomas, and Samuel Alito, who were qualified under the usual measures for the position. Another result of presidential deference is that the Supreme Court extended its reach into core disputes between the executive and the legislature over their constitutional powers. Courts, for example, traditionally waited until the passage of emergency or war before resolving disputes between the President and Congress. No longer.

During the Cold War, the courts made little effort to police the Constitution's limits on federal power. After the New Deal confrontation, the Court did not strike down another act of Congress for lack of authority for six decades. It almost gave up wholly the idea that individual economic rights were enforceable in court, except for government takings of real estate without just compensation. The courts focused their attention on incorporating the Bill of Rights against the states and resurrecting the Reconstruction amendments.

The first ten amendments to the Constitution — such as the right to free speech, freedom of religion, freedom from unreasonable searches, the jury trial guarantee, and the ban on cruel and unusual punishments — originally applied only to the federal government. In the 1930s and 1940s, the Court began to apply these rights to the states via the Due Process Clause of the Fourteenth Amendment. These decisions nationalized the rules that govern police investigations and criminal trials, such as the *Miranda* warning given at the time of arrest and *Mapp v. Ohio*'s exclusionary rule. The Court also intervened in matters of religion, sex, and privacy. The Justices banned prayer in schools and restrictions on the sale of contraceptives, gave First Amendment protection to pornography, and by 1973 recognized a woman's right to abortion.[82]

A second area of judicial activity was racial discrimination. In *Brown*, the Court held that segregation in the public schools violated the Fourteenth Amendment's Equal Protection Clause. In the face of Southern resistance, the Court called on the lower courts in *Brown II* to implement *Brown I* "with all deliberate speed." The Court followed by banning the use of race in other areas, such as access to public facilities, anti-miscegenation laws, and voting access. *Brown* did not immediately end Jim Crow laws, but it prompted massive Southern resistance, which itself advanced the Civil Rights movement. In a moment of opportunity tragically made possible by the Kennedy assassination, President Johnson led Congress to pass the Civil Rights Act of 1964 and the Voting Rights Act of 1965. The 1960s and 1970s witnessed unprecedented judicial intervention in the running of state institutions, primarily schools but also housing, prisons, police and fire departments, and hospitals, to enforce deseg-regation and civil rights. Busing to rebalance school enrollments between whites and minorities led to controversy and resistance in the North.[83]

Massive resistance in the Southern states caused the Court to go to extreme lengths to defend its decisions. As we have seen, resis-tance to *Brown* forced President Eisenhower to send the 101st Air-borne to escort black children to school in Arkansas. School board officials requested a delay in carrying out desegregation because of the state government's opposition. In *Cooper v. Aaron,* the Court ordered all state officials to fulfill their constitutional obligation to obey *Brown.* It declared the "basic principle" that "the federal judi-ciary is supreme in the exposition of the law of the Constitution," a conclusion that would have raised the hackles of Jefferson, Jackson, Lincoln, and FDR. "It follows that the interpretation of the Four-teenth Amendment enunciated by this Court in the *Brown* case is the supreme law of the land."

The Court's defense of its own supremacy might be politically understandable, as it came in response to outright defiance by South-ern officials. *Cooper* might even be correct as a principle of federal-ism: interpretation of the Constitution by any branch of the national government supersedes state decisions. But as an interpretation of the separation of powers, it was mistaken. While the constitutional structure allows the courts the power of judicial review, nothing gives their decisions supremacy over the other branches. Historically, neither Presidents nor Congresses had conceded to the judiciary the *sole* right to interpret the Constitution. To do so would have denied the example of past Presidents and the executive oath to support and defend the Constitution.[84] Yet, the Warren Court actually advanced the wishes of a majority of the nation by dismantling the racist social system localized in the South.[85]

No one understood *Cooper* at the time as a comment on presidential power, but it contained the kernel of judicial supremacy that would grow in *Nixon v. United States* and fully blossom during the Clinton and second Bush administrations. Presidents began to accept the decisions of the Court as binding, or at least refused to dispute them. To be sure, aside from the examples of Jefferson, Jackson, Lincoln, and FDR, Presidents had rarely challenged the Court to the point of ignoring its judgments or opinions, which worked to the political advantage of the executive and legislature.

No matter what principle the Justices choose, a significant portion of the electorate will oppose a decision in a controversial case. Abortion provides but one example. Groups of the electorate hold strong preferences on the abortion question, some to the point where it is the litmus test for office. No matter whether a President is pro-choice or pro-life, his position will generate substantial political opposition. Members of Congress and Presidents interested in re-election will seek to avoid, when possible, making clear decisions on these issues. The expansion of judicial review over abortion, affirmative action, or religion allows a President to take a stand on a controversial issue, but without the expectation of any immediate change in national policy. President Reagan, for example, could campaign on a constitutional amendment to overturn *Roe v. Wade*, but voters in favor of a right to abortion could discount the possibility of any change on the issue because of the Supreme Court.

The disintegration of the 1960s consensus over public values provided Presidents with the political support to exert a stronger

influence over the judiciary. The Supreme Court had associated itself
with the conventional liberal values of the Kennedy and Johnson
administrations, but the consensus broke down under the failure of
Johnson's Great Society programs and the Vietnam War.[86] While it
is true that Presidents could not affect the rules on abortion, affirmative action, or criminal procedure, they could affect the institutions
that made those rules. Even if they did not want to take a universal
stand on abortion, for example, Presidents could promise to appoint
judges who would support or reject *Roe v. Wade*. The politicization
of Supreme Court nominations occurred quickly.

Barry Goldwater became the first candidate to attempt to make
an issue of the Warren Court decisions, which he described as exercises of "raw and naked power" and examples of "obsessive concern
for the rights of the criminal defendant."[87] Although Goldwater was
overwhelmingly defeated, he introduced themes that would become
core features of the Republican agenda. Nixon truly made judicial
appointments a central part of his campaign. With a sharp rise in
crime rates and growing social disorder, Nixon promised to appoint
"law and order" judges.

Nixon explicitly linked the Supreme Court's decisions favoring
defendants to popular perceptions of a decline in policing. "Some of
the courts have gone too far in weakening the peace forces against the
criminal forces," he said in his standard stump speech. Riots in 1967
and 1968 — anti-war protesters, for example, fought pitched battles
with the Chicago police outside the Democratic convention — only
made Nixon's arguments more compelling. He promised that he
would appoint only "strict constructionists" to the bench who would
restore the ability of law enforcement to catch and convict criminals,
and thus reverse rising crime rates.[88] Nixon's approach to judicial
appointments fit neatly with his political strategy of appealing to
Southerners who opposed the expanded federal powers that had led

to school busing and liberal civil rights laws. His campaign themes, both political and constitutional, helped convert the solid South into the stronghold of Republican electoral campaigns, where it has remained for four decades.

Reagan built on Nixon's foundations. He openly criticized Supreme Court decisions on school prayer, abortion, busing, affirmative action, and the rights of criminal defendants. Nixon's appointments had stopped the Warren Court revolution in criminal procedure, but had produced no significant change of course in other areas of constitutional law. Nixon had appointed Chief Justice Burger, who was to be the leader of a conservative counter-revolution on the Court, but he followed up by appointing Harry Blackmun, who joined the liberal wing of the Court, and Lewis Powell, who would remain a moderate. Only the selection of William Rehnquist, who would become known as the "Lone Ranger" for his solitary dissents, would fulfill Nixon's promise to appoint strict constructionists.[89]

Reagan's efforts to reshape the judiciary went farther. On the campaign trail, he repeated Nixon's promise to appoint judges who "would interpret the laws, not make them." In May 1980, he said, "I think for a long time we've had a number of Supreme Court Justices who, given any chance, invade the prerogative of the legislature; they legislate rather than make judgments, and some try to rewrite the Constitution instead of interpreting it." The Reagan administration came to office with the intention not just of changing a vein of decisions, but of reorienting constitutional law. Faced with a Democratic-controlled House, the administration would have an easier time changing policy through a combination of executive orders, rule-making, and judicial appointments rather than new legislation. Selecting judges who would hold a more modest view of their role, and a narrower view of the Constitution, fit in well with Reagan's declared belief that "government is not the solution" and that the national authorities should leave more decisions to the marketplace and the states.[90]

Reagan fared somewhat better than Nixon in his appointments. In 1986, he elevated Rehnquist to Chief Justice. Rehnquist led an effort to limit federal power, attack racial preferences, and reverse the Warren Court's decisions in criminal procedure. In his place, Reagan appointed Antonin Scalia, a federal appeals judge on the D.C. Circuit and a former University of Chicago law professor who would become the Rehnquist Court's brightest conservative legal theorist. Both Rehnquist and Scalia were well-known adherents to the position that the original understanding of the Constitution's text should guide its interpretation. The effect of these appointments, however, was muted by the earlier 1981 selection of Sandra Day O'Connor, an Arizona state appeals judge who would become the Court's moderate swing vote. In 1987, Reagan attempted to build on Rehnquist and Scalia by appointing Robert Bork, a D.C. Circuit judge, former solicitor general, and Yale law professor, who was perhaps the leading exponent of a strict reading of the constitutional text based on the Framers' intentions.

Bork triggered a political explosion over judicial appointments the likes of which had never been seen in American politics. As recently as the nomination of Justice Byron White, nominees either did not appear before congressional committees or did so in a perfunctory manner. Justices often took their seats only a few days after their nomination, but that began to change at the end of the Johnson administration, with the Senate's rejection of Justice Abe Fortas as Chief Justice. The Senate also rejected Nixon's first two nominations to the Court, lower court judges Clement Haynsworth and Harrold Carswell, and fought over Rehnquist's elevation, which attracted 33 votes in opposition but ultimately survived attempts to dig through his past as a Supreme Court clerk and young lawyer.

Bork's nomination witnessed the first extensive use of political campaign techniques of the kind used for elections and legislation. While judges as individuals are not easily subject to the same type of compromise and give-and-take as a piece of legislation, their positions can be inferred from their judicial ideology, or at least interest groups think so. It was inevitable that, as the Court's expansion of its jurisdiction transferred contentious issues from the political arena to the judicial, the tactics used to pressure the government would follow. Interest groups formed, advertisements and editorials ran, and letter and phone campaigns were coordinated.[91]

Democrats, who had retaken control of the Senate in the 1986 elections, considered the Bork seat pivotal. He would replace Justice Powell, a moderate on the Court whose fifth vote decided the Court's outcomes on abortion, race, and privacy. Senate Democrats launched an aggressive stance that portrayed Bork's constitutional views as outside the mainstream. As a law professor, Bork had left a trail of academic writings that had questioned the Warren Court's methods and outcomes, but they bore little resemblance to the charges made against him.

The Judiciary Committee held hearings that featured the most extensive public testimony from a nominee in recent history. Senators held detailed exchanges with Bork on his theories of constitutional interpretation and his views on numerous Supreme Court cases. For his part, Bork did not shy away from the questions by claiming that they would come up before him as a judge, as most nominees do, but instead came out swinging. The Senate rejected Bork's nomination 58–42, and the President nominated in his place Anthony Kennedy, who joined O'Connor as a swing vote in the middle of the Court.

Bork's defeat politicized the appointments process. It has been much criticized by those who believe that the process has become too political or has failed to live up to the original constitutional design. Some believe that the Senate should confirm nominees based on their experience and qualifications, and that considerations of judicial ideology are inappropriate. The Appointments Clause gives the President the authority to nominate and appoint, subject only to the Senate's advice and consent. The clause's structure clearly gives the President the initiative and in this respect is similar to the Treaty Clause, in which the executive negotiates and makes the treaty.

During the Constitutional Convention, the Framers clearly moved the power to nominate from the Senate to the President because they feared that giving the legislature the upper hand would lead to factionalism and horse-trading. In *The Federalist 76*, Hamilton explained that a single person would be "better fitted to analyze and estimate the peculiar qualities" needed for a specific job, and "the sole and undivided responsibility of one man will naturally beget a livelier sense of duty and a more exact regard to reputation." On the other hand, there is little evidence that the Framers believed the Senate was limited in what it could consider. Under the objective qualifications approach, much of the politicization of the Senate's confirmation process has been illegitimate and directly harmful to the idea of the Court as a legal, rather than political, institution. But the only support for the deference that Senators have provided to the President's judicial nominees appears to be history.[92]

It is hard to feel much sympathy for the Court, because the politicization of appointments is a secondary effect of its own decisions. Judicial power has expanded to include more and more of society's most important questions. Today, the Court claims that its interpretations of the Constitution are supreme, not just over the states, but over the other branches.[93] It is only inevitable that players in the political system will seek to advance their agendas by influencing the only institution that can make many of society's fundamental choices on abortion, privacy, affirmative action, criminal procedure, and religion. The most direct way to change national policy on these issues is to change the makeup of the Supreme Court. Moving these issues into the courts did not remove them from politics; it only brought more politics into the courts.

The Court's drive for supremacy has increased executive power in the political short term at the expense of the long-term interests of the Presidency. Presidents have been able to put issues such as abortion or affirmative action on the back burner because there was little chance they could change national policy. Congress was in the same position: with the Court taking control of these issues, legislation could not change the outcomes. The executive has an advantage over Congress in pursuing policy changes through the judiciary, as the Appointments Clause gives the President the initiative in selecting the nominees. A Senate determined to advance a contrary view of constitutional law can only reject judicial nominees, not pick them. While the Senate has turned down a number of Supreme Court nominees, the President's selections have historically been confirmed at a rate of over 80 percent. To the extent that the Court has succeeded in achieving supremacy over many important social issues, it has tipped longer-term control over the issues in favor of the President at the expense of Congress.

Judicial supremacy, however, ultimately harms the Presidency. The President's first and most important job is to support and defend the Constitution, and performing that function requires the President to decide what the Constitution means. Presidents cannot grant that role to the judiciary, just as they cannot allow Congress to dictate how they will exercise their appointment, treaty, or Commander-in-Chief functions. The Constitution establishes a framework where each branch of the government must interpret the fundamental law in the course of carrying out its own unique functions.

The judiciary has an equal right to interpret the Constitution, but its opinions are no more binding on the other branches than the decisions of the President and Congress bind the courts. Supporters of judicial supremacy today either agree with the results of the Supreme Court's current opinions or see wisdom in having one institution decide the Constitution's final meaning. But they ignore the long historical practice of presidential interpretation of the Constitution, and they have no solution for mistaken judicial decisions like *Dred Scott* or *Plessy v. Ferguson*. As Lincoln showed, Presidents can present alternative meanings of the Constitution, ones that may be more true to the original understanding and may better apply to today's circumstances, than those of the Justices.

CONCLUSIONS

REGARDLESS OF POLITICAL party or electoral support, the great Cold War Presidents shared a common attitude toward presidential power. Presidential activism abroad was demanded by necessity, rather than adventurism. Presidents launched wars and covert actions throughout the world to contain the Soviet Union. The global reach of the Soviets and their possession of nuclear weapons seemed to call for greater centralization of policy in the branch best able to act with secrecy, speed, and decision. Congress could have chosen to stop the executive by refusing to provide funds and troops, but it preferred to keep a large standing military ready and available. Congress had every political incentive to allow the President to take the initiative, and to be blamed if war and national security went badly.

A similar dynamic characterized the Cold War Presidency at

home. Even though Congress held the constitutional upper hand over domestic affairs, the change in the nature of the federal government placed the President in the central role. Congress was only too happy to delegate to the executive branch the rule-making authority over issues with difficult trade-offs. Enhancing presidential control over the agencies helped coordinate decisions and ensure a common administrative policy. Congress naturally sought to maintain its ability to influence the agencies, leading to struggles over the removal power. The Supreme Court would uphold restrictions on removal, but the political system came to its senses and ended any new efforts to fragment the executive branch.

The Cold War witnessed the high and low points in the exercise of presidential power. Watergate ripped apart the political fabric of the nation and weakened popular trust in government, but the abuse of power by a single President in pursuit of his personal interests, as opposed to those of the nation, should not obscure the greater benefits from executive initiative. Because of the consistent application of force and pressure against the Soviet Union and its allies by Presidents of both parties, the United States was able to counter the most profound threat to its existence. While it fought several smaller wars and suffered its share of casualties, the United States achieved this result without losing the lives and treasure that come from a great power war. It would have been impossible without the exercise of presidential power from the Korean War, to the Cuban Missile Crisis, to the Reagan Doctrine.

This should give pause to critics who believe the problem with the modern Presidency is that it has grown too strong. Watergate understandably provoked a flurry of reforms designed to restrict presidential powers, but the problem with Watergate was not the Presidency itself, but the man who used the powers of the office to advance and protect his personal interests. While the Watergate reforms proved somewhat toothless, Congress has it well within its powers to stalemate any President. Luckily, the Cold War Congresses supported Presidents to bring the Cold War to a fortunate conclusion. Congress could have passed stricter laws that would have guaranteed that another Nixon could not abuse the powers of his office, but they would have come at the price of an energetic executive capable of defeating the Soviet Union. Executive power could have been domesticated, but only by depriving it of the very qualities that allowed it to respond successfully to the challenges of the Cold War.

CHAPTER 9

The Once and
Future Presidency

THE AMERICAN PRESIDENCY can provoke a schizophrenic
response in its students. Richard Neustadt's *Presidential Power*
portrays a Chief Executive whose formal weakness forces him
to advance his agenda by persuasion. He can bargain with other political actors, but he cannot command. By the end of the Vietnam War,
Arthur Schlesinger, Jr., was sounding the alarm against an *Imperial
Presidency* that had transformed the office into the supreme branch,
rather than a coordinate one. In the next decade, political scientists
described a *Resurgence of Congress* and left the President out of sophisticated models of legislative behavior.[1] By the late 1990s, political scientists began to include more vigorous accounts of the President's role
in exercising the veto and issuing executive orders. During President
George W. Bush's first term, scholars discussed the President's *Power
without Persuasion,* and others warned of the return of a *New Imperial
Presidency,* a *Terror Presidency,* and of a *Takeover* of democracy.[2]

No single work can fully grasp the Presidency in all of its dimensions. If the Presidency is both so strong as to be imperial, and so weak that it can only persuade, we are all looking at the same elephant through different pinholes and neglecting the possibility that the President's power fluctuates depending on the historical context. These works, illuminating though they may be, sometimes see these patterns in reverse. Neustadt viewed the Presidency of the 1950s and early 1960s as weak, but subsequent historical work showed Eisenhower to be in full command, and that Kennedy took advantage of his constitutional powers during his few years in office. Even as the phrase "imperial presidency" entered the political lexicon, President Nixon was headed for impeachment, followed by two Presidents who suffered from political and institutional handicaps and served only one term. As political scientists built their systems of congressional voting, Reagan was restoring presidential power after the drift of the 1970s. Even as books decrying the Bush Presidency arrived in the stores, Republicans lost the 2006 midterm elections and the Oval Office in 2008.[3]

These cycles reflect a permanent feature of the Presidency, rather than the character of individual Presidents. As some scholars have suggested, the Presidency contains a growing paradox.[4] Americans now expect their Chief Executives to secure economic growth and international peace, cure the credit problems in the housing market, reform the health care system, solve the challenges of terrorism and the Middle East, and even control global warming. On its own, the office of the President lacks the formal power to implement final policy in many of these areas. On domestic policy, Congress has the upper hand; the President's formal role is limited to making proposals and exercising a conditional veto. For foreign affairs, Presidents have the initiative and manage day-to-day policy, but Congress must provide the funds, change trade laws, and establish the size and shape of the military.

Presidents have relatively fixed powers but exaggerated responsibilities, for which they can blame their predecessors. Theodore Roosevelt transformed the office into a "rhetorical presidency," and his cousin made it a "plebiscitary presidency."[5] They both found that marshalling public opinion through direct communication with the electorate enhanced their ability to build political support for their agenda. Using public approval, however, has led the electorate to hold Presidents accountable for progress in areas outside their formal powers. Presidents of all stripes and parties have inevitably expanded their powers to meet their political responsibilities.

PRESIDENTIAL POWER IN THE MODERN AGE

ONE OF THE LESSONS of this book is that the Constitution creates a mass of executive power that can help Presidents rise to the challenges of the modern age. This power does not ebb and flow with the political tides, but finds its origins in the very creation of the executive. The Framers rejected the legislative supremacy of the revolutionary state governments in favor of a Presidency that would be independent of Congress, elected by the people, and possessed with speed, decision, and vigor to guide the nation through war and emergency. They did not carefully define and limit the executive power, as they did the legislative, because they understood that they could not see the future.

If Congress could enact legislation that successfully anticipated all possible circumstances that the nation might confront, or could act swiftly and decisively itself, a separate executive might be unnecessary. Those who wrote and ratified the Constitution, however, viewed untrammeled legislative power with deep suspicion. More often than not, the dominant state legislatures of the Revolution had failed to organize effective executives and had fallen into interest-group politics. The Continental Congress, which had no executive or judicial branch, suffered paralysis. Erecting an independent executive, and an independent judiciary, would allow the nation to act effectively and restore balance to its political system.

Use of presidential power does not signal failure — otherwise, Presidents like Washington, Jefferson, Jackson, Lincoln, and FDR would not merit their reputations today. Nor does executive action guarantee success. Instead, it sets the foundation for a President's ability to achieve. Our greatest Chief Executives have all vigorously exercised the powers of their office to the benefit of the nation — establishing the independence of the executive branch, purchasing Louisiana, blocking the politicization of the national bank, winning the Civil War, entering World War II, or containing the Soviet Union — but only in times of crisis. A branch headed by a single person, as Alexander Hamilton recognized, can act swiftly and decisively because it is not subject to the crippling decentralization of Congress. Emergencies and foreign affairs sit at the core of the purpose of the executive, and no President has successfully responded by passively following Congress's lead and forsaking his right to independent action.

Presidents have often wielded their powers in the face of congressional silence, and sometimes they have acted contrary to Congress to advance what they perceived to be the national interest. Obviously, Presidents will find governing easier when their political party enjoys large majorities in Congress. Some scholars link the growth in the Presidency to its position as party leader, and attribute the loss of executive influence to efforts to govern through an administrative state instead.[6] But even under unified government, Presidents have had to rely upon their constitutional powers when acting at odds with the wishes of their legislative supporters. Jefferson overcame constitutional qualms about the Louisiana Purchase; Lincoln rejected congressional Reconstruction plans; FDR tried to pack the Court and unseat leading Democrats in the South. Congress can still frustrate a President of the same party and doom him to failure, as was the case with Jimmy Carter and Herbert Hoover. Party government remains an important feature of the power of the modern Presidency, but it can act as a straightjacket just as easily as a lever.[7]

The same dynamic describes the relationship between the Presidency and the administrative state. Agencies facilitate the implementation of executive branch policy. Without the main cabinet departments, the President could not achieve priorities on finances, defense, law enforcement, or foreign policy, not to mention the broad array of decisions on economic and social issues delegated by Congress. On the other hand, the agencies create bureaucratic routines that hem in a President's ability to achieve swift change. While they are designed for rational, comprehensive planning, agencies and their processes inherently resist the ideas of a new President. The inertial weight, or even the outright opposition, of the bureaucracy — composed, after all, of career civil servants who have their own policy interests — is compounded by the emergence of powerful interest groups, congressional oversight committees, and a media culture focused on conflict. Presidents have responded by attempting to strengthen their control over the administrative state through their constitutional powers of removal, just as Congress has sought to keep agencies within its own political orbit.

While executive power is more general and open-ended than other powers in the Constitution, it is not undefined. Its general nature does not automatically subject it to congressional control, any more than the vesting of the "judicial power" in the federal courts makes judges the servants of Congress. The bulk of executive power rests in foreign affairs and national security, where it is most suited

to effective action. During peacetime, the Constitution limits the
Presidency to enforcing the law (which includes, as the highest law,
the Constitution itself) and managing the executive branch. While
executive power has grown throughout American history, its most
vigorous use appears sporadically. Only crises and challenges call
it forth.

World War II and the Cold War broke this pattern of peacetime
quiet punctuated by presidential action in times of crisis. The postwar growth in presidential power is not the result of the inexorable
and unwarranted aggression of an imperial executive, but America's
changing place in the world and its new ambitions at home. Foreign
policy has unquestionably become of vital importance to the nation.
By the end of World War II, American leaders finally understood
that events abroad dramatically affected the nation's security as
advances in transportation, communication, and technology eliminated the distance and security that the oceans once provided. Committing to the defense of Western Europe and East Asia required the
permanent mobilization of a large standing military. Containing the
Soviet Union and maintaining a liberal international order based on
free trade and democracy demanded the ability to exert military
and diplomatic force along many dimensions. As the executive was
designed to be continually "in being" and to have the leading constitutional role in foreign affairs, presidential power naturally increased
to match the demands on the government. What marks the postwar
period as a sharp break with the past is not presidential unilateral-
ism; rather, it is the change in circumstances that demanded executive initiative. It was not the Presidency that became imperial, it was
the United States that became an empire.

Rising expectations of government prompted a corresponding
jump in presidential power at home. The New Deal's goal of guaranteeing economic security demanded a massive expansion of federal

economic and social regulation. In the 1960s and 1970s, Congress broadened the role of the federal government into civil rights, the environment, consumer safety, poverty, housing, and crime. Extensive intervention called for bureaucratic resources that Congress simply does not have and would not want. Delegation to the executive branch agencies served multiple purposes. It allowed Congress to shift responsibility for decisions that are politically controversial, call for difficult choices based on technical and scientific information, and involve high but unpredictable stakes. Members of Congress could focus their limited time and energy on spending programs, earmarks, and tax breaks for constituents and interest groups who supported their reelection.[8]

A second lesson of this book is that the notion of an unchecked executive, wielding dictatorial powers to plunge the nation into disaster, is a myth born of Vietnam and Watergate. Congresses have always possessed ample ability to stalemate and check an executive run amok. Congress regularly ignores executive proposals for legislation, rejects nominees, and overrides vetoes. It can use its power over legislation, funding, and oversight to exercise significant control over the administrative state. There would be no agencies, no delegated powers, and no rule-making without Congress's basic decisions to create the federal bureaucracy. It can use these authorities even at the zenith of presidential power: foreign affairs. Congress can cut off war funding, shrink the military, stop economic aid, and block treaties. It used its sole control of the purse to limit the Mexican-American War and to end the Vietnam conflict, for example.

Of course, cooperation between the President and Congress on national security policy is politically desirable, but it has never been constitutionally necessary. As we have seen, our greatest Presidents have, at times, acted contrary to Congress to protect the nation. It was their judgment that the Constitution did not require the government to sit on its hands until both the President and Congress agreed on every particular. It is no doubt correct that requiring legislative consent would promote greater deliberation and slow down hasty decisions. But the collective-action problems that make the legislature slow bear costs, too — costs that can become acute when national security is involved, especially in light of technological change that has made weapons swifter and vastly more destructive. Expanding the numbers involved in decision-making does not guarantee that the results will prove more accurate. Congress makes mistakes just as the executive does, and the costs of national security paralysis might outweigh any marginal decrease in errors.

Political scientists are beginning to appreciate that the model of an institutionally weak executive cannot explain the growth of presidential power during the last half century. Recent works applying game theory to the separation of powers have recognized a large area for presidential action. According to these studies, the President will most often be able to succeed in areas where the stakes are high, the issues are complex and unpredictable, or political controversy means large portions of the electorate will disagree with any government decision. Congress has far more interest in awarding discrete benefits to constituents and supporting interest groups than in risking a serious mistake of national policy or generating political opposition. If the President acts first, Congress will have to take an affirmative step to overrule him. A presidential veto of that legislation will be sustained if more than one-third of the Senate agrees with him. Not surprisingly, legislative proposals to overrule executive orders rarely succeed.[9]

These approaches cannot work without a proper understanding of the President's constitutional authorities. Take the effort to model the President's role in the legislative process. During the 1980s and 1990s, political scientists developed rigorous frameworks to understand the movement of legislation through Congress. In these models, the role of the President was often an afterthought, an oversight since corrected by the work of the last decade. These scholars identify the conditions in which presidential vetoes, or even the threat of a veto, will win policy concessions from Congress.[10] For that variable to be significant, the President must have the power to veto legislation on policy, rather than just constitutional, grounds. Without that change in the understanding of the President's veto power, his ability to influence legislation would be dramatically reduced. Scholars also observe that Presidents prevail more often in foreign affairs than any other significant area. As with the veto, this would not be possible without an understanding of the President's constitutional authorities. One singular reason that the President may win more often in foreign affairs is simply that his constitutional powers, and hence his freedom of action, are greater beyond the nation's borders.

Exercise of these constitutional powers does not guarantee presidential greatness or success. Progressive scholars of the first half of the last century believed that the President should the play the role of a political hero who would represent the people better than a Congress beset by special interest groups. Chief Executives would use their constitutional powers to restore democracy and expand the powers of a national government that would respond to the people's wishes. But Andrew Johnson, Lyndon Johnson, and Richard Nixon demonstrated that not everyone would rise to this vision of the reformer President. Executive power does not inexorably bring progress. Constitutional power may not be enough to help the President overcome the many demands and obstacles placed in his way by the modern political system, and it certainly does not prevent a President from making poor decisions.

Yet, executive power remains the wellspring of a President's ability to play a transformative political role, which remains a key distinction between the great and the merely good. Stephen Skow-ronek has persuasively argued that the Presidency's political authority moves in cycles. Certain Presidents are "reconstructive" — they repudiate a vulnerable political order, often shown to be incompetent during times of crisis, and replace it with a new one. Other Presidents maintain the existing order and governing coalition, with their success declining rapidly if events have undermined the regime. A small set of Presidents come to office opposed to the existing political system, but that system is resilient, and efforts to preempt it will lead to conflict and often failure. A President's success depends on his matching his political "warrants" — in other words, his electoral and political support — to the circumstances of his day. According to Skowronek's retelling of presidential history, a deep structure generates recurring cycles of reconstruction, maintenance, and ultimately collapse. As the nation becomes institutionally richer, more populous, and more sophisticated, it becomes difficult for Presidents to overthrow the existing political order.[11]

The executive's constitutional powers provide the foundations for this dynamic. Skowronek's list of reconstructive Presidents is the same as this book's: Jefferson, Jackson, Lincoln, and FDR. Both lists track the Presidents usually rated as the greatest, and those elections considered pivotal in American history.[12] This book examines constitutional, rather than political, authority, but it is significant that the Presidents who established new governing regimes, some lasting almost 70 years (Lincoln), were also those who wielded their constitutional powers in the broadest ways. Because these Presidents came at the head of parties elected to sweep away a discredited political regime, their constitutional powers were critical to replacing the existing order. Executives dependent on Congress would find it far more difficult to establish the durable political orders of the Jeffersonian, Jacksonian, Republican, or New Deal periods. Congressional efforts to limit presidential power often represent the efforts of a status quo regime to prevent the rise of its successor.

Presidents achieve greatness for more than their reconstruction of the political system. Our best Chief Executives brought the nation safely through unprecedented crises and emergencies. Washington, Lincoln, and FDR remain the three greatest because they led the country through its birth, its rebirth, and its rise to great power status. Jefferson acquired the Louisiana territory, and Jackson started the drive toward the Pacific. Our Cold War Presidents patiently pursued the strategy of containment and eventually exhausted the Soviet Union. None of our great Presidents was a stranger to controversy. They relied heavily on their unique constitutional powers to take action — the very same powers that, in other hands, could produce disaster. At the time, they were often accused of dictatorship, tyranny, and acting above the law. History has proven them right, but it has taken decades or even centuries of perspective for their vindication.

Examples of presidential greatness caution against going beyond the Constitution to restrict executive power. After Watergate, Congress enacted a series of laws, such as the War Powers Resolution, intended to restrain the "imperial presidency." But within a decade, Presidents of both parties had worked around many of these statutes, without much opposition from Congress, to restore the capabilities of their office. But suppose Congress turned serious about altering the Presidency's institutional abilities. It could attach funding cutoffs to any laws creating military units or national security functions; reenact the independent counsel law; downsize the size and scope of the White House staff; and terminate delegated authority. The powers that some Presidents have abused, however, can be the very same ones that have allowed other Presidents to become great. Reducing presidential power for fear of another Nixon or Bush (depending on one's political perspective) could also cripple another Lincoln or Roosevelt. Critics of executive power desire a risk-free Presidency, but by creating a system designed to ensure against the risks of presidential action, they would defeat the very purpose of the executive.

Efforts at reform ignore the robustness of the original constitutional design. We have had poor Presidents, perhaps more than we like to admit, and we have had abusive Presidents, though perhaps fewer than commonly assumed. Our political system allows even these bad Presidents to stymie Congress and the courts, but when it comes to an unconstitutional abuse of authority, our system has shown the capacity to respond. Andrew Johnson and Congress fought to a standstill on Reconstruction, and eventually the Radical Republicans prevailed through impeachment and the next election. A combination of Justice Department investigation, media reports, and impeachment forced Nixon to resign. Impeachment by a Republican Congress placed Bill Clinton on the defensive for his second term, while the 2006 midterm elections forced George W. Bush to compromise and negotiate with a Democratic Congress. Bush's ability to continue the war in Iraq in the face of vigorous opposition serves as a reminder both of the President's constitutional preeminence in war and Congress's political reluctance to use its power of the purse to stop him.

THE BUSH PRESIDENCY

GEORGE W. BUSH has sparked a resurgence in popular interest in presidential power. Many of our great and near-great leaders have been wartime Presidents, but war has also led others, such as Johnson or Nixon, to make critical errors of judgment and policy. Partisanship and poll ratings will give way to the passage of time, just as they did to the benefit of Harry Truman and to the detriment of John F. Kennedy. What this book shows is that the claims of dictatorship or of a President acting above the law are exaggerations no different from the attacks on other vigorous Presidents. On some questions, the Bush administration acted well within the example of past Presidents; in others, it even sought greater accommodation with the other branches. Today's conflict over presidential power does not truly arise over whether the authorities in question exist, but whether now is the right time to exercise them.

War power is the most immediate and obvious example. Like Presidents before him, Bush claimed the authority to use force to defend the national security. But unlike his predecessors, he did not use it. In the wake of the September 11, 2001, terrorist attacks, the administration sought and received from Congress an Authorization to Use Military Force (AUMF). It was sweeping, perhaps the broadest grant of war power by Congress since World War II. It authorized the President "to use all necessary and appropriate force against those nations, organizations, or persons he determines planned, authorized, committed, or aided the terrorist attacks."[13]

The AUMF recognized that "the President has the authority under the Constitution to take action to deter and prevent acts of international terrorism against the United States." It was unlimited as to time or geography. Nor did Bush rely solely on his presidential power in Iraq. Again, the administration sought and received from Congress another AUMF, this time aimed at Iraq and Saddam Hussein. While not as broad as the September 11 resolution, it still granted significant power to the executive branch. Congress authorized the President to use the armed forces "as he determines to be necessary and appropriate" to achieve two objectives: "defend the national security of the United States against the continuing threat posed by Iraq" and "enforce all relevant United Nations Security Council resolutions regarding Iraq."[14]

Critics of the Iraq war have since claimed that the Bush administration provided misleading information to Congress. If it did so, it was nowhere as serious as President Polk's description of the events that led to the declaration of war against Mexico. But it is a mistake to think about the intelligence regarding Iraq in 2002 as the same in kind as the information about the Mexican-American War, Pearl Harbor, the Tonkin Gulf, or even Jefferson's war against the Barbary Pirates. In those conflicts, Presidents reported to Congress on events that had already occurred, and those facts either led Congress to authorize war or not. In contrast, the facts about Iraq involved prediction about the future. The decision on war did not focus on whether Iraq had aggressively acted to justify a military response, but whether the intentions and capabilities of its regime posed a sufficient threat to justify a preemptive attack. Such judgments will involve speculations, guesses, and estimates of future costs and benefits that may turn out to be wrong, but we should not confuse mistakes for a conspiracy.

If Congress were serious about claims that the executive branch deliberately misled it, it could have used its powers over funding, oversight, and legislation to influence the intelligence agencies. Select committees in the House and Senate had received classified briefings from the CIA on all covert operations and intelligence programs. If Congress believed that the executive branch deliberately manipulated information about Iraq, it could have restructured or cut funding for the national security agencies and programs. Or, ultimately, it could have impeached the President.

Putting the justification for war to one side, much of today's controversy over presidential power has settled on the conduct, rather than the initiation, of war. Critics of the Bush administration attacked the "surge" strategy of sending more troops to Iraq to secure Baghdad and its surrounding provinces. They argued that the executive branch cannot detain prisoners in the war on terrorism at the U.S. naval base at Guantanamo Bay, Cuba. They challenged the use of coercive interrogation measures on al Qaeda leaders and the establishment of military commissions for the trial of terrorists. They claimed that the National Security Agency's surveillance of the communications of suspected terrorists without a warrant, inside the United States, violated federal law and the Fourth Amendment.

Critics went to Congress to cut off funds for the Iraq war, but failed. Proposals to restrict the warrantless surveillance of suspected terrorists went nowhere. The opposition found more success in its efforts to seek legislation regulating military interrogation and trials. Critics have won some successes in the Supreme Court, which extended its jurisdiction in 2004 to hear cases arising out of Guantanamo Bay, blocked portions of the military commission rules in 2006, and expanded the right of the judiciary to review military detention decisions in 2008.

President Bush initially undertook many of these policies under his powers as Chief Executive and Commander-in-Chief. To be sure, the administration made broad claims about its powers under the President's constitutional authorities, but this book shows that it could look to past Presidents for support. Presidents have used force abroad without any legislative authorization at all, and several made the most important strategic decisions without any input from Congress. Lincoln and Roosevelt, for example, resisted or overrode efforts by Congress to interfere with their judgments about the steps necessary to protect the national security. The Emancipation Proclamation stands as a striking example of a presidential decision on the conduct of war — to free the slaves and undermine the Confederacy's vital labor source — which was inconsistent with Congress's preferences. Presidents have long exercised the widest discretion over the conduct of war and have fought jealously to defend their prerogatives. Congress, for the most part, has respected presidential discretion, and the times when it has not, as in the War of 1812 and the beginnings of World War II, it has done no better and sometimes much worse than the President. Congress simply does not have the ability to make effective, long-term national security decisions because of the difficulty in organizing 535 legislators and the political incentives that drive them toward short-term, risk-averse thinking.

Despite low approval ratings, President Bush succeeded in defending many of his war priorities. In Iraq, the administration won continued funding from Congress for the surge of troops, without any strings attached, such as a withdrawal date or a mandated reduction in operations. In the Detainee Treatment Act of 2005 and the Military Commission Act of 2006, Bush won support for the use of military commissions and the exclusion of the Supreme Court from reviewing the detention of terrorists. Congress did set rules for the interrogation of prisoners held by the U.S. armed forces, but it did not extend those guidelines to the CIA. Similarly, President Bush went to Congress to seek support for his warrantless surveillance program. In the Protect America Act, Congress responded by giving its temporary blessing and providing immunity to telecommunications companies that had helped carry out the surveillance after the 9/11 attacks.[15]

Other exercises of executive power have simply been blown out of proportion. A salient example is the issue of presidential signing statements. In 2006, a media report claimed that President Bush had used signing statements to claim "the authority to disregard more than 750 laws enacted since he took office." The American Bar Association assembled a task force that concluded that such statements were "contrary to the rule of law and our constitutional system of separation of powers." The Senate Judiciary Committee followed with hearings criticizing them as a "grave threat to our constitutional system of checks and balances." These reports would lead a stranger to this land to think that by issuing a statement when signing a bill, even one that provided an interpretation of the law or found parts of it unconstitutional, President Bush had brought down republican government.[16]

Careful examination of the issue shows that nothing of the sort has happened. Presidents have issued statements to explain their reasons for approving or disapproving a bill, almost from the beginning of the Republic. Jackson's lengthy message explaining his veto of the Bank of the United States was little different in purpose from a signing statement. To be sure, Presidents did not use statements frequently until the twentieth century. Beginning with Truman, Presidents issued statements that they would interpret laws to avoid causing constitutional problems, refuse to obey provisions that they believed violated the Constitution, or explain their preferred interpretation of ambiguous statutory language. By the Clinton administration, an average of between 35 and 60 were issued a year. Many of the statements discuss policy or feature political rhetoric rather than interpret legislation or comment on its constitutionality. It does not appear that courts give these declarations much, if any, weight. A more careful study of the Bush administration's practices finds that it issued signing statements challenging statutory provisions at a rate within the historical norms for postwar Presidents, though it questioned the constitutionality of more provisions per bill.[17]

Signing statements themselves can present reasonable defenses against legislative encroachments. In many, for example, President Bush objected to laws that required the executive branch to propose legislation to Congress — most would agree that Article II gives the President the discretion whether to do so. In others, Bush objected to congressional efforts to vest the power to appoint executive branch officers in people or entities outside the Appointments

Clause. Sometimes the administration challenged provisions ordering it to take a certain diplomatic position, vote a certain way in
an international organization, or limit the use of the armed forces
abroad. While Bush received criticism for signing the Military Commission Act with the proviso that he would interpret it consistent
with his Commander-in-Chief authority, President Clinton relied
on the same ground in refusing to obey a congressional prohibition
on placing American troops under foreign commanders. A recent
study finds that President Clinton issued signing statements virtually identical in substance, though fewer in number, on all of these
issues.[18] President Obama has issued signing statements in his first
few months in office that continue the Bush practice in form and
function, especially in the area of foreign affairs.

Bush's use of signing statements has been exaggerated into a
caricature. A desire to spin a story of an out-of-control President has
overlooked their modest purposes. Signing statements are not really
aimed at the courts, which do not take them into account, or even to
Congress, which is not bound by them. Instead, they communicate
presidential policy and interpretation to subordinate officers and
agencies within the executive branch. Presidents can just as easily
reach the same result by issuing a memorandum to cabinet secretaries and agency heads setting out the same instructions, minus the
public transparency of a public statement. The President need not
even declare that he believes a law violates the Constitution, the very
move that stoked the controversy in the first place. As we have seen,
the Constitution itself places the responsibility on the President to
execute the laws — and the Constitution is the supreme law. A presidential declaration that he will not enforce acts of Congress that violate the Constitution merely states a truism.

Some argue that the President has an obligation to veto an
unconstitutional law, rather than sign it and decline to enforce it. To

be true to his oath of office, the argument goes, the President cannot approve an unconstitutional act.[19] This argument ignores laws that were enacted before a President assumed office (as with Jefferson and the Alien and Sedition Acts) or laws passed over his veto (as with Nixon and the War Powers Resolution). But even if such a principle applied to bills signed during a President's own administration, it fails to take note of changes in the legislative process. Gone are the days when Congress enacted laws of brevity and conciseness. Congress today enacts massive omnibus legislation that combines provisions on multiple subjects along with spending needed to keep the government open. A President who signs legislation to keep normal functions going cannot thereby have his right to interpret the Constitution taken away. Members of Congress have a parallel obligation not to vote for bills that contain unconstitutional provisions, but they do so anyway for the same reason as the President's — they cannot vote against omnibus legislation containing vital appropriations. Today, it is not unusual to hear Congressmen declare that if part of a bill violates the Constitution, the Supreme Court should attend to the problems.

President Bush reached for a broad vision of executive power. Whether his claims ultimately have merit depends on whether they were used at the right moment. Our Framers designed the executive branch to be a government always in being that could respond quickly and with vigor to unforeseen emergencies and crises. Presidential power expands to meet them, and withdraws when they are over. During peacetime conditions, when there are few threats to the national security, the constitutional role of the President remains limited, and that of Congress is ascendant. During wartime, those roles are reversed, but that does not mean that the sudden expansion of presidential power in response to emergency ever occurs smoothly. Beginning with President Washington's declaration of neutrality in the European wars, the mobilization of the executive branch to meet crises has fallen under fire as dictatorial and tyrannical.

Two developments have contributed to the modern controversy over executive power. The first is the great expansion of economic and social regulation during the New Deal and postwar period. Critics of presidential power usually raise the specter of a massive executive branch that has broken free of its checks and balances, like a King Kong bursting his chains, but they are often silent when it comes to the changes that produced the massive bureaucracy of the New Deal state. If the executive branch has become a permanent establishment dwarfing Congress and the courts, it is in part because of Congress's delegation of power to the agencies to manage the economy and society. Those who worry about executive power often have no qualms about national education standards, pollution controls, or housing programs. If critics were to enforce the same standards about executive power in its domestic dimension that they would in foreign affairs, they would have to accept a return to a domestic regime of limited government and largely unregulated markets.

On the domestic front, the Bush administration's exercise of presidential power followed the path marked by its predecessors. Bush claimed privileges to shield discussions internal to the executive branch from Congress and private litigants, but he was not the first, nor even the most aggressive to do so. Eisenhower claimed a greater scope for secrecy, reaching down to anyone in the executive branch, while Clinton argued that it extended to activities that fell outside his official duties. Bush moved to make his mark on the judiciary by appointing Supreme Court Justices and lower court judges who shared his constitutional philosophy, but again, that made him no different from Presidents since at least Nixon. Bush used his position as Chief Executive and party leader to coordinate with his congressional majorities, but he was only following in the mold of Presidents since Jefferson. Like his predecessors, Bush sought to deepen his control so as to bring coherence and rationality to the administrative state. His exercise of power may have been different in amount, but not in kind.

The second, and sharper, area of controversy involved foreign affairs. President Bush's actions relied on broad claims of presidential power, but again they fell within the precedents set by earlier Presidents. President Bush, for example, terminated the Anti-Ballistic Missile Treaty with the Soviet Union without the approval of the House or the Senate, but Presidents have terminated treaties since at least President Lincoln. When Senator Barry Goldwater sued to block President Carter's decision to end the Mutual Defense Treaty with Taiwan, the federal appeals court in Washington, D.C., vindicated the President, and the Supreme Court refused to reach the merits. (Four Justices agreed that the case posed a political question that lay outside the judicial power.) President Bush declined to apply the Geneva Conventions' protections for prisoners of war to members of al Qaeda and the Taliban captured fighting in Afghanistan. He concluded that al Qaeda was not a signatory to the Conventions and that the Taliban did not meet the standards for lawful combatants, such as fighting in organized units with visible uniforms and arms in the open, while following the laws of war. Presidents have interpreted treaties since President Washington's proclamation of neutrality. President Clinton, for example, claimed that the ABM Treaty remained in existence even after the Soviet Union had collapsed into 15 independent states.[20]

Most of the opposition to the Bush administration's exercise of its powers focuses even more tightly not just on foreign affairs, but on the war on terrorism. The Framers vested the executive branch with a unitary design and broad authority precisely so it could respond to the demands of war. Structurally, a branch headed by a single person can process information more easily, analyze the situation and make decisions faster, and implement policies decisively and vigorously. In contrast, Congress's large numbers create severe transaction costs that prevent it from organizing and acting quickly, and the courts act slowly and address only issues that arise as a case or controversy under federal law. "Decision, activity, secrecy, dispatch will generally characterize the proceedings of one man, in a much more eminent degree, than the proceedings of any greater number," Hamilton reminds us in *Federalist 70*, "and in proportion as the number is increased, those qualities will be diminished."[21] The Framers vested the President with the executive power and the role of Commander-in-Chief so he could marshal the nation's military with speed and decision to defeat its external foes.

Every President since World War II has consistently argued that the Constitution gives him the right to use force abroad to protect the nation's security and interests. Presidents have consistently refused to obey the War Powers Resolution, and Congress has often recognized the President's right to use force, not just in the 2001 Authorization to Use Military Force, but in its acquiescence to the numerous presidentially led interventions abroad. Even the *Youngstown* case, much beloved by supporters of congressional authority, does not take away the President's powers abroad. *Youngstown* held that the regulation of the steel mills in wartime remained within Congress's power to legislate on domestic affairs. It did not address the scope of the President's authority over the armed forces in the theater of war, nor did it address the Commander-in-Chief's power to set military strategy or tactics, direct the military, or gather intelligence. *Youngstown* even acknowledges that if Congress attempts to limit presidential action, the executive could prevail by relying on "his own constitutional powers minus any constitutional powers of Congress over the matter."[22]

The Bush administration's claims of executive authority in the war on terrorism fell into the tactical and strategic decisions appropriate to the Commander-in-Chief. Commanders have long set the standards for the capture and treatment of enemy prisoners. The executive branch has played the leading role in the development and enforcement of the laws of armed conflict. The Lincoln administration issued the first code of the laws of war. The Wilson administration found that unrestricted submarine warfare was a *casus belli*. FDR approved the strategic bombing of Germany and Japan, even when hundreds of thousands of civilians were killed — a position put on stark display by President Truman's decision to drop the atomic bomb. President Reagan refused to adopt an international agreement extending the Geneva Conventions to irregular fighters because it would have given terrorists the same status as regular troops. While Congress has the power over funding, creation of the military, and the authority to pass laws for the "Government and Regulation of the land and naval Forces," it has never sought to prevent the President from making the critical decisions about the best means to prevail on the battlefield.

Even the Bush administration's domestic pursuit of al Qaeda terrorists, while controversial, followed the example of past Presidents confronted with grave security challenges. The military has detained hundreds of al Qaeda terrorists at Guantanamo Bay without access to civilian courts, and has established military commissions to try dozens of them for war crimes. Bush designated several U.S. citizens and permanent resident aliens as enemy combatants and ordered their detention without criminal trial as well. While not punitive, as is imprisonment in the civilian justice system, the detentions seek to prevent a member of the enemy from returning to the fight. President Bush ordered the warrantless interception of electronic communications involving suspected terrorists coming into or out of the

United States. Like detention, the warrantless Terrorist Surveillance Program does not seek information to use in convicting terrorists in court. It only intercepts communications that would allow the intelligence agencies or armed forces to take action to prevent an attack on the United States.

Earlier Presidents used similar means on the home front. President Lincoln detained thousands of citizens behind the Union lines, used military commissions to try suspected Confederate agents, and suspended habeas corpus. When the federal courts today have sought to extend habeas to broader classes, such as non–U.S. citizens held outside the United States at Guantanamo Bay, Congress and the President have joined together to overrule them, sparking yet another round of struggle with the courts.[23] FDR used military commissions to try U.S. citizens who had joined the Axis powers, interned 120,000 Japanese-American citizens, and instituted a sweeping surveillance program that intercepted all electronic communications within the nation's borders. This is not to argue that Bush's counterterrorism policies stand out because they reduced civil liberties less than these historical examples. Instead, the record of practice shows that the United States has always had to balance civil liberties and security interests and that in wartime, liberties will be narrowed to give the government broader freedom to win a war. Unless the government is to be prevented from making any adjustment in the trade-off between security and liberty, the executive will be the branch that often must strike that balance in wartime.

The war on terrorism provides a cautionary tale about current proposals to rein in executive power. Despite the executive's constitutional powers, Congress always has the ability to counter the President. Trying to force the President to assume less initiative may make the office more comfortable for the risk-averse, but it may also prevent the executive branch from rising to the great challenges confronting the nation. After Watergate, Congress embarked on a similar mission by passing a horde of statutes intended to hamstring future Presidents.

Some of the new statutes had little effect, some had a large one. One of those, the Foreign Intelligence Surveillance Act, required that Presidents obtain a warrant from the federal FISA court before they could pursue domestic wiretapping for national security purposes. The courts and the Justice Department read the law to prohibit the sharing of the fruits of such intelligence with domestic law enforcement officials. As American security agencies attempted to track down al Qaeda agents who had entered the country in the summer of 2001, FISA prevented the CIA from informing the FBI about the identities and photographs of some of the 9/11 hijackers already in the country. FISA was passed with the best of intentions, to prevent another Richard Nixon from ever using the intelligence agencies to harass his domestic opponents, but it also blocked the executive branch from taking the swift action necessary to prevent a devastating attack on the American homeland.[24]

No one wants another Nixon to abuse his powers to attack his political enemies, but the restraints necessary to prevent another Nixon or Andrew Johnson may sap the executive of those unique qualities that allow it to act decisively when the nation's security is at stake. The flexibility necessary for an energetic executive can serve bad as well as good ends. For the bad, our constitutional system seems up to the job. It has adequately handled the abusive Presidents with political resistance or by forcing them from office. While the poor Presidents have cost the nation dearly, Washington, Lincoln, and FDR brought the nation much more benefit, including national survival. If allowing Presidents to exercise their constitutional powers freely risks executive abuse, it also brings with it the promise of flexibility and energy to meet national emergencies and crises.

RETURNING TO FIRST THINGS

Bush's reputation will depend on whether future historians judge his exercise of presidential power to have been justified by the circumstances. If the September 11, 2001, attacks marked the emergence of a serious foreign threat to the nation's security, the invocation of broad presidential powers will have been appropriate. Presidents like Lincoln and FDR may have gone too far at times, but we forgive them their trespasses because they led us through the Civil War and World War II. If it turns out that the United States had overreacted to what was essentially an isolated event, the exercise of presidential power will prove to have been unnecessary and counterproductive. The difficulty in reaching a judgment now is that we are still living through the period of threat, and we cannot judge ex post whether the long-term reorientation of national security powers was necessary to meet it. This is not to argue that Bush is destined to rank among the great Presidents or even those considered above-average. It means that only when we have the benefit of distance will we know whether Bush's aggressive use of executive authority was too much, too little, or just right.

Understanding the contingency of our current circumstances brings us back to where we began, the purpose of the executive. As originally conceived, the need for the executive arose to respond to unforeseen dangers, unpredictable circumstances, and emergencies. It was given the virtues of speed, secrecy, vigor, and decisiveness to most effectively marshal society's resources in a time of crisis. The executive could correct for the instability, fractiousness, and inability to organize and decide (caused by what we today think of as transaction costs of a republican legislature) under time pressure. If the circumstances demand, the executive can even go beyond the standing laws in order to meet a greater threat to the nation's security.

It remains an open question whether the Constitution incorporated this prerogative. Hamilton believed that Article II's vesting of the executive power in the President necessarily included the ability to meet any challenge. To him, this power ought to "exist without limitation because" the "circumstances that endanger the safety of nations are infinite." There was no prerogative in the Lockean mold, only a President with open-ended powers in time of emergency. This broad conception of the executive underpinned the broader Hamiltonian program. A President of broad powers would guide the national government by developing proposals, managing legislation, and vigorously enforcing the law and setting foreign policy. In contrast, Jefferson believed that the President's ability to access the prerogative existed independent of the Constitution. To him, the natural right of self-preservation allowed the President to act beyond the Constitution itself when defending the nation. Whereas Locke believed that the executive would have to appeal to the heavens in the event of an exercise of the prerogative, Jefferson believed that an appeal to the nation was in order.

The prerogative allowed Jefferson to keep his devotion to a strict interpretation of the Constitution. If the prerogative could serve as a safety valve when emergency placed the government under stress, the Constitution would need no stretching. The government's powers would remain limited, rather than permanently extended, and individual liberty and hopefully state sovereignty would be preserved. The process for confirming the executive's use of the prerogative, an appeal to the people, advanced Jefferson's agenda to make the President the democratic representative of the nation as a whole. Jefferson did not believe that the approval of Congress or the courts alone was necessary, except insofar as they represented the will of the people.

History suggests that Hamilton had the better argument. The prerogative faces serious, perhaps fatal problems, chief of which is that it requires the executive to violate the Constitution. If the people bless executive lawbreaking, then they undermine the very purpose of the Constitution to bind future majorities. Although faced with the most serious threats to the nation's security, Lincoln and FDR did not claim a right to act outside the Constitution. While Lincoln suggested on several occasions that it might be necessary to violate the Constitution to save the nation, he never invoked the prerogative. In fact, he carefully argued that his every action, from using force against secession to the Emancipation Proclamation, was justified by his constitutional authorities. Roosevelt, too, never claimed the prerogative, and justified his actions by his authority as Commander-in-Chief. By the Cold War, the debate seemed to be over — the Constitution accommodated the need to respond to extraordinary events through the President's executive power.

At first glance, it might appear that this understanding of the Constitution could only work to the benefit of the President. It allows him to claim a reservoir of power to meet any serious threat to the national security. But subordinating the prerogative to the law may have come with costs as well — it has raised public expectations of the President to the point where no mere mortal can satisfy them. If the President has the constitutional authority to respond to any emergency, then the failure of the government to meet the latest national problem must be his fault.

A second effect may be the unwillingness of Presidents since FDR to challenge the Supreme Court. Presidents no longer claim an independent right to interpret the Constitution differently from the judiciary, giving up the inheritance of Jefferson, Jackson, Lincoln, and Roosevelt. There are understandable political reasons for this, but perhaps a deeper constitutional explanation lies in presidential adoption of the Hamiltonian theory of the executive. If the President accesses extraordinary power from the Constitution, he may seek judicial approval in order to address concerns that he is interpreting the Constitution solely for his own benefit. It is not clear whether this bargain is to the long-term benefit of the institution; abdicating the right to interpret the Constitution, in light of the President's obligation to enforce the laws, ultimately places the definition of his duties and powers solely in the hands of another branch. Presidents may have only won themselves the freedom to act in the short term, but they have left the long-term success in the hands of others.

The fundamental question of the prerogative lends presidential power a tragic quality. Due to the Constitution's design, the political system has great difficulty responding to unforeseen circumstances, fast-moving events, or decisions that require technical expertise or run high political risks. It will fall to the President to act at these times, which most often arise where the nation's foreign relations and national security are at stake. In exercising their constitutional powers, Presidents by definition act against the web of congressional statutes, court decisions, agency regulations, and interest groups that make up the political status quo. Invocation of executive authority is guaranteed to trigger a sharp response by the supporters of the governing regime.

In their own time, our greatest Presidents have been the subject of terrible attacks, ranging from accusations of personal immorality to the formation of opposition political parties. Nevertheless, our greatest Presidents have had to act because they have judged their actions necessary to benefit the nation or protect it from harm. Presidential power takes on a tragic dimension when our Chief Executives exercise their constitutional powers knowing that it could lead to their political ruin or damage their historical reputations. But as we have seen, presidential power moves in cycles, change is no doubt certain, and it is change that can bring out greatness in our Presidents.

AFTERWORD

"YOU NEVER WANT a serious crisis to go to waste," Rahm Emanuel, the new White House Chief of Staff, said in the early months of the Obama administration.[1] Barack Obama's election as America's forty-third President was historic for many reasons. Obama entered office amid what may be the worst economic recession since the Great Depression. Gross domestic product estimates nose-dived a stunning 6.3 percent in the fourth quarter of 2008 and fell another 5.7 percent in the first three months of 2009.[2] The stock market fell about one-third in 2008, destroying trillions in private wealth.[3] The unemployment rate leapt from 4.6 percent to 7.1 percent in 2008 — 2.7 million Americans lost their jobs, General Motors and Chrysler went bankrupt, while industrials like Alcoa and DuPont announced mass layoffs. Unemployment continued to rise after the inauguration, continuing upward to more than 9 percent by the middle of 2009.[4] Only the recessions of 1974–75 and 1982–83 threw a higher fraction of postwar Americans out of work.[5] Obama's assumption of office in the midst of trying economic times recalled the transitions between Hoover and FDR and between Carter and Reagan.

Foreign dangers also greeted the new President. Obama took the oath of office while the nation fought wars in Iraq and Afghanistan. Al Qaeda, which, along with its Taliban allies, continues to destabilize nuclear-armed Pakistan, remains a threat.[6] North Korea, the most brutal totalitarian dictatorship on the planet, successfully tested a nuclear weapon and continues its quest for a long-range ballistic missile capable of reaching the United States.[7] And Iran, another consistent foe of the United States, continued its own efforts to acquire nuclear weapons and ballistic missile technology in defiance of international sanctions.[8] The United States transferred power between the two major political parties during the Cold War, but it did not elect new regimes during any previous "hot" war except for the elections of Eisenhower during the Korean War and Nixon during the Vietnam conflict.

But as Emanuel's quip recognizes, crisis presents opportunity. Obama is the first African American elected to the nation's highest office, giving many hope of a post-racial future. His election might also portend, in the view of some, one of those rare realignments in American politics that have accompanied the elections of several of the great Presidents studied in this book — Washington, Jefferson, Jackson, Lincoln, FDR, and Reagan. Not only did Obama win the 2008 election decisively, by 52–46 percent of the popular vote and 365–173 in the Electoral College, but Democrats picked up 6 seats in the Senate and 20 in the House of Representatives. After the Minnesota Supreme Court declared Al Franken the winner of a Minnesota Senate seat in June 2009, Democrats gained a filibuster-proof majority in the Senate, in addition to their already secure 254–173 majority in the House.[9]

Obama, however, has a difficult course to chart. While he and his party won large majorities, he must navigate between overreaching and timidity. Americans of all stripes celebrated that the United States had elected the first African American to the Presidency. But Obama should resist the temptation to view his victory as a fundamental realignment of the political system. Obama is only the second Democratic presidential candidate to win more than 51 percent of the vote since FDR in 1944, and the first since Lyndon Johnson's landslide (Carter won in 1976 with only 50.1 percent). One of the Electoral College's effects is to magnify the political legitimacy of the winner beyond that bestowed by the popular vote alone. For example, even though he never won a popular majority, Bill Clinton won the 1992 election by 370 electoral votes to 168 for President George H. W. Bush, and four years later he won 379–159 over Senator Bob Dole.[10]

Realignments take more than a victory at the polls; they only occur after a critical election that represents a sea change in the nation's politics. Only two have occurred in the twentieth century: the elections of FDR in 1932 and Ronald Reagan in 1980. FDR's election rejected the laissez-faire philosophy of the Republican Party that had dominated politics since the Civil War. The 1932 realignment introduced the liberal New Deal state at home and an interventionist foreign policy abroad. The Reagan vote signaled skepticism of activist government, the rise of free market economics, and a focus on tax cuts, but maintained a muscular approach to foreign affairs. The only other realignments that scholars can agree upon occurred in 1800, 1828, and 1860.[11]

Misreading an electoral realignment can cause a President to over-reach without sufficient political support. FDR thought the results of the 1932 landslide justified his efforts to pack the Supreme Court and to challenge incumbent Southern senators in the mid-term elections. The New Deal stalled, and the economy would not recover until World War II. President Nixon believed that he represented a silent majority against a hostile, liberal Congress; he mistakenly turned to executive authority against his domestic political opposition. More recently, President Clinton read his 1992 election as a mandate to pursue higher taxes and a national health care plan that proved deeply unpopular, sparking the Republican takeover of Congress in 1994.

Current economic woes have brought comparisons with the Great Depression. FDR presents a worthy model of a Presidency more institutionally independent of Congress and more liberated from the political parties than ever before. Using every constitutional authority of the Presidency, FDR brought unprecedented leadership to the legislative process and led the nation through World War II. But Obama may make a fundamental mistake if he believes that he enjoys a mandate like FDR's. We still live in the era of Reagan — Obama himself campaigned on a platform of tax cuts and deficit reduction.[12] Any regulation of the financial system will be driven by a panicked response to the collapse of the credit markets, not a new philosophical dedication to an activist state. Obama may propose new spending on infrastructure, but only to stimulate the economy out of a recession, not because the American people have a newfound love of bigger federal government. Obama asked for a massive stimulus program in the first weeks after taking office "not because I believe in bigger government — I don't."[13]

To take just one sign that the election may not have ushered in a new political consensus, California voted for Obama by an amazing 61–37 percent.[14] But the bluest of blue states also prohibited same-sex marriage by 5 percent, enacted a crime victims' rights initiative by 7 percent, and defeated a proposal to limit minors' free access to abortions by only 4 percent.[15] Obama himself opposed gay marriage during the campaign[16] and called for the Supreme Court to overrule its decision banning the death penalty for child rapists.[17]

Obama would be better served by moving swiftly to cure the recession and then focus on moderate, bipartisan policies in areas such as education, spending, and entitlement reform. He might even pick a fight or two with a Congress that moves too far and too fast to nationalize health care or interfere with the free market. His picks of Hillary Clinton for Secretary of State and General James Jones as National Security Adviser, along with his decision to keep Robert Gates as Secretary of Defense, signal that he sees the virtues of a pragmatic foreign policy. Drawing down American forces in Iraq on the same timetable set by the Bush administration, and even increasing combat forces in Afghanistan, suggests that Obama intends no radical departures from national policy in these vital arenas.[18] While the new President has made diplomatic overtures to Iran and North Korea, these nations have shown no long-term desire to reach a permanent settlement of tensions with the United States.[19] If his feelers are rebuffed, Obama may well have to pursue the same policies as his predecessors toward these rogue nations. The realities of international power politics do not change on the timetable of American elections.

While avoiding the Scylla of overconfidence in his mandate, Obama almost must skirt the Charybdis of Congress. His victory over Hillary Clinton in the Democratic primaries raised the possibility that he might be beholden to congressional leaders, many of whom have decades more experience in Washington. One of the least understood aspects of the Democrats' primary system was the extraordinary role of the "superdelegates." Neither Obama nor Clinton could win their party's nomination through the allocation of delegates by direct election, because 795 superdelegates, all party insiders, held votes at the convention, far more than any one state. The important Pennsylvania primary on April 22, 2008, for instance, had only 158 delegates at stake.[20] Due to the closeness of the popular vote, the real battlefield in the Clinton-Obama contest moved from the voting booth to the superdelegates.

Democratic primary reforms in 1982 gave superdelegates about 20 percent of convention votes — precisely so that party graybeards could stop a popular, but politically extreme, candidate from seizing the nomination.[21] The Democrats deliberately rejiggered the rules to head off insurgent candidates like a George McGovern or a Jimmy Carter who might be crushed in the general election. Congressmen and other party leaders have more than twice the votes of the richest state prize, California.[22] If the popular vote is close, as it was in 2008, the superdelegate rules effectively give congressional incumbents a veto over the nomination.

The Framers did not envision this delegate dissonance. As we have seen, they believed that letting Congress choose the President was a dreadful idea. Without direct election by the people, the executive would lose its independence and vigor and become a mere servant of the legislature. They had the record of revolutionary America to go on. Recall Gouverneur Morris's explanation: if Congress picked the President, he "will not be independent of it; and if not independent, usurpation and tyranny on the part of the Legislature will be the consequence." Choosing the President would result from the "work of intrigue, of cabal, and of faction."[23] After weeks of debate, the Framers vested the Presidency with its own base of popular support by establishing a national election, so the President could represent the views of the entire people, not the wishes of Congress.

They kept the same rule when considering presidential reelection. Alexander Hamilton wrote in *Federalist 68* "that the executive should be independent for his continuance in office on all, but the people themselves," for otherwise, the President might "be tempted to sacrifice his duty to his complaisance for those whose favor was necessary to the duration of his official consequence."[24] The Framers were deeply concerned that a President chosen by Congress would keep his eye only on the happiness of legislators, turning our government into a parliamentary system like those of Europe today.

The Framers were right to worry. The Clinton and Obama campaigns competed hard to win superdelegates. No one knows whether members of Congress cut deals for themselves and their constituents in exchange for their vote, but it would have been difficult to resist. A water project here, some pet legislation there — surely such details were worth the Democratic nomination. Lose, and the candidate pays nothing. Win, and a Presidency is gained. Like shareholders deciding whether to sell in a tender offer, superdelegates would have bargained ferociously until the moment that the nominee secured a delegate majority. As the Democratic convention approached, the demand for superdelegates would have escalated, with the choice of the nominee becoming increasingly the work of political intrigue, inside deals, and power struggles among interest groups, just as the Framers feared.

The concern is that any nominee, not just Obama, who survived this process will come to the Presidency weighed down by dozens, if not hundreds, of commitments. Some may welcome such a development. Some students of American politics argue that the President and Congress should work more closely together, and may well prefer a President who obeyed congressional wishes. But as we have seen, the historical record is not heartening. During the reign of the Jeffersonians, the congressional caucus chose the party's nominee. It yielded mediocrity, even danger. James Madison deferred as Congress drove the nation into the disastrous War of 1812, which ended with a stalemate in Canada and the capture and torching of the U.S. capital.[25] "King Caucus" finally broke down when the system reached a peak of "cabal, intrigue, and faction" in the 1824 election, with Clay throwing the election in the House to Adams, allegedly in exchange for the post of Secretary of State. Jackson spent the next four years successfully attacking the legitimacy of the Adams administration and won his revenge in the election of 1828.[26]

It is unlikely that a candidate today would trade something as important as a cabinet post for a superdelegate's vote. But the election of 1824 ought to caution against allowing congressional leaders to play such a large role in choosing the President. Obama has advanced an ambitious domestic agenda, including an overhaul of national financial regulation, a national health care plan, large equity stakes in the banking and industrial sectors, and a huge economic stimulus. These are areas where the Constitution gives the legislature the primary authority, and where political scientists predict that members of Congress will have the greatest incentive to send money back to home districts or to favor political supporters at the expense of the public interest.[27] Obama would fulfill the role set out for him by the Framers by checking Congress's instinct to overregulate and hand out benefits to interest groups, rather than asking for stimulus bills and letting Congress fill in the details. The mode of his primary selection, however, will make it difficult for him to oppose the congressional leaders of his own party. That electoral system echoes failed models from the American past and threatens to sap the Presidency of its independence and authority by turning it into the handmaiden of Congress, instead of the choice of the American people.

Obama might be hampered by his origins as a member of Congress or his lack of executive experience. During the 2008 elections, John McCain accused Obama of lacking the maturity and experience to serve as President. The Obama-Biden campaign returned the same fire on Sarah Palin, who had been governor of Alaska for only two years and before that was mayor of tiny Wasilla, Alaska, and chair of the state oil and gas commission.

Because Obama's rise to the Presidency was truly meteoric, he avoided the legislative record that has doomed numerous presidential candidates from Bob Dole to John Kerry. Only three sitting Senators — Warren Harding, Kennedy, and now Obama — have ever been elected directly to the Presidency. In fact, Obama's lack of experience might have little impact on his success. Lincoln only won election to a single term in the House, and shot to fame by losing to Douglas in the 1858 Illinois Senate race. But that did not prevent him from becoming our greatest President. His predecessor, by contrast, had one of the most sterling resumes ever assembled by an occupant of the White House. James Buchanan had served as a member of the House for a decade, ambassador to Russia and Great Britain, a two-term Senator, and Secretary of State in the Polk administration.[28] Yet, scholars agree that Buchanan was the worst Chief Executive in American history because he did nothing to stop the South from leaving the Union.

History does not show any obvious link between experience and a President's effectiveness during times of crisis. Many of our worst performers in the office would have won the title of most qualified. James Madison wrote the first draft of the Constitution, coauthored *The Federalist Papers*, served in the House during the First Congress, cofounded the Jeffersonian party, and served as Secretary of State for two terms under Jefferson. He also allowed the nation to rush into an ill-advised war that saw Washington, D.C., conquered and burned and the nation itself almost dismembered.[29] Franklin Pierce served in both the House and Senate before serving as President from 1853–57, but a rigorous survey of scholars ranked him 38th out of 40 Presidents.[30] Andrew Johnson, who had been a member of the House and Senate, governor of Tennessee, and Vice President, came in at 37th for prompting impeachment by opposing Reconstruction.[31] Millard Fillmore, who checks in right before Johnson, had been Vice President, a member of the House, and a New York official before his Presidency from 1850–53.[32] The lack of correlation between experience and effectiveness is not merely a lesson from some far-off age in American history. Richard Nixon was one of our most qualified presidents, serving as Vice President and as a California Senator and Representative. He covered up Watergate, risked impeachment, and resigned from office.[33]

Extensive government experience does not bring any special ability to use presidential power to respond to crises. Herbert Hoover had been Secretary of Commerce and was known as the "Great Engineer" for his engineering company and his organization of the postwar relief effort in Europe.[34] He could do little to end the Great Depression. Woodrow Wilson had been president of Princeton University, governor of New Jersey, and the finest American political scientist of his day.[35] His failure over the Treaty of Versailles sparked a deep isolationism that ended only with the Japanese attack at Pearl Harbor.

Experience, no doubt, can help Presidents. Jefferson, Jackson, the two Roosevelts, and Eisenhower were prominent politicians, administrators, and soldiers before assuming the country's highest office. Jimmy Carter's inexperience — he had served only one term as governor of Georgia — left him unprepared for stagflation and the Iranian revolution. But experience is not a magic ingredient that can substitute for other important qualities. Electing candidates only because of their experience or charisma denies them a true mandate. A vote for ideology over experience produced the Reagan Revolution. Love him or hate him, Reagan's unerring commitment to a few simple principles — free markets, low taxes, and aggressive anti-communism — proved more critical to success than a long résumé.

The Framers invented the Presidency to ensure that government possessed the "decision, activity, secrecy, and dispatch" to lead the nation through the unforeseen circumstances of emergency, crisis, and war.[36] Judgment, character, and political principles, not how long he or she served on the Senate Foreign Relations Committee, will determine a President's success in acting swiftly and decisively. Congressional experience provides little preparation for executive

office. The legislative mind-set favors discussion over decision, deliberation over speed, and consensus over determination. Most of our
greatest Presidents spent little to no time in Congress. In fact, our
best modern executives have defined themselves through their opposition to Congress, not their deference.

We can see these dynamics at work in Obama's initial policies
on the war on terrorism, issues on which I worked during my service in the Bush administration. Obama has set his own course on
controversial issues such as the detention, interrogation, and trial of
terrorists, at first pleasing the base of the Democratic Party, but then
tacking back toward Bush policies as he became aware, I believe, of
the security challenges abroad.

During his first week as Commander-in-Chief, for example,
President Barack Obama ordered the closure of detention facilities
at Guantanamo Bay[37] and terminated the CIA's special authority
to question terrorists using tough interrogation methods that critics
have claimed amount to torture.[38] He suspended the military commissions that were in the middle of the trials of al Qaeda leaders for
war crimes.[39] His Department of Justice, led by Attorney General
Eric Holder, decided it would no longer use the phrase "enemy combatant" to describe terrorists nor describe the struggle with al Qaeda
as a "war."[40] Obama released several secret Bush legal memos, some
of which I worked on, regarding detention and interrogation policy,
and went head-to-head on May 21, 2009, in dueling speeches with
former Vice President Dick Cheney over whether the Bush administration policies on interrogation had proven effective.[41]

While these actions certainly pleased the left wing of the Democratic Party, they also threatened to handicap our intelligence
agencies from preventing future terrorist attacks. In issuing these
executive orders, Obama favored the law enforcement approach
to fighting terrorism that prevailed before September 11, 2001. He

also dried up the most valuable sources of intelligence on al Qaeda, which, according to former CIA Director Michael Hayden, has come largely out of the tough interrogation of high-level operatives.[42]

The question President Obama should have asked right after the inaugural parade was: "What will happen after we capture the next Khalid Sheikh Mohammed or Abu Zubaydah?" More careful review of terrorism policy would have made clear that the civilian law enforcement system cannot prevent terrorist attacks. What is needed are the tools to gain vital intelligence, which is why, under President Bush, the CIA could hold and interrogate high-value al Qaeda leaders. On the advice of his intelligence advisers, the President could authorize coercive interrogation methods like those used by Israel and Great Britain in their anti-terrorism campaigns. (He could even authorize waterboarding, which Bush did three times in the years after 9/11.)[43]

President Obama's stay of all military commission trials, and the transfer to the criminal justice system of the only al Qaeda operative held by the military on U.S. soil, might presage the shuttering of commissions entirely in favor of the exclusive use of U.S. civilian courts.[44] Military commission trials have been used in most American wars, and their rules and procedures are designed to protect intelligence sources and methods from revelation in open court. Obama has ordered that al Qaeda leaders be protected from "outrages on personal dignity" and "humiliating and degrading treatment" in accordance with the Geneva Conventions.[45] Obama might even be on the way to declaring terrorists to be equal to prisoners of war under the Geneva Conventions. The Bush administration classified terrorists — well supported by legal and historical precedent — like pirates: illegal combatants who do not fight on behalf of a nation and refuse to obey the laws of war.[46]

The CIA must now conduct interrogations according to the

rules of the Army Field Manual, which prohibits coercive techniques, threats and promises, and the good-cop, bad-cop routines used in police stations throughout America.[47] President Bush already banned torture or physical abuse in 2002,[48] but President Obama's new order amounts to requiring—on penalty of prosecution—that CIA interrogators be polite. Coercive measures are unwisely banned with no exceptions, regardless of the danger confronting the country.

Eliminating the Bush system entirely will mean that we will get little timely information from captured al Qaeda terrorists. Every prisoner will have the right to a lawyer (which they will surely demand), the right to remain silent, and the right to a speedy trial.[49] The first thing any lawyer will do is tell his clients to shut up. The KSMs or Abu Zubaydahs of the future will not respond to verbal questioning or trickery—which is precisely why the Bush administration felt compelled to use more coercive measures in the first place. Our soldiers and agents in the field will have to run more risks to secure physical evidence at the point of capture and maintain a chain of custody that will stand up to the standards of a civilian court.

Relying on the civilian justice system not only robs us of the most effective intelligence tool to avert future attacks, it also provides an opportunity for our enemies to obtain intelligence on us. If terrorists are now to be treated as ordinary criminals, their defense lawyers will insist that the government produce in open court all U.S. intelligence on their clients along with the methods used by the CIA and NSA to get it. A defendant's constitutional right to demand the government's files often forces prosecutors to offer plea bargains to spies rather than risk disclosure of intelligence secrets. Zacarias Moussaoui, the only member of the September 11, 2001 cell arrested before the attack, turned his trial into a circus by making such demands. He was convicted after four years of pretrial wrangling only because he chose to plead guilty.[50] Efforts to use the criminal justice system to try al Qaeda leaders will only lead to more of the same, but with far more valuable intelligence at stake.

It is naïve to say, as Obama did in his inaugural speech, that we can "reject as false the choice between our safety and our ideals."[51] That high-flying rhetoric means that we must give al Qaeda — a hardened enemy committed to our destruction — the same rights as garden-variety criminals at the cost of losing critical intelligence about real, future threats. All government policies involve trade-offs between competing values. As Obama has matured in office and learned more about the nation's security environment, he has adopted policies that suggest more continuity with the past. Obama has so far decided against ending the NSA's electronic surveillance program, which allows the warrantless interception of suspected terrorist communications entering or leaving the country.[52] The new administration not only kept in place, but even expanded, the use of unmanned aircraft to kill suspected al Qaeda leaders in civilian areas — a far greater deprivation of civil liberties than detention, interrogation, and trial by the military.[53] In May 2009, Obama reversed his decision to suspend military commissions, and even though he has proposed the transfer of enemy combatants from Guantanamo Bay to the United States, he also conceded that many will not be tried in civilian courts but will instead be detained as prisoners of war.[54] None of these policies would be legal unless the United States were at war.

In this, Obama bears similarity not to FDR or even Lincoln, to whom the new President is sometimes compared, but Eisenhower. Ike was another President whose personal popularity outstripped the public support for his policies. The Eisenhower administration continued the basic strategy developed by his immediate predecessor, Harry Truman, to address the dire security challenge posed by the Cold War. Eisenhower initially campaigned on the ground that the strategy of containment resigned millions to communist dictatorship, and his future Secretary of State, John Foster Dulles, promised "rollback" of Soviet control of Eastern Europe.[55] Once in office, however, Eisenhower kept in place the fundamental strategy of containment, though with a lower defense budget and without triggering an all-out war. As John Lewis Gaddis has shown, he changed the means from symmetric to asymmetric force, but he kept true to Truman's fundamental choice of containing the Soviet Union around its peripheries.[56]

Similarly, President Obama has come to have more in common with the ends of the Bush administration's terrorism policies than did Candidate Obama. It should be clear, further, that this would not be possible were it not for a broad view of presidential power. Obama has continued American occupation in Iraq and even increased deployment to Afghanistan, based on the view of his national security team — not Congress — that the battle against terrorism must be won there.[57] Continuing the NSA's warrantless wiretapping power is primarily the product of the President's decision to carry out intelligence against an enemy. Extensive use of predator drones is a tactic carried out by the military pursuant to the President's Commander-in-Chief authority. Suspending military commissions, which had received congressional authorization in 2006, could only be done pursuant to the President's Article II powers under the Constitution.[58] Even ordering the CIA to follow military rules in interrogating enemy combatants depends wholly on the President's authority to command the military and determine operational tactics and strategy. Congress itself refused to place the CIA under the rules of the Army Field Manual on interrogation.

It should be clear that regardless of any disagreement with these policies, the focus should remain on Obama's choices, not his constitutional power to adopt them. In making and implementing these terrorism policies, Obama has done nothing less than exercise many of the executive's broader powers in time of emergency of war. Counterterrorism policy also shows the effectiveness of Congress's powers. A signal element of Obama's plan is the decision to close the detention facilities at Guantanamo Bay and transfer the remaining prisoners to the U.S. prison system. Congress responded by requiring that no funds be used to allow any detainee from Guantanamo Bay to enter the United States.[59]

Obama's buildup in Afghanistan would be impossible without congressional funding for the new deployments, and his policies on targeted killings with Predator drones or NSA surveillance could not continue without Congress's financial support.[60] Obama's effort to recharacterize the status of enemy combatants or to try them in civilian courts will be tested in the federal courts and may even reach the U.S. Supreme Court. Both branches have the ability to impede, if not totally obstruct, President Obama's policies against the leading external security threat of our day.

Obama may have made his decisions on terrorism too swiftly after his inauguration. He may have opened the door to further terrorist acts on U.S. soil by shattering some of the nation's most critical defenses. Obama may even be right in reversing some of the Bush measures, if the classified threat assessments today report that the chances of a terrorist attack have sharply declined. What remains important is that Obama has relied on his constitutional authority, just as had Bush, to make policy on everything from the number of troops in Afghanistan, to warrantless wiretapping, to use of Predator drones. If Obama wishes to guide the nation successfully through its period of economic crash and foreign threat, he must draw on the mainspring of presidential power as deeply as his greatest predecessors. So far, he shows early signs that he has learned this lesson well.

ACKNOWLEDGMENTS

———✦———

THIS BOOK GREW out of an effort to reconcile personal experience with received teachings. As an immigrant from South Korea, I have long been conscious of President Harry Truman's use of his authority as Commander-in-Chief at the start of the 1950 Korean War. Were it not for his decision to send American troops immediately, I very well might have grown up in a real totalitarian dictatorship. The difference is strikingly illustrated by the satellite imagery of the thirty-eighth parallel at night, with the brilliantly lit cities of the South contrasting with the utter darkness of the North. Presidents throughout the Cold War pursued similar policies regardless of party, often risking their standing in the opinion polls steadily to contain the Soviet Union and to protect the Free World.

The benefits of vigorous presidential action did not accord with the conventional wisdom toward executive authority, at least as revealed at Harvard College in the 1980s or Yale Law School in the 1990s. In the classrooms of those days, it was *de rigueur* to criticize the Reagan and Bush administrations' exercise of their constitutional powers, arguments that became muted once President Clinton assumed office, but returned with a vengeance during the second Bush administration. For me, it was at least worth considering whether the modern Presidency had achieved better outcomes for the nation, and for the liberty of millions around the world. As I studied and thought more, it seemed to me that the Presidency of the twenty-first century falls well within the boundaries of its constitutional origins and political history and tradition than scholars commonly believe today. This book is the product of my thinking about the Presidency first sparked in my student days.

I have accumulated a number of intellectual debts in the course of writing this book. My greatest thanks go to colleagues and friends who have read and commented on some or all of the manuscript: Carlos Bea, Joseph Bessette, Jesse Choper, Robert Delahunty, Dan Farber, Mark Killenbeck, Sai Prakash, Dean Reuter, Ron Rotunda, Gary Schmitt, and Michael Uhlmann. I have also benefited from the excellent research assistance of Janet Galeria, Peter Gerra, Ben Peterson, Andrew Verriere, and Claire Yan. Dean Christopher Edley, Jr., provided financial support for summer research, and Dean John Eastman invited me to Chapman Law School for a semester when I put the finishing touches on the manuscript. Lynn Chu has been not just an agent, but a great editor and collaborator as well. Don Fehr of Kaplan has been a source of sage advice and editorial judgment.

I have been blessed to have the support of my wonderful parents, Drs. John Hyun Soo Yoo and Sook Hee Lee Yoo, and brother, Dr. Christopher J. Yoo. It has been my equally good fortune to spend the years since college with my wife, Elsa Arnett. She has combined the smarts, support, and strength for which every writer (or husband) could wish. This book, once again, is dedicated to her.

ENDNOTES

INTRODUCTION

[1] Stephen Skowronek, The Politics Presidents Make: Leadership from John Adams to George Bush (1993).

[2] Marc Landy & Sidney M. Milkis, Presidential Greatness (2000).

[3] John M. Cooper, The Warrior and the Priest: Woodrow Wilson and Theodore Roosevelt 118 (1983).

[4] See, e.g., Sidney Milkis & Michael Nelson, The American Presidency: Origins and Development, 1776–2007 (5th ed. 2007); and Michael A. Genovese, The Power of the American Presidency: 1789–2000 (2000).

[5] For excellent examples of such works (representing several different perspectives on the Presidency) that have been helpful to this study, see James D. Barber, Presidential Character: Predicting Performance in the White House (4th ed. 1992); James W. Caesar, Presidential Selection: Theory and Development (1979); Thomas E. Cronin, The Paradoxes of the American Presidency (2003); Fred I. Greenstein, The Presidential Difference: Leadership Style from FDR to George W. Bush (2004); Sidney M. Milkis, The President and the Parties: The Transformation of the American Party System since the New Deal (1993); Michael Nelson, The Presidency and the Political System; Skowronek, supra note 1; and Jeffrey K. Tulis, The Rhetorical Presidency (1988).

[6] Transcript of the third Nixon-Frost interview, N.Y. Times, May 20, 1977, p. A16.

[7] Richard E. Neustadt, Presidential Power from FDR to Carter xi (1980 ed.).

[8] Ibid. at 21.

[9] Greenstein, supra note 5.

[10] Woodrow Wilson, Congressional Government: A Study in American Politics (1885).

[11] Woodrow Wilson, Constitutional Government (1907).

[12] Clinton Rossiter, The American Presidency (1956).

[13] James MacGregor Burns, The Deadlock of Democracy 6 (1963); and James MacGregor Burns, Presidential Government (1965).

[14] Arthur M. Schlesinger, Jr., The Imperial Presidency viii (1973).

¹⁵ Alexis de Tocqueville, Democracy in America, v. 1, ch. 8 (Henry Reeve trans., 1835). I am grateful to Sandy Muir for pointing me to Tocqueville's thought on this issue.

¹⁶ Presidential Leadership: Rating the Best and the Worst in the White House 11 (James Taranto & Leonard Leo eds., 2005).

¹⁷ Dames & Moore v. Regan, 453 U.S. 654, 661 (1981).

¹⁸ Youngstown Sheet & Tube Co. v. Sawyer, 343 U.S. 579, 610 (1952) (Frankfurter, J., concurring). For views on the power of precedent in constitutional decision-making by courts, see David A. Strauss, Common Law Constitutional Interpretation, 63 University of Chicago Law Review 877 (1996); and Michael J. Gerhardt, The Power of Precedent (2008).

CHAPTER 1: BEGINNINGS

¹ Jack Rakove, Original Meanings: Politics and Ideas in the Making of the Constitution 245 (1996).

² See, e.g., Bruce Ackerman, Congressional Leadership is Necessary and Proper, Los Angeles Times, Apr. 2, 2007, at www.latimes.com/news/opinion/la-op-dustup2 apr02,0,3065343.story?coll=la-opinion-center.

³ Federalist No. 70, at 471 (Alexander Hamilton) (Jacob E. Cooke ed., 1961).

⁴ See Bernard Bailyn, Intellectual Origins of the American Revolution 31 (1967); Forrest McDonald, The American Presidency: An Intellectual History 4–5 (1994); and Gordon Wood, The Creation of the American Republic 1776–1789, at 10–18 (1969).

⁵ J. G. A. Pocock, The Machiavellian Moment: Florentine Political Thought and the Atlantic Republican Tradition (1975).

⁶ Harvey C. Mansfield, Jr., Taming the Prince: The Ambivalence of Modern Executive Power 121–149 (1989).

⁷ Ibid. at 135.

⁸ Ibid. at 142.

⁹ Federalist No. 70, at 472 (Alexander Hamilton) (Jacob E. Cooke ed., 1961).

¹⁰ See, e.g., McDonald, supra note 4, at 46.

¹¹ John Locke, Two Treatises of Government §145 (J. W. Gough ed., 3d ed. 1966) (1690). For Locke's development of the separation of powers and the definition of the executive power, see M. J. C. Vile, Constitutionalism and the Separation of Powers 60–61 (1967); and W. B. Gwyn, The Meaning of the Separation of Powers: An Analysis of the Doctrine from Its Origin to the Adoption of the United States Constitution 82–99 (1965).

¹² Locke, supra note 11, at § 146.

¹³ Ibid. at § 147.

¹⁴ Ibid. at § 160.

¹⁵ Charles Louis de Secondat, Baron Montesquieu, Spirit of the Laws, bk. 11, ch. 6 (Thomas Nugent trans., 1949) (1748). On Montesquieu's importance in the colonies, see Forrest McDonald, Novus Ordo Seclorum: The Intellectual Origins of the Constitution 80 (1985).

¹⁶ Donald S. Lutz, The Origins of American Constitutionalism 145 (1988).

¹⁷ 1 William Blackstone, Commentaries on the Laws of England 160.

[18] Ibid. at 249–50.

[19] Ibid. at 250.

[20] Ibid. at 244.

[21] McDonald, supra note 4, at 30–31.

[22] Bailyn, supra note 4, at 34–54.

[23] See ibid. at 36; see also Introduction to Cato's Letters (Ronald Hamowy ed., 1995) (1722).

[24] See, e.g., Arthur Bestor, Separation of Powers in the Domain of Foreign Affairs: The Intent of the Constitution Historically Examined, 5 Seton Hall Law Review 527, 568 (1974); and Raoul Berger, War-Making by the President, 121 University of Pennsylvania Law Review 29, 33 (1972).

[25] Andrew Rudalevige, The New Imperial Presidency 19 (2005).

[26] John Marshall, "A Friend of the Constitution Essays," reprinted in John Marshall's Defense of McCulloch v. Maryland 159 (Gerald Gunther ed., 1969); see also Akhil R. Amar, The Consent of the Governed: Constitutional Amendment Outside Article V, 94 Columbia Law Review 457, 465 (1994).

[27] On this point, see Jerrilyn Marston, King & Congress 297–309 (1987); Jennings B. Sanders, Evolution of Executive Departments of the Continental Congress 3 (1935); and Charles C. Thach, Jr., The Creation of the Presidency, 1775–1789, at 576 (1923).

[28] Articles of Confederation art. IX (1777).

[29] 1 Works of Alexander Hamilton 209 (Henry Cabot Lodge ed., 1904).

[30] For discussion of the problems in American foreign policy during the critical period, see John Yoo, The Powers of War and Peace: The Constitution and Foreign Affairs After 9/11, at 73–79 (2005); McDonald, supra note 4, at 143–53; and Frederick Marks, Independence on Trial: Foreign Affairs and the Making of the Constitution (1986).

[31] Wood, supra note 4, at 138.

[32] Pa. Const. § XIX (1776), reprinted in 5 Francis N. Thorpe, The Federal and State Constitutions, Colonial Charters, and Other Organic Laws of the States, Territories, and Colonies 3086–87 (1909).

[33] Thach, supra note 27, at 29.

[34] Thomas Jefferson, First Draft of the Virginia Constitution, art. II (1776), reprinted in 1 The Papers of Thomas Jefferson 337, 341 (Julian P. Boyd ed., 1950).

[35] The Constitution as Adopted by the Convention (1776), reprinted in 1 Ibid. at 377, 380. The Virginia constitution forbade the executive from exercising "any power or prerogative by virtue of any Law, statute, or Custom, of England." Va. Const. para. 9 (1776), reprinted in 7 Thorpe, supra note 32, at 3816–17.

[36] John Adams, Thoughts on Government (1776), reprinted in 4 Papers of John Adams 65, 89 (Robert J. Taylor ed., 1979).

[37] See Thach, supra note 27, at 34–35.

[38] N.Y. Const. arts. VIII & XVII (1777), reprinted in 5 Thorpe, supra note 32, at 2632. Although it did not establish a privy council, the New York constitution created two more specialized councils: the Council of Revision, which exercised the

veto power, and the Council of Appointment, which advised on appointments. N.Y. Const. arts. III, XXIII (1777), reprinted in 5 Ibid. at 2628, 2633–34.

[39] During the Revolution, George Clinton, the state's first governor, sent the militia on his sole authority to reinforce General Gates's campaign against British forces. He later notified the legislature of the move in his first inaugural address. Throughout the war, Clinton (himself a military officer) worked closely with General Washington and his subordinates to coordinate operations against the British. Although it expressed its views when appropriating funds for the war effort, the legislature generally obeyed Clinton's wishes. See E. Wilder Spaulding, His Excellency George Clinton: Critic of the Constitution 95–98, 114–18 (1938).

[40] Thach, supra note 27, at 37.

[41] See Clinton Rossiter, 1787: The Grand Convention 59, 65 (1966); and Thach, supra note 27, at 34–38.

[42] Federalist No. 26, at 167 (Alexander Hamilton) (Jacob E. Cooke ed., 1961).

[43] Thach, supra note 27, at 43.

[44] 2 The Records of the Federal Convention of 1787, at 35 (Max Farrand ed., 1911) (hereinafter "Farrand, Records").

[45] The important document revealing the Framers' thinking on the problem of state legislatures is Vices of the Political System of the United States (Apr. 1787), reprinted in 9 Papers of James Madison 349 (Robert A. Rutland et al. eds., 1975). See also Rakove, supra note 1, at 39–43; Charles F. Hobson, The Negative on State Laws: James Madison, the Constitution, and the Crisis of Republican Government, 36 Wm. & Mary Q. 215, 223–25 (1979) (discussing Madison's disillusionment with "turbulent majorities who ruled the state legislatures"). In examining Madison's thoughts during the Framing Period, I also have relied upon Lance Banning, The Sacred Fire of Liberty: James Madison and the Founding of the Federal Republic (1996); Drew R. McCoy, The Last of the Fathers: James Madison and the Republican Legacy (1989); and William Lee Miller, The Business of May Next: James Madison and the Founding (1992).

[46] The Essex Result, 1778, in The Popular Sources of Political Authority: Documents on the Massachusetts Constitution of 1780, at 324–65 (Oscar Handlin & Mary Handlin eds., 1966).

[47] Wood, supra note 4, at 434.

[48] Ibid. at 446–53.

[49] Willi Paul Adams, The First American Constitutions: Republican Ideology and the Making of the State Constitutions in the Revolutionary Era 271 (1980).

CHAPTER 2: CREATION

[1] 1 The Records of the Federal Convention of 1787, at 65 (Max Farrand ed., 1911) (hereinafter "Farrand, Records").

[2] Ibid. at 20–21.

[3] Ibid.

[4] Charles Thach, The Creation of the American Presidency, 1775–1789: A Study in Constitutional History 85 (1923).

[5] 1 Farrand, Records, supra note 1, at 66.

⁶ Ibid. at 65.

⁷ Ibid.

⁸ Ibid. at 65–66. Oddly, the notes of Rufus King of New York show Madison, rather than Pinckney or Wilson, raising the issue. King records Madison as saying that "executive powers ex vi termini, do not include the Rights of war & peace &c. but the powers shd. be confined and defined." Ibid. at 70.

⁹ Ibid. at 64–65; see also Ibid. at 65 (comments of John Rutledge); Ibid. at 65–66 (comments of James Wilson).

¹⁰ Ibid. at 244.

¹¹ Ibid.

¹² As James Wilson declared on June 26, the "Senate will probably be the depositary of the powers concerning" relations "to foreign nations" because of senators' longer terms in office. 1 Ibid. at 426. See also John C. Yoo, The Judicial Safeguards of Federalism, 70 Southern California Law Review 1311, 1366–74 (1997) (discussing dual role of the Senate).

¹³ 2 Farrand, Records, supra note 1, at 56–57.

¹⁴ 2 Jack Rakove, Original Meanings: Politics and Ideas in the Making of the Constitution 261–62 (1996).

¹⁵ 2 Farrand, Records, supra note 1, at 171–72.

¹⁶ 2 Ibid. at 300–01.

¹⁷ 2 Ibid. at 299–300.

¹⁸ 2 Ibid. at 318.

¹⁹ 2 Ibid. at 319.

²⁰ Ibid.

²¹ See John Yoo, The Powers of War and Peace: The Constitution and Foreign Affairs After 9/11, at 149–52 (2005). For contrary views, see Saikrishna Prakash, Unleashing the Dogs of War: What the Constitution Means by "Declare War," 93 Cornell Law Review 45 (2007); and Michael Ramsey, Textualism and War Powers, 69 University of Chicago Law Review 1543 (2002). For my responses, see Robert J. Delahunty & John Yoo, Making War, 93 Cornell Law Review 123 (2007); John Yoo, War and the Constitutional Text, 69 University of Chicago Law Review 1639 (2002).

²² Articles of Confederation art. IX (1777).

²³ 2 Farrand, Records, supra note 1, at 392.

²⁴ Jack N. Rakove, Solving a Constitutional Puzzle: The Treatymaking Clause as a Case Study, 1 Perspectives in American History 233, 240–41 (1984).

²⁵ See Yoo, Powers of War and Peace, supra note 21, at 182–214; and Saikrishna Prakash & Michael Ramsey, The Executive Power over Foreign Affairs, 111 Yale Law Journal 231 (2001). For a contrary view, see, e.g., Curtis A. Bradley & Martin S. Flaherty, Executive Power Essentialism and Foreign Affairs, 102 Michigan Law Review 545, 637–41 (2004); Harold H. Koh, The National Security Constitution: Sharing Power after the Iran-Contra Affair (1990); and Michael Glennon, Constitutional Diplomacy (1990).

²⁶ See, e.g., James W. Ceaser, Presidential Selection: Theory and Development 43 (1979).

27 Federalist No. 68, at 460–61 (Alexander Hamilton) (Jacob E. Cooke ed., 1961).

28 2 Farrand, Records, supra note 1, at 540.

29 Federalist No. 68, at 460 (Alexander Hamilton) (Jacob E. Cooke ed., 1961).

30 1 Farrand, Records, supra note 1, at 29.

31 2 Farrand, Records, supra note 1, at 540–41.

32 Clinton Rossiter, The American Presidency 67 (1956).

33 Edward S. Corwin, The President: Office and Powers, 1787–1984, at 201 (Randall W. Bland et al. eds., 1984).

34 2 Farrand, Records, supra note 1, at 648.

35 See Forrest McDonald: The American Presidency: An Intellectual History 181 (1994).

36 See, e.g., Arthur Schlesinger, Jr., The Imperial Presidency 1–12 (1973); and Michael Genovese, The Power of the American Presidency, 1789–2000, at 12–13 (2001).

37 See, e.g., Donald L. Robinson, "To the Best of My Ability": The Presidency and the Constitution 87–95 (1987); and Thach, supra note 4, at 139–40.

38 For excellent accounts of the political events and leaders of the ratification process, see Forrest McDonald, Novus Ordo Seclorum: The Intellectual Origins of the Constitution (1986); Forrest McDonald, We the People: The Economic Origins of the Constitution (1991); and Forrest McDonald, E Pluribus Unum (1979).

39 See Glenn Phelps, George Washington and American Constitutionalism (1994).

40 3 Farrand, Records, supra note 1, at 301–02.

41 George Mason, Objections to the Constitution (Oct. 7, 1787), reprinted in 13 Documentary History of the Ratification of the Constitution 349 (John P. Kaminski & Gaspare J. Saladino eds., 1986) (hereinafter "Documentary History"). Mason's objections were known to have been published in at least 27 newspapers from Maine to South Carolina and served as a sounding board for numerous Federalist and Anti-Federalist essays. See Ibid. at 348. As the influential Anti-Federalist "Federal Farmer" complained before the start of the Pennsylvania ratifying convention, "[I]n this senate are lodged legislative, executive and judicial powers..." Letter III from the Federal Farmer (Oct. 10, 1787), reprinted in 14 Ibid. at 32. The Letters from the Federal Farmer were published as 40-page pamphlets for sale, rather than as articles in newspapers. Apparently thousands of copies were sold throughout the states, and they appeared in Pennsylvania, New York, and Massachusetts before their ratifying conventions concluded. See John P. Kaminski & Gaspare J. Saladino, Editors' Note to Ibid. at 14–18. They are considered to be "one of the most significant publications of the ratification debate." Ibid. at 14.

42 6 The Complete Anti-Federalist 21 (Herbert J. Storing ed., 1981).

43 3 Ibid. at 115.

44 3 Ibid. at 38.

45 3 Ibid. at 414.

46 5 Ibid. at 145–46.

47 3 Ibid. at 233.

48 Federalist No. 23, at 147 (Alexander Hamilton) (Jacob E. Cooke ed., 1961).

49 Federalist No. 41, at 270 (James Madison) (Jacob E. Cooke ed., 1961).

50 Federalist No. 51, at 349 (James Madison) (Jacob E. Cooke ed., 1961).

51 Federalist No. 48, at 334 (James Madison) (Jacob E. Cooke ed., 1961).

52 Federalist No. 71, at 482 (Alexander Hamilton) (Jacob E. Cooke ed., 1961).

53 Federalist No. 70, at 471 (Alexander Hamilton) (Jacob E. Cooke ed., 1961).

54 Federalist No. 70, at 472 (Alexander Hamilton) (Jacob E. Cooke ed., 1961).

55 Federalist No. 70, at 480 (Alexander Hamilton) (Jacob E. Cooke ed., 1961).

56 2 Documentary History, supra note 41, at 495.

57 Ibid. at 579.

58 9 Ibid. at 1097–98.

59 See generally Douglass Adair, Fame and the Founding Fathers (1974).

60 Federalist No. 73, at 493 (Alexander Hamilton) (Jacob E. Cooke ed., 1961).

61 McDonald, supra note 35, at 206.

62 Federalist No. 75, at 504 (Alexander Hamilton) (Jacob E. Cooke ed., 1961).

63 Federalist No. 73, at 494 (Alexander Hamilton) (Jacob E. Cooke ed., 1961).

64 Akhil Reed Amar, America's Constitution: A Biography 184 (2005).

65 Federalist No. 73, at 495 (Alexander Hamilton) (Jacob E. Cooke ed., 1961).

66 See, e.g., Michael Rappaport, 16 Wm. & Mary Bill of Rights J. 113 (2007). For similar views, see Christopher N. May, Presidential Defiance of "Unconstitutional" Laws: Reviving the Royal Prerogative, 21 Hastings Const. L.Q. 865 (1994); Am. Bar Ass'n, Task Force on Presidential Signing Statements and the Separation of Powers Doctrine 5 (2006), available at www.abanet.org/op/signingstatements/aba_final_ statements_recommendation-report_ 7-24-06.pdf. Those taking a different view include Frank H. Easterbrook, Presidential Review, 40 Case Western Reserve Law Review 905 (1990); Gary Lawson & Christopher D. Moore, The Executive Power of Constitutional Interpretation, 81 Iowa Law Review 1267 (1996); and Michael S. Paulsen, The Most Dangerous Branch: Executive Power to Say What the Law Is, 83 Georgetown Law Journal 217 (1994).

67 See Saikrishna B. Prakash & John C. Yoo, The Origins of Judicial Review, 70 University of Chicago Law Review 887 (2003).

68 2 Documentary History, supra note 41, at 450–51.

69 Amar, America's Constitution, supra note 64, at 179.

70 Federalist No. 74, at 501 (Alexander Hamilton) (Jacob E. Cooke ed., 1961).

71 On this point, see generally Yoo, The Powers of War and Peace, supra note 21, at 30–87; Prakash & Ramsey, Executive Power over Foreign Affairs, supra note 25. For criticism of this theory, see Bradley & Flaherty, Executive Power Essentialism, supra note 25.

72 Thomas Schelling, The Strategy of Conflict 18 (1960).

73 Edward S. Corwin, The President: Office and Powers, supra note 33.

74 See, e.g., Frederick Marks, Independence on Trial: Foreign Affairs and the Making of the Constitution 52–95 (1986).

75 Federalist No. 74, at 500 (Alexander Hamilton) (Jacob E. Cooke ed., 1961).

76 3 Documentary History, supra note 41, at 59–60.

77 Rakove, supra note 14, at 276–77.

78 Ibid. at 1282.

79 10 Documentary History, supra note 41, at 1281.

[80] See John Yoo, Globalization and the Constitution, 99 Columbia Law Review 1955 (1999).

CHAPTER 3: GEORGE WASHINGTON

[1] See Glenn A. Phelps, George Washington and American Constitutionalism 44–46 (1993).

[2] Leonard D. White, The Federalists: A Study in Administrative History 27 (1948).

[3] Phelps, supra note 1, at 145–49.

[4] The story of the Washington-Hancock tiff is retold in James T. Flexner, Washington and the New Nation 230 (1970).

[5] See Forrest McDonald, The Presidency of George Washington 39–40 (1974).

[6] Ibid. at 39.

[7] 30 Writings of George Washington 344 (John C. Fitzpatrick ed., 1939).

[8] Ibid. at 334. For the view that Washington's move to control the machinery of the Continental Congress is more ambiguous because of the unusual change between forms of government, see Curtis Bradley & Martin Flaherty, Executive Power Essentialism and Foreign Affairs, 102 Michigan Law Review 545, 637–41 (2004).

[9] Myers v. United States, 272 U.S. 52, 151 (1926) (quoting Daniel Webster).

[10] 10 Documentary History of the First Federal Congress, 1789–1791, at 718–20 (Charlene Bangs Bickford et al. eds, 2004).

[11] Ibid. at 738–40.

[12] Ibid. at 868.

[13] I have been guided through the various debates and changes in the statutory proposals by Saikrishna B. Prakash, New Light on the Decision of 1789, 91 Cornell Law Review 1021, 1029–34 (2006). The debate is also recounted prominently by David Currie, The Constitution in Congress: The Federalist Period 1789–1801, at 36–41 (1997); Charles C. Thach, Jr., The Creation of the Presidency, 1775–1789, at 140–65 (1923); and James Hart, The American Presidency in Action 1789, at 155–89 (1948).

[14] Some have argued that Congress's actions indicate that the Treasury Department was not even an executive department, but rather an administrative agency outside of direct presidential control. See Lawrence Lessig & Cass R. Sunstein, The President and the Administration, 94 Columbia Law Review 1, 28 (1994). Steven Calabresi and Sai Prakash have shown their arguments on this score to be off the mark. See Steven G. Calabresi & Saikrishna B. Prakash, The President's Power to Execute the Laws, 104 Yale Law Journal 541 (1994). Indeed, Madison's arguments in the House that the Treasury Department ought to be unified under one secretary accountable to the President defeats their claim. For some interesting applications of this theme to Congress and the federal courts, see Saikrishna Prakash, Removal and Tenure in Office, 92 Virginia Law Review 1779 (2006). For the claim that the Decision of 1789 is more ambiguous, see Bradley & Flaherty, supra note 8, at 656–64.

[15] 1 Annals of Congress 379 (Joseph Gales ed., 1789).

[16] Ibid. at 463, 547.

[17] Letter from James Madison to Thomas Jefferson (June 30, 1789), in 16 Documentary History of the First Federal Congress, supra note 10, at 890, 893.

[18] Stanley M. Elkins & Eric L. McKitrick, The Age of Federalism: The Early American Republic, 1788–1800, at 53–54 (1993).

[19] Forrest McDonald: The American Presidency: An Intellectual History 227 (1994).

[20] George Washington to Henry Knox, Sept. 20, 1795, in 34 Writings of Washington, supra note 7, at 315.

[21] Various Senators and commentators have urged such a role for the Senate over the years. See, e.g., David A. Strauss & Cass R. Sunstein, The Senate, the Constitution, and the Confirmation Process, 101 Yale Law Journal 1491, 1502–12 (1992). Arguments against include John O. McGinnis, The President, the Senate, the Constitution, and the Confirmation Process: A Reply to Professors Strauss and Sunstein, 71 Texas Law Review 633, 638–39 (1993).

[22] Thomas Jefferson to Heads of Departments, Nov. 6, 1801, in 9 Writings of Thomas Jefferson 310–12 (Paul Leicester Ford ed., 1904).

[23] McDonald, Presidency of Washington, supra note 5, at 41.

[24] See Phelps, supra note 1, at 140–41.

[25] George Washington to Baron Poellnitz, Mar. 23, 1790, in 31 Writings of Washington, supra note 7, at 23–24.

[26] I have found invaluable Forrest McDonald's analysis of the Hamiltonian system, and its political effects, in McDonald, Presidency of Washington, supra note 5, at 47–88.

[27] Elkins & McKitrick, supra note 18, at 155–61.

[28] Federalist No. 44, at 302–05 (James Madison) (Jacob E. Cooke ed., 1961).

[29] 19 The Papers of Thomas Jefferson 275–80 (Julian P. Boyd ed., 1974).

[30] 8 The Papers of Alexander Hamilton 63-134 (Harold Syrett ed., 1965).

[31] McCulloch v. Maryland, 17 U.S. (4 Wheat.) 316 (1819).

[32] 19 Papers of Jefferson, supra note 29, at 280.

[33] 32 Writings of Washington, supra note 7, at 16–17.

[34] 19 Papers of Jefferson, supra note 29, at 280.

[35] Phelps, supra note 1, at 151–52.

[36] Ibid. at 153–54.

[37] See, e.g., Am. Bar Ass'n, Task Force on Presidential Signing Statements and the Separation of Powers Doctrine 5 (2006), available at www.abanet.org/op/signing statements/aba_final_statements_recommendation-report_7-24-06.pdf.

[38] See generally Lessig & Sunstein, supra note 14.

[39] See Jerry Mashaw, Recovering American Administrative Law: Federalist Foundations, 1787–1801, 115 Yale Law Journal 1256 (2006); and White, supra note 2.

[40] The discussion of the Whiskey Rebellion is taken from Elkins & McKitrick, supra note 18, at 461–88; McDonald, supra note 5, at 145–47; and Phelps, supra note 1, at 131–36. A sustained scholarly treatment can be found in Thomas P. Slaughter, The Whiskey Rebellion: Frontier Epilogue to the American Revolution (1988), and a recent journalistic retelling in William Hogeland, The Whiskey Rebellion: George Washington, Alexander Hamilton, and the Frontier Rebels Who Challenged America's Newfound Sovereignty (2006).

[41] Proclamation of September 15, 1792, in 32 Writings of Washington, supra note 7, at 150.

[42] A debate among historians continues to this day about the sources of the Whiskey Rebellion. McDonald has argued that Hamilton deliberately provoked a confrontation in order to create the opportunity for a show of force by the federal government. Others have argued that the sources were primarily economic, in that the tax hit certain classes of Western farmers particularly hard, while recent scholarship argues that the Whiskey Rebellion was the product of a number of social and political developments in the West that led to an uprising that was more popular in its roots.

[43] Stephen I. Vladeck, Emergency Power and the Militia Acts, 114 Yale Law Journal 149, 161–63 (2004).

[44] 32 Writings of Washington, supra note 7, at 455 (Whiskey Rebellion); and 32 Ibid. at 386 (Neutrality Proclamation).

[45] See Calabresi & Prakash, supra note 14, at 659 n. 547; see also Harold J. Krent, Executive Control over Criminal Law Enforcement, 38 American University Law Review 275 (1989).

[46] See, e.g., David Grady Adler, The President's Pardon Power, in Thomas E. Cronin ed., Inventing the American Presidency 209 (1989).

[47] See, e.g., Louis Henkin, Foreign Affairs and the U.S. Constitution (2d ed. 1996); Harold Hongju Koh, The National Security Constitution: Sharing Power after the Iran-Contra Affair (1990); and Michael J. Glennon, Constitutional Diplomacy (1990).

[48] Washington to Moultrie, Aug. 28, 1793, in 33 Writings of Washington, supra note 7, at 73.

[49] David Currie, Rumors of War: Presidential and Congressional War Powers, 67 University of Chicago Law Review 1, 2 (2000).

[50] See Richard H. Kohn, Eagle and Sword: The Federalists and the Creation of the Military Establishment in America, 1783–1802, at 92–93 (1975).

[51] Ibid. at 96.

[52] 1 Annals of Congress 715 (Joseph Gale ed., 1789).

[53] Act of Sept. 29, 1789, 1 Stat. 95.

[54] Kohn, supra note 50, at 97.

[55] 1 Annals of Congress 724 (Joseph Gale ed., 1789).

[56] Kohn, supra note 50, at 98.

[57] Ibid. at 96.

[58] Act of Apr. 30, 1790, 1 Stat. 119.

[59] Kohn, supra note 50, at 103.

[60] Ibid. at 104.

[61] See, e.g., George Washington to House of Representatives, Sept. 16, 1789, 1 Annals of Congress 927–28 (Joseph Gale ed., 1789).

[62] 1 Annals of Congress 1772.

[63] Kohn, supra note 50, at 115–17.

[64] 1 Stat. 241 (1792).

[65] Kohn, supra note 50, at 116–24.

[66] Abraham Sofaer, War, Foreign Affairs and Constitutional Power: The Origins 119 (1976).

[67] Errors of Government Towards the Indians, Feb. 1792, in 31 Writings of Washington, supra note 7, at 491.

[68] See, e.g., Fort Harmar Treaty of 1789, 7 Stat. 28 (Jan. 9, 1789); and Creek Treaty of 1790, 7 Stat. 35 (Aug. 7, 1790).

[69] Johnson v. M'Intosh, 21 U.S. (8 Wheat.) 543 (1823).

[70] Elkins & McKitrick, supra note 18, at 55–58.

[71] See Saikrishna Prakash & Michael Ramsey, The Executive Power over Foreign Affairs, 111 Yale Law Journal 231, 299–300 (2001).

[72] See Sofaer, supra note 66, at 65–78.

[73] Prakash & Ramsey, supra note 71, at 300–02.

[74] Thomas Jefferson, Opinion on the Powers of the Senate (Apr. 24, 1790), in 5 Writings of Jefferson, supra note 22, at 161.

[75] For the relevant historical details, I have relied on Elkins & McKitrick, supra note 18, at 303–73; McDonald, Presidency of Washington, supra note 5, at 113–37; Editorial Note, Jefferson's Opinion on the Treaties with France, reprinted in 25 Papers of Jefferson, supra note 29, at 597–602; and Letter from Alexander Hamilton to John Jay (Apr. 9, 1793), in 14 Papers of Hamilton, supra note 30, at 297, 298 n.4. These events are also discussed in David P. Currie, The Constitution in Congress: The Third Congress, 1793–1795, 63 University of Chicago Law Review 1, 4–16 (1996).

[76] Treaty of Alliance, Feb. 6, 1778, U.S.-Fr., Treaty Series 82, art. XI, 7 Bevans 777.

[77] Treaty of Amity and Commerce, Feb. 6, 1778, U.S.-Fr., 8 Stat. 12., art. XVII.

[78] Notes on Washington's Questions on Neutrality and the Alliance with France, May 6, 1793, in 25 Papers of Jefferson, supra note 29, at 665–66.

[79] See Letter from Hamilton to Jay (Apr. 9, 1793), in 14 Papers of Hamilton, supra note 30, at 297–98.

[80] Letter from Washington to Hamilton, Jefferson, Knox, and Randolph (Apr. 18, 1793), in ibid. at 326–27.

[81] Opinion on the Treaties with France, Apr. 28, 1793, in 25 Papers of Jefferson, supra note 29, at 608–18.

[82] Letter from Hamilton & Knox to Washington, May 2, 1793, in 14 Papers of Hamilton, supra note 30, at 367–96.

[83] Notes on Washington's Questions on Neutrality and the Alliance with France, reprinted in 25 Papers of Jefferson, supra note 29, at 666.

[84] 1 Compilation of the Messages and Papers of the Presidents: 1789–1897, at 156 (James D. Richardson ed., 1900).

[85] Neutrality Act, 1 Stat. 381 (June 5, 1794).

[86] See Jack N. Rakove, The Beginnings of National Politics: An Interpretive History of the Continental Congress 113–18 (1979); and Samuel F. Bemis, The Diplomacy of the American Revolution 58–69 (1957).

[87] Prakash & Ramsey, supra note 71, at 325–27.

[88] See Pacificus No. 1, reprinted in 15 Papers of Hamilton, supra note 30, at 33–43.

[89] Jefferson to Madison, June 13, 1793, 26 Papers of Jefferson, supra note 29, at 272–74; see also Jefferson to Madison, June 23, 1793, in 26 ibid. at 346.

[90] Jefferson to Madison, July 7, 1793, in 26 ibid. at 443–44.

91 See Helvidius Nos. 1–5, reprinted in 15 The Papers of James Madison 66–120 (Thomas Mason ed., 1985).

92 Helvidius No. 1, in 15 ibid. at 69.

93 Ibid.

94 Helvidius No. 4, in 15 ibid. at 108.

95 See Elkins & McKitrick, supra note 18, at 362 (noting Madison's weak performance); but cf. Lance Banning, The Sacred Fire of Liberty: James Madison and the Founding of the Federal Republic 527 n.18 (1995) (arguing that Madison demolished Hamilton's arguments).

96 Helvidius No. 2, in 15 Papers of Madison, supra note 91, at 82.

97 The Washington administration attempted to prosecute violators of neutrality in the absence of a statutory crime. See Stewart Jay, Origins of Federal Common Law: Part One, 133 University of Pennsylvania Law Review 1003, 1039–93 (1985). The issue was not finally resolved by the Supreme Court until 1812, in United States v. Hudson & Goodwin, 11 U.S. (7 Cranch) 32 (1812), in which the Court held that the federal government could not prosecute individuals for non-statutory common law crimes. See Gary D. Rowe, The Sound of Silence: United States v. Hudson & Goodwin, The Jeffersonian Ascendancy, and the Abolition of Federal Common Law Crimes, 101 Yale Law Journal 919 (1992).

98 These events are described in Jerald A. Combs, The Jay Treaty: Political Battleground of the Founding Fathers (1970); Samuel Flagg Bemis, Jay's Treaty (1923); Alexander DeConde, Entangling Alliance: Politics & Diplomacy under George Washington (1958); Bradford Perkins, The First Rapprochement: England and the United States, 1795–1805 (1955); and more recently by Todd Estes, The Art of Presidential Leadership: George Washington and the Jay Treaty, 109 Virginia Magazine of History and Biography 127 (2001); and Charles Ritcheson, Aftermath of Revolution: British Policy Toward the United States, 1783–1795 (1971).

99 Elkins & McKitrick, supra note 18, at 412; McDonald, Presidency of Washington, supra note 5, at 140.

100 Phelps, supra note 1, at 174–75.

101 35 Writings of Washington, supra note 7, at 2–5.

102 Ibid.

103 See United States v. Nixon, 418 U.S. 683 (1974). For critical discussion, see Akhil R. Amar, Nixon's Shadow, 83 Minnesota Law Review 1405 (1999); Michael S. Paulsen, Nixon Now: The Courts and the Presidency After Twenty-five Years, 83 Minnesota Law Review 1337 (1999). For analysis of the rise of executive privilege, see Mark J. Rozell, Executive Privilege: Presidential Power, Secrecy, and Accountability (2002); and Louis Fisher, The Politics of Executive Privilege (2003).

104 Abraham D. Sofaer, Executive Privilege: An Historical Note, 75 Columbia Law Review 1318 (1975).

105 On this point, see John Yoo, The Powers of War and Peace: The Constitution and Foreign Affairs after 9/11, at 242–43 (2005).

106 See, e.g., Ralph Ketcham, Presidents Above Party: The First American Presidency, 1789–1829 (1984).

CHAPTER 4: THOMAS JEFFERSON

1 The two magisterial works covering the Jefferson Presidency are Dumas Malone, Jefferson The President: The First Term 1801–05 (1970) (hereinafter "Malone, First Term") and Dumas Malone, Jefferson the President: The Second Term 1805–09 (1974) (hereinafter "Malone, Second Term"); and Henry Adams, History of the United States of America during the Administrations of Thomas Jefferson (1889–91) (Library of America ed., 1986). Helpful works include Joyce Appleby, Thomas Jefferson (2003); Jeremy D. Bailey, Thomas Jefferson and Executive Power (2007); Noble E. Cunningham, Jr., The Process of Government Under Jefferson (1978); Forrest McDonald, The Presidency of Thomas Jefferson (1976); Robert M. Johnstone, Jr., Jefferson and the Presidency: Leadership in the Young Republic (1978); David N. Mayer, The Constitutional Thought of Thomas Jefferson (1994); Merrill D. Peterson, Thomas Jefferson and the New Nation (1986); Ralph Ketcham, The Jefferson Presidency and Constitutional Beginnings, in Martin Fausold & Alan Shank eds., The Constitution and the American Presidency 5–27 (1991); Gary Schmitt, Thomas Jefferson and the Presidency in Thomas E. Cronin ed., Inventing the American Presidency 326 (1989); and Gary Schmitt, Jefferson and Executive Power: Revisionism and the "Revolution of 1800," 17 Publius 7 (1987).

2 First Draft of the Virginia Constitution (1776), in 1 The Papers of Thomas Jefferson 337, 341 (Julian P. Boyd ed., 1950).

3 Jefferson to Madison, Dec. 20, 1787, in 12 Ibid. at 442.

4 Jefferson to Madison, Sept. 6, 1789, in 15 Ibid. at 392, 397.

5 Jefferson to Roane, Sept. 6, 1819, 10 The Writings of Thomas Jefferson 140 (Paul L. Ford ed., 1904).

6 Hamilton to Bayard, Jan. 16, 1801, in 25 The Papers of Alexander Hamilton 319–24 (Harold Syrett ed., 1965).

7 Adams, supra note 1, at 354.

8 See, e.g., Sidney M. Milkis & Michael Nelson, The American Presidency: Origins & Development, 1776–1993, at 103–04 (2d ed. 1994).

9 See Ralph Ketcham, Presidents Above Party: The First American Presidency, 1789–1829, at 106 (1984); see also Bailey, supra note 1, at 5–27; Mayer, supra note 1, at 222–56; Schmitt, supra note 1, at 326–46. Bruce Ackerman traces the rise of "presidential democracy" under Jefferson to the failure of the Electoral College system in the election of 1800 and the embrace of popular majoritarianism to support Jefferson's selection. Bruce Ackerman, The Failure of the Founding Fathers: Jefferson, Marshall, and the Rise of Presidential Democracy 245–66 (2005).

10 See Bailey, supra note 1, at 16-20; Schmitt, supra note 1, at 341–43.

11 Federalist No. 23, at 147 (Alexander Hamilton) (Jacob E. Cooke ed., 1961).

12 Bailey, supra note 1, at 15–22.

13 11 Papers of Jefferson, supra note 2, at 679.

14 McDonald, Presidency of Jefferson, supra note 1, at 36.

15 Ibid. at 34–36; see also Peterson, supra note 1, at 680; Marc Landy & Sidney Milkis, Presidential Greatness 65 (2000).

16 Jefferson to Roane, Sept. 6, 1819, in 10 Writings of Jefferson, supra note 5, at 141.

17 Jefferson to Abigail Adams, Sept 11, 1804, in 8 Ibid. at 310–11.

18 Jefferson to Roane, Sept. 6, 1819, in 10 Ibid. at 141.

[19] Jefferson to Dickinson, Dec. 19, 1801, 10 The Writings of Thomas Jefferson 302 (Andrew A. Lipscomb ed., 1903–04).

[20] Richard E. Ellis, The Jeffersonian Crisis: Courts and Politics in the Young Republic 70 (1971).

[21] Quoted in McDonald, supra note 1, at 81.

[22] Jefferson to Hay, June 20, 1807, in 9 Writings of Jefferson, supra note 5, at 59–60.

[23] The Barbary Pirates are usefully discussed in Abraham Sofaer, War, Foreign Affairs, and Constitutional Power: The Origins 208–27 (1976); Schmitt, supra note 1, at 336–37; Gerhard Casper, Separating Power: Essays on the Founding Period 45–67 (1997); and Montgomery Kosma, Our First Real War, 2 Green Bag 2d 169 (1999).

[24] The Complete Annals of Thomas Jefferson 213 (Franklin B. Sawvel ed., 1903).

[25] Smith to Dale, May 20, 1801, in 1 Naval Documents Related to the United States Wars with the Barbary Powers 465 (1939).

[26] Kosma, supra note 23, at 174.

[27] President's Message, Dec. 8, 1801, in 7 Annals of Congress 11, 12 (Joseph Gale 2d ed., 1789).

[28] Act of Feb. 6, 1802, 2 Stat 129.

[29] The Examination No. 1, Dec. 17, 1801, in 25 Papers of Hamilton, supra note 6, at 444, 456.

[30] See Sofaer, supra note 23, at 216–21.

[31] See ibid. at 172–73; McDonald, supra note 1, at 135–37; and Bradford Perkins, Prologue to War, 1805–1812: England and the United States 142–44 (1961).

[32] The events surrounding the purchase are described in Robert Tucker & David Hendrickson, Empire of Liberty: The Statecraft of Thomas Jefferson 87–171 (1990); Malone, First Term, supra note 1, at 239–332; and McDonald, supra note 1, at 53–73.

[33] Quoted in Malone, First Term, supra note 1, at 285.

[34] Gary Lawson & Guy Seidman, The Constitution of Empire: Territorial Expansion and American Legal History 29 (2004).

[35] Malone, First Term, supra note 1, at 312.

[36] Jefferson to Dickinson, Aug. 9, 1803, in 8 Writings of Jefferson, supra note 5, at 262.

[37] Jefferson to Breckinridge, Aug. 12, 1803, in 8 Ibid. at 242.

[38] Jefferson to Breckinridge, Aug. 18, 1803, in 8 Ibid. at 245; see also Jefferson to Paine, in 8 Ibid. at 245.

[39] Jefferson to Nicholas, Sept. 7, 1803, in 8 Ibid. at 247.

[40] See Mayer, supra note 1, at 253.

[41] Jefferson to Colvin, Sept. 20, 1810, in 9 Writings of Jefferson, supra note 5, at 279.

[42] Bailey, supra note 1, at 15–22; and Schmitt, supra note 1, at 343–46.

[43] Quoted in Edwin Corwin, The President: Office and Powers, 1787–1984, at 18 (Randall W. Bland et al, eds., 5th ed. 1984).

[44] Richard Hofstadter, The Idea of a Party System: The Rise of Legitimate Opposition in the United States 122 (1969).

[45] See Harvey Mansfield, Thomas Jefferson, in Morton Frisch & Richard Stevens eds., American Political Thought: The Philosophic Dimension of Statesmanship 49 (1983); Landy & Milkis, supra note 15, at 41–43.

[46] Malone, First Term, supra note 1, at 93.

[47] Mayer, supra note 1, at 236–37.

[48] McDonald, Presidency of Jefferson, supra note 1, at 39; Mayer, supra note 1, at 238.

[49] See Casper, supra note 23, at 80–83.

[50] Tucker & Hendrickson, supra note 32, at 14–17.

[51] Ibid. at 18–21.

[52] Quoted in Ibid. at 190.

[53] Gallatin to Jefferson, Dec. 18, 1807, quoted in Malone, Second Term, supra note 1, at 482.

[54] 1 Compilation of the Messages and Papers of the Presidents: 1789–1897, at 422–24 (James D. Richardson ed., 1900); and 2 Stat. 451 (Dec. 22, 1807).

[55] 2 Stat. 453 (Jan. 9, 1808).

[56] 2 Stat. 473 (Mar. 12, 1808).

[57] 2 Stat. 499 (Apr. 25, 1808).

[58] Quoted in Leonard Levy, Jefferson and Civil Liberties: The Darker Side (1989).

[59] Insurrection Act of 1807, ch. 39, 2 Stat. 443.

[60] Leonard White, Jeffersonians: A Study in Administrative History, 1801–29, at 451 (1951).

[61] Quoted in Ibid. at 461.

[62] 2 Stat. 506 (Jan. 9, 1809).

[63] Levy, supra note 58, at 120.

[64] Garry Wills, James Madison 5–7 (2002). Wills's opinion is not universally shared, of course. For more positive biographies of Madison, see Irving Brant, James Madison: The President, 1809–1812 (1956); Ralph Ketcham, James Madison: A Biography (1971); Drew N. McCoy, The Last of the Fathers: James Madison and the Republican Legacy (1991); Jack N. Rakove, James Madison and the Creation of the American Republic (1990); Robert Rutland, The Presidency of James Madison (1990); and Robert Rutland, James Madison: The Founding Father (1987). For an interesting perspective on whether Madison's interest in political theory interfered with his ability to succeed as a president, see David J. Siemers, Theories About Theory: Theory-Based Claims about Presidential Performance from the Case of James Madison, 38 Pres. Studies Q. 78 (2007).

[65] Perkins, supra note 31, at 223–60.

[66] Rakove, supra note 64, at 151.

[67] Walter LaFeber, The American Age: U.S. Foreign Policy at Home and Abroad, 1750 to the Present 60–61 (1994).

[68] Third Annual Message, Nov. 5, 1811, in 1 Papers of the Presidents, supra note 54, at 491, 494 (James D. Richardson ed., 1900).

[69] Donald R. Hickey, The War of 1812: A Forgotten Conflict 29–37 (1990); LaFeber, supra note 67, at 63.

[70] Hickey, supra note 69, at 72-99, 126-58, 182–254.

[71] J.C.A. Stagg, Mr. Madison's War: Politics, Diplomacy, and Warfare in the Early American Republic, 1783–1830 (1983), provides a good historical account of the war.

[72] Rutland, Presidency of Madison, supra note 64, at 110.

CHAPTER 5: ANDREW JACKSON

[1] I have drawn on the wealth of Jackson histories in writing this article. Jackson's larger than life personality has made him the subject of several excellent works. Our generation's leading Jackson biographer, Robert V. Remini, provides great detail on Jackson's life in three volumes. Robert V. Remini, Andrew Jackson (1977–84) (hereinafter "Remini, Jackson"). Other helpful works include Gerard N. Magliocca, Andrew Jackson and the Constitution: The Rise and Fall of Generational Regimes (2007); H.W. Brands, Andrew Jackson: His Life and Times (2006); Sean Wilentz, Andrew Jackson (2005); and Donald B. Cole, The Presidency of Andrew Jackson (1993). Our leading history of the Jacksonian period is Daniel Walker Howe, What Hath God Wrought: The Transformation of America 1815–1848 (2007). Older works, such as Arthur M. Schlesinger, Jr., The Age of Jackson (1945), are less helpful in portraying Jackson as a proto-FDR and Jacksonian Democracy as a precursor for the New Deal.

[2] Andrew Jackson, First Annual Message to Congress (Dec. 8, 1829), in 2 Messages and Papers of the Presidents, 1789–1897, at 448 (James Richardson ed., 1896) (hereinafter "Jackson, First Annual Message to Congress") (emphasis in original).

[3] Ibid. at 447.

[4] Ibid.

[5] See Robert V. Remini, The Constitution and the Presidencies: The Jackson Era, in the Constitution and the American Presidency 29 (Martin L. Fausold & Alan Shank eds., 1991).

[6] See ibid. at 35.

[7] 1 Remini, Jackson, supra note 1, at 305.

[8] Ibid. at 305–07.

[9] Ibid. at 347.

[10] Ibid.

[11] Ibid. at 348–49.

[12] Ibid. at 349.

[13] Ibid. at 351–64.

[14] Ibid. at 367.

[15] Ibid. at 367–68.

[16] Ibid. at 371–74.

[17] Ibid. at 373.

[18] Ibid. at 374.

[19] Ibid.

[20] 3 Remini, Jackson, supra note 1, at 352.

[21] Ibid. at 354–55.

[22] Ibid. at 359–60.

[23] Ibid.

[24] The admission of Texas itself would mark an expansion of executive power. Initially, under President John Tyler, the Senate rejected a treaty annexing Texas by a vote of 35–16 on June 8, 1844. After James Polk defeated Henry Clay in the presidential election that November, Congress enacted a simple statute approving the annexation and admitting Texas as a state by a vote of 120–98 in the House and 27–25 in the Senate. President Tyler signed the law on March 1, 1845, just before Polk was inaugurated. See Vasan Kesavan & Michael Stokes Paulsen, Let's Mess With Texas, 82 Texas Law Review 1587, 1592–93 (2004).

[25] See Howe, supra note 1, at 342–57.

[26] Magliocca, supra note 1, at 14–15.

[27] Ibid. at 346.

[28] Howe, supra note 1, at 347.

[29] Ibid. at 14–15, 22–29.

[30] Jackson, First Annual Message to Congress, supra note 2, at 457–58. Article IV, Section 3 of the United States Constitution states that "New states may be admitted by the Congress into this Union; but no new State shall be formed or erected within the Jurisdiction of any other State...without the consent of the legislatures of the States concerned as well as of the Congress."

[31] Jackson, First Annual Message to Congress, supra note 2, at 458.

[32] Ibid.

[33] See Howe, supra note 1, at 348.

[34] Cherokee Nation v. Georgia, 30 U.S. 1 (1831).

[35] Howe, supra note 1, at 347.

[36] Ibid. at 352; Act of May 28, 1830, ch. 148, 4 Stat. 411, 21st Cong. (1st Sess. 1830).

[37] Cherokee Nation, 30 U.S. 1 (1831).

[38] Magliocca, supra note 1, at 36.

[39] Cherokee Nation, 30 U.S. at 17.

[40] Worcester v. Georgia, 31 U.S. 515, 561 (1832).

[41] Ibid. at 559. For an insightful discussion of Worcester, see Philip P. Frickey, Marshalling Past and Present: Colonialism, Constitutionalism, and Interpretation in Federal Indian Law, 107 Harvard Law Review 381 (1993).

[42] Cole, supra note 1, at 114.

[43] Howe, supra note 1, at 412.

[44] Ibid.

[45] Ibid.

[46] Ibid.

[47] Ibid. at 412–13.

[48] Ibid. at 415.

[49] Ibid. at 416.

[50] For the claim that Jackson's removal policy amounted to genocide, see Michael P. Rogin, Fathers and Children: Andrew Jackson and the Subjugation of the American Indian (1975).

[51] Howe, supra note 1, at 420.

⁵² Cole, supra note 1, at 34.

⁵³ 2 Remini, Jackson, supra note 1, at 62, 161.

⁵⁴ Cole, supra note 1, at 23–24.

⁵⁵ Ibid. at 35–36.

⁵⁶ Ibid.

⁵⁷ Ibid. at 38.

⁵⁸ Ibid. at 37.

⁵⁹ 2 Remini, Jackson, supra note 1, at 213–14.

⁶⁰ Andrew Jackson, First Inaugural Address (Mar. 4, 1829), in 2 Messages and Papers of the Presidents, 438 (James Richardson ed., 1896) (hereinafter "Richardson, Messages").

⁶¹ Remini, Jackson, supra note 1, at 183.

⁶² Jackson, First Annual Message to Congress, supra note 2, at 449.

⁶³ Ibid. at 448–49.

⁶⁴ Cole, supra note 1, at 41.

⁶⁵ Ibid.; Howe, supra note 1, at 333.

⁶⁶ Leonard White, The Jacksonians: A Study in Administrative History 327–32 (1954); Howe, supra note 1, at 334.

⁶⁷ Cole, supra note 1, at 80.

⁶⁸ Ibid. at 81 (Jackson to Calhoun, May 30, 1830).

⁶⁹ Ibid. at 82.

⁷⁰ Ibid. at 84–85.

⁷¹ Jackson, First Annual Message to Congress, supra note 2, at 462.

⁷² Ibid.

⁷³ Daniel Feller, King Andrew and the Bank, 29 Humanities (2008), at www.neh.gov/news/humanities/2008-01/KingAndrewandtheBank.html.

⁷⁴ Cole, supra note 1, at 57.

⁷⁵ Ibid.

⁷⁶ Ibid.

⁷⁷ James Madison, Veto Message (Jan. 30, 1815), in 1 Richardson, Messages, supra note 60, at 555.

⁷⁸ Ibid.

⁷⁹ McCulloch v. Maryland, 17 U.S. 316 (1819).

⁸⁰ Cole, supra note 1, at 57.

⁸¹ Ibid.

⁸² Ibid.

⁸³ Ibid.

⁸⁴ See ibid.; Wilentz, supra note 1, at 76; see generally Walter Smith, Economic Aspects of the Second Bank of the United States (1969).

⁸⁵ Robert V. Remini, Andrew Jackson and the Bank War: A Study in the Growth of Presidential Power 27 (1967) (hereinafter "Remini, Bank War").

⁸⁶ Ibid.

⁸⁷ Ibid. at 27–28.

[88] For one economist's account, see Murray Rothbard, Panic of 1819: Reactions and Policies (1962).

[89] Remini, Bank War, supra note 85, at 30–31.

[90] Ibid. at 32–33, 39.

[91] Ibid. at 37–38.

[92] Ibid. at 34–35.

[93] Ibid.

[94] Andrew Jackson, Second Annual Message to Congress (Dec. 6, 1830), in 2 Richardson, Messages, supra note 60, at 529.

[95] Remini, Bank War, supra note 85, at 74.

[96] Ibid. at 92.

[97] Ibid. at 75–76.

[98] Ibid. at 99.

[99] Ibid. at 77–78.

[100] Ibid. at 80, 93. To throw salt on Jackson's wounds, the Senate (with Vice President Calhoun casting the tie-breaking vote) at the same time rejected Van Buren's nomination as minister to Great Britain.

[101] Ibid. at 15–16 (emphasis added).

[102] Andrew Jackson, Veto Message (July 10, 1832), in 2 Richardson, Messages, supra note 60, at 576–91.

[103] Ibid. at 576–77.

[104] Ibid. at 578.

[105] Ibid. at 581.

[106] Ibid.

[107] Ibid. at 582.

[108] Ibid.

[109] Ibid.

[110] Ibid.

[111] Ibid.

[112] Ibid.

[113] Ibid. at 590.

[114] White, Jacksonians, supra note 66, at 29.

[115] See generally Charles M. Cameron, Veto Bargaining: Presidents and the Politics of Negative Power (2000).

[116] Remini, Bank War, supra note 85, at 84.

[117] Ibid. at 84–85.

[118] Ibid. at 84.

[119] Ibid. at 85.

[120] Ibid.

[121] Ibid.

[122] Ibid. at 87.

[123] Ibid. at 90–101.

[124] Ibid. at 101.

[125] Ibid.

[126] Ibid.

[127] Ibid. at 99–100.

[128] Ibid. at 98–99.

[129] Ibid. at 99.

[130] Ibid. at 103–04.

[131] Ibid. at 105.

[132] Ibid. at 106.

[133] Ibid. at 109.

[134] Ibid. at 111.

[135] Ibid. at 112–13.

[136] Ibid.

[137] Ibid. at 113.

[138] Ibid. at 113–14.

[139] Act of Apr. 10, 1816, § 16, 3 Stat. 266, 274, 14th Cong. (1st Sess. 1816).

[140] Remini, Bank War, supra note 85, at 111.

[141] Ibid. at 115.

[142] Ibid. at 116.

[143] Ibid. at 118.

[144] Ibid.

[145] Andrew Jackson, Removal of the Public Deposits (Sept. 18, 1833), in 3 Richardson, Messages, supra note 60, at 7.

[146] Remini, Bank War, supra note 85, at 122.

[147] Ibid. at 123.

[148] Ibid. at 124.

[149] Ibid. at 124.

[150] Ibid. at 126–27.

[151] Ibid. at 127.

[152] Ibid. at 126–27.

[153] Ibid. at 129 ("National Republicans, Bank men, nullifiers, tarriff men, states' righters, former Democrats and other dissidents joined together to form the 'Whig' party, adopting this name to designate their opposition to concentrated power in the hands of the chief executive.").

[154] Remini, Bank War, supra note 85, at 137–38.

[155] Andrew Jackson, Message to Senate (Dec. 12, 1833), in 3 Richardson, Messages, supra note 60, at 36.

[156] Ibid.

[157] Ibid.

[158] Remini, Bank War, supra note 85, at 138.

[159] Ibid.

[160] Ibid.

161 Ibid. at 138–39.

162 Ibid. at 140.

163 10 Reg. Deb. 1187 (1834).

164 Andrew Jackson, Protest (Apr. 15, 1834), in 3 Richardson, Messages, supra note 60, at 69 (hereinafter "Jackson, Protest"). See Steven G. Calabresi & Christopher S. Yoo, The Unitary Executive During the First Half-Century, 47 Case Western Reserve Law Review 1451, 1545–55 (1997).

165 Jackson, Protest, supra note 164, at 85.

166 Ibid. at 85–86.

167 Ibid. at 79.

168 Ibid.

169 Ibid. at 90.

170 Ibid.

171 Ibid.

172 Ibid. at 86.

173 Remini, Bank War, supra note 85, at 145.

174 Ibid.

175 Ibid.

176 Ibid. at 146.

177 Ibid.

178 Ibid.

179 Ibid.

180 10 Reg. Deb. 1575 (1834).

181 Ibid.

182 Ibid.

183 Ibid.

184 Remini, Bank War, supra note 85, at 160–68.

185 See Wilentz, supra note 1, at 150.

186 Remini, Bank War, supra note 85, at 166.

187 For historical background on the political and economic issues surrounding the tariff, see Howe, supra note 1, at 395–410; and Richard Ellis, The Union at Risk: Jacksonian Democracy, States' Rights, and the Nullification Crisis (1987).

188 See Wilentz, supra note 1, at 63.

189 Ibid.

190 See ibid. at 63–64.

191 John C. Calhoun, Exposition and Protest (Dec. 19, 1828), in Union and Liberty: The Political Philosophy of John C. Calhoun (Ross M. Lence ed., 1992).

192 It is difficult to escape the conclusion that the real issue behind nullification was not the tariff, but slavery. If a numerical majority in the North could enact a tariff over Southern objections, Southerners asked, what would prevent it from eradicating slavery, too?

[193] Daniel Webster, Speech on Mr. Foot's Resolution, in 2 American Eloquence: A Collection of Speeches and Addresses by the Most Imminent Orators of America 899 (Frank Moore ed., 1857).

[194] Wilentz, supra note 1, at 65 (emphasis added).

[195] James Parton, Life of Andrew Jackson 283 (1888).

[196] Wilentz, supra note 1, at 64.

[197] Andrew Jackson, Fourth Annual Message to Congress (Dec. 4, 1832), in 2 Richardson, Messages, supra note 60, at 598.

[198] Andrew Jackson, Proclamation (Dec. 10, 1832), in 2 ibid. at 641 (hereinafter "Jackson, Proclamation").

[199] Ibid. at 643 (emphasis in original).

[200] Ibid. at 645.

[201] Ibid. at 646.

[202] Ibid. at 643.

[203] Ibid.

[204] Ibid. at 642.

[205] Ibid. at 648.

[206] Ibid.

[207] Ibid.

[208] Ibid.

[209] 3 Remini, Jackson, supra note 1, at 22.

[210] Jackson, Proclamation, supra note 198, at 652.

[211] Ibid. at 654.

[212] Ibid.

[213] Ibid.

[214] Ibid.

[215] Ibid. at 654–55.

[216] Ibid. at 655.

[217] 3 Remini, Jackson, supra note 1, at 26.

[218] Ibid.

[219] Ibid. at 34.

[220] Ibid.

[221] Ibid. at 29.

[222] Andrew Jackson, Message to Congress (Jan. 16, 1833), in 2 Richardson, Messages, supra note 60, at 620–21.

[223] Ibid. at 631.

[224] Ibid. at 632.

[225] 3 Remini, Jackson, supra note 1, at 37.

[226] Ibid. at 38.

[227] See generally Paul Bergeron, The Presidency of James K. Polk 1–21 (1987).

[228] To the Senate and House of Representatives, May 11, 1846, in 5 Richardson, Messages, supra note 60, at 2292.

[229] Howe, supra note 1, at 731–91.

[230] See generally John S. D. Eisenhower, So Far From God: The U.S. War With Mexico, 1846–1848 (2000).

[231] Howe, supra note 1, at 797. See Third Annual Message, Dec. 7, 1847, in 5 Richardson, Messages, supra note 60, 2382, 2384–88; Speech in the U.S. House of Representatives on the War with Mexico, Jan. 12, 1848, in Abraham Lincoln Speeches and Writings, 1832–1858, at 161, 168 (Don E. Fehrenbacher ed., 1989); and David H. Donald, Lincoln 122–24 (1995).

[232] Howe, supra note 1, at 796–811.

[233] Ibid.

[234] Ibid. at 809.

[235] Ibid. at 808.

CHAPTER 6: ABRAHAM LINCOLN

[1] Lincoln to Albert G. Hodges, Apr. 4, 1864, in Don E. Fehrenbacher, ed., Abraham Lincoln, Speeches and Writings, 1859–1865, at 586 (1989) (hereinafter "Lincoln, Speeches and Writings"). There are a wide number of sources on Lincoln; he is reportedly the subject of the most books in the English language after Jesus and Shakespeare. Yet, there are relatively few books on Lincoln's performance of his role as President and Commander-in-Chief. I have relied in this chapter on a few outstanding works: David Donald, Lincoln (1995) (hereinafter "Donald, Lincoln"); Daniel Farber, Lincoln's Constitution (2003); Harold Hyman, A More Perfect Union: The Impact of the Civil War and Reconstruction on the Constitution (1975); James MacPherson, Battle Cry of Freedom (1988) (hereinafter "MacPherson, Battle Cry"); Mark Neely, The Fate of Liberty: Abraham Lincoln and Civil Liberties (1991); Phillip Shaw Paludan, The Presidency of Abraham Lincoln (1994); and J. G. Randall, Constitutional Problems Under Lincoln (1951). There are also a number of important articles on Lincoln's exercise of his constitutional powers, and whether they amounted to a dictatorship. In the chapters of the books on the Presidency that discuss Lincoln in detail, political scientists generally argue that Lincoln exercised powers approaching a dictatorship. Historians, on the other hand, seem to conclude that Lincoln's policies rested within his executive powers, broadly construed. See Herman Belz, Lincoln and the Constitution: The Dictatorship Question Reconsidered (1984); Michael Les Benedict, The Constitution of the Lincoln Presidency and the Republican Era, in Martin Fausold and Alan Shank eds., The Constitution and the American Presidency 45 (1991); David Donald, Lincoln Reconsidered: Essays on the Civil War Era 187 (1947) (hereinafter "Donald, Lincoln Reconsidered"); and Don Fehrenbacher, Lincoln in Text and Context: Collected Essays 113 (1987).

[2] Those deaths had a much greater impact than other wars, such as World Wars I and II, because the casualties represented a much larger share of the nation's smaller population in 1861 than more recent conflicts.

[3] 6 Messages and Papers of the Presidents, 1789–1897, at 277 (James D. Richardson ed., 1897) (hereinafter "Richardson").

[4] See, e.g., Arthur M. Schlesinger, Jr., The Imperial Presidency 59 (1973); Clinton Rossiter, Constitutional Dictatorship: Crisis Government in the Modern Democra-

cies (1948); and Edward S. Corwin, The President: Office and Powers, 1787–1984, at 20–22 (5th ed. 1984).

[5] Lincoln to Hodges, Apr. 4, 1864, in Lincoln, Speeches and Writings, supra note 1, at 586.

[6] Ibid.

[7] Donald, Lincoln Reconsidered, supra note 1, at 191–96.

[8] 60 U.S. (19 How.) 393 (1857).

[9] Lincoln, First Inaugural Address, Mar. 4, 1861, in Lincoln, Speeches and Writings, supra note 1, at 221.

[10] See Texas v. White, 74 U.S. 700, 725 (1869) ("The Constitution, in all its provisions, looks to an indestructible Union, composed of indestructible States.").

[11] Power of the President in Executing the Laws, 9 Op. Att'y Gen. 516–24 (Nov. 20, 1860). See also Farber, supra note 1, at 75–76.

[12] James Buchanan, Fourth Annual Message, Dec. 3, 1860, in 5 Richardson, supra note 3, at 626, 635–36. See also Farber, supra note 1, at 76.

[13] James Buchanan, Special Message to Congress, Jan. 8, 1861, in 5 Richardson, supra note 3, at 656.

[14] Lincoln, Speeches and Writings, supra note 1, at 215–222.

[15] Ibid. at 224. See Michael Stokes Paulsen, Review: The Civil War as Constitutional Interpretation, 71 University of Chicago Law Review 691, 706–07 (2004) (explaining Lincoln's belief in a duty to defeat secession).

[16] McPherson, Battle Cry, supra note 1, at 313.

[17] There is some dispute as to whether Taney was sitting as a judge on circuit or as a Supreme Court Justice in chambers at the time. For a more detailed discussion of the Merryman case, see John Yoo, Of Merryman and Milligan, __ Journal of Supreme Court History __ (forthcoming 2010). The facts of the case are described in Ex Parte Merryman, 17 F. Cas. 144 (C.C.D.Md. 1861) (No. 9487). No good history focuses on John Merryman and the history of the case, aside from a helpful essay. See Arthur T. Downey, The Conflict between the Chief Justice and the Chief Executive: Ex Parte Merryman, 31 Journal of Supreme Court History 262 (2006).

[18] Merryman, 17 F. Cas. at 152.

[19] Ibid.

[20] Paludan, supra note 1, at 76.

[21] Act of Aug. 6, 1861, 12 Stat. 326.

[22] The Prize Cases, 67 U.S. (2 Black) 635, 666 (1862).

[23] Ibid. at 666–67.

[24] Ibid. at 668.

[25] Ibid. at 670.

[26] To Lyman Trumbull, Dec. 10, 1860, in Lincoln, Speeches and Writings, supra note 1, at 190.

[27] Paludan, supra note 1, at 33–34.

[28] Ibid. at 84–87.

[29] Ibid. at 108–18.

[30] Ibid. 98, 104.

31 Ibid. at 105.

32 Eliot Cohen, Supreme Command: Soldiers, Statesmen, and Leadership in Wartime (2002).

33 To Edwin M. Stanton, May 17, 1864, in Lincoln, Speeches and Writings, supra note 1, at 594.

34 For general discussion, see Donald, Lincoln, supra note 1, at 367; and MacPherson, Battle Cry, supra note 1, at 515.

35 Ibid. at 83.

36 Farber, supra note 1, at 153.

37 See discussion in Randall, supra note 1, at 342–70.

38 Paludan, supra note 1, at 84.

39 Confiscation Act, 12 Stat. 319 (Aug. 6, 1861); and Second Confiscation Act, 12 Stat. 589 (July 17, 1862). See Randall, supra note 1, at 351–63.

40 Militia Act, 12 Stat. 597 (July 17, 1862).

41 Preliminary Emancipation Proclamation, Sept. 22, 1862, in Lincoln, Speeches and Writings, supra note 1, at 368.

42 Paludan, supra note 1, at 155.

43 Final Emancipation Proclamation, Jan. 1, 1863, in Lincoln, Speeches and Writings, supra note 1, at 424.

44 To Horace Greeley, Aug. 22, 1862, in Ibid. at 358.

45 To James C. Conkling, Aug. 26, 1863, in Ibid. at 497.

46 See, e.g., Randall, supra note 1, at 374–404.

47 See, e.g., Miller v. United States 78 U.S. 268 (1870) (confiscation of property); Ford v. Surget, 97 U.S. 594 (1878) (destruction of property); and New Orleans v. The Steamship Co., 87 U.S. 387 (1874) (transfer of property).

48 Annual Message to Congress, Dec. 6, 1864, in Lincoln, Speeches and Writings, supra note 1, at 658.

49 On this point, see Harry Jaffa, A New Birth of Freedom: Abraham Lincoln and the Coming of the Civil War (2000); and Harry Jaffa, Crisis of the House Divided: An Interpretation of the Issues in the Lincoln-Douglas Debates (1959).

50 Address at Gettysburg, Pennsylvania, Nov. 19, 1863, in Lincoln, Speeches and Writings, supra note 1, at 536.

51 See James McPherson, Abraham Lincoln and the Second American Revolution 75–76 (1990).

52 Ibid. at 84.

53 Donald, Lincoln, supra note 1, at 523.

54 Ibid.

55 Annual Message to Congress, Dec. 6, 1864, in Lincoln, Speeches and Writings, supra note 1, at 660.

56 Paludan, supra note 1, at 73–74.

57 Lincoln to Erastus Corning and Others, June 12, 1863, in Lincoln, Speeches and Writings, supra note 1, at 458.

58 Special Message to Congress, July 4, 1861, in Ibid. at 252–53.

CRISIS AND COMMAND

59 Suspension of the Privilege of the Writ of Habeas Corpus, 10 U.S. Op. Att'y Gen. 74 (July 5, 1861).

60 Luther v. Borden, 48 U.S. 1 (1849); and Moyer v. Peabody, 212 U.S. 78 (1909). For discussion, see Farber, supra note 1, at 148–49.

61 Lincoln, Speeches and Writings, supra note 1, at 371.

62 Neely, supra note 1, at 168–69.

63 See ibid. at 28, 65–68.

64 Ex Parte Vallandigham, 68 U.S. 243 (1863).

65 Lincoln to Erastus Corning and Others, June 12, 1863, in Lincoln, Speeches and Writings, supra note 1, at 456–60.

66 Ibid. at 461–62.

67 Reply to Ohio Democrats, June 29, 1863, in Lincoln, Speeches and Writings, supra note 1, at 466–69; and Paludan, supra note 1, at 201–02.

68 Habeas Corpus Act, 12 Stat. 755 (Mar. 3, 1863).

69 Randall, supra note 1, at 166–67.

70 No good biography exists of Milligan, but there are several helpful articles about him and his case. See, e.g., Frank L. Klement, The Indianapolis Treason Trials and Ex Parte Milligan, in American Political Trials 101 (Michael R. Belknap ed., 1981); Allan Nevins, The Case of the Copperhead Conspirator, in Quarrels That Have Shaped the Constitution 101 (John A. Garraty ed., 1962); and Kenneth M. Stampp, The Milligan Case and the Election of 1864 in Indiana, 31 Mississippi Valley Historical Review 41 (1944). One short book is Darwin Kelley, Milligan's Fight Against Lincoln (1973).

71 Ex Parte Milligan, 71 U.S. 2 (1866).

72 Quoted in 3 Charles Warren, The Supreme Court in United States History, 1856–1918, at 151 (1922).

73 3 Ibid. at 154.

74 3 Ibid. at 149–50 (describing Republican reaction); Ex Parte McCardle, 74 U.S. (7 Wall.) 506 (1868) (upholding constitutionality of repeal of appellate jurisdiction over military commissions).

75 For a contrary view, see Stanley I. Kutler, Ex Parte McCardle: Judicial Impotency?: The Supreme Court and Reconstruction Reconsidered, 72 American Historical Review 835 (1967); and William W. Van Alstyne, A Critical Guide to Ex Parte McCardle, 15 Arizona Law Review 229 (1973).

76 Neely, supra note 1, at 113–38.

77 See, e.g., Geoffrey Stone, Perilous Times: Free Speech in Wartime 94–120 (2004).

78 For discussions of the law and policy of Reconstruction, see generally Herman Belz, Reconstructing the Union: Theory and Policy During the Civil War (1969); Michael Les Benedict, A Compromise of Principle: Congressional Republicans and Reconstruction, 1863–1869 (1974); and Harold Hyman, A More Perfect Union: The Impact of the Civil War and Reconstruction on the Constitution (1975).

79 See generally Eyal Benvenisti, The International Law of Occupation (1992).

80 Paludan, supra note 1, at 235.

81 Randall, supra note 1, at 225–27.

82 The Grapeshot, 76 U.S. (9 Wall.) 129 (1869); and United States v. Diekelman, 92 U.S. 520 (1875).

83 The Grapeshot, 76 U.S. at 132.

84 Paludan, supra note 1, at 244.

85 Annual Message to Congress, Dec. 8, 1863, in Lincoln, Speeches and Writings, supra note 1, at 552.

86 Proclamation of Amnesty and Reconstruction, Dec. 8, 1863, in Ibid. at 555–58.

87 Paludan, supra note 1, at 265.

88 Donald, Lincoln, supra note 1, at 511.

89 Wade-Davis Manifesto, Aug. 5, 1864, available at www.vlib.us/amdocs/texts/1864wade.html.

90 Memorandum on Probable Failure of Re-election, Aug. 23, 1864, in Lincoln, Speeches and Writings, supra note 1, at 624.

91 Response to Serenade, Washington, D.C., Nov. 10, 1864, in Ibid. at 641.

92 Paludan, supra note 1, at 290.

93 Response to Serenade, Nov. 10, 1864, in Lincoln, Speeches and Writings, supra note 1, at 641.

94 Donald, Lincoln, supra note 1, at 561.

95 Eric Foner exemplifies the academic consensus that views Reconstruction as a noble effort to expand the civil rights of black freemen in the South. Eric Foner, Reconstruction: America's Unfinished Revolution 1863–1877 (1988).

96 Donald, Lincoln, supra note 1, at 562.

97 Annual Message to Congress, Dec. 6, 1864, in Lincoln, Speeches and Writings, supra note 1, at 660.

98 Second Inaugural Address, Mar. 4, 1865, in Ibid. at 686–87.

99 Ibid. at 687.

100 Speech on Reconstruction, Apr. 11, 1865, in Ibid. at 698.

101 Donald, Lincoln, supra note 1, at 592.

102 See Michael Les Benedict, The Impeachment and Trial of Andrew Johnson 1–25 (1973).

103 Ibid.

104 Ibid. at 13.

105 Ibid. at 22.

106 Ibid. at 60.

107 Ibid. at 89–180.

108 Myers v. United States, 272 U.S. 52 (1926) (observing that the Tenure in Office Act violated the Constitution).

109 Foner, supra note 95, at 602–03.

CHAPTER 7: FRANKLIN D. ROOSEVELT

1 There are a great number of works on Roosevelt, with more appearing all of the time. I have relied on general works for the background to this chapter. Conrad Black, Franklin Delano Roosevelt: Champion of Freedom (2005); James MacGregor

Burns, Roosevelt: The Lion and the Fox 1882–1940 (1956); James MacGregor Burns, FDR: Soldier of Freedom 1940–1945 (1970); 1–5 Kenneth S. Davis, FDR (1972–2000); Frank Freidel, Franklin D. Roosevelt: A Rendezvous with Destiny (1991); George McGimsey, The Presidency of Franklin Delano Roosevelt (2000); 1–3 Arthur M. Schlesinger, Jr., The Age of Roosevelt (1957–60); and Geoffrey C. Ward, A First-Class Temperament: The Emergence of Franklin Roosevelt (1990). Similarly, there are a multitude of works on the New Deal. Some that have been particularly helpful are Alan Brinkley, Voices of Protest: Huey Long, Father Coughlin, and the Great Depression (1983); Alan Brinkley, The End of Reform: New Deal Liberalism in Recession and War (1996); Barry Cushman, Rethinking the New Deal Court: The Structure of a Constitutional Revolution (1998); David M. Kennedy, Freedom from Fear: The American People in Depression and War, 1929–1945 (2001); William E. Leuchtenburg, Franklin D. Roosevelt and the New Deal (1963); Sidney M. Milkis, The President and the Parties: The Transformation of the American Party System Since the New Deal (1993); and G. Edward White, The Constitution and the New Deal (2002).

[2] See, e.g., Milkis, supra note 1, at 98–124; Theodore Lowi, The Personal President: Power Invested, Promise Unfulfilled (1985).

[3] To understand the economics of the Great Depression and the New Deal, see 1 Allan Meltzer, A History of the Federal Reserve, 1913–1951 (2003); Peter Temin, The Great Depression, in 3 The Cambridge Economic History of the United States 301 (Stanley Engerman & Robert Gallman eds., 2000); Thomas Hall & David Ferguson, The Great Depression: An International Disaster of Perverse Economic Policies (1998); Richard Vedder & Lowell Gallaway, Out of Work: Unemployment and Government in Twentieth Century America (1997); Barry Eichengreen, Golden Fetters, The Gold Standard and the Great Depression, 1919–1939 (1995); and Milton Friedman & Anna Schwartz, A Monetary History of the United States, 1867–1960, at 299–301 (1963). John Kenneth Galbraith, The Great Crash 1929 (2d ed. 1961), remains a classic treatment, but one that has been surpassed by more recent work.

[4] Ben Bernanke, Essays on the Great Depression (2000).

[5] Kennedy, supra note 1, at 164–65.

[6] See Friedman & Schwartz, supra note 3; Meltzer, supra note 3, at 271.

[7] Ellis Hawley, The Constitution of the Hoover and Franklin Roosevelt Presidency During the Depression Era, 1930–1939, in The Constitution and the American Presidency 83, 90–91 (Martin Fausold & Alan Shank eds., 1991).

[8] 2 The Public Papers and Addresses of Franklin D. Roosevelt 14–15 (Samuel I. Rosenman ed., 1938–1950).

[9] Trading with the Enemy Act of 1917, 50 U.S.C. app. § 1 (2000).

[10] Hawley, supra note 7, at 92.

[11] See Thomas Hall & David Ferguson, The Great Depression: An International Disaster of Perverse Economic Policies 124–26 (1998).

[12] William Leuchtenberg, The FDR Years: On Roosevelt and His Legacy 53 (1995).

[13] United States v. E. C. Knight, 156 U.S. 1 (1895).

[14] Hammer v. Dagenhart, 247 U.S. 251 (1918).

[15] Bailey v. Drexel Furniture Co., 259 U.S. 20 (1922).

[16] Lochner v. New York, 198 U.S. 45 (1905).

[17] See, e.g., Adair v. United States, 208 U.S. 161 (1908) (federal labor law); Adkins v. Children's Hospital, 261 U.S. 525 (1923) (minimum wages); Williams v. Standard Oil Co., 278 U.S. 235 (1929) (setting prices of gasoline); New State Ice Co. v. Liebmann, 285 U.S. 262 (1932) (limiting entry into business); Jesse Choper, et al., Constitutional Law—Cases, Comments, Questions 292 (9th ed. 2001).

[18] Robert Stern, The Commerce Clause and the National Economy, 1933–1946, 59 Harvard Law Review 645, 883 (1946).

[19] William Leuchtenburg, The Supreme Court Reborn: The Constitutional Revolution in the Age of Roosevelt 83–84 (1995).

[20] Home Building & Loan Ass'n v. Blaisdell, 290 U.S. 398 (1934); Nebbia v. New York, 291 U.S. 502 (1934).

[21] Panama Refining Co. v. Ryan, 293 U.S. 388 (1935).

[22] U.S. 495 (1935).

[23] Ibid. at 528.

[24] Franklin D. Roosevelt, The 209th Press Conference (May 31, 1935), in 4 The Public Papers and Addresses of Franklin D. Roosevelt 1935, at 221 (1938).

[25] Ibid.

[26] William Leuchtenburg, The Origins of Franklin D. Roosevelt's "Court-Packing" Plan, 1966 Supreme Court Review 347, 351–54 (hereinafter "Leuchtenburg, Court-Packing").

[27] Norman v. B. & O. R.R., 294 U.S. 240 (1935).

[28] 297 U.S. 1 (1936).

[29] 298 U.S. 238 (1936).

[30] 298 U.S. 1 (1936).

[31] 298 U.S. 587 (1936).

[32] 81 Cong. Rec. 878 (1937) (reprinting FDR's message to Congress).

[33] Ibid.

[34] Barry Cushman, Rethinking the New Deal Court, 80 Virginia Law Review 201, 212 (1994).

[35] Ibid. at 214–15.

[36] Ibid. at 221.

[37] West Coast Hotel Co. v. Parrish, 300 U.S. 379 (1937).

[38] NLRB v. Jones & Laughlin Steel Corp., 301 U.S. 1 (1937); NLRB v. Fruehauf Trailer Co., 301 U.S. 49 (1937); NLRB v. Friedman-Harry Marks Clothing Co., 301 U.S. 58 (1937); and Associated Press v. NLRB, 301 U.S. 103 (1937); and Washington, Virginia & Maryland Coach Co. v. NLRB, 301 U.S. 142 (1937).

[39] 301 U.S. 1, 41 (1937).

[40] Cushman, supra note 34, at 222–23.

[41] See, e.g., Steward Machine Co. v. Davis, 301 U.S. 548 (1937); and Helvering v. Davis, 301 U.S. 619 (1937).

[42] See, e.g., Joseph Alsop & Turner Catledge, The 168 Days (1938); and Merlo Pusey, The Supreme Court Crisis (1937).

[43] 1 Bruce Ackerman, We the People: Foundations 105–30 (1991).

[44] See generally Cushman, supra note 1.

[45] See, e.g., United States v. Darby, 312 U.S. 100 (1941).

[46] See, e.g., David M. Kennedy, Over Here: The First World War and American Society (1980); Stephen Skowronek, Building a New American State: The Expansion of National Administrative Capacities 1877–1920 (1982); Robert H. Wiebe, The Search for Order, 1877–1920 (1966).

[47] Marc Landy & Sidney Milkis, Presidential Greatness 153–54 (2000).

[48] Burns, Roosevelt: The Lion and the Fox, supra note 1, at 174.

[49] Ibid. at 150.

[50] Christopher Yoo, Steven Calabresi & Laurence Nee, The Unitary Executive During the Third Half-Century, 1889–1945, 80 Notre Dame Law Review 1, 83–84 (2004).

[51] The classic work on the origins of the independent agencies remains Robert E. Cushman, The Independent Regulatory Commissions (1941). For more recent analyses, see Geoffrey P. Miller, Independent Agencies, 1986 Supreme Court Review 41; Peter L. Strauss, The Place of Agencies in Government: Separation of Powers and the Fourth Branch, 84 Columbia Law Review 573 (1984); and Paul R. Verkuil, The Status of Independent Agencies after Bowsher v. Synar, 1986 Duke Law Journal 779.

[52] Steven G. Calabresi & Christopher S. Yoo, The Unitary Executive: Presidential Power from Washington to Bush 284–88 (2008).

[53] Humphrey's Executor v. United States, 295 U.S. 602, 620 (1935).

[54] Yoo, Calabresi & Nee, supra note 50, at 85.

[55] Myers v. United States, 272 U.S. 52, 117 (1926).

[56] Humphrey's Executor, 295 U.S. 602, 629 (1935).

[57] See, e.g., Morrison v. Olson, 529 U.S. 654 (1988); and Mistretta v. United States, 488 U.S. 361 (1989).

[58] Compare Hadley Arkes, The Return of George Sutherland (1997).

[59] Yoo, Calabresi & Nee, supra note 50, at 88–89.

[60] The federal courts upheld FDR's decision, ultimately holding that Congress had failed to clearly prevent the President from firing on other grounds in addition to criteria it listed. See Morgan v. TVA, 28 F. Supp. 732 (E.D. Tenn. 1939), aff'd, 115 F.2d 990 (6th Cir. 1940); and Yoo, Calabresi & Nee, supra note 50, at 89–90.

[61] See Peri Arnold, Making the Managerial Presidency: Comprehensive Reorganization Planning, 1905–1996, at 103–17 (1986).

[62] See Matthew Dickinson, Bitter Harvest: FDR, Presidential Power, and the Growth of the Presidential Branch 104–10 (1996).

[63] Arnold, supra note 61, at 103–17.

[64] Dickinson, supra note 62, at 111.

[65] Leuchtenburg, supra note 1, at 277–80.

[66] See, e.g., Christopher C. DeMuth & Douglas H. Ginsburg, White House Review of Agency Decisionmaking, 99 Harvard Law Review 1075 (1986); Alan B. Morrison, OMB Interference with Agency Rulemaking: The Wrong Way to Write a Regulation, 99 Harvard Law Review 1059 (1986); Terry Eastland, Energy in the Executive: The Case for the Strong Presidency 163 (1992); and Elena Kagan, Presidential Administration, 114 Harvard Law Review 1075, 2245 (2001).

[67] On the way that Presidents today manage policy development through the White House and the Executive Office of the President, see Andrew Rudalevige, Managing

the President's Program: Presidential Leadership and Legislative Policy Formation 18–62 (2002).

[68] United States v. Lovett, 328 U.S. 303 (1946).

[69] Plessy v. Ferguson, 163 U.S. 537 (1896).

[70] Exec. Order No. 8802, 6 Fed. Reg. 3109 (June 25, 1941).

[71] Exec. Order No. 9346, 8 Fed. Reg. 7183 (May 27, 1943).

[72] See, e.g., Barry D. Karl, Constitution and Central Planning: The Third New Deal Revisited, 1988 Supreme Court Review 163, 188; Peter Evans et al. eds., Bringing the State Back In (1985); and Theda Skocpol, Protecting Soldiers and Mothers: The Political Origins of Social Policy in the United States (1995).

[73] For a more extensive discussion of the transformation of American politics wrought by the New Deal, see Milkis, supra note 1, at 21–51, 149–183; and Theodore J. Lowi, The End of Liberalism: The Second Republic of the United States (2d ed. 1979).

[74] Important historical works on FDR and American entry into World War II include Robert Dallek, Franklin D. Roosevelt and American Foreign Policy, 1932–45 (1979); Robert Divine, The Illusion of Neutrality (1962); Waldo Heinrichs, Threshold of War: Franklin D. Roosevelt and American Entry into World War II (1988); Patrick Hearden, Roosevelt Confronts Hitler: America's Entry into World War II (1987); Warren Kimball, The Juggler: Franklin Roosevelt as Wartime Statesman (1991); Frederick W. Marks III, Wind Over Sand: The Diplomacy of Franklin Roosevelt (1988); David Reynolds, The Creation of the Anglo-American Alliance, 1937–1941: A Study in Competitive Co-operation (1982); and Akira Iriye, The Origins of the Second World War in Asia and the Pacific (1987). The day-to-day events of American entry into World War II are traced in William Langer & S. Everett Gleason, The Undeclared War: 1940–1941 (1953), and the events leading up to World War II are described in Donald C. Watt, How War Came: The Immediate Origins of the Second World War, 1938–1939 (1990); and John Keegan, The Second World War (2005). U.S. diplomacy in the war itself is discussed by Akira Iriye, The Globalizing of America, 1913–1945 (1995).

[75] For a summary of the debates, see Gordon Prange, et al., At Dawn We Slept (2001).

[76] See Marc Trachtenberg, The Craft of International History: A Guide to Method 79–139 (2006).

[77] See, e.g., Marks, supra note 74, at 163.

[78] Arkes, supra note 58.

[79] 299 U.S. 304 (1936).

[80] Curtiss-Wright, Our History, available at www.curtisswright.com/history.asp.

[81] Curtiss-Wright Export Corp., 299 U.S. at 318. Scholars have not been kind to Justice Sutherland's analysis. For critical discussion of Curtiss-Wright, see David M. Levitan, The Foreign Relations Power: An Analysis of Mr. Justice Sutherland's Theory, 55 Yale Law Journal 467 (1946); Charles A. Lofgren, United States v. Curtiss-Wright Export Corp.: An Historical Reassessment, 83 Yale Law Journal 1 (1973); and Louis Henkin, Foreign Affairs and the Constitution 19–20 (2d ed. 1996).

[82] United States v. Belmont, 301 U.S. 324, 331 (1937). See also Michael D. Ramsey, Executive Agreements and the (Non)Treaty Power, 77 North Carolina Law Review 133 (1998); and Joel R. Paul, The Geopolitical Constitution: Executive Expediency and Executive Agreements, 86 California Law Review 671 (1998).

[83] Congressional Research Service, Treaties and Other International Agreements: The Role of the United States Senate, S. Prt. 106–71, 106th Cong., 2d Sess. 39 (2001).

[84] Dames & Moore v. Regan, 453 U.S. 654 (1981) (Iranian hostages); American Insurance Association v. Garamendi, 539 U.S. 396 (2003) (Holocaust-survivor claims).

[85] Dallek, supra note 74, at 102.

[86] See, e.g., Robert Kagan, Dangerous Nation: America's Foreign Policy from Its Earliest Days to the Dawn of the Twentieth Century (2007); and John Lewis Gaddis, Surprise, Security, and the American Experience (2005).

[87] Trachtenberg, supra note 76, at 118.

[88] Ibid. at 118–19.

[89] Fireside Chat 16: On the Arsenal of Democracy, Dec. 29, 1940, at http://millercenter .org/scripps/archive/speeches/detail/3319.

[90] Dallek, supra note 74, at 267.

[91] Ibid. at 109.

[92] Neutrality Act of 1935, ch. 837, 49 Stat. 1081 (1935).

[93] Dallek, supra note 74, at 110.

[94] Neutrality Act of 1936, ch. 106, 49 Stat. 1152 (1936).

[95] Neutrality Act of 1937, ch. 146, 50 Stat. 121 (1937).

[96] Dallek, supra note 74, at 285.

[97] Neutrality Act of 1939, ch. 2, 54 Stat. 4 (1939).

[98] Aaron X. Fellmeth, A Divorce Waiting to Happen: Franklin Roosevelt and the Law of Neutrality, 1935–1941, 3 Buff. J. Int'l L. 414, 451 (1996–97).

[99] Ibid. at 457.

[100] Dallek, supra note 74, at 190.

[101] Ibid. at 222.

[102] Fellmeth, supra note 98, at 464.

[103] Dallek, supra note 74, at 221–22.

[104] Address at University of Virginia, June 10, 1940, in The Public Papers and Addresses of Franklin D. Roosevelt 1940, at 259, 261–62 (Samuel I. Rosenman ed., 1941).

[105] Dallek, supra note 74, at 232.

[106] Ibid. at 243.

[107] Ibid.

[108] Fellmeth, supra note 98, at 467–68.

[109] Act of June 28, 1940, § 14, 54 Stat. 676, 681 (1940); and Espionage Act of 1917, ch. 30, 40 Stat. 222 (1917).

[110] Dallek, supra note 74, at 244.

[111] Fellmeth, supra note 98, at 476–78.

[112] Acquisition of Naval and Air Bases in Exchange for Over-Age Destroyers, 39 Opp. Atty'y Gen. 484, reprinted in H. Jefferson Powell ed., The Constitution and the Attorneys General 307, 308 (1999).

[113] Training of British Flying Students in the United States, 40 Op. Att'y Gen. 58 (May 23, 1941), reprinted in Ibid. at 316, 317.

[114] Dallek, supra note 74, at 245.

[115] Quoted in Kenneth S. Davis, FDR: Into the Storm 1937–40, at 611 (1993).

[116] Edwin Borchard, The Attorney General's Opinion on the Exchange of Destroyers for Naval Bases, 34 Am J Int'l L 690, 691 (1940).

[117] Edward S. Corwin, Executive Authority Held Exceeded in Destroyer Deal, N.Y. Times, Oct. 13, 1940.

[118] Davis, supra note 115, at 608.

[119] Ibid. at 603–04.

[120] Quoted in Ibid. at 614.

[121] Campaign Address at Boston, Massachusetts, Oct. 30, 1940, in FDR Papers 1940, supra note 104, at 514, 517.

[122] Hearden, supra note 74, at 192.

[123] Kenneth S. Davis, FDR: The War President, 1940–43, at 63 (2000).

[124] Ibid. at 65.

[125] The Seven Hundred and Second Press Conference, Dec. 17, 1940, in FDR Papers 1940, supra note 104, at 604, 607–08.

[126] Fireside Chat on National Security, Dec. 29, 1940, in Ibid. at 633.

[127] Dallek, supra note 74, at 257.

[128] 55 Stat. 31 (1941). For the lengthy congressional discussions, see Davis, supra note 123, at 92–136.

[129] Fellmeth, supra note 98, at 485–86.

[130] Radio Address Announcing the Proclamation of an Unlimited National Emergency, May 27, 1941, in The Public Papers and Addresses of Franklin D. Roosevelt 1941, at 181, 189 (1950).

[131] Dallek, supra note 74, at 275–77.

[132] Fellmeth, supra note 98, at 466–67.

[133] Trachtenberg, supra note 76, at 80–139.

[134] Colin S. Gray, The Implications of Preemptive and Preventive War Doctrines: A Reconsideration 23 (2007), available at www.strategicstudiesinstitute.army.mil/pubs/display.cfm?pudID=789. See also Hew Strachan, Preemption and Prevention in Historical Perspective, in Preemption: Military Action and Moral Justification 23 (Henry Shue & David Rodin eds., 2007).

[135] The Atlantic Charter, in FDR Papers 1941, supra note 130, at 314.

[136] Dallek, supra note 74, at 285.

[137] Fireside Chat to the Nation, Sept. 11, 1941, in FDR Papers 1941, supra note 130, at 384, 390.

[138] Dallek, supra note 74, at 289.

[139] Navy and Total Defense Day Address, Oct. 27, 1941, in Ibid. at 438, 439.

[140] Dallek, supra note 74, at 300.

[141] Ibid. at 304.

[142] Ibid. at 307.

[143] For a critical review of the history, compare John Yoo, War by Other Means: An Insider's Account of the War on Terror 204–230 (2006) with Louis Fisher, Military Tribunals & Presidential Power: American Revolution to the War on Terrorism (2005).

[144] See David Danelski, The Saboteurs' Case, 1 Journal of Supreme Court History 61, 61–65 (1996).

[145] Ibid. at 65–66.

[146] Ibid. at 66–67.

[147] 7 Fed. Reg. 5101 (1942); see also Fisher, supra note 143, at 98–99.

[148] 7 Fed. Reg. 5103 (1942); see also Fisher, supra note 143, at 99–100.

[149] Ex Parte Milligan, 71 U.S. 2, 121–22 (1866).

[150] Danelski, supra note 144, at 68–69.

[151] Ibid. at 69.

[152] See Peter Irons, Justice at War: The History of the Japanese American Internment Cases 19 (1983).

[153] 7 Fed. Reg. 1407.

[154] Greg Robinson, By Order of the President: FDR and the Internment of the Japanese Americans (2003).

[155] See, e.g., Irons, supra note 152; Robinson, supra note 154; and Erik Yamamoto et al., Race, Rights & Reparation: Law and the Japanese American Internment (2001).

[156] Robinson, supra note 154, at 95.

[157] Ibid. at 104.

[158] Davis, supra note 123, at 424.

[159] Robinson, supra note 154, at 118.

[160] Act of Mar. 21, 1942, ch. 191, Pub. L. No. 77-503, 56 Stat. 173.

[161] Korematsu v. United States, 323 U.S. 214 (1944).

[162] Ibid. at 217–18.

[163] Ibid. at 218 (quoting Hirabayashi v. United States, 320 U.S. 81 (1943)).

[164] Ibid. at 223–24.

[165] Ibid. at 226 (Roberts, J., dissenting).

[166] Ibid. at 234 (Murphy, J., dissenting).

[167] Ibid. at 235–36 (Murphy, J., dissenting).

[168] Ibid. at 244 (Jackson, J., dissenting).

[169] Ex Parte Endo, 323 U.S. 283 (1944); see Brief for the United States, Korematsu (No. 22), reprinted in 42 Landmark Briefs and Arguments of the Supreme Court of the United States: Constitutional Law 197 (Philip B. Kurland & Gerhard Casper eds., 1975); and Robinson, supra note 154, at 210.

[170] Act of July 6, 1798, ch. 66, §1, 1 Stat. 577 (codified at 50 U.S.C. § 21). After the war, the Supreme Court upheld the use of the Alien Enemies Act during World War II in the case of a German national detained in the United States. See Ludecke v. Watkins, 335 U.S. 160 (1948).

[171] Christopher Andrew, For the President's Eyes Only, at 6–9, 76 (1995).

[172] Ibid. at 88, 94.

[173] Ibid. at 92.

[174] Reprinted in Appendix A, United States v. United States District Court, 444 F.2d 651, 669–70 (6th Cir. 1971) (hereinafter "Roosevelt 1940 Memorandum").

[175] Olmstead v. United States, 277 U.S. 438 (1928).

[176] 389 U.S. 347 (1967).

[177] United States v. Nardone, 302 U.S. 379 (1937).

[178] United States v. Nardone, 308 U.S. 338 (1939).

[179] Robert H. Jackson, That Man: An Insider's Portrait of Franklin D. Roosevelt 68–69 (2003).

[180] Roosevelt 1940 Memorandum, supra note 174.

CHAPTER 8: THE COLD WAR PRESIDENTS

[1] 5 Historical Statistics of the United States, Millennial Edition Online 5-353-36 (Susan Carter et al. eds., 2006).

[2] John Lewis Gaddis, Surprise, Security, and the American Experience (2004); and Walter McDougall, Promised Land, Crusader State: The American Encounter with the World Since 1776 (1998).

[3] The classic analysis of containment along these lines is John Lewis Gaddis, Strategies of Containment: A Critical Appraisal of Postwar American National Security Policy (1982) (hereinafter "Gaddis, Strategies").

[4] Ibid. at 127–97.

[5] Marc Trachtenberg, A Constructed Peace: The Making of the European Settlement 1945–1963, at 15–41 (1999).

[6] See Michael Hogan, A Cross of Iron: Harry S. Truman and the Origins of the National Security State, 1945–9154 (1998); and Melvyn Leffler, A Preponderance of Power: National Security, the Truman Administration, and the Cold War (1993).

[7] Gaddis, Strategies, supra note 3, at 89–109.

[8] 5 Historical Statistics, Millennial Edition, supra note 1, at 5–350 (Korean War statistics).

[9] Dean Acheson, Present at the Creation: My Years in the State Department 415 (1969).

[10] David McCullough, Truman 780 (1992). The events of the decision to go to war in Korea are usefully reviewed in Robert Turner, Truman, Korea, and the Constitution: Debunking the "Imperial President" Myth, 19 Harv. J. L. & Pub. Pol'y 533 (1996). For a differing account, see Louis Fisher, Presidential War Power 70–91 (1995).

[11] Fisher, supra note 10, at 89–90.

[12] McCullough, supra note 10, at 814–855 (firing of MacArthur), 855 (Truman quote).

[13] Ibid. at 630–31, 734–35; Trachtenberg, supra note 5, at 78–91.

[14] Arthur Schlesinger, The Imperial Presidency 135–36 (1973); Trachtenberg, supra note 5, at 85–125, 156 (figures on spending); and 5 Historical Statistics, supra note 1, at 5–367.

[15] Schlesinger, supra note 14, at 136–38.

[16] Youngstown Sheet & Tube Co. v. Sawyer, 343 U.S. 579, 587 (1952).

[17] Ibid. at 634–39 (Jackson, J., concurring).

[18] Louis Henkin, Foreign Affairs and the U.S. Constitution (1996); Harold Hongju Koh, The National Security Constitution: Sharing Power after the Iran-Contra Affair (1990); and Michael J. Glennon, Constitutional Diplomacy (1990).

19 Youngstown, 343 U.S. at 645 (Jackson, J., concurring). For useful discussion, see Jesse Choper, Judicial Review and the National Political Process: A Functional Reconsideration of the Role of the Supreme Court 315–25 (1980).

20 See 2 Stephen E. Ambrose, Eisenhower: The President 51 (1984); See also Burton I. Kaufman, The Korean War: Challenges in Crisis, Credibility, and Command 305 (1986).

21 Ibid. at 52.

22 Stephen Ambrose, Rise to Globalism: American Foreign Policy Since 1938, at 132–33 (6th ed. 1991).

23 Gaddis, Strategies, supra note 3, at 127–50.

24 Public Papers of the Presidents of the United States, Dwight D. Eisenhower 1955, at 209.

25 2 Ambrose, Eisenhower, supra note 20, at 232–33.

26 2 Ibid. at 239–45.

27 Quoted in Fisher, supra note 10, at 107–08.

28 H.J. Res. 117, 85th Cong. (1957).

29 Fred Greenstein, The Hidden-Hand Presidency: Eisenhower as Leader (1982).

30 On Kennedy's handling of these crises, see Lawrence Freedman, Kennedy's Wars: Berlin, Cuba, Laos, and Vietnam (2000); on the Kennedy administration's version of containment, see Gaddis, Strategies, supra note 3, at 198–236.

31 See John Yoo, Using Force, 71 University of Chicago Law Review (2004).

32 The events of the Cuban Missile Crisis have been exhaustively detailed in numerous books. See, e.g., Graham Allison & Philip Zelikow, Essence of Decision: Explaining the Cuban Missile Crisis (2d ed., 1999).

33 See, e.g., John Hart Ely, War and Responsibility: Constitutional Lessons of Vietnam and Its Aftermath 4 (1995).

34 The constitutional and legal issues on Vietnam are discussed in Ibid. at 12–46, 68–104.

35 Ibid. at 27–28. George Herring, America's Longest War: The United States and Vietnam, 1950–1975, at 135, 174–75, 243–44 (1985).

36 William H. Rehnquist, The Constitutional Issues—Administration Position, 45 New York University Law Review 628 (1970); and Herring, supra note 35, at 252–54.

37 See War Powers Resolution, Pub. L. No. 93-148, 87 Stat. 555 (codified at 50 U.S.C. §§ 1541–48). Presidents Ford and Carter never expressly recognized the resolution's binding force, and President Reagan refused to comply with the resolution when he ordered the use of force in Lebanon, Grenada, Libya, and the Persian Gulf. President George H. W. Bush sent messages notifying Congress of military interventions in Panama and the Persian Gulf that were "consistent with" the WPR, but that did not obey it. During the Gulf War, President Bush dispatched troops to the Middle East for well longer than permitted by the WPR's 60-day clock. President Bush sent troops to Saudi Arabia within days of the August 2, 1990, Iraqi invasion of Kuwait, and engaged in a buildup that reached more than 430,000 troops by November 8, but did not receive a congressional resolution of support until January 12, 1991, more than five months after the first American deployment. American troops invaded Kuwait and Iraq shortly thereafter. Even as he asked for a congres-

sional sign of support, President Bush argued that he already had the constitutional authority as President and Commander-in-Chief to implement UN Security Council Resolution 678, which asked member states to use "all necessary means" to force Iraqi troops out of Kuwait. When he signed Congress's joint resolution supporting the use of force to implement UN Resolution 678, H.R.J. Res. 77, 102d Cong., 1st Sess. (1991), Bush declared that "my signing this resolution does not constitute any change in the long-standing positions of the executive branch on either the President's constitutional authority to use the Armed Forces to defend vital U.S. interests or the constitutionality of the War Powers Resolution." Statement on Signing the Resolution Authorizing the Use of Military Force against Iraq, 27 Weekly Comp. Pres. Doc. 48 (Jan. 14, 1991). President Clinton followed this example in Somalia, Haiti, Bosnia, and Kosovo. John C. Yoo, Kosovo, War Powers, and the Multilateral Future, 148 University of Pennsylvania Law Review 1673, 1681 (2000); William Michael Treanor, "The War Powers Outside the Courts," 81 Ind. L.J. 1333 (2005) (former Clinton deputy assistant attorney general discussing Clinton OLC positions). For a view supporting the constitutionality of the War Powers Resolution, see John Hart Ely, War and Responsibility: Constitutional Lessons of Vietnam and Its Aftermath (1995); and Louis Fisher, Presidential War Power (2004).

[38] The historical writing on Reagan remains colored by the political controversies from the 1980s, which is not surprising, given that Reagan left office in 1989. Some of the journalistic accounts of his Presidency are helpful, especially Richard Reeves, President Reagan: The Triumph of Imagination (2005); and Lou Cannon, President Reagan: The Role of a Lifetime (1991). With Reagan's death, historians are beginning to provide more detail about his life and Presidency. See, e.g., John P. Diggins, Ronald Reagan: Freedom, Fate, and the Making of History (2008).

[39] John Lewis Gaddis, The Cold War: A New History (2005).

[40] 5 Historical Statistics, Millenial Edition, supra note 1, at 5–368 (Reagan defense spending); John Yoo, Politics as Laws?: The Anti-Ballistic Missile Treaty, the Separation of Powers, and Treaty Interpretation, 89 California Law Review 851 (2001) (discussion of the Strategic Defense Initiative); and Frances Fitzgerald, Way Out There in the Blue: Reagan, Star Wars and the End of the Cold War (2000).

[41] See Gaddis, supra note 39, at 223–28, 234–36.

[42] Fisher, supra note 10, at 140–45.

[43] Ibid. at 140–41.

[44] See, e.g., Sanchez-Espinoza v. Reagan, 770 F.2d 202 (D.C. Cir. 1985) (Central America); Crockett v. Reagan, 720 F.2d 1355 (D.C. Cir. 1983), cert. denied 467 U.S. 1251 (1984) (Central America); Lowry v. Reagan, 676 F.Supp. 333 (D.D.C. 1987), aff'd, No. 87-5426 (D.C. Cir. 1988) (per curiam) (Kuwaiti tankers operation).

[45] The story is told in Report of the Congressional Committees Investigating the Iran-Contra Affair, H. Rep. No. 433 & S. Rep. No. 216, 100th Cong., 1st Sess. (1987).

[46] CBS News, A Look Back at the Polls: Reagan's High Approval Rating Was Matched Only by Clinton and FDR, June 7, 2004, available at www.cbsnews.com/stories/2004/06/07/opinion/polls/main621632.shtml.

[47] Fisher, supra note 10, at 149–51.

[48] The events and Bush's perspectives are retold in George H.W. Bush & Brent Scowcroft, A World Transformed (1999).

[49] Ely, supra note 33, at 3.

50 For current data on Germany, Japan, and Italy, see Central Intelligence Agency, The World Factbook, at www.cia.gov/library/publications/the-world-factbook/index.html. For earlier data, see U.S. Census Bureau, International Data Base, Country summaries, at www.census.gov/ipc/www/idb/summaries.html.

51 See William Howell, Power without Persuasion: The Politics of Direct Presidential Action (2003); and David Epstein & Sharyn O'Halloran, Delegating Powers: A Transaction Cost Politics Approach to Policy Making under Separate Powers (1999).

52 Richard Neustadt, Presidential Power 5–6 (1960); see also Theodore Lowi, The Personal President: Power Invested, Promise Unfulfilled (1985); Stephen Skowronek, The Politics Presidents Make: Presidential Leadership from John Adams to George Bush (1993); and Thomas E. Cronin & Michael A. Genovese, The Paradoxes of the American Presidency (2003). On the President's legislative program, see Andrew Rudalevige, Managing the President's Program: Presidential Leadership and Legislative Policy Formation (2002).

53 The trend toward broad delegation is criticized on constitutional political grounds by Theodore Lowi, The End of Liberalism: The Second Republic of the United States (2d ed. 1979); Martin H. Redish, The Constitution as Political Structure 135–61 (1995); David Schoenbrod, Power Without Responsibility: How Congress Abuses the People Through Delegation (1993), and on constitutional law grounds by Larry Alexander & Saikrishna Prakash, Reports of the Nondelegation Doctrine's Death are Greatly Exaggerated, 70 University of Chicago Law Review 1297 (2003); and Gary Lawson, Delegation and Original Meaning, 88 Virginia Law Review 327 (2002). For a defense, see Eric Posner & Adrian Vermeule, Interring the Nondelegation Doctrine, 69 University of Chicago Law Review 1721 (2002).

54 See Elena Kagan, Presidential Administration, 114 Harvard Law Review 2245, 2277–88 (2001).

55 The classic explanation of OMB cost-benefit review remains Christopher C. DeMuth & Douglas H. Ginsburg, White House Review of Agency Rulemaking, 99 Harvard Law Review 1075 (1986). For a more recent investigation, see Steven Croley, White House Review of Agency Rulemaking: An Empirical Investigation, 70 University of Chicago Law Review 821 (2003). A description of the Reagan administration's overall approach to the constitutional issues can be found in Terry Eastland, Energy in the Executive: The Case for the Strong Presidency (1992). For criticism of the constitutional reach of White House cost-benefit analysis, see Richard H. Pildes & Cass R. Sunstein, Reinventing the Regulatory State, 62 University of Chicago Law Review 1, 25 (1995).

56 See generally The Executive Office of the President: A Historical, Biographical, and Bibliographic Guide (Harold C. Relyea ed., 1997).

57 See Kenneth Mayer, With the Stroke of a Pen: Executive Orders and Presidential Power (2001) (describing growth of executive orders); and Curtis Bradley & Eric Posner, Presidential Signing Statements and Executive Power, 23 Const. Commentary 307 (2006).

58 2 Ambrose, supra note 20, at 190.

59 Ibid.

60 2 Ibid. at 419–23.

⁶¹ See David E. Lewis, Presidents and the Politics of Agency Design: Political Insulation in the United States Government Bureaucracy, 1946–1997, at 21–38 (2003).

⁶² See Christopher Yoo, Steven Calabresi & Anthony Colangelo, The Unitary Executive in the Modern Era, 90 Iowa Law Review 601, 633–34 (2005).

⁶³ Ethics in Government Act of 1978, Pub. L. No. 95-521, tit. VI, 92 Stat. 1824, 1867 (1978). The independent counsel provision was reauthorized in 1983, 1987, and 1994. See Ethics in Government Act Amendments of 1982, Pub. L. No. 97-409, 96 Stat. 2039 (1983); Independent Counsel Reauthorization Act of 1987, Pub. L. No. 100-191, 101 Stat. 1293 (1987); and Independent Counsel Reauthorization Act of 1994, Pub. L. No. 103-270, 108 Stat. 732 (1994). See William K. Kelley, The Constitutional Dilemma of Litigation under the Independent Counsel System, 83 Minnesota Law Review 1197 (1999) (discussing constitutional issues raised by independent counsels); Ken Gormley, An Original Model of the Independent Counsel Statute, 97 Michigan Law Review 601 (1999) (describing history); and Julie O'Sullivan, The Independent Counsel Statute: Bad Law, Bad Policy, 33 American Criminal Law Review 463 (1996).

⁶⁴ Inspectors General Act of 1978, Pub. L. No. 95-452, § 3, 92 Stat. 1101, 1102; see also Paul C. Light, Monitoring Government: Inspectors General and the Search for Accountability (1993).

⁶⁵ See National Emergencies Act, Pub. L. No. 94-412, 90 Stat. 1255 (1976); International Emergency Economic Powers Act, Pub. L. No. 95-223, 91 Stat. 1626 (1977); Foreign Intelligence Surveillance Act, Pub. L. No. 95-511, 92 Stat. 1783 (1978); and Intelligence Oversight Act of 1980, Pub. L. No. 96-450, 94 Stat. 1975; and Case-Zablocki Act, 1 U.S.C. § 112b (1972).

⁶⁶ Buckley v. Valeo, 424 U.S. 1 (1976).

⁶⁷ Federal Election Campaign Act of 1971, Pub. L. No. 92-225, 86 Stat. 3 (1972) (codified as amended in 47 U.S.C.); Presidential Records Act, 44 U.S.C. § 2201; Freedom of Information Act, 5 U.S.C. § 552 (1995); Privacy Act, 5 U.S.C. § 552a. Government in the Sunshine Act, 5 U.S.C. § 552b (1995); and Federal Advisory Committee Act, 5 U.S.C.A. App. § 1 (1995).

⁶⁸ See generally Steven G. Calabresi & Christopher Yoo, The Unitary Executive (2009).

⁶⁹ See Koh, supra note 18, at 117–33.

⁷⁰ Dames & Moore v. Regan, 453 U.S. 654 (1981).

⁷¹ INS v. Chadha, 462 U.S. 919 (1983).

⁷² Bowsher v. Synar, 478 U.S. 714, 722, 726–27 (1986).

⁷³ In re Sealed Case, 838 F.2d 476 (D.C. Cir. 1988).

⁷⁴ Brief for the United States as Amicus Curiae Supporting Appellees, Morrison v. Olson, No. 87-1279, 1988 WL 1031600 (April 8, 1988).

⁷⁵ Morrison v. Olson, 487 U.S. 654, 691–96 (1988).

⁷⁶ See Richard A. Posner, An Affair of State: the Investigation, Impeachment, and Trial of President Clinton (2000).

⁷⁷ See generally Mark J. Rozell, Executive Privilege: Presidential Power, Secrecy, and Accountability (2d ed., 2002). For an older, less balanced approach, see Raoul Berger, Executive Privilege: A Constitutional Myth (1974).

78 Letter to the Secretary of Defense Directing Him to Withhold Certain Information from the Senate Committee on Government Operations, May 17, 1954, Public Papers of the Presidents of the United States, Dwight D. Eisenhower 1954, at 483.

79 Rozell, supra note 77, at 38–40 (describing executive privilege claims of Truman and Eisenhower); Greenstein, supra note 29, at 205–08 (discussing Eisenhower's indirect attack on McCarthyism).

80 Rozell, supra note 77, at 60–61. James T. Patterson, Grand Expectations: The United States, 1945–1974, at 775–78 (1997); Stephen E. Ambrose, Nixon: Ruin and Recover, 1973–1990, at 289–445 (1992); and Stanley I. Kutler, The Wars of Watergate: the Last Crisis of Richard Nixon 443–550 (1992).

81 United States v. Nixon, 418 U.S. 683, 703–13 (1974).

82 See generally Lucas A. Powe, Jr., The Warren Court and American Politics (2000).

83 Brown v. Board of Education, 347 U.S. 483 (1954); Brown v. Board of Education II, 349 U.S. 294 (1955). On the resistance to Brown and the reaction of the Civil Rights Movement and Congress, see Michael Klarman, From Jim Crow to Civil Rights: The Supreme Court and the Struggle for Racial Equality (2004).

84 Cooper v. Aaron, 358 U.S. 1, 18 (1958).

85 See Powe, supra note 82, at 485–501. For prominent defenses of the Warren Court, see Jesse H. Choper, Judicial Review and the National Political Process: A Functional Reconsideration of the Role of the Supreme Court 60–128 (1980); John Hart Ely, Democracy and Distrust: A Theory of Judicial Review (1980).

86 See generally Allen J. Matusow, The Unraveling of America: A History of Liberalism in the 1960s (1985).

87 Powe, supra note 82, at 495 (quoting Goldwater).

88 Ibid. at 474 (quoting Nixon); see also Ibid. at 467–75 (Fortas nomination).

89 See generally Bernard Schwartz, The Ascent of Pragmatism: The Burger Court in Action (1989); and The Burger Court: Counter-Revolution or Confirmation (Bernard Schwartz ed., 1998).

90 Eastland, supra note 55, at 236 (quoting Reagan); David A. Yalof, Pursuit of Justices: Presidential Politics and the Selection of Supreme Court Nominees 97–98, 133–35 (1999); see also Henry Abraham, Justices, Presidents, and Senators (2001).

91 See generally David Yalof, Pursuit of Justices: Presidential Politics and the Selection of Supreme Court Nominees (1999); Henry J. Abraham, Justices, Presidents and Senators: A History of the U.S. Supreme Court Appointments Process from Washington to Clinton (1999); and Lee Epstein & Jeffrey Segal, Advice and Consent: The Politics of Judicial Appointments (2007).

92 Federalist No. 76, at 510–11 (Alexander Hamilton) (Jacob E. Cooke ed., 1961). On the appointments process for Supreme Court justices, see Stephen Carter, The Confirmation Mess, 101 Harvard Law Review 1185 (1988); John McGinnis, The President, the Senate, the Constitution and the Confirmation Process, 71 Texas Law Review 633 (1993); Henry Monaghan, The Confirmation Process: Law or Politics?, 101 Harvard Law Review 1202 (1988); Robert F. Nagel, Advice, Consent, and Influence, 84 Northwestern University Law Review 858 (1990); David A. Strauss & Cass R. Sunstein, The Senate, the Constitution, and the Confirmation Process, 101 Yale Law Journal 1491 (1992); and John C. Yoo, Choosing Justices: A Political Appointments Process and the Wages of Judicial Supremacy, 98 Michigan Law Review 1436 (2000).

[93] See, e.g., City of Boerne v. Flores, 521 U.S. 507 (1997). For criticism of the modern version of judicial supremacy, see Saikrishna B. Prakash & John Yoo, Against Interpretational Supremacy, 103 Michigan Law Review 1539 (2005).

CHAPTER 9: THE ONCE AND FUTURE PRESIDENCY

[1] James L. Sundquist, The Decline and Resurgence of Congress (1981).

[2] See, e.g., Richard E. Neustadt, Presidential Power from FDR to Carter (1980 ed.); Arthur M. Schlesinger, Jr., The Imperial Presidency (1973); James L. Sundquist, The Decline and Resurgence of Congress (1981); William G. Howell, Power without Persuasion: The Politics of Direct Presidential Action (2003); Peter Irons, War Powers: How the Imperial Presidency Hijacked the Constitution (2005); Andrew Rudalvige, The New Imperial Presidency: Renewing Presidential Power after Watergate (2006); Jack L. Goldsmith, The Terror Presidency: Law and Judgment Inside the Bush Administration (2007); and Charlie Savage, Takeover: The Return of the Imperial Presidency and the Subversion of American Democracy (2007).

[3] Compare Samuel Huntington, American Politics: The Promise of Disharmony 75–77 (1981).

[4] Thomas E. Cronin & Michael A. Genovese, The Paradoxes of the American Presidency (2d ed. 2004).

[5] See Jeffrey K. Tulis, The Rhetorical Presidency (1987); Theodore J. Lowi, The Personal President: Power Invested, Promise Unfulfilled (1986).

[6] See Marc Landy & Sidney M. Milkis, Presidential Greatness (2000); and Sidney M. Milkis, The President and the Parties: The Transformation of the American Party System since the New Deal (1993).

[7] Cf. Stephen Skowronek, The Politics Presidents Make: Leadership from John Adams to Bill Clinton (1997).

[8] David Epstein & Sharyn O'Halloran, Delegating Powers: A Transaction Cost Politics Approach to Policy Making under Separate Powers (1999).

[9] For works in this vein, see William G. Howell, Power without Persuasion: The Politics of Direct Presidential Action (2003); Kenneth R. Mayer, With the Stroke of a Pen: Executive Orders and Presidential Power (2001); Charles M. Cameron, Veto Bargaining: Presidents and the Politics of Negative Power (2000); Terry M. Moe, Presidents, Institutions, and Theory, in George C. Edwards, et al., Researching the Presidency: Vital Questions, New Approaches (1993); and Terry M. Moe, The Politicized Presidency, in John E. Chubb & Paul E. Peterson eds., The New Direction in American Politics 238 (1985).

[10] See, e.g., Howell, supra note 9; Cameron, supra note 9.

[11] Stephen Skowronek, The Politics Presidents Make: Leadership from John Adams to Bill Clinton (1997). For a further articulation of his theory, see Stephen Skowronek, Presidential Leadership in Political Time: Reprise and Reappraisal (1997).

[12] Walter Dean Burnham, Critical Elections and the Mainsprings of American Politics (1970).

[13] Authorization to Use Military Force, Pub. L. No. 107-40, 115 Stat. 224 (2001).

[14] Authorization for Use of Military Force against Iraq Resolution of 2002, H.R.J. Res. 114, 107th Cong. § 3, 116 Stat. 1498 (2002).

[15] Pub. L. 110-55, 121 Stat. 552 (2007).

16   Charlie Savage, Bush Challenges Hundreds of Laws: President Cites Powers of His Office, Boston Globe, Apr. 20, 2006, at A1; American Bar Association, Task Force on Presidential Signing Statements and the Separation of Powers Doctrine, www.abanet.org/op/signingstatements; and Jonathan Weisman, Bush's Challenges of Laws He Signed Is Criticized, Wash. Post, June 28, 2006, at A9. For earlier defenses of the practice, see Mark Killenbeck, A Matter of Mere Approval?: The Role of the President in the Creation of Legislative History, 48 Ark. L. Rev. 239 (1995) (defending signing statements as legitimate under text and history of Constitution); Daniel B. Rodriguez, Statutory Interpretation and Political Advantage, 12 Int'l Rev. Law & Econ. 217 (1992); Frank B. Cross, The Constitutional Legitimacy and Significance of Presidential "Signing Statements," 40 Admin. L. Rev. 209 (1988). For early criticism, see Kathryn Marie Dessayer, Note, The First Word: The President's Place in "Legislative History," 89 Mich. L. Rev. 399 (1990); William D. Popkin, Judicial Use of Presidential Legislative History: A Critique, 66 Ind. L.J. 699 (1991); Marc N. Garber & Kurt A. Wimmer, President Signing Statements as Interpretation of Legislative Intent: An Executive Aggrandizement of Power, 24 Harv. J. Legis. 363 (1987).

17   See Curtis A. Bradley & Eric A. Posner, Presidential Signing Statements and Executive Power, 23 Const. Comment. 307, 309–15 (2007).

18   Ibid. at 324–34.

19   See American Bar Association, Task Force on Presidential Signing Statements and the Separation of Powers Doctrine, available at www.abanet.org/op/signingstatements.

20   See John Yoo, The Powers of War and Peace: The Constitution and Foreign Affairs after 9/11, at 182–214 (2005).

21   Federalist No. 70, at 472 (Alexander Hamilton) (Clinton Rossiter ed., 1961).

22   Youngstown Sheet & Tube Co. v. Sawyer, 343 U.S. 579, 637 (1952) (Jackson, J., concurring).

23   See, e.g., Boumediene v. Bush, 128 S. Ct. 2229 (2008). See also J. Andrew Kent, "A Textual and Historical Case Against a Global Constitution," 95 Geo. L.J. 463 (2007) (presidents have unvaryingly declined to confer constitutional rights or habeas corpus review on aliens abroad).

24   See John Yoo, War by Other Means: An Insider's Account of the War on Terrorism (2006).

AFTERWORD

1   Rahm Emanuel, Speech on "Era of Reform" at the Wall Street Journal CEO Council in Washington, D.C., Nov. 19, 2008.

2   See Bureau of Economic Analysis, Gross Domestic Product Estimates (June 25, 2009), available at www.bea.gov/newsreleases/national/gdp/gdpnewsrelease.htm.

3   Mark Hulbert, "2008 by the Numbers," Market Watch, Dec. 31, 2008, available at www.marketwatch.com/story/a-review-of-the-stock-market-in-2008 (reporting that the Dow dropped 33.8% in 2008).

4   Bureau of Labor Statistics, Chart 1: Unemployment Rate May 2007–May 2009 (June 5, 2009), available at www.bls.gov/news.release/pdf/empsit.pdf (reporting an increase in unemployment from 7% in December 2008 to 9.5% in June 2009).

5   Bureau of Labor Statistics, Employment Status of the Civilian Noninstitutional Population, 1940 to date, available at www.bls.gov/cps/cpsaat1.pdf.

6   Mark Mazzetti & Eric Schmitt, "Shaky Pakistan Is Seen as Target of Qaeda Plots," N.Y. Times, May 11, 2009, at A1.

7   Choe Sang-Hun, "North Korea Claims to Conduct 2nd Nuclear Test," N.Y. Times, May 25, 2009, at A1.

8   Glenn R. Simpson & Jay Solomon, "Fresh Clues of Iranian Nuclear Intrigue," Wall St. J., Jan. 16, 2009, at A1.

9   Election Results 2008, Wash. Post, available at www.washingtonpost.com/wp-srv/politics/interactives/campaign08.

10   See U.S. Electoral College, Historical Election Results, available at www.archives.gov/federal-register/electoral-college/scores.html.

11   See generally Stephen Skowronek, The Politics Presidents Make: Leadership from John Adams to Bill Clinton (1997).

12   Obama promised to "cut[] taxes below the level under Ronald Reagan while restoring fiscal responsibility." See Obama '08, Barack Obama's Comprehensive Tax Plan, available at www.barackobama.com/pdf/taxes/Factsheet_Tax_Plan_FINAL.pdf.

13   Remarks of President Barack Obama—As Prepared for Delivery Address to Joint Session of Congress, Feb. 24, 2009, available at www.whitehouse.gov/the_press_office/remarks-of-president-barack-obama-address-to-joint-session-of-congress.

14   California Secretary of State, Statement of Vote: Nov. 4, 2008, at 8, available at www.sos.ca.gov/elections/sov/2008_general/sov_complete.pdf.

15   Ibid. at 13.

16   Barack Obama, Interview with Reverend Rick Warren at Saddleback Presidential Candidates Forum, Aug. 17, 2008, available at http://transcripts.cnn.com/TRANSCRIPTS/0808/17/se.01.html.

17   Susan Davis, "Obama Condemns Supreme Court Decision in Child Rape Case," Washington Wire, June 25, 2008, available at blogs.wsj.com/washwire/2008/06/25/obama-condemns-supreme-court-decision-in-child-rape-case.

18   Message from the President and Notice of Continuation of the National Emergency with Respect to the Stabilization of Iraq, May 20, 2009, available at www.whitehouse.gov/the_press_office/Message-from-the-President-and-Notice-of-Continuation-regarding-Iraq. See also Statement by the President on Afghanistan, Feb. 17, 2009, available at www.whitehouse.gov/the_press_office/Statement-by-the-President-on-Afghanistan.

19   A New Year, A New Beginning, Mar. 19, 2009, available at www.whitehouse.gov/Nowruz. See also Statement by the President from Prague, Czech Republic, Apr. 5, 2009, available at www.whitehouse.gov/the_press_office/Statement-by-the-President-North-Korea-launch. For a response to President Obama's diplomacy efforts, see Ali Khamenei, Response to President Obama's Nowruz Statement: Change in Words is Not Enough, Mar. 23, 2009, available at www.memritv.org/clip/en/2059.htm.

20   Election Guide 2008, Pennsylvania Primary Results, N.Y. Times, available at http://politics.nytimes.com/election-guide/2008/results/states/PA.html.

21   Carl Hulse, "In Open Nomination, 'Superdelegates' May Hold Key to Victory," N.Y. Times, Jan. 28, 2008, available at www.nytimes.com/2008/01/28/us/politics/

28superdelegates.html.; see also Adam Nagourney & Carl Hulse, "Neck and Neck, Democrats Woo Superdelegates," N.Y. Times, Feb. 10, 2008, available at www. nytimes.com/2008/02/10/us/politics/10superdelegates.html.

22 Election Guide 2008, California Primary Results, N.Y. Times, available at http:// politics.nytimes.com/election-guide/2008/results/states/CA.html.

23 2 The Records of the Federal Convention of 1787, at 29, 31 (Max Farrand ed., 1911).

24 Federalist No. 68, at 460 (Alexander Hamilton) (Jacob E. Cooke ed., 1961).

25 Robert Rutland, The Presidency of James Madison 110 (1990).

26 See Robert V. Remini, Andrew Jackson (1977–84).

27 See, e.g., Kenneth A. Shepsle & Barry R. Weingast, Political Preferences for the Pork Barrel: A Generalization, 25 American Journal of Political Science 96 (1981); and Mancur Olson, The Logic of Collective Action: Public Goods and the Theory of Groups (1965).

28 See Elbert Smith, The Presidency of James Buchanan (1975).

29 See Robert Rutland, The Presidency of James Madison (1990).

30 See Larry Gara, The Presidency of Franklin Pierce (1991).

31 See Albert Castel, The Presidency of Andrew Johnson (1979).

32 See Elbert Smith, The Presidencies of Zachary Taylor and Millard Fillmore (1988).

33 See Richard Small, The Presidency of Richard Nixon (2003); see generally Leonard Leo & James Taranto eds., Presidential Leadership: Rating the Best and Worst in the White House (2005) (providing rankings of presidents).

34 See Martin Fausold, The Presidency of Herbert Hoover (1988).

35 See Kendrick Clements, The Presidency of Woodrow Wilson (1992).

36 Federalist No. 70, at 472 (Alexander Hamilton) (Jacob E. Cooke ed., 1961).

37 Executive Order, Review and Disposition of Individuals Detained at the Guantanamo Bay Naval Base and Closure of Detention Facilities, Jan. 22, 2009, available at www.whitehouse.gov/the_press_office/ClosureOfGuantanamoDetentionFacilities.

38 Executive Order, Ensuring Lawful Interrogations, Jan. 22, 2009, available at www. whitehouse.gov/the_press_office/EnsuringLawfulInterrogations.

39 Executive Order, Review and Disposition of Individuals Detained at the Guantanamo Bay Naval Base and Closure of Detention Facilities, supra note 37.

40 Department of Justice, Press Release #09-232 Withdrawing "Enemy Combatant" Definition for Guantanamo Detainees, Mar. 13, 2009, available at www.usdoj.gov/ opa/pr/2009/March/09-ag-232.html.

41 See Remarks by the President on National Security, May 21, 2009, available at www. whitehouse.gov/the_press_office/Remarks-by-the-President-On-National-Security-5-21-09 and Remarks by Richard B. Cheney at the American Enterprise Institute for Public Policy Research, May 21, 2009, available at www.aei.org/speech/ 100050.

42 Michael Hayden & Michael B. Mukasey, "The President Ties His Own Hands on Terror," Wall St. J., Apr. 17, 2009, at A13 (explaining that "fully half of the government's knowledge about the structure and activities of al Qaeda came from [enhanced] interrogations").

43 See John Yoo, War by Other Means: An Insider's Account of the War on Terror 165–203 (2006).

44 Memorandum for the Attorney General, Secretary of Defense, Secretary of State, Secretary of Homeland Security, and Director of National Intelligence, From: President Barack Obama, Re: Review of the Detention of Ali Saleh Kahlah al-Marri (Jan. 22, 2009), available at www.whitehouse.gov/the_press_office/ReviewoftheDetention ofAliSalehKahlah.

45 Executive Order, Ensuring Lawful Interrogations, supra note 38.

46 See Yoo, War by Other Means, supra note 43, at 18–48.

47 Executive Order, Ensuring Lawful Interrogations, supra note 38; U.S. Army Interrogation Field Manual 34–52 (May 8, 1987).

48 Memorandum for the Vice President, Secretary of State, Secretary of Defense, Attorney General, Chief of Staff to the President, Direct of the Central Intelligence, Assistant to the President for National Security Affairs, and Chairman of the Joint Chief of Staffs, From: President George W. Bush, Re: Humane Treatment of al Qaeda and Taliban Detainees (Feb. 7, 2002), available at www.dod.gov/pubs/foi/detainees/dia_previous_releases/fourth_release/DIAfourth_release.pdf.

49 For example, according to former CIA Director George Tenet, 9/11 mastermind Khalid Sheikh Mohammed said, "I'll talk to you guys after I get to New York and see my lawyer," after being captured. See George Tenet, 60 Minutes Interview with Scott Pelley, April 29, 2007.

50 For discussion of the trial, see Yoo, War by Other Means, supra note 43, at 210–17.

51 Barack Obama, Inaugural Address (Jan. 21, 2009), available at www.whitehouse.gov/blog/inaugural-address.

52 The Department of Justice asserted the state secrets privilege to defend the NSA surveillance program. See, e.g., Government Defendants' Memorandum in Support of Motion to Dismiss and For Summary Judgment, Jewel v. National Security Agency, No. C:08-cv-4373-VRW, (June 25, 2009) (arguing that the case must be dismissed because Congress has not waived sovereign immunity for plaintiffs' statutory claims, and state secrets are needed to litigate plaintiffs' claims).

53 Tim Reid, "President Obama 'orders Pakistan drone attacks,'" Times Online, Jan. 23, 2009, available at www.timesonline.co.uk/tol/news/world/us_and_americas/article5575883.ece. See also Mark Mazzetti & Eric Schmitt, "Shaky Pakistan Is Seen as Target of Qaeda Plots," N.Y. Times, May 11, 2009, at A1 (reporting that the "United States has conducted 17 drone attacks [from January to May 2009] compared with 36 strikes in all of 2008").

54 Statement of President Barack Obama on Military Commissions (May 15, 2009), available at www.whitehouse.gov/the_press_office/Statement-of-President-Barack-Obama-on-Military-Commissions.

55 Stephen Ambrose, Rise to Globalism: American Foreign Policy Since 1938, at 132–33 (6th ed. 1991).

56 John Lewis Gaddis, Strategies of Containment: A Critical Appraisal of Postwar American National Security Policy 127–97 (1982).

57 Remarks by the President on a New Strategy for Afghanistan and Pakistan, Mar. 27, 2009, available at www.whitehouse.gov/the_press_office/Remarks-by-the-President-on-a-New-Strategy-for-Afghanistan-and-Pakistan.

58 See Military Commissions Act of 2006 ("MCA"), § 3, 10 U.S.C. § 948c.

[59] David M. Herszenhorn, "Funds to Close Guantanamo Denied," N.Y. Times, May 20, 2009.

[60] See Letter from the President to the Speaker of the House of Representatives, Re: Request for Supplemental Appropriations for the Armed Forces, April 9, 2009, available at www.whitehouse.gov/the_press_office/Text-of-Letter-from-the-President-to-the-Speaker-of-the-House-of-Representatives (requesting supplemental appropriations to fund military, diplomatic, and intelligence operations in Iraq, Pakistan, and Afghanistan).

BIBLIOGRAPHY

———•———

PRIMARY SOURCES

Abraham Lincoln Speeches and Writings, 1832–1858 (Don E. Fehrenbacher ed., 1989).

Annals of Congress (Joseph Gales ed., 1789).

Blackstone, William. Commentaries on the Laws of England (1765–69).

Compilation of the Messages and Papers of the Presidents: 1789–1897 (James Richardson ed., 1900).

The Complete Anas of Thomas Jefferson (Franklin B. Sawvel ed., 1903).

The Complete Anti-Federalist (Herbert J. Storing ed., 1981).

Documentary History of the First Federal Congress, 1789–1791 (Charlene Bangs Bickford et al. eds., 2004).

Documentary History of the Ratification of the Constitution (John P. Kaminski & Gaspare J. Saladino eds., 1986)

The Federal and State Constitutions, Colonial Charters, and Other Organic Laws of the States, Territories, and Colonies (Francis N. Thorpe ed., 1909).

Hamilton, Alexander, John Jay & James Madison. The Federalist Papers (1787–88) (Jacob E. Cooke ed., 1961).

John Marshall's Defense of McCulloch v. Maryland (Gerald Gunther ed., 1969).

Locke, John. Two Treatises of Government (1690) (J. W. Gough ed., 3d ed., 1966).

Montesquieu, Charles Louis de Secondat, Baron. Spirit of the Laws (1748) (Thomas Nugent trans., 1949).

The Papers of Alexander Hamilton (Harold Syrett ed., 1965).

The Papers of James Madison (Robert A. Rutland et al. eds., 1975–85).

The Papers of John Adams (Robert J. Taylor ed., 1979).

The Papers of Thomas Jefferson (Julian P. Boyd ed., 1950).

The Popular Sources of Political Authority: Documents on the Massachusetts Constitution of 1780 (Oscar Handlin & Mary Handlin eds., 1966).

The Public Papers and Addresses of Franklin D. Roosevelt (Samuel I. Rosenman ed., 1938–1950).

Public Papers of the Presidents of the United States, Dwight D. Eisenhower (1955).

The Records of the Federal Convention of 1787 (Max Farrand ed., 1911).

de Tocqueville, Alexis. Democracy in America (1835).

Union and Liberty: The Political Philosophy of John C. Calhoun (Ross M. Lence ed., 1992).

Works of Alexander Hamilton (Henry Cabot Lodge ed., 1904).

Writings of George Washington (John C. Fitzpatrick ed., 1939).

Writings of Thomas Jefferson (Paul Leicester Ford et al. eds., 1903–04).

MONOGRAPHS

Abraham, Henry. Justices, Presidents, and Senators (2001).

Acheson, Dean. Present at the Creation: My Years in the State Department (1969).

Ackerman, Bruce. The Failure of the Founding Fathers: Jefferson, Marshall, and the Rise of Presidential Democracy (2005).

Adams, Henry. History of the United States of America during the Administrations of Thomas Jefferson (1889–91) (Library of America ed., 1986).

Adams, Willi Paul. The First American Constitutions: Republican Ideology and the Making of the State Constitutions in the Revolutionary Era (1980).

Adler, David Grady. The President's Pardon Power, in Thomas E. Cronin, ed., Inventing the American Presidency (1989).

Allison, Graham & Philip Zelikow. Essence of Decision: Explaining the Cuban Missile Crisis (2d ed., 1999).

Alsop, Joseph & Turner Catledge. The 168 Days (1938).

Amar, Akhil Reed. America's Constitution: A Biography (2005).

Ambrose, Stephen E. Eisenhower: The President (1984).

Ambrose, Stephen E. Nixon: Ruin and Recovery, 1973–1990 (1992).

Ambrose, Stephen E. Rise to Globalism: American Foreign Policy Since 1938 (6th ed., 1991).

Andrew, Christopher. For the President's Eyes Only (1995).

Appleby, Joyce. Thomas Jefferson (2003).

Arnold, Peri. Making the Managerial Presidency: Comprehensive Reorganization Planning, 1905–1996 (1986).

Bailey, Jeremy D. Thomas Jefferson and Executive Power (2007).

Bailyn, Bernard. Intellectual Origins of the American Revolution (1967).

Banning, Lance. The Sacred Fire of Liberty: James Madison and the Founding of the Federal Republic (1996).

Barber, James D. Presidential Character: Predicting Performance in the White House (4th ed., 1992).

Belz, Herman. Lincoln and the Constitution: The Dictatorship Question Reconsidered (1984).

Bemis, Samuel F. The Diplomacy of the American Revolution (1957).

Bemis, Samuel F. Jay's Treaty (1923).

Les Benedict, Michael. The Constitution of the Lincoln Presidency and the Republican Era, in Martin Fausold & Alan Shank, eds., The Constitution and the American Presidency (1991).

Bergeron, Paul. The Presidency of James K. Polk (1987).

Bernanke, Ben. Essays on the Great Depression (2000).

Bessette, Joseph M. & Jeffrey Tulis, eds. The Presidency in the Constitutional Order (1981).

Black, Conrad. Franklin Delano Roosevelt: Champion of Freedom (2005).

Brant, Irving. James Madison: The President, 1809–1812 (1956).

Brinkley, Alan. The End of Reform: New Deal Liberalism in Recession and War (1996).

Brinkley, Alan. Voices of Protest: Huey Long, Father Coughlin, and the Great Depression (1983).

Burnham, Walter D. Critical Elections and the Mainsprings of American Politics (1970).

Burns, James MacGregor. The Deadlock of Democracy (1963).

Burns, James MacGregor. FDR: Soldier of Freedom 1940–1945 (1970).

Burns, James MacGregor. Presidential Government (1965).

Burns, James MacGregor. Roosevelt: The Lion and the Fox 1882–1940 (1956).

Bush, George H. W. & Brent Scowcroft. A World Transformed (1999).

Caesar, James W. Presidential Selection: Theory and Development (1979).

Calabresi, Steven G. & Yoo, Christopher S. The Unitary Executive (2009).

Cameron, Charles M. Veto Bargaining: Presidents and the Politics of Negative Power (2000).

Cannon, Lou. President Reagan: The Role of a Lifetime (1991).

Casper, Gerhard. Separating Power: Essays on the Founding Period (1997).

Choper, Jesse. Judicial Review and the National Political Process: A Functional Reconsideration of the Role of the Supreme Court (1980).

Cohen, Eliot. Supreme Command: Soldiers, Statesmen, and Leadership in Wartime (2002).

Cole, Donald B. The Presidency of Andrew Jackson (1993).

Combs, Jerald A. The Jay Treaty: Political Battleground of the Founding Fathers (1970).

Cooper, John M. The Warrior and the Priest: Woodrow Wilson and Theodore Roosevelt (1983).

Cooper, Phillip J. By Order of the President: The Use and Abuse of Executive Direct Action (2002).

Corwin, Edward S. The President: Office and Powers, 1789–1984 (Randall W. Bland et al. eds., 1984).

Cronin, Thomas E. The Paradoxes of the American Presidency (2003).

Cunningham, Noble E., Jr. The Process of Government Under Jefferson (1978).

Currie, David. The Constitution in Congress: The Federalist Period 1789–1801 (1997).

Cushman, Barry. Rethinking the New Deal Court: The Structure of a Constitutional Revolution (1998).

Dallek, Robert. Franklin D. Roosevelt and American Foreign Policy, 1932–45 (1979).

Davis, Kenneth S. FDR: The War President, 1940–43 (2000).

DeConde, Alexander. Entangling Alliance: Politics & Diplomacy under George Washington (1958).

Dickinson, Matthew. Bitter Harvest: FDR, Presidential Power, and the Growth of the Presidential Branch (1996).

Diggins, John P. Ronald Reagan: Freedom, Fate, and the Making of History (2008).

Divine, Robert. The Illusion of Neutrality (1962).

Donald, David. Lincoln (1995).

Donald, David. Lincoln Reconsidered: Essays on the Civil War Era (1947).

Eastland, Terry. Energy in the Executive: The Case for the Strong Presidency (1992).

Edwards, George C., et al. Researching the Presidency: Vital Questions, New Approaches (1993).

Eichengreen, Barry. Golden Fetters: The Gold Standard and the Great Depression, 1919–1939 (1995).

Eisenhower, John S.D. So Far From God: The U.S. War With Mexico, 1846–1848 (2000).

Elkins, Stanley & Eric L. McKitrick. The Age of Federalism: The Early American Republic, 1788–1800 (1993).

Ely, John Hart. War and Responsibility: Constitutional Lessons of Vietnam and Its Aftermath (1995).

Epstein, David & Sharyn O'Halloran. Delegating Powers: A Transaction Cost Politics Approach to Policy Making under Separate Powers (1999).

Epstein, Lee & Jeffrey Segal. Advice and Consent: The Politics of Judicial Appointments (2007).

Evans, Peter, et al., eds., Bringing the State Back In (1985).

Farber, Daniel. Lincoln's Constitution (2003).

Fisher, Louis. Constitutional Conflicts Between Congress and the President (5th ed., 2007).

Fisher, Louis. Military Tribunals & Presidential Power: American Revolution to the War on Terrorism (2005).

Fisher, Louis. The Politics of Executive Privilege (2003).

Fisher, Louis. Presidential War Power (1995).

Fitzgerald, Frances. Way Out There in the Blue: Reagan, Star Wars and the End of the Cold War (2000).

Flexner, James T. Washington and the New Nation (1970).

Foner, Eric. Reconstruction: America's Unfinished Revolution 1863–1877 (1988).

Freedman, Lawrence. Kennedy's Wars: Berlin, Cuba, Laos, and Vietnam (2000).

Freidel, Frank. Franklin D. Roosevelt: A Rendezvous with Destiny (1991).

Friedman, Milton & Anna Schwartz. A Monetary History of the United States, 1867–1960 (1963).

Gaddis, John Lewis. The Cold War: A New History (2005).

Gaddis, John Lewis. Strategies of Containment: A Critical Appraisal of Postwar American National Security Policy (1982).

Gaddis, John Lewis. Surprise, Security, and the American Experience (2004).

Galbraith, John Kenneth. The Great Crash 1929 (2d ed., 1961).

Genovese, Michael A. The Power of the American Presidency: 1789–2000 (2000).

Gerhardt, Michael J. The Power of Precedent (2008).

Glennon, Michael J. Constitutional Diplomacy (1990).

Goldsmith, Jack L. The Terror Presidency: Law and Judgment Inside the Bush Administration (2007).

Gould, Louis L. The Modern American Presidency (2004).

Gray, Colin S. The Implications of Preemptive and Preventive War Doctrines: A Reconsideration (2007).

Greenstein, Fred I. The Presidential Difference: Leadership Style from FDR to George W. Bush (2004).

Gwyn, W. B. The Meaning of the Separation of Powers: An Analysis of the Doctrine from Its Origin to the Adoption of the United States Constitution (1965).

Hall, Thomas & David Ferguson. The Great Depression: An International Disaster of Perverse Economic Policies (1998).

Hart, James. The American Presidency in Action 1789 (1948).

Hearden, Patrick. Roosevelt Confronts Hitler: America's Entry into World War II (1987).

Heinrichs, Waldo. Threshold of War: Franklin D. Roosevelt and American Entry into World War II (1988).

Henkin, Louis. Foreign Affairs and the U.S. Constitution (2d ed., 1996).

Herring, George. America's Longest War: The United States and Vietnam, 1950–1975 (1985).

Hickey, Donald R. The War of 1812: A Forgotten Conflict (1990).

Hofstadter, Richard. The Idea of a Party System: The Rise of Legitimate Opposition in the United States (1969).

Hogan, Michael. A Cross of Iron: Harry S. Truman and the Origins of the National Security State, 1945–1954 (1998).

Hogeland, William. The Whiskey Rebellion: George Washington, Alexander Hamilton, and the Frontier Rebels Who Challenged America's Newfound Sovereignty (2006).

Howe, Daniel Walker. What Hath God Wrought: The Transformation of America 1815–1848 (2007).

Howell, William. Power Without Persuasion: The Politics of Direct Presidential Action (2003).

Huntington, Samuel. American Politics: The Promise of Disharmony (1981).

Hyman, Harold. A More Perfect Union: The Impact of the Civil War and Reconstruction on the Constitution (1975).

Iriye, Akira. The Globalizing of America, 1913–1945 (1995).

Iriye, Akira. The Origins of the Second World War in Asia and the Pacific (1987).

Irons, Peter. Justice at War: The History of the Japanese American Internment Cases (1983).

Irons, Peter. War Powers: How the Imperial Presidency Hijacked the Constitution (2005).

Jackson, Robert H. That Man: An Insider's Portrait of Franklin D. Roosevelt (2003).

Jaffa, Harry. A New Birth of Freedom: Abraham Lincoln and the Coming of the Civil War (2000).

Jaffa, Harry. Crisis of the House Divided: An Interpretation of the Issues in the Lincoln-Douglas Debates (1959).

Johnstone, Robert M., Jr. Jefferson and the Presidency: Leadership in the Young Republic (1978).

Jones, Charles O. The Presidency in a Separated System (1994).

Kaufman, Burton I. The Korean War: Challenges in Crisis, Credibility, and Command (1986).

Keegan, John. The Second World War (2005).

Kelley, Darwin. Milligan's Fight Against Lincoln (1973).

Kennedy, David M. Freedom from Fear: The American People in Depression and War, 1929–1945 (2001).

Kennedy, David M. Over Here: The First World War and American Society (1980).

Ketcham, Ralph. James Madison: A Biography (1971).

Ketcham, Ralph. The Jefferson Presidency and Constitutional Beginnings, in Martin Fausold & Alan Shank, eds., The Constitution and the American Presidency (1991).

Ketcham, Ralph. Presidents Above Party: The First American Presidency, 1789–1829 (1984).

Kimball, Warren. The Juggler: Franklin Roosevelt as Wartime Statesman (1991).

Klarman, Michael. From Jim Crow to Civil Rights: The Supreme Court and the Struggle for Racial Equality (2004).

Koh, Harold H. The National Security Constitution: Sharing Power after the Iran-Contra Affair (1990).

Kohn, Richard H. Eagle and Sword: The Federalists and the Creation of the Military Establishment in America, 1783–1802 (1975).

Kutler, Stanley I. The Wars of Watergate: The Last Crisis of Richard Nixon (1992).

LaFeber, Walter. The American Age: U.S. Foreign Policy at Home and Abroad, 1750 to the Present (1994).

Lammers, William W. & Michael A. Genovese. The Presidency and Domestic Policy: Comparing Leadership Styles, FDR to Clinton (2000).

Landy, Marc & Sidney M. Milkis. Presidential Greatness (2000).

Langer, William & Everett S. Gleason. The Undeclared War: 1940–1941 (1953).

Lawson, Gary & Guy Seidman. The Constitution of Empire: Territorial Expansion and American Legal History (2004).

Leffler, Melvyn. A Preponderance of Power: National Security, the Truman Administration, and the Cold War (1993).

Leuchtenberg, William. The FDR Years: On Roosevelt and His Legacy (1995).

Leuchtenburg, William. Franklin D. Roosevelt and the New Deal (1963).

Leuchtenburg, William. The Origins of Franklin D. Roosevelt's "Court-Packing" Plan (1996).

Leuchtenburg, William. The Supreme Court Reborn: The Constitutional Revolution in the Age of Roosevelt (1995).

Levy, Leonard. Jefferson and Civil Liberties: The Darker Side (1989).

Lewis, David E. Presidents and the Politics of Agency Design: Political Insulation in the United States Government Bureaucracy, 1946–1997 (2003).

Light, Paul C. Monitoring Government: Inspectors General and the Search for Accountability (1993).

Lowi, Theodore J. The End of Liberalism: The Second Republic of the United States (2d ed., 1979).

Lowi, Theodore J. The Personal President: Power Invested, Promise Unfulfilled (1985).

Lutz, Donald S. The Origins of American Constitutionalism (1988).

Malone, Dumas. Jefferson the President: The First Term 1801–05 (1970).

Malone, Dumas. Jefferson the President: The Second Term 1805–09 (1974).

Mansfield, Harvey C., Jr. Taming the Prince: The Ambivalence of Modern Executive Power (1989).

Mansfield, Harvey C., Jr. Thomas Jefferson, in Morton Frisch & Richard Stevens, eds., American Political Thought: The Philosophic Dimension of Statesmanship (1983).

Marks, Frederick W. Independence on Trial: Foreign Affairs and the Making of the Constitution (1986).

Marks, Frederick W. Wind Over Sand: The Diplomacy of Franklin Roosevelt (1988).

Marston, Jerrilyn. King & Congress (1987).

Matusow, Allen J. The Unraveling of America: A History of Liberalism in the 1960s (1985).

May, Ernest R., ed., The Ultimate Decision: The President as Commander in Chief (1960).

Mayer, David N. The Constitutional Thought of Thomas Jefferson (1994).

Mayer, Kenneth. With the Stroke of a Pen: Executive Orders and Presidential Power (2001).

McCoy, Drew R. The Last of the Fathers: James Madison and the Republican Legacy (1989).

McDonald, Forrest. The American Presidency: An Intellectual History (1994).

McDonald, Forrest. E Pluribus Unum (1979).

McDonald, Forrest. Novus Ordo Seclorum: The Intellectual Origins of the Constitution (1985).

McDonald, Forrest. The Presidency of Thomas Jefferson (1976).

McDonald, Forrest. We the People: The Economic Origins of the Constitution (1991).

McDougall, Walter. Promised Land, Crusader State: The American Encounter with the World Since 1776 (1998).

McPherson, James. Abraham Lincoln and the Second American Revolution (1990).

McPherson, James. Battle Cry of Freedom (1988).

Meltzer, Allan. A History of the Federal Reserve, 1913–1951 (2003).

Milkis, Sidney M. & Michael Nelson. The American Presidency: Origins and Development, 1776–2007 (5th ed., 2007).

Milkis, Sidney M. The President and the Parties: The Transformation of the American Party System since the New Deal (1993).

Miller, William Lee. The Business of May Next: James Madison and the Founding (1992).

Moe, Terry M. The Politicized Presidency, in John E. Chubb & Paul E. Peterson, eds., The New Direction in American Politics (1985).

Neely, Mark. The Fate of Liberty: Abraham Lincoln and Civil Liberties (1991).

Nelson, Michael. The Presidency and the Political System (2006).

Neustadt, Richard E. Presidential Power from FDR to Carter (1980 ed.).

Nevins, Allan. The Case of the Copperhead Conspirator, in John A. Garrety, ed., Quarrels That Have Shaped the Constitution (1962).

Paludan, Phillip Shaw. The Presidency of Abraham Lincoln (1994).

Perkins, Bradford. The First Rapprochement: England and the United States, 1795–1805 (1955).

Peterson, Merrill D. Thomas Jefferson and the New Nation (1986).

Pfiffner, James P. The Modern Presidency (2007).

Phelps, Glenn. George Washington and American Constitutionalism (1994).

Pious, Richard M. The Presidency (1995).

Pocock, J.G.A. The Machiavellian Moment: Florentine Political Thought and the Atlantic Republican Tradition (1975).

Posner, Richard A. An Affair of State: the Investigation, Impeachment, and Trial of President Clinton (2000).

Pusey, Merlo. The Supreme Court Crisis (1937).

Rakove, Jack N. The Beginnings of National Politics: An Interpretive History of the Continental Congress (1979).

Rakove, Jack N. James Madison and the Creation of the American Republic (1990).

Rakove, Jack N. Original Meanings: Politics and Ideas in the Making of the Constitution (1996).

Randall, J.G. Constitutional Problems Under Lincoln (1951).

Redish, Martin H. The Constitution as Political Structure (1995).

Reeves, Richard. President Reagan: The Triumph of Imagination (2005).

Remini, Robert V. Andrew Jackson and the Bank War: A Study in the Growth of Presidential Power (1967).

Remini, Robert V. The Constitution and the Presidencies: The Jackson Era, in Martin L. Fausold & Alan Shank, eds., The Constitution and the American Presidency (1991).

Reynolds, David. The Creation of the Anglo-American Alliance, 1937–1941: A Study in Competitive Co-operation (1982).

Ritcheson, Charles. Aftermath of Revolution: British Policy Toward the United States, 1783–1795 (1971).

Robinson, Donald L. "To the Best of My Ability": The Presidency and the Constitution (1987).

Robinson, Greg. By Order of the President: FDR and the Internment of the Japanese Americans (2003).

Rogin, Michael P. Fathers and Children: Andrew Jackson and the Subjugation of the American Indian (1975).

Rossiter, Clinton. 1787: The Grand Convention (1966).

Rossiter, Clinton. The American Presidency (1956).

Rossiter, Clinton. Constitutional Dictatorship: Crisis Government in the Modern Democracies (1948).

Rothbard, Murray. Panic of 1819: Reactions and Policies (1962).

Rozell, Mark J. Executive Privilege: Presidential Power, Secrecy, and Accountability (2d ed., 2002).

Rudalevige, Andrew. Managing the President's Program: Presidential Leadership and Legislative Policy Formation (2002).

Rudalevige, Andrew. The New Imperial Presidency (2005).

Rutland, Robert. James Madison: The Founding Father (1987).

Rutland, Robert. The Presidency of James Madison (1990).

Sanders, Jennings B. Evolution of Executive Departments of the Continental Congress (1935).

Savage, Charlie. Takeover: The Return of the Imperial Presidency and the Subversion of American Democracy (2007).

Schelling, Thomas. The Strategy of Conflict (1960).

Schlesinger, Arthur, Jr. The Age of Jackson (1945).

Schlesinger, Arthur, Jr. The Imperial Presidency (1973).

Schmitt, Gary. Thomas Jefferson and the Presidency, in Thomas E. Cronin, ed., Inventing the American Presidency (1989).

Schoenbrod, David. Power Without Responsibility: How Congress Abuses the People Through Delegation (1993).

Schwartz, Bernard. The Ascent of Pragmatism: The Burger Court in Action (1989).

Schwartz, Bernard. The Burger Court: Counter-Revolution or Confirmation (1998).

Skocpol, Theda. Protecting Soldiers and Mothers: The Political Origins of Social Policy in the United States (1995).

Skowronek, Stephen. Building a New American State: The Expansion of National Administrative Capacities 1877–1920 (1982).

Skowronek, Stephen. The Politics Presidents Make: Leadership from John Adams to George Bush (1993).

Smith, Walter. Economic Aspects of the Second Bank of the United States (1969).

Sofaer, Abraham D. War, Foreign Affairs and Constitutional Power: The Origins (1976).

Spaulding, E. Wilder. His Excellency George Clinton: Critic of the Constitution (1938).

Stagg, J. C. A. Mr. Madison's War: Politics, Diplomacy, and Warfare in the Early American Republic, 1783–1830 (1983).

Stone, Geoffrey. Perilous Times: Free Speech in Wartime (2004).

Strachan, Hew. Preemption and Prevention in Historical Perspective, in Henry Shue & David Rodin, eds., Preemption: Military Action and Moral Justification (2007).

Sundquist, James L. The Decline and Resurgence of Congress (1981).

Taranto, James & Leonard Leo. Presidential Leadership: Rating the Best and the Worst in the White House (2005).

Temin, Peter. The Great Depression, in Stanley Engerman & Robert Gallman, eds., The Cambridge Economic History of the United States (2000).

Thach, Charles. The Creation of the American Presidency, 1775–1789: A Study in Constitutional History (1923).

Trachtenberg, Marc. A Constructed Peace: The Making of the European Settlement 1945–1963 (1999).

Trachtenberg, Marc. The Craft of International History: A Guide to Method (2006).

Tucker, Robert & David Hendrickson. Empire of Liberty: The Statecraft of Thomas Jefferson (1990).

Tulis, Jeffrey K. The Rhetorical Presidency (1988).

Vedder, Richard & Lowell Gallaway. Out of Work: Unemployment and Government in Twentieth Century America (1997).

Vile, M. J. C. Constitutionalism and the Separation of Powers (1967).

Ward, Geoffrey C. A First-Class Temperament: The Emergence of Franklin Roosevelt (1990).

Warren, Charles. The Supreme Court in United States History, 1856–1918 (1922).

Watt, Donald C. How War Came: The Immediate Origins of the Second World War, 1938–1939 (1990).

White, G. Edward. The Constitution and the New Deal (2002).

White, Leonard D. The Federalists: A Study in Administrative History (1948).

White, Leonard D. The Jacksonians: A Study in Administrative History (1954).

Wiebe, Robert H. The Search for Order, 1877–1920 (1966).

Wilentz, Sean. Andrew Jackson (2005).

Wilson, Woodrow. Congressional Government: A Study in American Politics (1885).

Wilson, Woodrow. Constitutional Government (1907).

Wood, Gordon. The Creation of the American Republic 1776–1789 (1969).

Yalof, David A. Pursuit of Justices: Presidential Politics and the Selection of Supreme Court Nominees (1999).

Yamamoto, Erik, et al. Race, Rights & Reparation: Law and the Japanese American Internment (2001).

Yoo, John. The Powers of War and Peace: The Constitution and Foreign Affairs after 9/11 (2005).

Yoo, John. War by Other Means: An Insider's Account of the War on Terror (2006).

JOURNALS

Alexander, Larry & Saikrishna B. Prakash. Reports of the Nondelegation Doctrine's Death are Greatly Exaggerated, 70 U. Chi. L. Rev. 1297 (2003).

Amar, Akhil R. The Consent of the Governed: Constitutional Amendment Outside Article V, 94 Colum. L. Rev. 457 (1994).

Amar, Akhil R. Nixon's Shadow, 83 Minn. L. Rev. 1405 (1999).

Berger, Raoul. War-Making by the President, 121 U. Pa. L. Rev. 29 (1972).

Bestor, Arthur. Separation of Powers in the Domain of Foreign Affairs: The Intent of the Constitution Historically Examined, 5 Seton Hall L. Rev. 527 (1974).

Borchard, Edwin. The Attorney General's Opinion on the Exchange of Destroyers for Naval Bases, 34 Am J Int'l L 690 (1940).

Bradley, Curtis & Martin Flaherty. Executive Power Essentialism and Foreign Affairs, 102 Mich. L. Rev. 545 (2004).

Calabresi, Steven G. & Christopher S. Yoo. The Unitary Executive During the First Half-Century, 47 Case W. Res. L. Rev. 1451 (1997).

Calabresi, Steven G. & Saikrishna B. Prakash. The President's Power to Execute the Laws, 104 Yale L.J. 541 (1994).

Carter, Stephen. The Confirmation Mess, 101 Harv. L. Rev. 1185 (1988).

Croley, Steven. White House Review of Agency Rulemaking: An Empirical Investigation, 70 U. Chi. L. Rev. 821 (2003).

Currie, David. Rumors of War: Presidential and Congressional War Powers, 67 U. Chi. L. Rev. 1 (2000).

Danelski, David. The Saboteurs' Case, 1 J. S. Ct. Hist. 61 (1996).

Delahunty, Robert J. & John Yoo. Making War, 93 Cornell L. Rev. 123 (2007).

DeMuth, Christopher C. & Douglas H. Ginsburg. White House Review of Agency Decisionmaking, 99 Harv. L. Rev. 1075 (1986).

Downey, Arthur T. The Conflict between the Chief Justice and the Chief Executive: Ex Parte Merryman, 31 J. S. Ct. Hist. 262 (2006).

Easterbrook, Frank H. Presidential Review, 40 Case W. Res. L. Rev. 905 (1990).

Estes, Todd. The Art of Presidential Leadership: George Washington and the Jay Treaty, 109 Va. Mag. Hist. 127 (2001).

Fellmeth, Aaron X. A Divorce Waiting to Happen: Franklin Roosevelt and the Law of Neutrality, 1935–1941, 3 Buff. J. Int'l L. 414 (1996–97).

Frickey, Philip. Marshalling Past and Present: Colonialism, Constitutionalism, and Interpretation in Federal Indian Law, 107 Harv. L. Rev. 381 (1993).

Gormley, Ken. An Original Model of the Independent Counsel Statute, 97 Mich. L. Rev. 601 (1999).

Hobson, Charles F. The Negative on State Laws: James Madison, the Constitution, and the Crisis of Republican Government, 36 Wm. & Mary Q. 215 (1979).

Jay, Stewart. Origins of Federal Common Law: Part One, 133 U. Pa. L. Rev. 1003 (1985).

Kagan, Elena. Presidential Administration, 114 Harv. L. Rev. 2245 (2001).

Karl, Barry D. Constitution and Central Planning: The Third New Deal Revisited, 1988 S. Ct. Rev. 163.

Kelley, William K. The Constitutional Dilemma of Litigation under the Independent Counsel System, 83 Minn. L. Rev. 1197 (1999).

Kesavan, Vasan & Michael S. Paulsen. Let's Mess With Texas, 82 Tex. L. Rev. 1587 (2004).

Kosma, Montgomery. Our First Real War, 2 Green Bag 2d 169 (1999).

Krent, Harold J. Executive Control over Criminal Law Enforcement, 38 Am. U. L. Rev. 275 (1989).

Kutler, Stanley I. Ex Parte McCardle: Judicial Impotency?: The Supreme Court and Reconstruction Reconsidered, 72 Am. Hist. Rev. 835 (1967).

Lawson, Gary. Delegation and Original Meaning, 88 Va. L. Rev. 327 (2002).

Lawson, Gary & Christopher D. Moore. The Executive Power of Constitutional Interpretation, 81 Iowa L. Rev. 1267 (1996).

Lessig, Lawrence & Cass R. Sunstein. The President and the Administration, 94 Colum. L. Rev. 1 (1994).

Levitan, David M. The Foreign Relations Power: An Analysis of Mr. Justice Sutherland's Theory, 55 Yale L.J. 467 (1946).

Lofgren, Charles A. United States v. Curtiss-Wright Export Corp.: An Historical Reassessment, 83 Yale L.J. 1 (1973).

Mashaw, Jerry. Recovering American Administrative Law: Federalist Foundations, 1787–1801, 115 Yale L.J. 1256 (2006).

May, Christopher N. Presidential Defiance of "Unconstitutional" Laws: Reviving the Royal Prerogative, 21 Hastings Const. L.Q. 865 (1994).

McGinnis, John O. The President, the Senate, the Constitution, and the Confirmation Process: A Reply to Professors Strauss and Sunstein, 71 Tex. L. Rev. 633 (1993).

Monaghan, Henry. The Confirmation Process: Law or Politics?, 101 Harv. L. Rev. 1202 (1988).

Morrison, Alan B. OMB Interference with Agency Rulemaking: The Wrong Way to Write a Regulation, 99 Harv. L. Rev. 1059 (1986).

Nagel, Robert F. Advice, Consent, and Influence, 84 Nw. U. L. Rev. 858 (1990).

O'Sullivan, Julie. The Independent Counsel Statute: Bad Law, Bad Policy, 33 Am. Crim. L. Rev. 463 (1996).

Paul, Joel R. The Geopolitical Constitution: Executive Expediency and Executive Agreements, 86 Cal. L. Rev. 671 (1998).

Paulsen, Michael S. The Most Dangerous Branch: Executive Power to Say What the Law Is, 83 Geo. L.J. 217 (1994).

Paulsen, Michael S. Nixon Now: The Courts and the Presidency After Twenty-Five Years, 83 Minn. L. Rev. 1337 (1999).

Paulsen, Michael S. Review: The Civil War as Constitutional Interpretation, 71 U. Chi. L. Rev. 691 (2004).

Pildes, Richard H. & Cass R. Sunstein. Reinventing the Regulatory State, 62 U. Chi. L. Rev. 1 (1995).

Posner, Eric & Adrian Vermeule. Interring the Nondelegation Doctrine, 69 U. Chi. L. Rev. 1721 (2002).

Prakash, Saikrishna B. New Light on the Decision of 1789, 91 Cornell L. Rev. 1021 (2006).

Prakash, Saikrishna B. Removal and Tenure in Office, 92 Va. L. Rev. 1779 (2006).

Prakash, Saikrishna B. Unleashing the Dogs of War: What the Constitution Means by "Declare War," 93 Cornell L. Rev. 45 (2007).

Prakash, Saikrishna B. & John Yoo. Against Interpretational Supremacy, 103 Mich. L. Rev. 1539 (2005).

Prakash, Saikrishna B. & John Yoo. The Origins of Judicial Review, 70 U. Chi. L. Rev. 887 (2003).

Prakash, Saikrishna B. & Michael Ramsey. The Executive Power over Foreign Affairs, 111 Yale L.J. 231 (2001).

Rakove, Jack N. Solving a Constitutional Puzzle: The Treatymaking Clause as a Case Study, 1 Persp. Am. Hist. 233 (1984).

Ramsey, Michael. Executive Agreements and the (Non)Treaty Power, 77 N.C. L. Rev. 133 (1998).

Ramsey, Michael. Textualism and War Powers, 69 U. Chi. L. Rev. 1543 (2002).

Rappaport, Michael. The Unconstitutionality of "Signing and Not Enforcing," 16 Wm. & Mary Bill of Rights J. 113 (2007).

Rehnquist, William H. The Constitutional Issues—Administration Position, 45 N.Y.U. L. Rev. 628 (1970).

Rowe, Gary D. The Sound of Silence: United States v. Hudson & Goodwin, The Jeffersonian Ascendancy, and the Abolition of Federal Common Law Crimes, 101 Yale L.J. 919 (1992).

Schmitt, Gary. Jefferson and Executive Power: Revisionism and the "Revolution of 1800," 17 Publius 7 (1987).

Siemers, David J. Theories About Theory: Theory-Based Claims about Presidential Performance from the Case of James Madison, 38 Pres. Studies Q. 78 (2007).

Sofaer, Abraham D. Executive Privilege: An Historical Note, 75 Colum. L. Rev. 1318 (1975).

Stampp, Kenneth M. The Milligan Case and the Election of 1864 in Indiana, 31 Miss. Valley Hist. Rev. 41 (1944).

Stern, Robert. The Commerce Clause and the National Economy, 1933–1946, 59 Harv. L. Rev. 645 (1946).

Strauss, David A. Common Law Constitutional Interpretation, 63 U. Chi. L. Rev. 877 (1996).

Strauss David A. & Cass R. Sunstein. The Senate, the Constitution, and the Confirmation Process, 101 Yale L.J. 1491 (1992).

Turner, Robert. Truman, Korea, and the Constitution: Debunking the "Imperial President" Myth, 19 Harv. J. L. & Pub. Pol'y 533 (1996).

Van Alstyne, William W. A Critical Guide to Ex Parte McCardle, 15 Ariz. L. Rev. 229 (1973).

Vladeck, Stephen I. Emergency Power and the Militia Acts, 114 Yale L.J. 149 (2004).

Yoo, Christopher, Steven Calabresi & Anthony Colangelo. The Unitary Executive in the Modern Era, 90 Iowa L. Rev. 601 (2005).

Yoo, Christopher, Steven Calabresi & Laurence Nee. The Unitary Executive During the Third Half-Century, 1889–1945, 80 Notre Dame L. Rev. 1 (2004).

Yoo, John C. Choosing Justices: A Political Appointments Process and the Wages of Judicial Supremacy, 98 Mich. L. Rev. 1436 (2000).

Yoo, John C. Globalization and the Constitution, 99 Colum. L. Rev. 1955 (1999).

Yoo, John C. The Judicial Safeguards of Federalism, 70 S. Cal. L. Rev. 1311 (1997).

Yoo, John C. Kosovo, War Powers, and the Multilateral Future, 148 U. Pa. L. Rev. 1673 (2000).

Yoo, John C. Politics as Laws?: The Anti-Ballistic Missile Treaty, the Separation of Powers, and Treaty Interpretation, 89 Cal. L. Rev. 851 (2001).

Yoo, John C. War and the Constitutional Text, 69 U. Chi. L. Rev. 1639 (2002).

CASES

Adair v. United States, 208 U.S. 161 (1908).

Adkins v. Children's Hospital, 261 U.S. 525 (1923).

American Insurance Association v. Garamendi, 539 U.S. 396 (2003).

Associated Press v. NLRB, 301 U.S. 103 (1937).

Bailey v. Drexel Furniture Co., 259 U.S. 20 (1922).

Boumediene v. Bush, 128 S. Ct. 2229 (2008).

Bowsher v. Synar, 478 U.S. 714, 722 (1986).

Brown v. Board of Education, 347 U.S. 483 (1954).

Brown v. Board of Education II, 349 U.S. 294 (1955).

City of Boerne v. Flores, 521 U.S. 507 (1997).

Crockett v. Reagan, 720 F.2d 1355 (D.C. Cir. 1983).

Dames & Moore v. Regan, 453 U.S. 654 (1981).

Ex Parte Endo, 323 U.S. 283 (1944).

Ex Parte McCardle, 74 U.S. (7 Wall.) 506 (1868).

Ford v. Surget, 97 U.S. 594 (1878).

Hammer v. Dagenhart, 247 U.S. 251 (1918).

Helvering v. Davis, 301 U.S. 619 (1937).

Home Building & Loan Ass'n v. Blaisdell, 290 U.S. 398 (1934).

Humphrey's Executor v. United States, 295 U.S. 602 (1935).

INS v. Chadha, 462 U.S. 919 (1983).

Johnson v. M'Intosh, 21 U.S. (8 Wheat.) 543 (1823).

Lochner v. New York, 198 U.S. 45 (1905).

Lowry v. Reagan, 676 F.Supp. 333 (D.D.C. 1987).

Ludecke v. Watkins, 335 U.S. 160 (1948).

Luther v. Borden, 48 U.S. 1 (1849).

McCulloch v. Maryland, 17 U.S. (4 Wheat.) 316 (1819).

Miller v. United States 78 U.S. 268 (1870).

Mistretta v. United States, 488 U.S. 361 (1989).

Morgan v. TVA, 28 F. Supp. 732 (E.D. Tenn. 1939).

Morrison v. Olson, 529 U.S. 654 (1988).

Moyer v. Peabody, 212 U.S. 78 (1909).

Myers v. United States, 272 U.S. 52 (1926).

Nebbia v. New York, 291 U.S. 502 (1934).

New Orleans v. The Steamship Co., 87 U.S. 387 (1874).

New State Ice Co. v. Liebmann, 285 U.S. 262 (1932).

NLRB v. Friedman-Harry Marks Clothing Co., 301 U.S. 58 (1937).

NLRB v. Fruehauf Trailer Co., 301 U.S. 49 (1937).

NLRB v. Jones & Laughlin Steel Corp., 301 U.S. 1 (1937).

Norman v. B. & O. R.R., 294 U.S. 240 (1935).

Olmstead v. United States, 277 U.S. 438 (1928).

Panama Refining Co. v. Ryan, 293 U.S. 388 (1935).

Plessy v. Ferguson, 163 U.S. 537 (1896).

Sanchez-Espinoza v. Reagan, 770 F.2d 202 (D.C. Cir. 1985).

Steward Machine Co. v. Davis, 301 U.S. 548 (1937).

Texas v. White, 74 U.S. 700 (1869).

United States v. Belmont, 301 U.S. 324 (1937).

United States v. Darby, 312 U.S. 100 (1941).

United States v. Diekelman, 92 U.S. 520 (1875).

United States v. E.C. Knight, 156 U.S. 1 (1895).

United States v. Hudson & Goodwin, 11 U.S. (7 Cranch) 32 (1812).

United States v. Lovett, 328 U.S. 303 (1946).

United States v. Nardone, 302 U.S. 379 (1937).

United States v. Nardone, 308 U.S. 338 (1939).

United States v. Nixon, 418 U.S. 683 (1974).

United States v. United States District Court, 444 F.2d 651 (6th Cir. 1971).

Washington, Virginia & Maryland Coach Co. v. NLRB, 301 U.S. 142 (1937).

West Coast Hotel Co. v. Parrish, 300 U.S. 379 (1937).

Williams v. Standards Oil Co., 278 U.S. 235 (1929).

Youngstown Sheet & Tube Co. v. Sawyer, 343 U.S. 579 (1952).

INDEX